MICHAEL JACKSON'S
Complete Guide to
SINGLE MALT SCOTCH

MICHAEL JACKSON'S
Complete Guide to
SINGLE MALT SCOTCH

UPDATED BY DOMINIC ROSKROW
AND GAVIN D. SMITH

DK INDIA
Senior Editor Dorothy Kikon
Senior Art Editor Balwant Singh
Deputy Managing Editor Bushra Ahmed
Managing Editor Alicia Ingty
Managing Art Editor Navidita Thapa
Senior DTP Designer Neeraj Bhatia
DTP Designer Manish Chandra Upreti
Pre-production Manager Sunil Sharma

DK UK
US Editor Jane Perlmutter
US Senior Editor Shannon Beatty
Managing Editor Dawn Henderson
Managing Art Editor Christine Keilty
Senior Jacket Creative Nicola Powling
Producer, Pre-production Rebecca Fallowfield
Category Publisher Peggy Vance

First American edition published by Running Press, 1989

A Penguin Random House Company

This revised edition published in the United States in 2015 by
Dorling Kindersley Limited

15 16 17 18 19 10 9 8 7 6 5 4 3 2 1
001-193006-September/2015

A WORLD OF IDEAS:
SEE ALL THERE IS TO KNOW

www.dk.com

CONTENTS

INTRODUCTION
MICHAEL JACKSON'S LEGACY

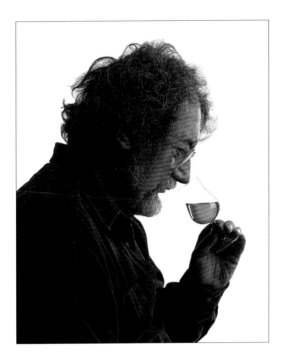

THE SEVENTH EDITION of this Companion, first published more than a quarter of a century ago, coincides with what is arguably the most dynamic, diverse, and purely exciting time in the history of whisky. The Scotch whisky industry is booming, with many existing distilleries being expanded, and a plethora of fledgling and start-up distilling ventures being developed, in a wide variety of locations. The youthful "make" of some of these distilleries will no doubt make its way into the eighth edition.

There have, however, been boom times for Scotch whisky in the past, just as there has for Irish, bourbon, and rye. What makes the present situation so different is the increasing number of countries around the world that have little or no tradition of making whisky, but which are now developing whisky industries of their own on varying scales. In the past, consumers in these countries might have drunk whisky, but now they are making their own. And when it comes to single malts, this edition embraces the best and most interesting, just as it does with Scotch malts.

The aim throughout is not to be inclusive, as there are now simply too many expressions of malt whisky available, but to be selective and representative, and feature whiskies that readers should be able to locate and sample for themselves. Due attention has been paid to malt whiskies exclusive to the burgeoning travel retail sector.

Were Michael Jackson with us today, it seems certain that he would have embraced the "world of whisky" with his customary thirst for knowledge and new experiences, boarding planes for Tasmania or Taiwan, just as he once did for Aberdeen and the distilling delights of nearby Speyside or Louisville, and the whiskey jewels of Kentucky.

THE MAN HIMSELF

Nothing remains the same for very long, and as time passes a new generation is discovering Michael's work for the first time. So it seems appropriate to offer for their benefit, some brief biographical information on the man whose name graces this book. As cold, hard facts rarely do anyone full justice, we have also invited a number of people professionally associated with whisky and whisky making, who knew Michael well, to offer some personal reminiscences about him.

To begin with the cold, hard facts, Michael was born in Wetherby, Yorkshire, on March 27, 1942, and brought up in nearby Leeds, where his family moved after the war. His father was a Lithuanian Jew who had changed his name from Jakowitz when the family migrated to Yorkshire. Michael began his career in journalism on the Huddersfield Examiner, and as the beer writer Roger Protz noted in his Guardian obituary of Michael in September 2007, "Jackson's writing style was deeply influenced by his early journalism—short sentences shorn of adornment."

Moving to London, Michael wrote his first book, *The English Pub*, published in 1976, followed a year later by *The World Guide to Beer*, which set a benchmark for the subject and became a much reprinted classic. Turning to whisky, the first edition of this best-selling Companion was published in 1989, and since then, various other titles followed.

The whisky legend

THE WHISKY INDUSTRY is full of wonderful characters whose talents are matched only by their modesty. Michael, as unpretentious and unassuming as the characters he met and interviewed, was the perfect person to bring their talents to a wider audience. He built bridges within the industry, linking whisky makers and whisky devotees around the world. He gave us access to the world's great distilleries, and the people who create great whisky within them.

AT HEART, MICHAEL was a traditionalist. His values harked back to a time when the pace of life was slower and more considered. He fought with quiet determination to preserve the things he loved, and saw as threatened. He wrote for *Slowfood* magazine, eschewed marketing terms such as "brand" and "product," and had little time for the insincerity and disposability of modern consumerism.

On the subjects of both beer and whisky, Michael was one of the first commentators to really address issues of flavor and diversity, and paved the way for so much that has subsequently been written about alcohol. He was responsible for developing and refining regional classifications for malt whiskies, and wrote extensively and perceptively for the first time about the distilleries within those classifications. His reputation and influence were truly global. He died of a heart attack on August 30, 2007, having suffered from Parkinson's disease for the previous 10 years.

THIS EDITION

As in the sixth edition, we have attempted to remain faithful to Michael's traditional values, modesty, and positivity. He was respectful and careful about what he said and how he said it. He held the view that there were very few bad malt whiskies, and sought to find something positive about all of them, or to say nothing at all. He set about his tasting notes with almost scientific precision, describing the flavors he encountered while avoiding subjective indulgences.

We have also tried to be as true to Michael's precise and frugal writing style as possible, and to score whiskies in the same way as he did. This hasn't been easy because scoring is highly subjective, and each of us found malts in the old editions that we would have scored differently from Michael. When scoring other malts from the same distillery, were we to give them the score we felt they justified, or align them with Michael's other scores? We went with the latter approach.

Michael also scored most malts in a very tight band. With some notable exceptions, he rarely scored below 60 or above 85. The scoring must therefore be seen in this context. Where other writers often score whiskies over 90, and even 95, this book does so only rarely. And while other books pass judgment on malts, both good and bad, we have sought to do what Michael did and merely describe their properties.

The way to approach this book is to accept that if a malt has been included at all, we consider that it is of sufficient quality to justify being sought after and tasted. A score of 65 suggests a good, decent, but unexceptional whisky. A score of 75 represents a Grade A malt. A score of 85 is a Grade A with distinction, and a whisky that is warmly recommended by the authors. Anything above that is in an elite class of the very finest malts.

In updating this book, we have been helped by countless people within the industry, and we would particularly like to thank those, who went to the trouble of expressing support for what we were doing. Hopefully, we have repaid their faith by producing a book that still represents Michael and all that he stood for, a book in which the seams don't show, and in which Michael's personality and values shine bright.

This *Malt Whisky Companion* is very much Michael Jackson's book, and may it always remain so.

Dominic Roskrow
Gavin D. Smith

September 2015

MICHAEL REMEMBERED

MICHAEL JACKSON was a quiet and modest man, but touched the lives of scores of whisky fans who had the fortune to meet him. He was a constant surprise, and passionate about, among other things, old-fashioned rugby league and the great hot-metal-and-dirty-print days of journalism. We asked three people who knew him for many years for a snapshot recollection of him.

"*Michael was already a legend in Japan when we first met him, and one of the longest queues I've ever seen was for one of his books. Masterclasses and presentations had to be rescheduled to accommodate the sheer number of people who wanted to make a purchase and shake his hand!*"

DAVID CROLL, Organizer, Whisky Live Tokyo

"*Michael once signed a copy of the Complete Guide to Single Malt Scotch for me, adding the inscription, "The future is in the past, lead them to it." By this he meant that we should capitalize on the rich heritage of the distillery, and I suppose, also my own long-term experience of the place, and the brand.*"

DENNIS MALCOLM, Distillery Manager at Glen Grant, with which he has enjoyed a lifelong association

"*A particular gift was his ability to fall asleep in a meeting, from a combination of jet lag and apparent narcolepsy, then to suddenly awake in order to answer a specific question, or contribute to the conversation, without skipping a beat. Like many, I still miss him.*"

MARCIN MILLER, Former Whisky Magazine editor, and founder of media relations company Quercus Communications Ltd

◄ **Lighted aids**
Built across the sea inlet of Loch Indaal, the lighthouse at Bruichladdich faces the sea-bordered, classic Islay distillery, Bowmore.

WHY MALTS?

AN INSTANT GUIDE TO THE PLEASURES OF THE PURSUIT

A T ITS SIMPLEST, MALT WHISKY HAS A STARTLING PURITY. The snow melts on the mountains, filters through rock for decades, perhaps even centuries, bubbles out of a spring, then tumbles down a hillside, until it finds land flat enough and warm enough to grow barley. The water irrigates the barley in the field; persuades it to germinate in the maltings; infuses its natural sugars in the mash tun; becomes beer when the yeast is added; vaporizes in the still; becomes liquid once more in the condenser; enters the cask as spirit, and leaves it as whisky.

THE FLAVOR

Malted barley is always present to a degree, clean, sweet, and restorative, but there are many other elements. The rock from which the water rises will influence the character of the whisky. The vegetation over which it flows can also be an influence. In the process of malting, the partially germinated grain is dried, sometimes over a peat fire, and this will impart smokiness. The yeasts used in fermentation can create fruity, spicy flavors. Similar characteristics can be influenced by the size and shape of the stills, which also affect the richness and weight of the spirit. Further aromas and flavors are assumed during maturation in the cask, from the wood used, its previous contents, and the atmosphere it breathes (see pp. 68–69).

For people who enjoy a spirit with flavor, malt whisky at its most robust is a world champion. The flavors in a blended Scotch are usually more restrained, as they might be in a cognac. Those who suffer from fear of flavor might feel safer with white rums or vodkas.

THE INDIVIDUALITY of malts is what makes each so different. Naturally enough, they appeal to people who are individualists. A smoky, earthy, seaweedy, medicinal malt from the coasts or islands of Scotland is a spirit of unrivaled power on the palate. A Speysider

◀ **Glasses from a distillery tasting session**
Tasting glasses after a master class at Bruichladdich. Malt lovers like to learn—classes, tastings, and whisky festivals are popular. Finding flavors and aromas is a sensuous activity.

Malt

The original Scotch whisky—or *uisge beatha* ("water of life" in Gaelic)—from the 15th century or earlier, would have been a single malt. That is, distillation made from barley, and the product of just one distillery, rather than a blend or vatting of whiskies of different kinds or provenances. However, it would be different from the malt we know today. It would not have been aged in oak casks but instead be drunk hot from the still.

may be sherryish, honeyed, flowery, and often very complex. Lowlanders are few, but they can be appetizingly grassy and herbal. Malt whiskies from other countries may produce flavors that differ entirely from those of Scotland, as we shall see.

THE MOMENT for a malt may simply be the occasion for a social drink, but some pleasures are more particular: the restorative after a walk in the country or a game of golf; the aperitif; even, occasionally, the malt with a meal; the digestif; the malt with a cigar, or with a book at bedtime.

THE MEAL Although malt whiskies are more commonly served before or after a meal, as an aperitif or digestif, they very happily accompany some dishes. Some malt-loving chefs also like to use their favorite spirit as an ingredient.

THE EXPLORATION Malt drinkers rarely stick to one distillery. They enjoy comparing malts from different regions, and familiarizing themselves with the aromas and flavors of each. To do this is to explore the world by nosing glass. This armchair exploration often leads on to the real thing.

THE DISTILLERIES are often in beautiful locations. Some have their own distinctive architecture. Most are quite small, and it is not unknown for visiting malt lovers to strike up long-term friendships with distillery managers or workers.

THE VISIT Malt lovers often become passionate about Scotland and other whisky-producing countries. Whisky tourism extends beyond visits to distilleries. The principal whisky regions (the Highlands, especially Speyside; and the Islands, especially Islay) are set in countryside offering outstanding opportunities for hiking, climbing, bird-watching, and fishing.

THE CONNOISSEUR Just as wine enthusiasts progress from comparing vineyards or châteaux to assessing vintages, so malt lovers develop their own connoisseurship. A single distillery may offer malts of different ages, vintage-dated malts, a variety of strengths, and a diversity of wood finishes. Since new bottlings are constantly being released, there is no end to this pleasure.

COLLECTING WHISKY Every lover of malt whiskies sooner or later becomes, to some extent, a collector. It may not be a conscious decision. It can just happen. A few casual purchases, the occasional gift. For the collector's friends, birthdays are suddenly easy. Some collectors have backgrounds in the trade. Some buy two of every bottle: one to drink, the other to keep. Such collectors pour scorn on those who do not drink any of their whisky. The most serious collections are often found in countries with a nostalgia for the Britain of gentlemen's clubs, leather-upholstered Bentleys, and rugby union. There are famous collectors in Brazil, Italy, and Japan.

WHISKY AS INVESTMENT

Even if it was not bought for that purpose, a collection soon begins to represent a valuable asset. Collections that began after World War II started to come up for sale in the 1980s, and ever since then the size of the whisky auction market has grown and grown.

In 2009 it reached unprecedented heights when McTear's expanded its stand-alone whisky auctions to four a year. At the same time, Bonhams recruited former McTear's auction expert Martin Green and also began to hold whisky auctions quarterly. With uncertainty in many financial markets, whisky began to attract a new breed of investor—one who is more interested in pecuniary gain than any love of malt. Whisky may change hands for thousands of dollars, and the possibility of a bottle selling for $120,000 (£100,000) is considered realistic. There are a handful of "grand cru" distilleries and rare bottles from distilleries such as Ardbeg, Springbank, The Macallan, and The Dalmore that will always attract big investments.

If you are considering developing a collection of your own, you might want to think about a theme, based on a specific distillery or geographical region; or you might want to opt for limited edition bottlings. Though whisky is more robust than wine, high temperatures and direct sunlight should be avoided, and bottles should be stored upright, not lying down, as with wine.

THE ORIGINS OF
MALT WHISKY

W HILE GRAPE VINES HAVE their roots in prehistory, barley staked out the beginning of civilization. As hunter-gatherers, human beings picked wild fruit such as grapes, but this source of refreshment and nutrition had a short season and a propensity to rot (or spontaneously ferment) into wines. Fruit absorbs rainfall from the soil and turns it into highly fermentable, sugary juice. Wild yeasts trigger fermentation, and this process creates alcohol. Perhaps the hunter-gatherers enjoyed the effect, but wine did not provide them with any much needed protein.

When human beings ceased to be nomadic and settled in organized societies they did so in order to cultivate crops. The earliest evidence of this, between 13000 and 8000 years ago, occurs at several sites in the fertile crescent of the Middle East. The first crop was a prototype barley, and the first explanation of its use is a depiction in Sumerian clay tablets of beer making. This is sometimes described as the world's first recipe of any kind.

HALFWAY TO WHISKY

To grow barley, transform it into malt and then into beer, is halfway toward the making of whisky. While it is easy to obtain the sugars from fruit—peel me a grape, take a bite from an apple—grain is less yielding. The first step toward the unlocking of the sugars in barley and several other grains is the process of malting. This means that the grain is steeped in water, partially germinated, and then dried. The Sumerian civilization was on land that today is Iraq. It may be that malting occurred naturally while the barley was still in the field, as the water rose and fell in the flood plains of this land. This is described poetically on clay tablets in "A Hymn to Ninkasi" *(see p. 18)*.

It seems likely that at this stage the Sumerians had no more precise goal than to make grain edible. They did so in the form of beer, though pictograms and relics suggest a grainy, porridgey beverage consumed through straws. This depiction bears a startling resemblance to the "traditional" beer still brewed in villages in some parts of Africa.

◀ **Road to the Isles**
A few miles from the Bushmills distillery in Ireland, this remarkable rock formation heads for Fingal's Cave, Staffa, and Mull. The first whisky road … or the first whisky legend?

When you pour out the filtered beer of the collector vat,
It is [like] the onrush of Tigris and Euphrates. Ninkasi, you are
the one who pours out the filtered beer of the collector vat,
It is [like] the onrush of Tigris and Euphrates.

Grain and water meet ...
*... in the "Hymn to Ninkasi" (c. 1800BC), found on tablets at several sites
in Iraq. Translated in 1964, by Miguel Civil, of the Oriental Institute of the
University of Chicago. The first evidence of malting?*

GRAIN OR GRAPE

If the cultivation of grain originated from the first civilization of the
ancient world, the crop itself varied from place to place. To the east, the
Chinese and Japanese grow rice, which is fermented to produce saké.
To the north, the Russians use rye to make kvass. To the west, barley is
brewed. The words "brewed" and "bread" have the same etymology,
and, in Germany, beer is sometimes known as "liquid bread."

The soft, sensuous, delicate, capricious grape and the tall, spiky,
resilient grain compete to make the world's greatest drinks:
fermented and distilled. The weather divides temperate Europe into
wine and beer belts. Wine is made in the grape-growing south:
Greece, Italy, France, Iberia. Beer belongs to the grainy north: the
Czech Republic, Germany, Belgium, and the British Isles. All of
these countries also produce distilled counterparts, but the real
emphasis on spirits is in the colder countries. The spirits belt links
Russia, Poland, the Baltic and Nordic states, and Scotland.

BARLEY WATER

Modern-day Iraq is due south of Armenia, and the Greek historian
Herodotus tells us that the Armenians made "barley water." So perhaps
the brewing of barley malt spread by way of Armenia, Georgia, and
Ukraine. The Greeks also called all "strangers" Celts. The Romans called
them Gallic people, and a part of Turkey is known as Galatia. The term
"Galatian" was also used by the Roman author Columella to describe
the two-row "race" of barley, preferred today by many brewers.

Sites that were Celtic settlements are even today known for the
brewing of beer, notably sites in Bohemia, Bavaria, and Belgium.
Many of these sites later gave rise to abbeys, with breweries. Most
of the early brewing sites in England, Scotland, and Ireland are on
the locations of former abbeys. So are the distilling towns of Cork
and Midleton in Ireland. The northeast of Ireland and the western

isles of Scotland have associations with St. Columba, who urged his community of Iona to grow barley. In 1494, Friar Cor, of Lindores Abbey in Fife, placed on record in the rolls of the Scottish Exchequer the purchase of malt "to make *aqua vitae*." He probably wasn't the first malt distiller, but he left us the first evidence.

THE ART OF DISTILLATION

It is easy to see how spontaneous fermentation provides a natural model for the first brewers. Evaporation and condensation occur in nature, too, but it is not clear when, or where, distillation was first practiced. To distill is to boil the water, wine, or beer, collect the steam, and condense it back into liquid. This drives off certain substances (for example, the salt in water) and concentrates others (such as the alcohol in wine or beer). The process was used by Phoenician sailors to render sea water drinkable, by alchemists, by makers of perfumes and, eventually, in the production of medicines and alcoholic drinks.

One theory has the Phoenicians bringing distillation to Western Europe, via the Mediterranean and Spain, whence it crossed the sea again to Ireland. Another theory has the art spreading by way of Russia and the Nordic countries to Scotland.

WATER OF LIFE

The fermented raw material—wine or beer—is boiled to make steam, which, being wraithlike, may have given rise to the English word "spirit" or to the German "*Geist*" (ghost), especially since condensation brings it back to life in a restored (and restorative) form. The "water of life" they call it: vodka, a diminutive form, in Slavic countries; aquavit, in various spellings, in Nordic lands; *eau-de-vie* in French; and *usquebaugh*, in various spellings, in Gaelic. This last became *usky*, then whisky, in English. All of these terms at first simply indicated a distillate, made from whatever was local.

All spirit drinks were originally made in a batch process in a vessel that superficially resembles a kettle or cooking pot, and malt whisky is still made in this way today. But this "pot still" was an inefficient purification vessel, and, in the early days, if the spirit emerged with flavors that were considered disagreeable, they were masked with spices, berries, and fruit.

"PLAIN MALT"

In the mid-1700s, a distinction was made in Scotland between flavored spirits and "plain malt." As the first industrial nation, Britain shaped its beer and whisky with the early technologies of the

Industrial Revolution: England's "bright beer" was a copper-colored pale ale, rather than the more "evolved" golden lager of continental Europe, which was made using more advanced techniques. Scotland's whisky remained a pot-still product, with its own inherent flavors, turned to an attractive complexity.

Most of the northern European countries use a generic term such as "schnapps" for a spirit, and offer both plain and flavored examples. More specific flavorings include caraway and dill, traditional in the aquavit of Scandinavia; and juniper, together with botanical flavorings such as iris root and citrus peel, in the gins of northern Germany, the Low Countries, northern France, and England. Flavored or not, many grain-based spirits outside Britain employ a column still, and most are not aged.

The elements that go into making a Scottish malt whisky are the local water; a grist comprising malted barley only; traditionally, a degree of peat; pot stills, usually designed and built in Scotland; and aging in oak casks. The last of these elements gradually became more significant from the late 1700s onward.

BLENDED SCOTCH

Like most alcohol production, the distilling of malt whisky in Scotland was originally a sideline for farmers. In the coastal coves and Highland glens, illicit distillation was rife. Legislation in 1824 to regulate this activity began the shaping of today's industry. That process was largely finished by the legislation of 1909–15, which initially arose from a trading standards case in the London borough of Islington.

For the farmer-distiller, a few casks of malt whisky might be a hedge against a rainy day. A farm distillery would not have a bottling line. The casks could be sold directly to wealthy householders, to hotels or pubs, or to a licensed grocer, a Scottish institution similar to an

Blending the bottles
The "medicine bottles" on Richard Patterson's workbench contain the latest samples taken from casks of malt whiskies normally included in Whyte and Mackay's blended Scotch. Every cask is slightly different. Patterson checks color, nose, palate—and adjusts accordingly.

American country store. (The outstanding example of such a shop, and still active, is Gordon & MacPhail of Elgin.) One or two renowned distillers might sell their whisky to a wine merchant, sometimes as far away as Edinburgh or London.

BLENDING BEGINS

Each farmer's whisky would vary from one year to the next, and supply would be irregular. So rather than run out of farmer McSporran's fine dram, the licensed grocers would vat the malts and sell the result under their own label. Some became famous: names such as Chivas Brothers, Johnnie Walker, and George Ballantine. Among the wine merchants known for their bottlings, two in London are still active: Justerini & Brooks and Berry Brothers & Rudd.

Vatting turned to blending when, in the mid-1800s, the column-shaped continuous still was patented. This type of still, operated on an industrial scale, can produce whisky that is lighter in flavor and body. It can also produce whisky more quickly, at a lower cost, and in larger quantities than a pot still. Column-still whisky provides the bulk of a blend, while a combination of pot-still malt whiskies add character and individuality. The volume afforded by blended Scotches, and their less challenging style, helped them become the world's most popular spirits at a time when much of the globe was embraced by the British Empire.

Mountainous Scotland, with its long coastline, had provided mariners, explorers, engineers, teachers, soldiers, and administrators for the empire. Each turned out also to be a propagandist for the virtues of his country's greatest product.

BORN-AGAIN MALTS

More than 90 percent of malt whisky still goes into blends. Scotland has about 100 malt distilleries, of which about two thirds are working at any one time. All but a handful are owned by international alcohol companies whose products include blended Scotches. A blend can contain anything from six or seven malts to 30 or 40. The companies like to own the distilleries whose malt whiskies are vital to their blends. They also exchange malts with one another.

The big companies have been growing through mergers since the 1920s. A round of mergers after World War II left the handful of remaining independent distillers feeling vulnerable. William Grant & Sons, producers of Glenfiddich and Balvenie, decided they no longer wished to rely on supplying blenders, but to actively market their whisky as a single malt.

ABERLOUR

<small>ESTᵈ 1879</small>

WAREHOUSE №1
SINGLE CASK SELECTION

SPEYSIDE MALT SCOTCH WHISKY
AGED 11 YEARS

BOURBON CASK MATURED

FILL DETAILS

☑ 1ST ☑ 2ND ☐ REFILL

CASK NUMBER...10122.........

FILLED INTO CASK...61/1/199d...

BOTTLE NUMBER...PRESELECTION...

70cl

HAND FILLED AT ABERLOUR DISTILLERY
THE ABERLOUR GLENLIVET DISTILLERY CO. LTD.
ABERLOUR ~ SPEYSIDE ~ SCOTLAND

57.2 VOL

THE LANGUAGE OF
THE LABEL

CONTROVERSY was aroused in 2003 when Cardhu single malt was relaunched as a pure malt. What is the difference, and why did it matter? This book is primarily concerned with malt whisky, but also looks briefly at grain whisky. Much of the book, the A–Z section, is devoted to single malt Scotches, but a substantial section deals with products from other countries—these are malt whiskies, but not Scotches. All of these overlapping terms are employed in labeling. What do they say about the liquid in the bottle?

MALT

Cereal grain that has been partially sprouted—in preparation for the release of its fermentable sugars—then dried in a kiln. The grains look drier and slightly darker after being malted for distillation. The grain is always barley if the end result is to be malt whisky in the Scottish or Irish style. Other grains can be malted and used in other whiskies, as in the case of rye.

For the beer brewer or whisky distiller, the process of malting in part parallels the crush in wine making or brandy distilling. The premises in which it takes place is called a maltings. The grains are first steeped in water, to encourage their sprouting (or partial germination). Traditionally, the sprouting continues with the grains spread on a stone floor. They are constantly raked, or turned with a shovel, to keep them aerated. Floor malting requires a lot of space and is labor-intensive, but is felt by many to produce the most delicious result. There are several other methods, including ventilated boxes and rotating drums.

BARLEY TYPES

Just as grapes are also eaten or used to provide juice, so malted barley is used, either as whole grains or milled, in breads, cakes, and milk shakes. A syrupy, water-based extract of malt sugars is sold as a tonic. An ever-evolving series of barley varieties is used for malting. These are required to produce plump kernels and clean, sweet malt sugars. The farmer distinguishes between malting barley and feed barley for cattle.

◄ **Detailed dram**
Malt lovers like to know what they are drinking, and Aberlour provides every last detail when you make your own vatting and bottling at the distillery's visitor center.

Almost all types of whisky employ a proportion of malt. Those that employ no other grain are known as malt whisky. Single malt whiskies are often referred to simply as "malts."

WHISK(E)Y A spirit drink originating from Scotland and Ireland—but produced in a variety of styles in other countries— distilled from malted barley and other grains, and matured in oak. Its complex aromas and flavors originate from the raw materials, manufacturing process, and maturation. These distinguish whiskies from the more neutral grain spirits in the schnapps and vodka families.

There is a misunderstanding that there are British and American spellings of this term. However, it is not the nationality of the writer, or the country of publication, that should determine the spelling. It is the type of whisk(e)y: thus Scottish and Canadian "whisky," but Irish "whiskey." American styles, such as Kentucky Bourbon and Tennessee whiskey, generally favor the "e," but some labels dissent.

MALT WHISKY Whisky made only from malted barley. Typically distilled in a batch process, in a copper vessel resembling a kettle or cooking pot.

SINGLE MALT WHISKY Malt whisky produced in a single distillery, and not vatted or blended with whisky made in any other distillery. Scotland has by far the most malt distilleries: in the region of a hundred, of which between 80 and 90 percent are operating at any one time. Ireland has one distillery that can produce only malt whisky, namely Bushmills. Malt whiskies are also distilled on a more limited scale at Cooley and Midleton in Ireland, though both of these distilleries also produce a range of other styles of whisky. Some very serious malt whiskies are made in Japan, which has seven malt-producing distilleries, and a scattering elsewhere in the world.

Mountain men?
These potbellied creatures are the whisky stills at Ben Nevis. The pot-still shape is more evident when the whole vessel is visible.

BOURBON Aging

WHY THE NAME BOURBON? The French helped the Americans in the Revolutionary War, and the Americans acknowledged this by naming towns and counties after the French royal family. Bourbon County, in Kentucky, was known for shipping whiskey down the Ohio and Mississippi rivers to New Orleans and other big cities. (Whiskey had been introduced to the US by Northern Irish immigrants of Scottish origin.)

LOCAL CORN is always used to make bourbon, along with rye or wheat, and the bourbon is then matured in a fresh oak barrel. The inside of the barrel is charred to help the whiskey permeate the wood. After only one use in Kentucky, the barrel may be sent to Scotland and used to mature Scottish whiskey. It will still retain enough of its typical vanilla-like flavors to impart some of these to the first fill of this whiskey; and along with the vanilla, there may be caramel-toffee flavors, dessert apple, and a touch of tannin. There will still be some lively flavor contribution in a second fill. By the third fill the barrel may be relatively neutral. Some barrels are recharred in Scotland.

SCOTCH WHISKY This term can be applied only to whisky made in Scotland, and matured for at least three years. No other nation can call a product "Scotch," although any nation can call a product whisky. Scotland's status is not widely understood beyond its borders. It is not a region but a nation, and has been for almost 1000 years. For the past 300 years, it has been part of a union. Scotland, England, and Wales share an island called Great Britain. These three nations with Northern Ireland (a six-county province) form the United Kingdom.

SINGLE MALT SCOTCH WHISKY Single malt whisky made in Scotland.

SINGLE CASK A bottling made from just one cask.

VATTED MALT If malt whiskies from different distilleries are combined, the result will be called a vatted malt. This might be done to create a desired character, perhaps the flavor of a region. This term assumes that all the whiskies in the vatting are malts.

BLENDED MALT Exactly the same as a vatted malt, this is the term adopted by the whisky industry. It is not the same as a blended Scotch whisky or a blended whisky because there is no grain whisky in a blended malt. Some whisky makers use the old terminology, insisting the term blended malt is confusing. You be the judge.

BLENDED SCOTCH WHISKY A stroke of Scottish genius, devised in the Victorian era. Craft producers, mainly in the Highlands and Islands, make small quantities of flavorful malt whisky. Much larger, more industrial distilleries, mainly in the Midlands and the south, produce large quantities of more neutral grain whiskies to add volume to the malt. The result is a blended Scotch.

GRAIN WHISKY These may be produced from corn, wheat, or raw barley. A small amount of malted barley is required to provide the enzymes needed in fermentation, in a continuous process, in a column-shaped still. Grain whiskies are light in body and flavor, but not neutral, and are matured for a minimum of three years in oak.

SINGLE GRAIN WHISKY There have been attempts to market single grain whisky as a more interesting alternative to vodka, or perhaps as a Scottish "grappa"? Occasional independent bottlings are also of interest to collectors.

OTHER LABEL TERMS

PEATING When maltsters kilned their grains over open fires, the fuel was whatever could easily be found. In Poland, a style of beer was made from oak-smoked malt. In Franconia, in Germany, beechwood was favored. In Scotland, whisky malt was traditionally kilned over peat fires. The peat gave an especially distinct smokiness to Scotch whisky, and has to varying degrees been retained. Serious whisky lovers have come to cherish peatiness, and demand more, since many of the popular malts have become less smoky to appease consumers who fear flavor. Within the industry, the peat-smoke character is measured in parts per million (ppm) of phenol. The smokiness can be accentuated or softened by the design, shape, and configuration of the stills, the woods used in aging, and so on.

Sherry Aging

THE WORD "SHERRY" derives from English attempts to pronounce the Spanish place name Jerez. The wine makers of the Jerez area, in the southwest, near Cadiz and Seville, have a long relationship with the British Isles. Large quantities of their fortified Jerez wines were for a long time shipped to Cork, Bristol (the closest English port), and Leith (the port that adjoins Edinburgh). Instead of being shipped empty back to Spain, the drained butts and hogsheads were snapped up by whisky distillers. Today, this wine is bottled in Spain, and sherry wood is expensive. Nonetheless some distillers feel that its influence is important. They make the investment (see pp. 66–67), and are precise in their requirements. Most sherry is made from the Palomino grape. There are several styles—fino: dry, delicate and fresh; manzanilla: a saltier coastal cousin; amontillado: darker and nuttier; palo cortado: aromatic, complex, and cookielike; oloroso: rich, creamy, and fruity; Pedro Ximénez (made with the grape of the same name, and not the Palomino): intensely raisiny, syrupy and dark.

Oak versus glass
Whisky is legally acknowledged as "whisky" after it has matured for a period in oak casks. The fact that the flavors of malt spirit improve if stored for a time in wooden casks was most likely discovered only by accident.

DOUBLE/TRIPLE DISTILLATION Most Scottish malt whisky is run through a pair of stills, but a handful of distilleries have used a system of three linked stills (*see* Springbank). Triple distillation was once traditional in the Lowlands of Scotland (*see* Auchentoshan). It is also favored in Ireland. In theory, the more thorough the distillation, the lighter and cleaner the spirit. While this is broadly true, the still's influence on flavor is not completely understood.

CASK STRENGTH A spirit enjoys a number of potencies on its way to the bottle. When it is first distilled it will have a strength around 140 proof. It is sometimes reduced with water to a casking strength of about 126 proof because distillers feel this is the ideal strength to open the spirit up for maturation.

During the maturation process in Scotland and some other countries, a proportion of the spirit's strength is lost through evaporation. This is known as the "angels' share." The amount of loss depends on a number of factors, including the position of the cask in the warehouse, the type of warehouse, the ambient temperature and humidity, the size of cask, and the length of maturation.

At the end of maturation the whisky will be considerably stronger than the common bottling strength of 80–92 proof. Water is normally added to the whisky to bring it down to this strength. However, the bottler may choose to bottle the whisky at the strength it came out of the cask, in which case it is known as a cask strength whisky.

UN-CHILL-FILTERED When whisky is chilled some proteins, fats, and congeners effectively solidify and make the whisky cloudy. To avoid this and keep the whisky bright and clear, many distillers chill the whisky and filter out the compounds. But it is increasingly common to leave them in, as it is thought they include flavor compounds. This is referred to as "un-chill-filtered" or "non-chill-filtered" on the label.

FLAVORS

THE INFLUENCE OF THE LANDSCAPE

THE UNIVERSE OF SPIRITS BEGAN to change when the word "designer," having become an adjective, attached itself to the word "vodka." Then, some of the most famous names in the world of distillation became better known for their "ready-to-drink" confections, misleadingly known in the United States as "malternatives." Now a new generation of consumers faces a choice between drinks that come from nowhere, taste of nothing much, and have a logo for a name; and drinks that come from somewhere, have complex aromas and flavors, and may have a name that is hard to pronounce.

Such drinks reflect their place of origin. They have evolved. They have a story to tell. They are good company, and they require something of the drinker in return: that he or she experiences the pleasure of learning to drink. Real, evolved drinks begin as the gift of God. They are grown, whether from grapes, grain, sugar cane, or, for example, the agave plant. They arise from their own *terroir*: geology, soil, vegetation, topography, weather, water, and air. To what extent they are influenced by each of these elements is a matter for debate, often passionate. People care about real drinks.

BRANDY AND WHISKY

The most sophisticated of real drinks are the brandies of France and the whiskies of the British Isles. The most complex brandies are the cognacs and armagnacs. The most complex whiskies are those of Scotland, Ireland, Japan, and Kentucky in the US.

Within these two duopolies, cognac and Scotch are the best known. In Cognac, the regions of production are contiguous, stretch about 90 miles (144 kilometers) from one end to the other, and are all in flat countryside. The whisky distilleries of Scotland, on the other hand, are spread over an area of about 280 miles (448 kilometers) from one end of the country to the other, from the Lowlands in the south to the northern Highlands, from mountain to

◄ **Under the volcano**
Scotland's landscape can be silent and still, yet the evidence of eruptions, glaciations, and rocky collisions is everywhere. The dews and frosts, the marine plants and mountain forests—each valley or island has its own flavor. Arran, left, has extinct volcanoes and a newish distillery.

shore, and from the Hebrides in the west to Orkney in the northeast. Theirs is surely the greater complexity. Scotland is the perfect place to study how landscape influences these complex flavors.

Whisky is a real drink. A single malt is as real as it gets. There are many potential influences on its character, and much dispute as to the relative importance—if any—of each.

On these and other issues ever more research is carried out, but an apparent insight into one stage of the whisky-making process may raise new questions about the next. In production, if a procedure is changed, the result may not be apparent until the whisky is mature, perhaps 10 years hence.

TASTING THE *TERROIR*

Scotland seems like a machine for the making of whisky: a nation on a small island, awaiting the vapors of the sea; providing summits to unlock their precipitation, which then filters through a diversity of rock, via springs and mountain streams, over peat and heather, to the fields of barley and the distilleries.

Scotland's heather-clad hillsides, its peaty moorlands, and its seaweed-fringed islands all contribute to the character of its national drink. To sample some of the more pungent malts is to taste the *terroir*. But to what extent are the aromas and flavors carried by the mountain streams or burns that feed the distilleries? Is the greater influence in the peat that is used to dry the malt? Then there is the question of the atmosphere in the damp, earth-floored warehouses, and its influence on the whisky.

Heather, peat, and seaweed are not unique to Scotland, but the country is unusually rich in all three. Their local variations, their proportion, their juxtaposition, and their relationship with the rest

The blood of …
… John Barleycorn was spilled by Robert Burns, a Lowlander but from the West. This field of barley is in the East, near the Lowland distillery, Glenkinchie.

"Scandinavian Scotland"

IN ITS TOPOGRAPHY, its use of Viking words, its Protestant rigor (with some ambivalence toward alcohol), Scotland can resemble Norway, the nearest of the Scandinavian countries. Scotland seems to reach northward, higher into the spirits belt, while its Celtic cousin Ireland (more especially the Republic) appears to lean south, toward the Roman Catholic countries of mainland Europe.

SCOTLAND IS BIGGER in both land area and population than Ireland. It also has 20 or 30 times as many distilleries. At one stage, for a brief period, the numbers of stills in each of the countries were close, but Ireland's industry spent decades in decline before rediscovering itself in recent years. Whichever country "discovered" the barley distillate, and this is contentious, Scotland is today's preeminent "Land of Whisky."

of the landscape are unique. Every landscape is. The color of a person's hair or eyes, or the shape of a nose or jawline, are not unique, but the face is, and it derives from them all.

On the map, Scotland presents a weatherbeaten face. The outline—the coast—is penetrated by endless inlets from the sea. These inlets are variously known as "sea lochs" or "firths"; the latter word has the same roots as the Norwegian "fjord."

SCOTCH

Only whisky made there can be called Scotch. For many years, the industry repeated this without making clear its meaning. Were their spokesmen simply repeating an appellation? Or did they mean that no other country could make a comparable product? Scotch whiskies all taste of their homeland to varying degrees, but in many the taste is so subtle as to be scarcely evident, while in others the aromas of peat and seaweed, for example, are wonderfully shocking.

The handful of malt whiskies (as opposed to the "pot-still Irish" type) made at Bushmills and Cooley in Ireland are similar in style to their Scottish counterparts; as are the handful of Japanese malts, though some have distinct local features. But a whisky cannot taste of Scotland if it is made in Ireland or Japan, however similar the *terroir*. The most characterful whiskies taste of the *terroir*, wherever it is. They are real drinks.

ROCK

Geology as a discipline began in Scotland—with the book *Theory of the Earth*, published in 1788. The author, Dr. James Hutton, was a Scot, inspired in part by the natural landscape of his homeland. The geology of Scotland is more varied than that of any country of a

Rosebank
Roses once bloomed
at Rosebank. Now rosebay
willowherb has taken over.
The whisky tastes of camomile
… or carboniferous rock.

similar size. Much of this diversity arises from a spectacular collision 400–500 million years ago. The part of the earth's crust that is now Scotland was at that time attached to North America. It was in collision with a European plate that included England, Wales, and Ireland. The fault line where the two plates met was more or less followed a few million years later by Hadrian's Wall, and the border between England and Scotland has rarely strayed more than a few miles from this line since. The geological turbulence continued, with everything from volcanoes to glaciers, until 20,000 years ago.

Thus not only did geology begin with Scotland, but Scotland began with geology: with the thrusts, intrusions, eruptions, and glaciations. It came to rest, semantically, as a Gaelic-language landscape, with "corries" (hollows in the mountainside); "lochans" (small lakes) and "lochs" in a wide range of sizes (sometimes stretching for many miles, and possibly with a small opening to the sea); "straths" (broad valleys); and the "glens" (or narrower valleys) that appear on every other label. *This* is the whisky-making machine.

In 1990, geologists Stephen Cribb and Julie Davison made a study of rock formations in Scotland's whisky regions, and compared them with tasting notes in books on the drink, including this one. Their findings suggested that the similar tastes in certain whiskies produced near each other might in part be due to the similar rock from which the water rose. For example, in the Lowlands, the crisp, dry Glenkinchie and Rosebank share the same carboniferous rock. The oldest rock is that which supplies water to the Bowmore and Bruichladdich distilleries on Islay, off the west coast of Scotland; it was formed about 600–800 million years ago, and seems to contribute an ironlike flavor.

GRAY GRANITE

For many years, whisky makers always spoke of granite. Being so hard, granite does not donate minerals to the water. Thus hard rock means soft water, and vice versa. Granite is the principal rock of the Grampians, the group of mountains and subranges that dominates the Highlands, and from which the Spey River flows. Every Speyside distiller seemed to claim that he had soft water, "rising from granite and flowing over peat." In looking at the Grampians, the Cribbs' book *Whisky on the Rocks* identified Ben Rinnes and the Conval Hills as sources of the typical Speyside water, feeding distilleries such as Glenfarclas, Aberlour, and Craigellachie. The study went on to point out that the region's geology is diverse, embracing substantial areas of limestone and sandstone. One distillery that has, sensibly, made a virtue of its sandstone water source is Glenmorangie, located in the northern Highlands.

Mineral flavors—and textures—are familiar from bottled waters, and also seem evident in some malt whiskies. Water is used to steep the grain at maltings (though only a handful of these are attached to distilleries). It is employed in the mash tun at every distillery to extract the sugars from the malted barley. It is used to reduce the strength of spirit in the cask to aid maturation. It is also used to reduce mature whisky to bottling strength. For this last stage the local water is influential only in the handful of distilleries that bottle on site, and in those cases, it is very influential indeed.

SNOW

Vodka marketeers love to promote their products with suggestions of snowy purity, whether they are distilled in St. Petersburg, Poznan, or in Peoria, Illinois. Some vodkas are distilled in one place and rectified in another. Others have Slavic origins, but are produced under license in North America or elsewhere.

Snowmelt is more reliably found in Scottish malt whisky. There is typically snow on Scotland's highest mountain, Ben Nevis (measuring 4410 feet or 1344 meters high), for six to seven months of the year, and occasionally for longer: perhaps from September to May, or even all year. The same can be true in the Grampians, though three or four months is more common.

SNOWMELT

At sea level, especially in the drier east, Scotland may have less than 32 inches (800 millimeters) of rain and snow a year. In the mountains, that figure can more than triple. Once the snow melts, it descends

descends by a variety of routes, filtering through fissures in the rock, emerging from springs, swelling streams or burns, or gushing into rivers like the Spey, Livet, and Fiddich.

High in the hills, distilleries like Dalwhinnie or Braeval might regard their water as snowmelt. By the time it has swollen the Spey, then been tapped by Tamdhu, it is regarded as river water. If it filters through the Conval Hills in search of Glenfiddich, Balvenie, or Kininvie, it emerges as the spring water of Robbie Dubh. Every distillery knows where it collects its water, and protects its source as a critical asset. Distillers know where their water arrives, but it may be impossible to say whence it came, or how long its journey was, except that it was once rain or snow.

WATER

The worry over water concerns not only quality, but also quantity. A great deal is required, not only for the steeps at the maltings and the mash tun at the distillery, but also to cool the condensers or worm tubs, to wash vessels, and to reduce the strength of the spirit in the cask or the mature whisky at bottling.

Not only must water for malting and mashing be available in volume, it must also be consistent in character. If a source threatens to run dry in the summer, the distillery may stop production and devote a few weeks' "silent season" to annual maintenance and vacations. If the water runs unusually slowly, or quickly, it may become muddy or sandy. If the water source is endangered by a project in the next county upstream, that could be a critical problem. And it is certainly critical if the distillery's production is outstripping the water source. Even the most sophisticated of distillery companies has been known to hire a water diviner to find an additional nearby source. Every effort will be made to match the character of the principal water used.

The issue of soft water versus hard goes beyond the flavor of any salts naturally occurring in the water. Calcium, for example, increases the extract of malt sugars in the mash tun, and may also make for a cleaner, drier whisky. Whether it does— whether, indeed, such influences could survive distillation—is hotly debated.

PRESENCE OF PEAT

Visitors to distilleries are sometimes invited to sample the water. It can taste intensely peaty. Yet the whisky may be barely peaty at all. This is the case at the famous Speyside distillery, Glen Grant. The

Snow on the Spey
The river Spey rises south of the Dalwhinnie distillery, one of Scotland's highest. Clearly whisky made from snowmelt, but also with some peaty complexity. Absolut Scotland ...

explanation would seem to be that the peaty taste does not survive distillation. Speyside is also rich in heather. Is that why its whiskies are so floral? The circumstantial evidence is strong, but some distillers might argue that the flowery character actually results from reactions during maturation.

On the island of Islay, even the tap water can be tinged a peaty brown or ironstone red. Perhaps the water flowed over peat for a longer distance. Did it linger, and absorb more peatiness? Or flow faster and dig up its peaty bed? The bed may also have contributed some ironstone, or some green, ferny, vegetal character. This time, the flavors do seem to carry over into the whisky. Perhaps the flavors were absorbed when the peaty water was used to steep the barley at the beginning of the malting process. Unlike the maltings on the mainland, those on Islay highlight the intensity of local peat. It is the use of peat fires in the drying of the grains that imparts the greatest degree of smokiness and "Islay character" to the malt. The peat in the kiln is the smoking gun. The Islay distiller has the soul of an outlaw.

PEAT

Not only is aroma the bigger part of taste—the drinks and foods that arouse the appetite and the imagination are often fragrant—but these same foods are in fact frequently grilled, barbecued, roasted, toasted, or smoked: the bacon, toast, and coffee; the steak sizzling on a charcoal grill; the chestnuts roasting on an open fire. Of all the techniques historically used to kiln malt in different parts of Europe, the peat fires of Scotland surely produce the most evocative aromas. While some devotees of single malts have a broad view, many take sides: will it be the peaty, briney whiskies of the islands and coasts; or the flowery, honeyed, sometimes sherried Speysiders?

The partisans for peat lust for its intensity (and love quoting ppm), but it also imparts a number of complex flavors and aromas. At least 80 aroma compounds have been found in peated malt.

While peatiness excites connoisseurs, it can alienate first-time tasters. When people say they "don't like" Scotch whisky, they often refer to a "funny taste," which turns out to mean peat. To take exception to such a fundamental element of the drink may seem odd, but distinctive, powerful flavors, especially if they are dry, can be challenging. Very hoppy beers are a perfect parallel. In a pinch, heavily oaked wines might also be drawn into the discussion.

In whisky, the dryness of peat provides a foil for the sweetness of barley malt, but that is a bonus, as is peat's rich content of antioxidants, the enemy of free radicals.

PLENTIFUL PEAT

Peat was used in the first place because it is a convenient and plentiful fuel. Ninety percent of the world's peat bogs are in temperate-to-cold parts of the northern hemisphere. Two-thirds of

Tasting the terroir
The basis of terroir is the earth. Here, it is sliced, and placed on a fire, so that its smoke pervades the malt. Some peat cutting on Islay is still done by hand.

Britain's bogland is in Scotland, which in land area is half the size of England. Scotland's northern Highlands has Europe's largest expanse of blanket bogs. These bogs, in the counties of Caithness and Sutherland, are said to set a standard in the worldwide study of the phenomenon.

The peat that seduces whisky lovers is on the distillery islands of Orkney and Islay. In both cases, the sea air and high winds add salty flavors to the peat. The coast of Islay is heavily fringed with seaweed, which adds an iodine, medicinal character to the atmosphere. This, too, penetrates the peat. The Orcadian peat is younger, more heathery, and incorporates a wide range of salt-tolerant maritime plants. In the western islands, especially Islay, the peat is rich in bog myrtle (*Myrica gale*), also known as sweet gale, which has a sweet, cypresslike aroma and bitter flavor. Bog myrtle was one of the flavorings used in beer before the hop plant was adopted, and clearly influences the flavors imparted by the peat.

When peat is being cut by hand, the spade digs out a cube with surfaces as shiny and dark as a bar of very dark chocolate. It sometimes looks as edible as Mississippi mud pie. A closer look at the muddy block sometimes reveals the fossil-like remains of mosses. The principal component is sphagnum, a spongy moss that intertwines with other plants to form a fibrous soil, which, under pressure, will eventually become coal. The peat bogs of Scotland began to grow between 7000 and 3000 years ago, and are up to 23 feet (7 meters) deep.

Ireland is also famously boggy, and no doubt its rural whisky makers burned peat, but distilling quickly moved to an industrial scale, concentrated in the few big cities, and the lack of peat became a defining characteristic of the "smooth" Irish whiskies. The large, urban distillers used coke to fire smokeless maltings. Having been overtaken in volume long ago by the country next door, the Irish are now rediscovering the merit of variety. A peated single malt called Connemara was launched in 1995–96 by the Cooley distillery, and has gone on to win several judgings.

BARLEY

Everyone knows that wines and brandies are made from grapes, but what about beer or whisky? Many consumers are unsure. Beer is often thought, mistakenly, to be made from hops. And whisky?

In explaining, and therefore promoting, its natural qualities, the grape does rather better than the grain. Wine makers often indicate on their labels which varieties of grape they have used. They may do this even if the wine is not a varietal. They might even discuss their choice of grape varieties on a back label or hang tag, and in their public relations and advertising.

Whisky makers do not in general do this. Why not? Are they using poor-quality barley? No. Malting requires barley of good quality. The argument for reticence is threefold: barley's contribution to flavor in whisky is less than it would be in beer, and even less than that of the grapes in wine. Second, perhaps simply as a reflection of the above, the difference between varieties is less obvious when it comes to flavor. Third, perhaps explaining this, the act of distillation removes some characteristics, and others are masked by the flavors gained during maturation. All of this is true up to a point, but what the distiller puts into his vessels must be a factor in the liquid that issues from them.

GOLDEN PROMISE

Almost all whisky distillers buy their barley according to a set of technical criteria (grain size, nitrogen, moisture content, etc.), rather than by variety. Some varieties bred or selected in the period of innovation after World War II are still legends. The last of that line, Golden Promise, represented 95 percent of the harvest at its peak. Its short straw stands up to the wind; it ripens early (in August); and it produces nutty, rich flavors.

The color purple
Heather is a distinctive feature of the Scottish landscape. Its color does not affect the whisky, but the floral and honey aromas often seem to have jumped into the glass.

Heather

IN THE UNOFFICIAL NATIONAL ANTHEM, the "Flower of Scotland" is Robert the Bruce; in heraldry, it is the thistle; in the world of drinks, it is surely heather. While the thistle is Scotland (prickly, defensive, and looking for a fight), heather is attractive and lucky. In Scotland, especially Orkney, it was traditionally the flavoring for an ale. When a whisky has a floral aroma, the flower is frequently heather. Often, it is not the flower itself but heather honey.

THESE CHARACTERISTICS are especially notable on Speyside and Aberdeenshire, where the hills are dense with heather. Glen Elgin and Balvenie are two whiskies with a notably heather-honey character. In Aberdeenshire, Glendronach and Glen Garioch have an enjoyable touch of heather, balancing their dry maltiness.

HEATHER IS A SIGNIFICANT COMPONENT of much peat in Scotland. At some distilleries, notably Highland Park, lore has it that sprigs of heather were thrown on to the peat fire in the maltings. Water flows over heather to several distilleries. Besoms, or brooms, made of heather twigs were once commonplace in Scotland, and were typically used to clean wooden washbacks (fermenting vessels). Whether their effect was to sanitize or inadvertently to inoculate with microorganisms is a piquant question. Wild yeast activity is at its height in summer, when bees are pollinating, and heather is a favorite source of nectar.

THE GREEK FOR THE WORD "BRUSH" gives us the botanical name Calluna vulgaris for the purple ling heather, which carpets the hillsides from mid-August into September. The brighter, redder bell heather (Erica cinerea) and the pinker, cross-leafed variety (Erica tetralix) flower about a month earlier. The English name for this group of small evergreen shrubs derives from their liking of heaths, but they also grow in bogs and on mountainsides. All three occur in Scotland, where heather covers between 4 to 5 million acres (1.6 and 2 million hectares).

SOME VARIETIES ARE FOUND throughout northern Europe, others are native to Scotland, which has the greatest abundance of the plants. Scottish settlers introduced heather to North America.

As the industry has grown, farmers have switched to varieties that give them more grain per acre, and therefore increase their profitability, while distillers have sought varieties that yield more fermentable sugars. These, however, do not necessarily produce delicious flavors, any more than do bigger, redder strawberries out of season. Nor do the varieties last much more than four or five seasons before being overtaken by something "better."

SEAWEED

The medicinal note in most Islay malts, especially Laphroaig, surely derives from seaweed, a source of iodine. The sea washes against the walls at all the distilleries, except Bruichladdich and Kilchoman,

Whisky and water
The village and distillery of Bowmore face the sea loch around which Islay wraps itself. Some of the distillery's warehouses are below sea level. Even on a calm day, the atmosphere is rich in the aromas of seaweed.

and the coast is enwrapped with seaweed. How do the seaweedy, ironlike aromas get into the spirit? It seems likely that they are carried ashore by the winds and the rain, and permeate the peaty surface of the island. Then, when the rivers and burns flow over the peat to the distilleries, they pick up these flavors and impart them in the steep or the mash tun. If the boggy surface is, indeed, impregnated with the seaweedy rain, then a further opportunity will arise when the peat is cut and burned in the distillery's maltings.

BREATHING SPIRIT

The greatest scepticism concerns the belief that the casks in the warehouses "breathe in" the atmosphere. Distillers who use centralized warehouses, away from the distillery, especially favor this argument. Some age on site spirit which is destined to be bottled as single malt, but send to centralized warehouses spirit that is destined for blending.

Seaweed has been described as one of Scotland's most abundant natural resources. The harvesting of seaweed was once a significant industry in Scotland. There is some circumstantial evidence that the practice was introduced by monks on the islands of the west. This is the part of Scotland with the most seaweed. Skye has especially dense kelp forests, sometimes stretching 3 miles (5 kilometers) offshore and more than 65 feet (20 meters) deep. In the islands, kelp was traditionally used as a fertilizer. It was also collected as a source of iodine. More recently, it was used to provide alginates to clarify beer and set jellies and desserts.

DISTILLERY FLAVORS

In the balance of influences, much more importance has been accorded in recent years to the way in which the distillery works. Twenty-eight malt distilleries, (about a third of the industry's working total) are owned by Diageo, the world's biggest spirits group; and Diageo argues strongly that the most important influences on flavor come from within the distillery itself.

The basic process of making malt whisky is the same throughout Scotland, but there are endless small but significant areas of variation. The degree of peating in the malt is one, similar to the choice of roasts in coffee. Another example is the density (or original gravity) of the malt-and-water mixture that goes into the mash tun (the "coffee filter"). The time the mixture spends in the mash tun, the temperatures to which it is raised, and the duration of each stage, all vary slightly from one distillery to the next. Inside a traditional mash tun is a system of revolving rakes to stir the mixture. In the more modern lauter system, developed in the German brewing industry, a system of knives is used. The German word "lauter" means pure or transparent, and refers to the solution of malt sugars that emerges from the vessel.

WHISKY RISING

As in cooking, every variation affects everything that follows, so that the permutations are infinite. It can be very difficult to determine which aspect of procedure has what effect. Despite that, the industry in general has over the years adopted a rather casual attitude toward yeast's use in fermentation. The view taken was that yeast's influence on flavor would largely be lost in distillation, and that its job was simply to produce as much alcohol as possible.

For years, almost all of Scotland's malt distillers employed the same two yeast cultures. An ale yeast from one of the big brewers

The infusion
Like coffee in a filter, the ground grains of malted barley are soaked in warm water, in a vessel with a sievelike base. The stirring mechanism rotates and can be lowered so that its blades prevent the mixture from solidifying.

was used because it started quickly. Then there was a second pitching with a whisky yeast from Distillers' Company Limited (now long subsumed into a component of Diageo). This had less speed but more staying power. Mergers and changes in ownership resulted in different yeasts coming into the industry. Many distilleries now use only one yeast culture.

The action of yeast in fermentation creates flavor compounds called "esters," which are variously fruity, nutty, and spicy. It is difficult to accept that none of these would survive distillation. Most distillers believe that the amount of time spent in the fermenter is critical to the individuality of each distillate. The effect of a new yeast culture can be tasted in new make, but the final result will not be determined until the whisky is mature.

Fermentation vessels in Scottish malt distilleries are known as "washbacks." Some are closed vessels made of metal, usually stainless steel. These are easy to clean and relatively safe from contaminants. Despite this, some distilleries prefer wooden washbacks, usually made from larch or Oregon pine. These are open, with a movable lid. Although they are cleaned thoroughly, it is hard to believe that they accommodate no resident microflora. Perhaps these contribute to the house character of some of the more interesting whiskies. Meanwhile, whether the microclimate in and around the distillery has an influence is hotly debated.

Storing The Spirit

IN MATURATION, most distillery managers prefer a stone-built, earth-floored, cool, damp warehouse. Such an atmosphere is felt to encourage the casks to breathe. In this type of structure, known as a dunnage warehouse, the casks are normally stacked only three high, usually with planks between them as supports. The more modern type of warehouse has a concrete floor and fixed racking, and can contain several stories of maturing casks. The atmosphere is generally warmer and drier than in dunnage warehouses. As is often the case, the old, inefficient system, more vulnerable to the vagaries of nature, produces the more characterful result.

INTO THE STILLS

Anyone who cooks will know that a recipe, however rigidly followed, will produce different results every time, depending upon the source of heat, the utensils, the cook, and so forth. The design of the stills is a factor increasingly emphasized by Diageo, but even this has an element of location. Some farmhouse distilleries clearly had stills designed to fit their limited space. Elsewhere, several distilleries in the same valley will have the same shape of still (in much the same way that train stations on the same line may look alike). Obviously, the local coppersmith had his own way of doing things. Distilleries are reluctant to change the shape or size of their stills when wear and tear demands replacement, or when an expansion is planned. The legend is that if a worn-out still has been dented at some time, the

Water music?
Not a French horn, or any musical instrument, but the unromantically named worm tub. This is Edradour's. The coil is 80 ft (24.5 m) long. The diameter starts at 8 inches (20 cm) and finishes at 2 inches (5 cm).

Still life
The creaminess of Macallan is attributed in part to its short, fat stills. In this picture, the stillman provides a sense of scale. The stills at Glenmorangie are twice as tall, and produce a spirit of legendary delicacy.

coppersmith will beat a similar blemish into its replacement, in order to ensure that the same whisky emerges.

Illegal distillers used just one small (and therefore portable), copper pot. Since then stills have grown, and are typically run in pairs (or occasionally threesomes), but the principles have not changed. It is clear that design has been largely empirical, with experiments and innovations introduced by individuals. It is often hard to imagine how a bit of extra piping here or there can make a difference. The ratio of surface areas to heat, liquid, vapor, and condensate have infinite effects that are not fully understood.

SHAPELY STILLS

It is argued that in a tall, narrow still, much of the vapor will condense before it can escape. The condensate will fall back into the still and be redistilled. This is known as reflux. The result is a more thorough distillation and a more delicate spirit. Because there is far less reflux in a short, fat still, the spirit will be oilier, creamier, and richer. This is just the simplest example of how the still shape influences the character of the whisky.

Stills vary enormously in size and shapes range from "lantern" or "lamp" to "onion" or "pear." Some have a mini-column above the shoulders or, more often, a "boil ball." Others have pipes known as "purifiers" in order to create reflux. The pipe that carries the vapor to the condenser is sometimes at an upward angle, or it can be straight, or point downward. The first will create the most reflux and the last little or none.

COOLING IT

The traditional method of condensing is in a worm tub. The vapors pass through a wormlike coil of copper piping in a tub of cold water. This tends to produce a more pungent, characterful spirit, with a heavier, maltier, cereal-grain character.

The more modern system has the opposite relationship between vapor and water. It involves a single large tube, inside which are packed smaller tubes. The small tubes are circulated with cold water, while the vapor passes through the large tube. This is called a shell-and-tube condenser. It is more efficient, and is said to produce lighter, grassier, fruitier spirits.

At a time when the industry was moving from worm tubs to shell-and-tube, Diageo made this change at its Dalwhinnie distillery. It was subsequently decided that the spirit had changed character to an unacceptable degree, and the distillery reverted to worm tubs.

One of the most important judgments in influencing flavor is deciding the speed at which the stills are run. A slower distillation leads to more contact between the liquid and the copper than a faster distillation, and this is usually desirable. Only part of the distillation is kept as useable spirit, though. Known at "the cut," this is the middle section of the distillation run. Judging the cut points is crucial.

REGIONAL VARIATIONS
SCOTLAND

L IKE WINES—AND MANY OTHER DRINKS—the single malts of
Scotland usually identify in their labeling not only their country
of origin but also the region within it. To know where in Scotland a
whisky was produced is to have a very general idea of its likely
character. The differences arise from *terroir* and tradition; there are
no regional regulations regarding production methods. In their a
roma and palate, some whiskies speak of their region more clearly
than others, as is the case with wines. Within Bordeaux, a particular
Pomerol, for example, might have a richness more reminiscent of
Burgundy; similar comparisons can be made in Scotland.

THE LOWLANDS

These are the most accessible whiskies, both in terms of palate
and geography, but sadly they are few in number. From the border
town of Carlisle, it is less than 100 miles (160 kilometers) to the
southernmost Scottish distillery, Bladnoch, which has been back in
production since December 2000.

Only two Lowlanders are in constant production. One of these is
Auchentoshan, sometimes billed as "Glasgow's only working
distillery." It is on the edge of the city, at Dalmuir, across the
Dunbartonshire county line. In Lowland tradition, the whisky is
light in both flavor and body, but surprisingly complex and herbal.
Auchentoshan is now the sole practitioner of the Lowland tradition
of triple distillation. The distillery does not have a visitor center, but
professional tours are possible by arrangement. With its galleried
mash house and uncluttered still-house, it is very visitor-friendly.

The other thriving Lowlander, at the opposite side of the country,
is Glenkinchie, "The Edinburgh Malt." This pretty distillery is about
15 miles (25 kilometers) southeast of the city, in the direction of the
border. Its spicy whisky has a popular following, and the distillery
has a visitor center.

In the last couple of years, hope has faded for the reopening of
the Lowland distilleries Littlemill and Rosebank, although various
bottlings of both are still available. There is a possibility, too, that

◄ **Maritime malt**
Riveted, not welded, this pot still has a marine appearance
befitting its region. Campbeltown's heyday was the era of
coastal steamers. Fat stills make oily, muscular whiskies.

Rosebank's equipment may find future use in a planned new distillery at Falkirk. Rosebank, which triple distilled, was widely regarded as a classic, and its whisky is collectible. Half a dozen more whiskies are still to be found from Lowland distilleries, some of which closed as long ago as the 1970s.

There were never a great many Lowland malts, but to have only three active distilleries is perilously few. The delicacy of the Lowlanders makes its own contribution to the world of single malts. This style can be very attractive, especially to people who find the Highlanders and Islanders too robust.

The Lowlanders' problem has been that the Highlanders and Islanders have the romance. Many consumers like a gentle, sweetish malt such as is typical in the Lowlands, but they want the label to say it came from the Highlands. This is analogous with the wine industry, where consumers who like sweetish Chardonnays nevertheless insist that they are drinking a "dry white."

The notion of the Lowlands as a whisky region would be reinforced if it could annex two distilleries that are barely across the Highland line: Glengoyne and Loch Lomond. The first is very pretty, can be visited, and is barely outside Glasgow. Its malty whisky would be perfectly acceptable as a Lowlander. The second is a more industrial site, but a much more attractive distillery than it once was, and it makes a variety of whiskies. Pressed to "defect," both would probably cling to the Highland designation.

THE HIGHLANDS

The border between the Lowland and Highland distilleries is surprisingly southerly, following old county boundaries, stretching across the country between the rivers Clyde and Tay. Some commentators talk of a "southern Highlands," embracing the Tullibardine distillery and Deanston. Beyond these two, the spread is clearly eastern.

THE EASTERN HIGHLANDS includes, among others, the newly independent Edradour, the smallest distillery in Scotland. Another tiny, farm-style distillery, Glenturret, now finds itself greeting visitors as "The Famous Grouse Experience." The much larger but handsome Aberfeldy distillery has a similar role as "Dewar's World of Whisky." All of these, together with Blair Athol, are in Perthshire. Any of them could comfortably be visited in a day trip from Edinburgh (about 70 miles, or 112 kilometers, away), and all are on or near the main road north to Speyside. Perhaps for reasons of

The border
It is neither the Berlin Wall nor Hadrian's, but it is Border country. The outer wall of a warehouse is turned to brash advertisement at the otherwise discreet Bladnoch distillery. Several distilleries identify themselves with such bold wall paintings.

geology, several distilleries in this region have notably fresh, fruity whiskies. Farther north, in barley-growing Aberdeenshire, some heftier whiskies emerge from handsome distilleries such as Royal Lochnagar, Glen Garioch, and Glendronach.

SPEYSIDE is not precisely defined, but it embraces between a half and two-thirds of Scotland's distilleries, including the most widely recognized whisky names. A generous definition of Speyside is assumed in this book. Strictly speaking, the long-gone distilleries of Inverness were regarded as Highlanders, not Speysiders.

Again for the convenience of the visitor, this book divides the region into a series of river valleys. In some of these valleys, there do seem to be similarities between the whiskies of neighboring distilleries.

The Spey River itself is lined with distilleries on both banks, but a number of tributaries and adjoining rivers frame the region. Speyside's ascendancy rested not only on the Grampian mountain snowmelt and the malting barley of Banff and Moray, but also on the railroad era. Trains on a rustic branch alongside the Spey took workers and barley or malt to the distilleries, and returned with whisky for the main line to Edinburgh, Glasgow, and London. Only vestiges of the Speyside railroad survive today, though it is a popular walk. The active line from Aberdeen to Inverness

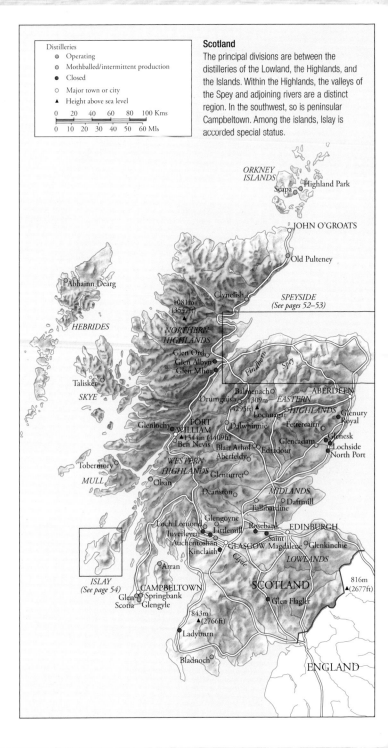

Distilleries
- ◉ Operating
- ◉ Mothballed/intermittent production
- ● Closed
- ○ Major town or city
- ▲ Height above sea level

0   20   40   60   80   100 Kms

0   10   20   30   40   50   60 Mls

Scotland

The principal divisions are between the distilleries of the Lowland, the Highlands, and the Islands. Within the Highlands, the valleys of the Spey and adjoining rivers are a distinct region. In the southwest, so is peninsular Campbeltown. Among the islands, Islay is accorded special status.

ORKNEY
ISLANDS
Scapa Highland Park

JOHN O'GROATS

Old Pulteney

Abhainn Dearg

Clynelish

SPEYSIDE
(See pages 52–53)

1081m
(3547ft)
▲

HEBRIDES

NORTHERN
HIGHLANDS

Glen Ord
Glen Albyn
Glen Mhor

Findhorn   Spey

Talisker

SKYE

Balmenach   ABERDEEN

Drumguish   1309m   EASTERN
▲4295ft)   HIGHLANDS   Glenury
Lochnagar   Royal
Dalwhinnie   Fettercairn
Glenlochy   Glenesk
FORT   Glencadam   Lochside
WILLIAM   North Port
▲1344m (4409ft)
Ben Nevis   Blair Athol
Aberfeldy   Edradour

WESTERN
HIGHLANDS   Glenturret

Tobermory

MULL   Oban

Deanston   MIDLANDS

Tullibardine

Daftmill

Glengoyne
Loch Lomond   Rosebank   EDINBURGH
Inverleven   Littlemill
Auchentoshan   Saint
Kinclaith   GLASGOW   Magdalene   Glenkinchie

Arran   LOWLANDS

816m
▲(2677ft)

ISLAY
(See page 54)   CAMPBELTOWN   SCOTLAND
Glen Springbank
Scotia Glengyle   Glen Flagler

843m
▲(2766ft)

Ladyburn

Bladnoch

ENGLAND

(just over 100 miles or 160 kilometers) follows the main road. The rivers are crossed as follows:

DEVERON: This valley has Glendronach distillery and Macduff. There are five or six distilleries in the general area, but these are quite widely dispersed. Most produce firm, malty whiskies.

ISLA: This has nothing to do with island (it has a different spelling; there's no "y"). Dominican monks brewed here in the 1200s, and there is mention of heather ale in the records. The oldest distillery on Speyside is Strathisla (founded in 1786), showpiece of Chivas Brothers, in the town of Keith in the Isla Valley. There are four or five distilleries in this area, and some of its whiskies have a cedary dryness.

FIDDICH AND DULLAN: These rivers meet at Dufftown, one of the claimants to be the whisky capital of Scotland. There are still six working distilleries in the area, despite the loss of Pittyvaich in 2002. A couple more are currently silent. Some classically rounded, malty Speysiders are produced here, including the secret star, Mortlach.

LIVET: The most famous distillery is named after the river valley itself, and there are three others in the area, all producing light, soft, delicate whiskies. The Livet appellation was once widely copied, but has been increasingly protected. The hill town, Tomintoul, is a base for exploration.

SPEY: Macallan, Aberlour, and Glenfarclas, three of the heavier interpretations of Speyside malts, are all to be found on the most heavily whiskied stretch of the Spey. There are about 12 distilleries, each less than a mile from the next, immediately upstream of the village of Craigellachie, home to a famous hotel and whisky bar.

ROTHES BURN: Actually no more than a stream, this river is one of several that reach the Spey at Rothes, another whisky "capital." This one-street town has five distilleries, producing some very nutty whiskies. Speyburn, usually shot through the trees, is the most photographed distillery in Scotland, while Glen Grant has a spectacular "tropical" garden, a coppersmith's, and a "dark grains" plant, which turns residual malt into cattle feed.

LOSSIE: Was it the water that first attracted the Benedictines of Pluscarden to this region? They no longer brew there, but they still

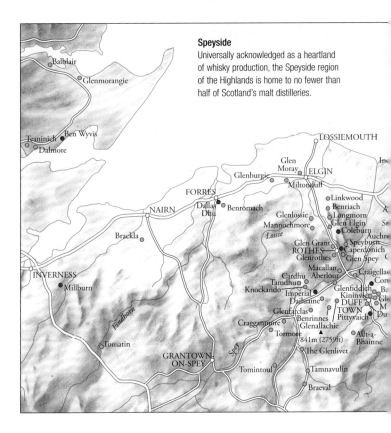

Speyside
Universally acknowledged as a heartland of whisky production, the Speyside region of the Highlands is home to no fewer than half of Scotland's malt distilleries.

have a priory next door to the Miltonduff distillery. Two secret stars, Longmorn and Linkwood, are among the eight distilleries just south of Elgin. The world's most famous whisky store, Gordon & MacPhail, is in Elgin itself which is the undisputed commercial capital of Speyside and the county seat of Moray. The Lossie whiskies are sweetish and malty.

FINDHORN: Born-again Benromach is near the town Forres. Production restarted in 1998: the new make tasted creamy and flowery. The museum distillery of Dallas Dhu is nearby, and in the distance is Tomatin.

THE NORTHERN HIGHLANDS is a geographically clear-cut region, which runs from Inverness, straight up the last stretch of the east coast. The region's water commonly runs over sandstone, and there is a gentle maritime influence. There are four or five distilleries in short order; including the energetic Glenmorangie and the rich

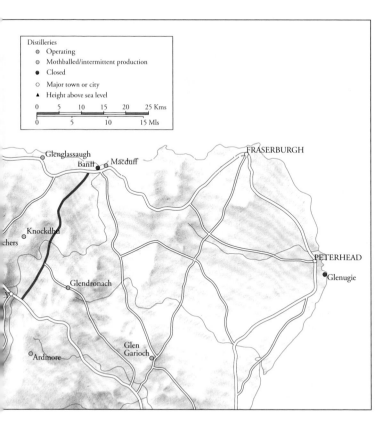

Distilleries
- ◉ Operating
- ◎ Mothballed/intermittent production
- ● Closed
- ○ Major town or city
- ▲ Height above sea level

0 5 10 15 20 25 Kms
0 5 10 15 Mls

Glenglassaugh
Banff Macduff
FRASERBURGH
Knockdhu
chers
Glendronach
PETERHEAD
Glenugie
Glen Garioch
Ardmore

Dalmore. Then there is a gap before the connoisseurs' favorite, Clynelish, and an even bigger gap before the famously salty Old Pulteney in Wick. As its distilleries have become more active, the northern Highlands has gained more recognition as a region. Its whiskies tend toward firm, crisp dryness and a light saltiness.

WESTERN HIGHLANDS The far northwest is the only sizeable stretch of the country with no legal whisky makers. It is just too rugged and rocky. Even the center cut has only two distilleries. On the foothills of Scotland's (and Britain's) highest mountain, Ben Nevis, the eponymous distillery can be regarded as being "coastal," according to its manager, Colin Ross. Why? Because it is on a sea loch. The Oban distillery certainly does face the sea, and has the flavors to prove it.

The other active mainland distilleries, Loch Lomond and Glengoyne, are so close to Glasgow that they might attract more attention reclassified as Lowlanders. In 2003, Glengoyne was acquired by Ian Macleod Ltd.

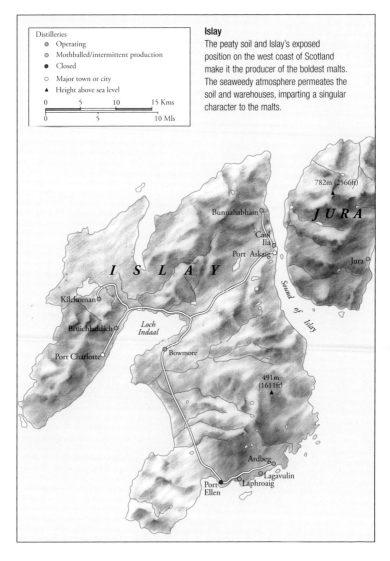

Distilleries
- ◉ Operating
- ◉ Mothballed/intermittent production
- ● Closed
- ○ Major town or city
- ▲ Height above sea level

0   5   10   15 Kms
0   5   10 Mls

Islay
The peaty soil and Islay's exposed position on the west coast of Scotland make it the producer of the boldest malts. The seaweedy atmosphere permeates the soil and warehouses, imparting a singular character to the malts.

THE ISLANDS

The greatest whisky island by far is Islay (above), with its eight distilleries—the newest being Kilchoman. The others have one apiece, except for Orkney, which has two distilleries.

ORKNEY For the moment, Highland Park is Scotland's northernmost distillery. Its whisky is one of the greats: peaty and smoky, and univerally superb. Saltier whiskies from the Scapa distillery—slightly to the southwest of Highland Park—have a strong following.

SKYE Talisker whisky from Skye is a classic—volcanic, explosive, and peppery. The taste reflects the wild, looming *terroir*.

MULL Tobermory is a restrained islander, but the distillery also produces the peatier, smokier whisky called Ledaig.

JURA The decidedly piney Isle of Jura whisky has appeared in more expressions and has been better promoted since the owning group, Whyte and Mackay, seceded from its American parent, Jim Beam.

ISLAY There are currently eight distilleries bottling whisky on Islay now that Kilchoman is on line, and nine if you count the Bruichladdich bottlings under the Port Charlotte name. The Islay Festival in late May has established itself as an annual favorite.

ARRAN The first spirit from the Isle of Arran distillery ran in 1995. Its small stills produce a creamy spirit with only faint touches of island character: a touch of flowery pine in the finish.

LEWIS Became a legal whisky-making island for the first time since around 1840, when Abhainn Dearg started production in 2008. Stylistically, early expressions released have been light and easy-drinking, with the promise of more substantial things to come.

CAMPBELTOWN

A temporary cessation in production occurred at Springbank and its associated companies in 2008, but production began again in 2009. The first new distillery of the new millennium, Glengyle, opened in 2004 and there has subsequently been a series of limited releases from the plant under the Kilkerran single malt name.

The Springbank distillery itself produces three whiskies, using entirely its own malt—the Springbank maltings was restored a decade ago. This distillery has on occasion also assisted with the management of the other Campbeltown distillery, Glen Scotia, which is currently also in production.

Springbank, independent bottlers Cadenhead, and the Eaglesome store are related businesses. The whisky veteran behind them, Hedley Wright, has been determined to keep Campbeltown on the whisky map. Its history is evidenced by fragments of about 20 distilleries converted to other uses. There are said to have been 32 distilleries in 1759. The town at the foot of the Kintyre peninsula provides not only a harbor, but a location surrounded by the sea often shrouded in mist.

EVOLUTION OF
WORLD WHISKIES

THE EXPLOSION IN WORLD WHISKIES in the last decade has been huge. In the last edition, we introduced a dedicated world whisk(e)y section for the first time, and including Irish malts, it consisted of nine pages. Today, it would be possible to fill this whole book with non-Scottish malts.

That is not an exaggeration. If you take America alone, the last edition had four entries under the heading US microdistillers. Today, there are more than 700 craft distilleries. Many of them aren't making malt whisky and some of the ones that are don't yet warrant comparison with the fine whiskies that make up this book's 448 pages. But there are some that do. It's not just America, either. Indeed, there are many territories, from Taiwan and India to Australia and New Zealand, and up to Sweden and Denmark, which are making exceptional malt whiskies, and are now knocking on the doors of the fortress that is Scottish single malt.

There are two ways you can make single malt whisky: like the Scots do, in which case you'd better be very, very good indeed. Or by trying to do something genuinely different.

Once upon a time, Scotland bossed the world of whisky. If you made single malt whisky, you did it the Scottish way. Japan's whiskies are modeled on Scotch, and Canada's one single malt distillery, in Nova Scotia, was somewhat ironically accused of passing off its whisky as Scottish single malt. But with the "new world" distilleries, part of a surprisingly wide diaspora, come new rules.

The regulations introduced by the Scotch Whisky Association and adopted by the European Union, apply only in Europe, and some of them apply only in Scotland. So the minimum maturation of spirit for three years is a given. But the type of wood you mature your spirit in, or how you dry your barley, isn't. So while some follow the Scottish route, many others are setting it in a totally different direction.

The extremes in different approaches are best summarized by probably the two best "new world whisky" exponents, Sweden and Australia. Swedish whisky fans treat Scottish single malts with deference and reverence. Their distillers set out to make malt that

◄ **Whisky, the Kiwi way**
Stunning landscapes and temperate climate characterize New Zealand's South Island, which is home to great whisky.

Back to tradition
Nant in Australia has been using its water-driven flour mill from the 1800s as part of the whisky-making process.

matches Scottish single malt as closely as possible. They bring precision and science to their efforts, and are sourcing the finest ingredients including low-yield, high-quality barleys that have long gone from Scottish distilleries. The results so far have been outstanding, with four distilleries now bottling, and another handful on their way.

At the other end of the world, the Australians are taking a very different approach. They are exuberant, loud, and brash, with powerful, full-flavored whiskies, often matured in unusual casks at unusual sizes. The Australians do not making waves, and are questioning the way whisky is made, asking why they must be bound by some of malt whisky's traditions. If they can't get sherry wood they use port. They are raising questions about the size of cask used, and the climate it is used in, not just in terms of heat, but extremes of heat and humidity. And they are confident enough to stand up for their malts—with very good reason—when they are criticized by some of the traditionalists.

REGIONAL VARIATION

What comes next is regional whiskies reflecting where they are produced. The peat in Australia is sweet and clean from the vegetation that has been crushed over the centuries, whereas

Swedish peat is salty because at one time it came from under the Baltic sea. Salt is a characteristic of food preservation in Scandinavia, so the Swedish palate is used to saltiness, and it is a natural fit in the country's whisky. Some Swedish whisky contains malted barley dried over juniper twigs—a traditional way of smoking Swedish food. Swedish whisky, therefore, tastes Swedish.

Oak is another area where regionalism will impact. Hungarian, Russian, and East European oak has a massively different impact on malt spirit than French oak will. We're already familiar with the different effects of American and European oak. The new distillers will offer many other options, as well as maturation in many different wood types.

The picture is a rapidly changing one. Barely a week goes by without a new distillery opening for the first time, and another releasing its first expression. Many will sell to a very localized community, and many have no great designs on world domination. Several have reached the point where they are having to pause, consolidate, and expand. But others, including most of the ones featured in this edition, are reaching out across the world.

Whisky in India
The affluent state of Karnataka is home to India's
IT boom and now malt whisky!

TUN No 92 9
ROTATION No 0
BULK LTRS 2130/1 2115/2
G/F 12 Y.O. SPECIAL RESERVE

AGED TO
PERFECTION

IT'S NOT UNCOMMON FOR A WHISKY MAKER to decide to change the age of the whisky sold as its core expression. As whisky enthusiasts have become more knowledgeable, it has become more widely understood that malt is an organic and evolving product, and advances in knowledge and technology have meant that while in the past many saw the age on the label as a statement of authenticity, in fact even relatively young whisky can have a strong and full flavor.

Glenfiddich, the world's biggest-selling malt, has changed its mind about age on more than one occasion, and other malts have moved to a different age. Some companies have left the age alone but have changed the liquid in the bottle markedly.

There is another trend going on too, driven by shortages of malt. Increasingly distillers are focusing on taste and moving away from age statements. The intention is to persuade drinkers that even a young whisky can taste great—and that's all that really matters.

THE IMPOSSIBLE DECISION

Upgrading the age is not easy. Most distilleries have some reserves of maturing whisky that is older than they strictly need, but these stocks would not be sufficient to support such a major change. Had sales been falling sharply, a backlog of stock would have built up, but this was not the case. The decision to increase the age would have required sufficient stock to be laid down 12 years earlier, probably with a view to the change.

The person who makes such decisions has an impossible job. However good their judgment, knowledge, and understanding of the industry; however thorough the company's market research; and however many futurologists it consults, it is simply impossible to predict how much whisky will be required in five, ten or fifteen years. When the time comes, there is always too little or too much. Across the industry this is why distilleries open, close, are mothballed, and so frequently change ownership.

◀ **Single but married**
Glenfiddich Special Reserve is already 12 years old when it goes into this marrying tun for about four months. The object is to iron out natural differences and ensure a consistent product.

IN THE VAT

The components of a bottling may also embrace casks of various sizes and with different histories. Although the contents of the casks will be vatted according to a "recipe," adjustments will have to be made to account for the way in which the whisky has developed during maturation. No two casks, even with the same origin, are alike. Casks from the bottom of the warehouse will have matured at a different rate from those in the airier racks at the top. A warehouse closer to the sea may impart brinier characteristics. Some distilleries have only the classically damp, earth-floored, stone-built warehouses, with casks stacked three high, separated by planks of wood; others have built-in racking, with casks nine high; some have both. All of these factors may affect the distillers' choice of casks for a bottling.

Ages around six, seven, and eight years are commonly used in blends, but could be used in a vatting for a single malt. If it carries an age statement, regulations demand that it be based on the youngest age, but since "6-year-old" might sound callow, the producer might prefer to do without an age statement. When Glenfiddich was marketed as an 8-year-old, it probably included whiskies of nine and ten years or more. Now it is a 12-year-old and probably includes whiskies of up to 15 years old. Some of the lighter-bodied malts hit their stride at eight or ten years old, while 12 is so common as to be regarded by consumers in some markets as a standard for mature malt.

While some distillers such as Chivas Brothers continue to make a virtue of age statements, an increasing number of their competitors are freeing themselves from what they see as the shackles of specified ages. The argument goes that you don't pick an apple after a certain number of days, but when it is at its best. Though we should not shy away from the fact that non-age-statement (NAS) bottlings are ultimately about a shortage of aged stock, due to increased demand for Scotch whisky in a recent year, which has outstripped supply. Distillers are making the best of the situation, and many of their NAS creations are very good. However, we have to wait for posterity to judge whether the "freedom" provided by this trend ultimately damages the integrity of Scotch single malts.

Away from Scotland, with the emergence of new whisky countries, a straightforward age statement is seen by many as increasingly irrelevant. Producers in countries such as Australia, India, and Taiwan point out that without considering other factors, such as type and size of cask used, temperature and extremes of temperature in the country of maturation, humidity and atmospheric pressure, and type of oak involved, it is impossible to discern much about quality.

Glenfiddich

TAKING GLENFIDDICH as an example, in addition to the "standard" 12-year-old, there is a 14-year-old Rich Oak (finished in virgin American and European oak cask), a 15-year old Solera Reserve (using the solera system, common in the world of sherry), and a 21-year-old Gran Reserva (finished in rum casks), along with several dated vintages.

WHEN FORMER GLENFIDDICH Malt Master David Stewart formulated his 12-year-old, he might as well have preferred to approach the task from a wider angle: retaining some younger malts from the previous 8-year-old variant, but increasing the proportion of older malts (or increasing their ages). Young malts can inject liveliness to a vatting, while the older ones add complexity. Would this have produced an even more complex whisky? Why did he not follow that course? Because it would have precluded the use of the age statement "12 years old." So we return to the potential merits of NAS whiskies, when created with skill and integrity.

We already know this from the way bourbon, matured in Kentucky's very hot summers and very cold winters, matures faster than Scottish single malt. Many world whiskies are ready to release at less than six years old. The oldest ever Indian single malt released was eight years old, and three-quarters of the cask's contents was lost to the angels. But it was a stunning whisky, at the peak of maturation. It has been argued that Scotch whisky at a similar age is not of the same quality.

DEVELOPING A RANGE

If there were a "best" age for malt whisky, it would be universally adopted. In Italy, where the words "malt whisky" are potent, devotees are delighted with a 5-year-old. In Japan, where age is respected, a 30-year-old is appreciated. However, the trend for NAS expressions has thrown the whole business of building a range of whiskies, based on age, into question. To take one high-profile example, Ardbeg now offers a core portfolio in which only one expression—the entry level 10-year-old—carries an age statement.

Regardless of the issue of ages, in recent years distillers have expanded their ranges by varying strengths, types of cask, and finishes. For those consumers bored with consistency, there is the merit of greater individuality in some of the more unusual bottlings, particularly vintages, and those at cask strength.

A whisky can be too woody at 21 years, or it can still be enjoyable at 50, but—like death and taxes—evaporation eventually takes its toll. Unlike a human being, a whisky that has overstayed its time on earth is sure to meet the angels. Just as humans in ancient cultures revered trees, especially oaks, so *Quercus robur* and *Quercus alba* are the greatest influences on the maturation of *aqua vitae*.

THE PERFECT WOOD

D ID THE FLAVORS IN YOUR GLASS begin a dozen years ago, with the sowing of barley on the Black Isle? Or decades earlier, as a blizzard on the Grampians? If the malt was peated, you could be enjoying a few leaves of bog myrtle that have been waiting 7000 years for your rendezvous. Or did your favorite flavors emerge a century ago on a forest slope in Galicia, Spain? Or perhaps in the Ozark Mountains of Missouri?

The creation of alcoholic drinks in different parts of the world employs in various roles a whole alphabet of trees: for their fruit and berries; to make charcoal, to act as a filter; as a fuel in the kilning of malt; to provide vessels for fermentation or maturation, or simply to act as containers. Various drinks are stored in (or consumed from) cedar, juniper, and chestnut, but the wood most commonly used for all those purposes is oak. Its most attractive property is its pliability. It must bend to make a barrel, and the elegant curves of this traditional vessel strengthen it, just as an arch reinforces a building. Even in the most mechanized distillery, casks are rolled and occasionally dropped or bounced. They must be tough and not split or leak. They contain an increasingly precious product.

United States regulations insist that bourbon is matured in new oak, but the cask may subsequently cross the Atlantic and be filled three or four times with the spirit of Scotland. If each of those fillings is matured for only six or seven years, the cask will see two or three decades' service. If a cask is tapped at 25 years, then repeats the performance, it already has half a century under its belt. It must be tough, yet also able to breathe during the maturation of the whisky, and perhaps also have some flavors and aromas to donate.

OAK AND FLAVOR

Wooden casks were originally regarded simply as containers. Whisky was sold in the cask to inns and country houses, and customers noted that it mellowed in the cellar. Over the years, it has increasingly been recognized that the character of the wood plays a big part in the development of the whisky's aromas and flavors, but how big? The perceived importance of wood has

◀ **Tough but pliable**
Oak does not break under torture, but it bends to provide the elegant, strengthening curves of the cask. This cooperage is in Andalusia. Charring to enhance flavor is more typical in Kentucky.

greatly increased across the industry in recent years, yet opinions differ more widely than ever.

SWEET SHERRY The issue was not much discussed while former sherry casks were readily available for the maturation of whisky. These casks seem to have been accepted without much question, though they must have imparted a variety of characteristics. Some had been used in fermentation, others in maturation, others for transportation. They had contained different styles of sherry—and sometimes other fortified wines.

As sherry fell out of fashion, exports to the United Kingdom diminished. Meanwhile, the dictator Franco died in 1975, Spain became a democracy, and its trade unions insisted that the bottling of wines be carried out by local labor in Spain.

Distilleries anxious to continue sherry aging now had to work directly with the bodegas in Jerez. Macallan has been the most consistently active proponent of this approach. So through several changes of control at Macallan, its top managers have each year swapped the granite and heather of Speyside for the orange trees and Moorish architecture of Jerez.

WHICH VARIETY OF OAK?

Setting aside those that grow as shrubs and bushes, there are more than half a dozen European species of oak tree. Two have traditionally been used in cooperage. The second choice is usually *Quercus petraea*, known as the sessile oak, for the way the acorns "sit" on the twigs. The first choice is *Quercus robur*, the pendunculate oak. The epithet refers to the way the acorns are suspended on stalks.

The *Q. robur* tolerates a wide range of growing conditions, and is typically found in England, France, and Iberia. In France, where region appellations are used, Limousin and Tronçais oaks are usually of the *Q. robur* variety.

SPANISH OAK The principal growing area in Spain is the northwest corner of the country, where the coast between the cities of Santander and Corunna faces the Bay of Biscay and the Atlantic. Behind the coast rise stony hills, the valleys between them dappled with oaks. These once fed shipyards making galleons; then Spanish oak was turned into barrels for wine; and now its final destination is Scotland.

The center of the lumber industry is the city of Lugo, in the province of the same name, in the region of Galicia. A sawmill there cuts staves for Macallan. The staves are air-dried for 12 to 15 months by being left outdoors. The weather washes out some of the tannins, moderating the intensity of the wood, and the staves then become casks at a cooperage in Jerez. They are filled with newly pressed cloudy grape juice, for between two weeks and six months, and then used a second time, to mature sherry, before being sent to Scotland. The casks are shipped whole, thus maintaining the sherryish character of the wood. This would diminish if they were broken down into staves.

Spanish wine makers, such as those of Jerez, increasingly prefer the sweeter, more vanilla-like character of American oak.

BUTTS, BARRELS, OR HOGSHEAD?

The casks used for the maturation of sherry are known as butts, and typically have a capacity of 132 gallons (500 liters or 110 UK gallons). There is a beauty and an integrity to such vessels, but their size and weight make them difficult to handle.

The term "hogshead" refers to a traditional cask size of 66 gallons (250 liters or 55 UK gallons). Sherry hogsheads can be found, but the designation is more commonly applied to a Scottish adaptation of an American barrel. In this instance, the barrel is broken down in the US and shipped as staves. It is then reassembled in Scotland with new heads (barrel ends) to increase the capacity of the cask. The new heads also freshen up the wood influence. The term "American

Iron lady
Torture continues … this machine forces the hoops to hold the staves in position.

oak" is sometimes used to indicate a bourbon barrel, which typically has a capacity of around 53 gallons (200 liters or 44 UK gallons). Many single malts are vatted from a combination of sherry butts and bourbon barrels, usually with the latter in the majority.

BOURBON BARRELS Many producers of lighter-bodied, more delicate-tasting whiskies feel that they express their aromas and flavors more successfully when matured in bourbon barrels. A long-time proponent of this approach is the Glenmorangie distillery.

The man in charge of distillation and maturation for Glenmorangie, Bill Lumsden, has worked with the Blue Grass Cooperage in Louisville to develop a bourbon barrel that perfectly suits both sides of the Atlantic. More than 225 miles (360 kilometers) southwest and 100 miles (160 kilometers) south of St. Louis, Missouri, oak for the casks is grown around Altenburg, a town settled by immigrants from Saxony in Germany. The town sign still uses the word *"Stadt"* for "city."

This is an area of mixed deciduous woodland, with small, privately owned lots. The soil is very well drained. The part of the country has four definite seasons, but the winter cold has enough restraint not to damage the crop. The wood is clean, without knots, and with good pores. This is white oak, *Quercus alba*.

LIGHT, MEDIUM, OR ALLIGATOR?

Bourbon barrels are toasted or charred on the inside to enable the whisky to permeate the wood. There are stories of this happy discovery having arisen from an accidental fire, but it seems more likely to have emerged from the technique of toasting the wood to make it pliable.

Charring gives the spirit access to positive properties and flavors in the wood, but also enables it better to expel undesirable flavors.

Steam heat
Scalded into submission … after these sequences of tortures, the casks can settle down to a life of sipping sherry, then whisky.

The Aging Process

SEVERAL PROCESSES take place during maturation. While the new distillate may have some harsh, "spirity" flavors, these can be lost by evaporation. With the expansion and contraction of the wood, caused by seasonal changes in temperature, spirit flavors may be exhaled and the natural aromas of the environment taken into the cask: piney, seaweedy, and salty "sea-air" characteristics can all be acquired in this way. Flavors are also imparted by the cask: sherry wood may add the nutty note of the wine; and bourbon barrels can impart caramel flavors, vanillins, and tannins.

PERHAPS THE MOST IMPORTANT influence on the flavor is that of a very slow, gentle oxidation of the whisky. While oxygen is regarded as an "enemy" by brewers and some wine makers, because it can cause "stale" flavors, its influence is also a part of the character of other drinks such as Madeira wines. The importance of oxidation in the maturation of whisky has been the subject of much work by Dr. Jim Swan, originally at the Pentlands Scotch Whisky Research Institute, and more recently by his own company. Dr. Swan argues that oxidation increases the complexity and intensity of pleasant flavors in whisky, especially fragrant, fruity, spicy, and minty notes.

AS IN THE PRODUCTION of all alcoholic drinks, the flavors emerge from a complex series of actions and reactions. Traces of copper from the stills are the catalyst. They convert oxygen to hydrogen peroxide, which attacks the wood, releasing vanillin. This promotes oxidation, and additionally pulls together the various flavors present. These processes vary according to the wood's region of origin, and its growth patterns. Vanillin is a component that occurs naturally in oak. As its name suggests, it imparts a vanilla-like flavor.

IN SPAIN, trees from the most mountainous districts of Galicia are more resiny. In the US, growth is mainly in a belt across Ohio, Kentucky, Illinois, Missouri, and Arkansas. The western part of this contiguous region has the poorest soil and the most arid climate, and therefore the trees have to fight to survive. This optimizes spring growth, which has the most open texture and is the most active in the maturation process.

American cooperages typically offer three degrees of char: light, medium, and alligator. The latter, the heaviest, leaves the wood looking like a log so heavily burned that it has formed a pattern of squares reminiscent of an alligator's skin.

A sherry butt or bourbon barrel will impart considerable aroma and flavor to its first fill of whisky. "First-fill sherry casks were used in the maturation of this whisky" is the type of claim that appears on the neck label of an especially voluptuous malt. Some distillers feel that the more restrained second fill provides a better balance. A third fill will impart little, but let the character of the spirit speak for itself. If there is a fourth fill, it is likely to go for blending after which, 30 or 40 years later, the inside of the cask might be recharred. The preferred word is "rejuvenated."

A–Z
OF SINGLE MALTS

WHATEVER THE ARGUMENTS about their relative prices, no one denies that a Château Latour is more complex than a mass-market table wine. The fine wines of the whisky world are the single malts. Some malts are made to higher standards than others, and some are inherently more distinctive than their neighbors. This cannot be obscured by the producers' blustery arguments about "personal taste." A tasting note cannot be definitive, but it can be a useful guide, and will tell you, for example, if the whisky is a light, dry malt, or if it is rich and sherryish, or peaty and smoky.

The tasting notes start with a comment on the house style—a quick, first, general indication of what to expect from each distillery's products, before looking at the variations that emerge in different ages and bottlings. I also suggest the best moment for each distillery's whiskies (such as before dinner, or with a book at bedtime). These suggestions are meant as an encouragement to try each in a congenial situation. They are not meant to be taken with excessive seriousness.

Tasting note example:
AUCHENTOSHAN 18-year-old, 43 vol

COLOR Deep gold.
NOSE Fresh fruit, honey, almonds, spices, and vanilla.
BODY Oily and quite full.
PALATE Initially fresh and floral, with developing maltiness, fresh oak, and ginger.
FINISH Comparatively lengthy, with raisins, nutmeg, and a final dry oak note.

SCORE **86**

COLOR The natural color of a malt matured in plain wood is a very pale yellow. Darker shades, ranging from amber to ruby to deep brown, can be imparted by sherry wood. Some distilleries use casks

◀ **A character-forming home**
Skye forms a natural crucible, in which the flavors of a great whisky are fused. Living in the mountains and surrounded by sea, the whisky assumes a gusty salt-and-pepper house character.

that have been treated with concentrated sherry, and this can cause a caramel-like appearance and palate. Some add caramel to balance the color. I do not suggest that one color is in itself better than another, though a particular subtle hue can heighten the pleasure of a fine malt. We enjoy food and drink with our eyes as well as our nose and palate.

NOSE Anyone sampling any food or drink experiences much of the flavor through the sense of smell. Whisky is highly aromatic, and the aromas of malts include peat, flowers, honey, toasty maltiness, coastal brine, and seaweed, for example.

BODY Lightness, smoothness, or richness might refresh, soothe, or satisfy. Body and texture (sometimes known as "mouthmfeel") are distinct features of each malt.

PALATE In the enjoyment of any complex drink, each sip will offer new aspects of the taste. Even one sip will gradually unfold a number of taste characteristics in different parts of the mouth over a period of, say, a minute. This is notably true of single malts. Some present a very extensive development of palate. A taster working with an unfamiliar malt may go back to it several times over a period of days, in search of its full character. I have adopted this technique in my tastings for this book.

FINISH In all types of alcoholic drinks, the "finish" is another stage of the pleasure. In most single malts, it is more than a simple aftertaste, however important that may be. It is a crescendo, followed by a series of echoes. When I leave the bottle, I like to be whistling the tune. When the music of the malt fades, there is recollection in tranquillity.

SCORE The pleasures described above cannot be measured with precision, if at all. The scoring system is intended merely as a guide to the status of the malts. Each tasting note is given a score out of 100. This is inspired by the system of scoring wines devised by the American writer Robert Parker. In this book, a rating in the 50s indicates a malt that in my view lacks balance or character, and which—in fairness—was probably never meant to be bottled as a single. The 60s suggest an enjoyable but unexceptional malt. Anything in the 70s is worth tasting, especially above 75. The 80s are, in my view, distinctive and exceptional. The 90s are the greats.

A modest score should not dissuade anyone from trying a malt. Perhaps I was less than enthusiastic; you might love it.

ABERFELDY

PRODUCER John Dewar & Sons Ltd. (Bacardi)
REGION Highlands DISTRICT Eastern Highlands
ADDRESS Aberfeldy, Perthshire, PH15 2EB
TEL 01887 822010 WEBSITE www.dewarswow.com
EMAIL worldofwhisky@dewars.com VC

THE ORIGINAL JOHN DEWAR was born on a small tenant farm near Aberfeldy in 1806, and was introduced to the wine trade at the age of 22 by a distant cousin. The family moved into blending whisky, and, in 1896–98, established their own distillery at Aberfeldy. From the start, its job was to provide the heart of the malt whisky content of the Dewar's blends; it continued to do so in recent years under the ownership of United Distillers, and it persists with this role today, under the umbrella of Bacardi. Perhaps it is the Aberfeldy malt that imparts to Dewar's that fresh, lively crispness.

The hard water used at the distillery rises from whinstone flecked with iron and gold, and runs through pine, spruce, birch, and bracken on its way to the distillery. It is piped from the ruins of Pitilie, an earlier distillery, which closed for good in 1867. It took its name from the source of the water, the Pitilie Burn.

Aberfeldy still has its pagoda roof, though malting on site stopped in 1972. The owner at the time, DCL, was closing distillery maltings in favor of centralized sites for providing the malted barley. Some of the space liberated at the distilleries was then used to expand still-houses, at a time when production was being increased to meet demand. The upgraded still-house at Aberfeldy is in the classic design of the period. The stills themselves are tall, with a gentle contour. The distillery also has a small steam locomotive, no longer in operation.

When UD merged with IDV in 1998 and became Diageo, the new business had an embarrassment of distilleries. Then Aberfeldy, Aultmore, Craigellachie, and Royal Brackla were sold to become John Dewar & Sons, under the ownership of Bacardi.

HOUSE STYLE Oily, cleanly fruity, vigorous. Social, with dessert, or book-at-bedtime, depending upon ascending age.

ABERFELDY 12-year-old, 40 vol

COLOR Warm gold to bronze.

NOSE Lively. Orange zest. A hint of smokiness. Warm.

BODY Light on the tongue. Oily.

PALATE Emphatically clean fruitiness. Tangerines. English trifle.

FINISH Like biting into a kumquat. Dust. Spicy. Gently warming.

SCORE **76**

ABERFELDY 15-year-old, Flora and Fauna, 43 vol

COLOR Amber.

NOSE Oil, incense, heather, lightly piney, and peaty
(especially after water is added).

BODY Medium, very firm.

PALATE Very full flavors. Light peat, barley. Fresh, clean touches
of Seville orange. Rounded.

FINISH Sweetness moves to fruitiness, then to firm dryness.

SCORE **77**

ABERFELDY 16-year-old, Bits of Strange, 55.1 vol

COLOR Deep copper.

NOSE Polished wood, syrup, orange blossom, and burned molasses.

BODY Waxy, feisty, and oily.

PALATE Toasted almonds on fruitcake. Burned raisins.
Challenging but enjoyable mix of floral and sweet notes
and burned toffee and dark molasses. Nutty.

FINISH Big, oaky, and sherried.

SCORE **90**

ABERFELDY 1980, 17-year-old, Bottled 1997,
Cask Strength Limited Bottling, 62 vol

COLOR Pale gold.

NOSE Restrained, fragrant, pine, and heather. Dry.

BODY Medium, smooth, and distinctly oily.

PALATE Creamy. Nutty. Hint of orange toffee. Still lively, but two or three years in the cask have brought more tightly combined flavors.

FINISH Nutty, late pine. Leafy, peppery dryness.

 SCORE **77**

ABERFELDY 21-year-old, 40 vol

COLOR Warm gold to bronze. Very similar to the Aberfeldy
12-year-old, but a touch darker.

NOSE Soft, sweet, and warming. Notes of honey, vanilla, and oranges.

BODY Soft, yet robust. Slight oiliness.

PALATE A trace of peat, with notes of honey, oak, and Seville oranges.

FINISH Dry. Lingers for a short moment, then drifts off
in a puff of smoke.

SCORE **77**

AN INDEPENDENT BOTTLING
ABERFELDY 1994, 13-year-old, Duncan Taylor NC2, 46 vol

COLOR Yellowy green.

NOSE Melon and grapefruit hard candy. Clean, sweet, and zesty.

BODY Gentle and medium full.

PALATE Honey. Citrus fruit. Very clean. Fresh currants. Cooking apples.

FINISH Sharp fruit, some spice. Medium length.

SCORE **73**

ABERLOUR

PRODUCER Chivas Brothers (Pernod Ricard)
REGION Highlands DISTRICT Speyside (Strathspey)
ADDRESS Aberlour, Banffshire, AB3 9PJ
TEL 01340 881249 WEBSITE www.aberlour.co.uk VC

A NY FEARS THAT ABERLOUR'S parent company Pernod Ricard would pay less attention to its favorite malt since acquiring a host of neighboring brands eight years ago have long since been dispelled, and the French love affair with Aberlour has continued unabated.

Aberlour is at least a super-middleweight in body. With medals galore in recent years, it competes as a light-heavyweight, standing up well against bigger names, much as Georges Carpentier did. Aberlour rhymes with "power" in English, but most French-speakers make it sound more like "amour."

The regular range in Scotland and the rest of the United Kingdom comprises the 10-year-old, the a'bunadh, and the 15-year-old sherry-wood finish, but there are larger selections in duty-free stores and in France. The overall range includes a great many minor variations.

Since 2002, visitors to the distillery have been able to hand fill their own personally labeled bottle of Aberlour, from an identified single cask. A sherry butt and a bourbon barrel, each felt to provide a good example of its style, are set aside for this purpose. As each is exhausted, it is replaced by a similar cask. This personalized whisky is bottled at cask strength.

On the main road (A95) that follows the eastern bank of the Spey, an 1890s lodge signals the distillery, which is hidden a couple of hundred yards into the glen of the Lour River (little more than a stream). The Lour flows into the Spey. The site was known for a well associated with St. Drostan, from the epoch of St. Columba. The distilling water is soft. It rises from the granite of Ben Rinnes, by way of a spring in the glen of the Allachie, and is piped to the distillery.

HOUSE STYLE Soft texture, medium to full flavors,
nutty, spicy (nutmeg?), sherry accented. With dessert,
or after dinner, depending upon maturity.

ABERLOUR a'bunadh ("The Origin"), No Age Statement, 59.6 vol

A single malt comprising Aberlours from less than 10 to more than 15 years, vatted together. All sherry aging, with an emphasis on second-fill dry oloroso. No chill filtration.

COLOR Dark orange.

NOSE Sherry, mint, and pralines. Luxurious, powerful.

BODY Full, creamy, textured, and layered.

PALATE Rich, luxurious, and creamy, with a hint of mint
and cherries behind.

FINISH Nougat, cherry brandy, ginger, and faint smoke.
Definitely after dinner.

SCORE **86**

ABERLOUR Warehouse No. 1 Hand filled
First-fill Bourbon Cask No. 1684, 63.5 vol

A special treat reserved for distillery visitors. Filled into cask in 1994, bottled in 2009.

COLOR Bright gold.

NOSE Sweet, rock candy. Raw sugar with light vanilla.
Wonderfully rich, yet airy. Notes of lemons linger in the glass.

BODY Full, mouth coating, and rich.

PALATE Rich, floral, and sweet. Violets, hard candy, and hints of
green apples. Full-flavored, but also light and delicate, exhibiting lovely floral
notes mixed with ripe green apples. Like a female ninja—delicate,
beautiful, yet nimble and strong.

FINISH Long and sweet. Apples.

SCORE **91**

ABERLOUR Warehouse No. 1 Hand filled
First-fill Sherry Cask No. 9643, 62.6 vol

A special treat reserved for distillery visitors. Filled into cask in 1993, bottled in 2009.

COLOR Light mahogany.

NOSE Hot varnish and coffee grounds. Leather and pencil erasers.

BODY Robust and creamy.

PALATE Well-balanced sherry; pronounced, but not overpowering.
Hints of cloves and cardamom, pecans with a dusting of nutmeg.
Striking a match from afar.

FINISH Lingering and spicy, with the nutty warmth of a tawny port.

SCORE **89**

ABERLOUR 12-year-old, 40 vol

COLOR Deep bronze.

NOSE Red berries. Black currant. Floral. Summer meadow.

BODY Medium rich and sweet.

PALATE Classic Speyside. Summer fruit. Clean and fresh.
Trace of menthol. Sweet spices. Vanilla.

FINISH Medium sweet and addictive.

SCORE **84**

ABERLOUR White Oak, 43 vol

COLOR Rich orange.

NOSE Orange, toffee, pastry cream, and vanilla.

BODY Rich, sweet, and creamy.

PALATE Coconut. Banana sundae. Fresh cream.
Vanilla and jam tart. Menthol.

FINISH Medium long, sweet, and satisfying.

SCORE **88**

ABHAINN DEARG

PRODUCER Mark Tayburn
REGION Highlands ISLAND Lewis
ADDRESS Carnish, Isle of Lewis, HS2 9EX
TEL 01851 672429 WEBSITE www.abhainndearg.co.uk

Gaelic for "red river," Abhainn Dearg is Scotland's westernmost distillery, situated on the Atlantic coast of the Outer Hebridean island of Lewis. Production commenced in September 2008. The founder is one-time construction worker turned recycling merchant Mark "Marko" Tayburn, who developed his distillery on the site of a former salmon hatchery.

The pair of stills is truly idiosyncratic and reminiscent of old-fashioned, domestic hot-water tanks, with necks like elongated witches' hats, linked to lyne arms that twist dramatically before descending into a pair of wooden worm tubs. In addition to the steam-heated "formal" pair of stills, Abhainn Dearg also boasts a genuine former illicit still, which takes an 80-liter charge and is used from time to time, with the make being filled into oloroso sherry casks. Additionally, around five tons of peated malt is distilled each year, with a peating level of between 35 and 40 ppm. A "standard" bottling can be expected when the whisky reaches an age of seven to 10 years, with a number of limited releases along the way.

For now, Abhainn Dearg retails "Spirit of Lewis," which is new spirit filled into ex-Pedro Ximénez sherry casks for a three-month period of maturation, while 2,011 bottles of three-year-old Abhainn Dearg Single Malt Special Edition were released in 2011. This expression is not chill filtered or colored, and was bottled by hand, with each bottle being numbered and signed by Mark Tayburn.

HOUSE STYLE Light and sweet when young. An aperitif whisky.

ABHAINN DEARG Single Malt Special Edition, 46 vol

COLOR Pale straw.

NOSE Linseed, then soft fudge and faint orchard fruit.

BODY Light.

PALATE Light and easy drinking, with some nutty spice and a hint of anise.

FINISH Watery mint fudge.

SCORE **74**

ALLT-A-BHAINNE

PRODUCER Chivas Brothers (Pernod Ricard)
REGION Highlands DISTRICT Speyside (Fiddich)
ADDRESS Glenrinnes, Dufftown, Banffshire, AB55 4DB
TEL 01542 783200

A FLURRY OF CONSTRUCTION enlivened Speyside in the mid-1970s, with four or five new distilleries built. It was one of those periods when the industry tries to catch up with underestimated demand. This distillery and the present Braeval were built by Seagrams. Their light, airy architecture is a happy marriage of traditional allusions and modern ideas, but they are lacking in humanity. Both are designed to operate with minimal staff, and their spirit is matured in central warehousing elsewhere.

In Gaelic, Allt-á-Bhainne means "the milk stream," and the distillery lies to the west of the Fiddich River in the foothills of Ben Rinnes, near Dufftown. Its malt whisky is a component of the Chivas blends. There have been no official bottlings, so malt lovers curious to taste the whisky have had to rely on independents.

HOUSE STYLE Light, slightly vegetal, flowery-spicy. Aperitif.

ALLT-A-BHAINNE Provenance (Douglas Laing), 46 vol

COLOR Light honey.

NOSE Soft sawed wood, honey, breakfast cereal, and paprika.

BODY Sweet, firm, and medium full.

PALATE Sweet, with soft toffee. Orange gummy bears.
Ginger barley candy.

FINISH Soft and sweet with vanilla and light tannin.

SCORE **82**

ARDBEG

PRODUCER Glenmorangie PLC
REGION Islay   DISTRICT South Shore
ADDRESS Port Ellen, Islay, Argyll, PA42 7EA
TEL 01496 302244   WEBSITE www.ardbeg.com
EMAIL oldkiln@ardbeg.com VC

ALREADY ONE OF THE WORLD'S GREAT DISTILLERIES in the days when single malts were a secret, and revived at a cost of millions (whether dollars or euros), Ardbeg shines ever more brightly. Its reopening was one of the first signs of the Islay revival, of which it has become both a principal element and a beneficiary. Its owners' ambitions for the distillery are being rewarded.

When Ardbeg reopened, one of the former kilns was turned into a shop, also offering tea, coffee, a dram, and a clootie (dumpling). The Old Kiln now serves meals and is used by local people as well as visitors to the distillery.

Ardbeg aficionados still cling to the hope that the second kiln may one day return to use. The maltings were unusual in that there were no fans, causing the peat smoke to permeate very heavily. This is evident in very old bottlings. The peaty origins of the water are also a big influence in the whisky's earthy, tarlike flavors. Some lovers of Ardbeg believe that an applewood, lemon-skin fruitiness derives from a recirculatory system in the spirit still.

The distillery traces its history to 1794. The maltings last worked in 1976–77, though supplies of their malted barley were no doubt eked out a little longer. Ardbeg closed in the early 1980s, but toward the end of that decade began to work again, albeit very sporadically, using malt from Port Ellen. Whisky produced at that time, but released by the new owners, is less tarlike than the old Ardbeg. Such heavily peated whisky as was inherited has been used in some vattings. Under the ownership by Glenmorangie, Ardbeg has released a significant number of innovative bottlings, and the iconic Islay distillery and its whisky seem in good hands.

HOUSE STYLE Earthy, very peaty, smoky, salty, robust. A bedtime malt.

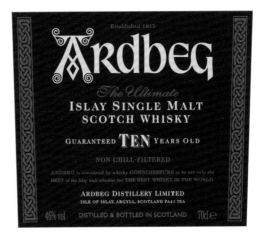

ARDBEG 10-year-old, 46 vol

COLOR Pale gold.

NOSE Sweet, with soft peat, carbolic soap, and smoked fish.

BODY Medium, firm.

PALATE Burning peats and dried fruit, followed by malt
and a touch of licorice.

FINISH Long and smoky. Fine balance of cereal sweetness,
iodine, and dry peat.

SCORE **87**

ARDBEG Ardbog, 52.1 vol

*Matured for 10 years in American oak ex-bourbon barrels
and ex-Spanish Manzanilla sherry butts.*

COLOR Deep ocher.

NOSE Brine, earthy peat, damp fabric Band-Aid, old leather,
violet candy, and lime.

BODY Supple.

PALATE Buttery and fruity, with salted nuts, coffee, caramel,
ginger, and ashy peat.

FINISH Long and warming, with cloves and cinnamon.

SCORE **88**

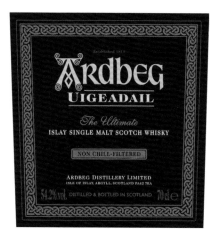

ARDBEG Uigeadail, 54.2 vol

COLOR Pale gold.

NOSE Intensely smoky. Dry, clean, tangy barbecue smoke.

BODY Light, firm.

PALATE Firm, very smooth, then explodes on the tongue.

FINISH Hot. Alcoholic. A shock to the system.

SCORE **92**

ARDBEG Blasda, No Age Statement, 40 vol

Distilled from lightly peated malt.

COLOR Chardonnay.

NOSE Light and gently peaty, with a hint of lemon juice.

BODY Light, but not entirely unsubstantial.

PALATE Sweet peat and canned peaches, moving to ripe apples.

FINISH Initially fresh, with developing and intensifying spicy peat.

SCORE **86**

ARDBEG Corryvreckan, No Age Statement, 57.1 vol

COLOR Gold.

NOSE Buttered preserved herring, freshly dug soil, citrus fruit, ginger, and medicine cabinets.

BODY Full and viscous.

PALATE Quite dry, spicy, and nutty, with savory and licorice notes, plus muted, background fruit, salt, and peat.

FINISH Long, with peppery peat.

SCORE **88**

ARDBEG 1990, Airigh Nam Beist, 46 vol

COLOR Ripening straw.

NOSE Soft, sweet, and medicinal, with nuttiness and subtle peat.

BODY Medium, oily.

PALATE Burning peat and seaweed. Oily and slightly peppery.
Cough lozenges. A hint of vanilla.

FINISH Lengthy, with strong coffee and licorice,
but predominantly bonfire smoke.

SCORE 92

ARDBEG Supernova SN2014 (Committee Release), 55 vol

COLOR Pale gold.

NOSE Sweet peat, iodine, ginger, vanilla, and roasted chestnuts.

BODY Full.

PALATE Bitter peat smoke, more vanilla, with antiseptic
and black pepper.

FINISH Long, spicy, and very dry.

SCORE 92

ARDBEG 1977, 46 vol

COLOR Pale gold.

NOSE Delicate peat smoke blends with ripe pears, ginger,
and mildly medicinal notes.

BODY Medium.

PALATE Sweet peat, freshly squeezed lemon, and ultimately bonfire smoke.

FINISH Long, smoky, and spicy, with aniseed and licorice.

SCORE **90**

ARDBEG Alligator (Committee Release), 51.2 vol

*A cask strength expression that employs some recharred American
oak casks for maturation.*

COLOR Bright gold.

NOSE Beach bonfires, ozone, and a savory note, plus
Balkan Sobranie tobacco.

BODY Firm.

PALATE Sweet and smoky, with chili, ginger, and dark tea.

FINISH Spicy smoke, with a final citric and medicinal tang.

SCORE **89**

ARDBEG Rollercoaster (Committee Release), 57.3 vol

Comprising a quantity of malt distilled every year from 1997 to 2006; 15,000 bottles.

COLOR Pale gold.

NOSE Sweet peat, bonfire smoke, freshly sawed pine,
preserved herring, damp tweed, and a hint of honey.

BODY Smooth.

PALATE Classic Ardbeg intense fruitiness and peat, with spicy
antiseptic notes and rock salt.

FINISH Long and peaty, with coal soot and dark fruit-and-nut chocolate.

SCORE **89**

ARDBEG Galileo, 49 vol

Distilled in 1999, bottled in 2012.

COLOR Amber.

NOSE Smoked fish, drying fishing nets, seaweed, and lemon,
along with sweeter fruit notes and then a blast of peat.

BODY Luscious.

PALATE Sweet peat, with apricot and banana, fabric Band-Aid,
pepper, ginger, and aniseed.

FINISH Long, with more pepper, licorice, and persistent smoked fruitiness.

SCORE **88**

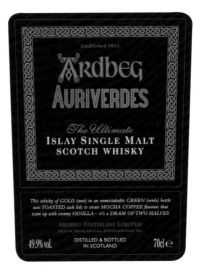

ARDBEG Auriverdes, 49.9 vol

Matured in American oak casks with bespoke toasted cask lids.

COLOR Gold.

NOSE Rolling tobacco, hot tar, green tea, lemon, vanilla, and coffee.

BODY Firm.

PALATE Notably fruity and quite medicinal, with ginger, vanilla, more coffee, and smoked ham.

FINISH Long and peppery, with vanilla, cocoa, and peat smoke.

SCORE **91**

ARDBEG Supernova SN2010, 60.1 vol

COLOR Pale gold.

NOSE Brine, preserved herring in butter, apricots, and freshly wiped ashtrays.

BODY Full.

PALATE Sweet and mashy, with fierce bonfire smoke, orange peel, and almonds.

FINISH Medium in length and ashy with chili powder.

SCORE **90**

ARDMORE

PRODUCER Suntory Holdings Ltd.
REGION Highlands   DISTRICT Speyside (Bogie)
ADDRESS Kennethmont, by Huntly, Aberdeenshire, AB54 4NH
TEL 01464 831213   VC

ARDMORE LIES ON THE EASTERN FRINGE of Speyside where Aberdeenshire barley country begins. Although not very well known, it is a sizeable distillery, makes a major contribution to Teacher's, and enjoys a healthy reputation as a single malt within some circles. When Allied broke up, it was taken over by Beam Global, who also owned Teacher's and Laphroaig. However, in 2014 Japan's Suntory Holdings Ltd. acquired what had been rebranded Beam Inc., bringing Ardmore and Laphroaig distilleries into the same fold as Fowmore, Auchentoshan, and Glen Garioch.

HOUSE STYLE Malty, creamy, fruity. After dinner.

ARDMORE Traditional Cask, 46 vol

COLOR Gold.

NOSE Rooty, savory, wet vines, bamboo, vanilla, and toffee.

BODY Medium full, savory.

PALATE A delicatessen of savory flavors, olive, and artichoke;
waves of grungy peat; oily, full, and demanding.

FINISH Delightfully peaty, briny, long, and full.

SCORE **82**

ARDMORE 25-year-old, 51.4 vol

COLOR Yellow gold.

NOSE Sweet barley, graham crackers, ripe apples, and fragrant peat.

BODY Rich.

PALATE Pineapple, honey, and smoky spices. Soft.

FINISH Medium to long, gentle oak, and persistent sweet peat.

SCORE 85

ARDMORE 30-year-old, 53.7 vol

COLOR Bright gold.

NOSE Fragrant, with honey, citrus fruit, and discreet smokiness.

BODY Rounded.

PALATE Toffee, cocoa powder, and more citrus fruit.

FINISH Lengthy, with dry peat, licorice, and developing oak.

SCORE 86

ARDMORE Legacy, 40 vol

80 percent lightly peated malt, 20 percent unpeated malt.

COLOR Light honey.

NOSE Vanilla, caramel, and sweet peat smoke.

BODY Smooth.

PALATE Vanilla and honey contrast with quite dry peat notes,
plus ginger and dark berries.

FINISH Medium to long, spicy, with persistently drying smoke.

SCORE 83

ARRAN

PRODUCER Isle of Arran Distillers Ltd.
REGION Highlands   ISLAND Arran
ADDRESS Lochranza, Isle of Arran, Argyll, KA27 8HJ
TEL 01770 830264   WEBSITE www.arranwhisky.com
E-MAIL arran.distillers@arranwhisky.com   VC

S INCE IT OPENED IN 1995, and released its first whisky in 1998, the Isle of Arran distillery has inspired several similar projects elsewhere in Scotland. Its launch effectively marked the start of a prosperous and fertile spell in whisky's history.

The island, a favorite with hikers and bird-watchers, is easily accessible. From Glasgow it is a short drive south to the Ayrshire port of Ardrossan, from where a frequent ferry runs to Brodick, on the east of the island. A narrow road then winds its way around the north coast to the distillery, in the village of Lochranza. There is accommodation in Lochranza, and a ferry to Kintyre, for those who want to visit the Campbeltown distilleries. A couple more ferries can be taken to extend the trip to Islay and Jura.

Arran has dramatic granite mountains, peaty land, and good water. The island was once known for its whisky, but spent a century and a half without a legal distillery. The inspiration for a new distillery came after a talk given at the Arran Society in 1992. Industry veteran Harold Currie, a retired managing director of Chivas, put together a plan in which 2000 bonds were sold in exchange for whisky from the new distillery. Since the Isle of Arran has many visitors, the distillery was seen as an additional attraction for tourists. It has a store and a restaurant with an excellent kitchen.

HOUSE STYLE Creamy, leafy. Restorative or with dessert.
No obvious island character.

ISLE OF ARRAN 10-year-old, 46 vol

COLOR Rich gold.

NOSE Light. Spearmint, vanilla, and butterscotch.

BODY Creamy, oily, and full.

PALATE Big rich melon, fresh barley, and confectionery.
Clean, sweet, and chewy.

FINISH Vanilla, gentle spice. Rich.

SCORE **83**

ISLE OF ARRAN 12-year-old, 46 vol

COLOR Rich copper.

NOSE Barley sugar, crystallized ginger, fresh mandarin, and incense spices.

BODY Full, rich, sweet, and creamy.

PALATE Tangerine. Orange liqueur, spice, and some tannins.

FINISH Quite long, spicy, fruity, and rich.

SCORE **79**

ISLE OF ARRAN 14-year-old, 46 vol

COLOR Copper.

NOSE Fragrant, with ripe peaches, baked apples, vanilla, and ginger.

BODY Creamy.

PALATE Vanilla and malt, citric, spicy oak, and finally, white pepper.

FINISH Graham crackers and nutmeg.

SCORE **85**

ISLE OF ARRAN 16-year-old, 46 vol

9,000 bottles.

COLOR Full amber.

NOSE Milk chocolate, sherry, and honey, with a citric edge.

BODY Smooth.

PALATE Malt, honey, and more milk chocolate, plus ginger and spicy oak.

FINISH Relatively long, fruity, and spicy.

SCORE **87**

ISLE OF ARRAN 17-year-old, 46 vol

9,000 bottles.

COLOR Gold.

NOSE Ripe pineapple, Jaffa oranges, malt, and slight licorice.

BODY Luscious.

PALATE Orchard fruit, Cuban cigars, sherry, and dark chocolate.

FINISH Lengthy, spicy, and warming.

SCORE **88**

ISLE OF ARRAN Robert Burns, 43 vol

COLOR White wine.

NOSE Fresh and fruity, with pears, toffee apples, and vanilla.
Cinnamon and ginger notes in time.

BODY Medium.

PALATE Sweet and honeyed, with spicy oak.

FINISH Nutty, with milk chocolate and lively spices.

SCORE **77**

ISLE OF ARRAN 1999, 11-year-old, Single Bourbon Cask No. 77, 57 vol

206 bottles.

COLOR Amber.

NOSE Barley, vanilla, and spicy oak.

BODY Medium.

PALATE Lots of malt, with pineapple and a hint of aniseed.

FINISH Tropical fruit and cereal notes.

SCORE **85**

ISLE OF ARRAN 1998, Single Sherry Cask No. 049, 53.6 vol

590 bottles.

COLOR Deep amber.

NOSE Orange peel, nutmeg, vanilla, and sweet sherry.

BODY Creamy.

PALATE Figs, golden raisins, dates, and more sherry.

FINISH Long and spicy, with drying sherry.

SCORE **86**

ISLE OF ARRAN Sauternes Cask Finish, 50 vol

COLOR Bright gold.

NOSE Grassy and spicy, with lemon and a contrasting marzipan note.

BODY Viscous.

PALATE Baked apple tart, honey, vanilla and contrasting cranberries, and a hint of rock salt.

FINISH Long and rich.

SCORE **85**

ISLE OF ARRAN Port Cask Finish, 50 vol

COLOR Deep bronze.

NOSE Rich, with vanilla, hazelnuts, and Mandarin oranges, plus developing honey.

BODY Full.

PALATE Sweet apples, cinnamon, golden raisins, and port wine.

FINISH Lengthy, warming, sweet, and spicy.

SCORE **84**

ISLE OF ARRAN **Amarone Cask Finish, 50 vol**

COLOR Deep copper.

NOSE Fragrant, with an obvious wine influence, plus cinnamon,
pepper, plums, raspberries, and cinnamon candy.

BODY Muscular.

PALATE Sweet and rounded, with blackberries and rosewater.

FINISH Medium in length, with stewed fruit, oak, and spices,
especially cloves.

SCORE **85**

ISLE OF ARRAN **The Devil's Punch Bowl Chapter III, 53.4 vol**

*Matured in oloroso sherry butts, French oak barriques,
and bourbon barrels; 6,660 bottles.*

COLOR Pale gold.

NOSE Figs, dates, citrus fruit, and honey. Developing savory notes.

BODY Oily.

PALATE Silky sherry, lively cinnamon, and red berries,
with a hint of wood smoke.

FINISH Lengthy, with spicy oak.

SCORE **89**

ISLE OF ARRAN **Machrie Moor (Fourth Edition), 46 vol**

COLOR Ripe hay.

NOSE Dry peat merges with coconut and toffee.

BODY Soft.

PALATE Spicy citrus fruit, vanilla, and bonfire smoke.

FINISH Long, spicy, and citric.

SCORE **83**

ISLE OF ARRAN **Orkney Bere, 46 vol**

Distilled in 2004, bottled in 2012; 5,800 bottles.

COLOR Ripe barley.

NOSE Peaches, vanilla, and fudge. Slightly herbal. Wet grass
and homemade lemonade.

BODY Oily.

PALATE New oak, cloves, and wild berries.

FINISH Drying, addictive.

SCORE **86**

AUCHENTOSHAN

PRODUCER Morrison Bowmore Distillers Ltd.
REGION Lowlands   DISTRICT Western Lowlands
ADDRESS Dalmuir, Clydebank, Dunbartonshire, G81 4SJ
TEL 01389 878561   WEBSITE www.auchentoshan.com   VC

THIS IS A CLASSIC LOWLAND DISTILLERY, not only in its location, but also in its adherence to triple distillation. Light-bodied whiskies result; light in flavor, too, but by no means bland. If you enjoy single malts, but do not care for intensity, Auchentoshan offers the perfect answer: subtlety. Stan Getz rather than Sonny Rollins; Vivaldi, as opposed to Beethoven.

Auchentoshan ("corner of the field") is pronounced "och'n'tosh'n," as though it were an imprecation. The distillery is at the foot of the Kilpatrick Hills, just outside Glasgow. There are suggestions of a distillery on the site around 1800, but 1825 is the "official" foundation date. The distillery was rebuilt after World War II, reequipped in 1974, and further overhauled ten years later, when it was acquired by Stanley P. Morrison. The acquisition provided a Lowland partner for their Islay and Highland distilleries, Bowmore and Glen Garioch. The company is now called Morrison Bowmore, and is controlled by Suntory. The Japanese cherish the distilleries, and the upkeep is superb. Much has been done to highlight the equipment at Auchentoshan and to show how the whisky is made.

HOUSE STYLE Light, lemongrassy, herbal, oily. Aperitif or restorative.

AUCHENTOSHAN 12-year-old, 40 vol
A replacement for the now discontinued 10-year-old.
Contains a higher percentage of sherry wood matured spirit.

COLOR Honey gold.

NOSE Floral and fruity, with mashed banana and nutty malt.

BODY Smooth, slightly oily.

PALATE Malt, caramel, oranges, and a hint of sherry.

FINISH Medium in length and malty.

SCORE **85**

AUCHENTOSHAN 18-year-old, 43 vol

COLOR Deep gold.

NOSE Fresh fruit, honey, almonds, spices, and vanilla.

BODY Oily and quite full.

PALATE Initially fresh and floral, with developing maltiness,
fresh oak, and ginger.

FINISH Comparatively lengthy, with raisins, nutmeg,
and a final dry oak note.

SCORE **86**

AUCHENTOSHAN 21-year-old, 43 vol

COLOR Full, deep gold.

NOSE Orange zest, date boxes, cedar, and oil.

BODY Light to medium. Oily. Very smooth indeed.

PALATE Oily. Citrussy. Orange peel. Lightly spicy. Lots of flavor
development. Oaky character. Fresh, with no obtrusive woodiness.

FINISH Cedar, vanilla, beautifully rounded, and aromatic.

SCORE **86**

AUCHENTOSHAN American Oak, 40 vol

COLOR Corn syrup.

NOSE Pine workshop. Bay leaves. Flower regarded in the rain.

BODY Medium and savory. Not cloying.

PALATE Damson and gooseberry. Green banana. Quite savory
with a late dash of pepper.

FINISH Quite short and gentle.

SCORE **81**

AUCHENTOSHAN 1975, 38-year-old, 45.6 vol

COLOR Rich lemon.

NOSE Polished wood. Scented church pew. Red licorice rancio.
Gentle citrus.

BODY Medium full and oily.

PALATE Honey, mandarin, and guava. Menthol. Amazingly
clean and fruity. Nutmeg. Flowery.

FINISH Very addictive. Elegant and stately finish, which fades
but stays for a long time in the mouth.

SCORE **93**

AUCHENTOSHAN 1988, Wine Finish, 47.6 vol

COLOR Reddish gold.

NOSE Very winey. Musk. Black currants. Rose garden.

BODY Firm and full for an Auchentoshan.

PALATE Berry fruit. Orange. Raspberry English trifle. Some late spice.

FINISH Sweet, spicy, and full.

SCORE **84**

AUCHENTOSHAN Valinch No. 1, 57.5 vol

COLOR Pale lemon.

NOSE Very sweet, with lemon and kitchen pantry spices.
Dried flowers. Dustiness.

BODY Light, clean, and sweet.

PALATE Sweet and satisfying. Lemon and honey toddy.
Cherry candy. Menthol.

FINISH Big and full, with citrus sweetness coming through.

SCORE **86**

TRAVEL RETAIL

AUCHENTOSHAN Springwood, 40 vol

COLOR Pale lemon.

NOSE Allspice. Lemon. Grapefruit. Zesty.

BODY Quite thin, cordial-like, and refreshing.

PALATE Sappy and young. Quite sharp. Grape, lime, and other citrus fruit. Some pepper but all gentle.

FINISH Quite short and gentle.

SCORE **79**

AUCHENTOSHAN Heartwood, 43 vol

COLOR Golden honey.

NOSE Banana toffee. Soft. Clean. Sweet grape.

BODY Medium full and sweet.

PALATE More banana toffee. Banana split. Vanilla. Some spearminty notes.

FINISH Sweet, medium, and fruity.

SCORE **83**

AUCHENTOSHAN Solera, 48 vol

COLOR Mahogany.

NOSE Wood-paneled study. Dusty. Damp forest.

BODY Soft and rounded.

PALATE Prune. Overripe apple. Soft toffee. Burned molasses. Date cake.

FINISH Sweet with cracked pepper.

SCORE **83**

AUCHENTOSHAN 14-year-old, Cooper's Reserve, 46 vol

COLOR Gold.

NOSE Maple syrup. Toffee. Hazelnut. Tangerine. Canned strawberries. Winey. Rosewater.

BODY Creamy, intense, and full.

PALATE Intense. Bananas, apricot, almond, and chestnut. A big chili hit.

FINISH Very spicy and quite long.

SCORE **87**

AUCHENTOSHAN 22-year-old, Silveroak, 50.9 vol

COLOR Gold.

NOSE Dusty study. Herb garden. Thyme, tarragon, and mint.
Perfume notes.

BODY Quite thin but refreshing.

PALATE Mushy peas. Apricot juice. Tangerine. Tangy.

FINISH Short and refreshing.

SCORE **82**

AUCHENTOSHAN Three Wood, 43 vol

*Released without an age statement, this whisky has at least 10 years in bourbon wood,
a good year in oloroso, and six months in the hefty Pedro Ximénez. In addition to offering
an unusual array of wood characteristics, it fills a gap in Auchentoshan's age range.*

COLOR Orange liqueur.

NOSE Soft. Orange zest, apricot, dates, and marshmallow.

BODY Oily. Marshmallow-like.

PALATE Perfumy. Lemongrass and cashews. A delicate interplay
of flavors, but the whisky struggles to assert itself among the woods.
Better with little or no water.

FINISH Long and creamy. Raisins, aniseed, and fresh oak.
Sappy dryness.

SCORE **85**

AUCHROISK

PRODUCER Diageo
REGION Highlands   DISTRICT Speyside
ADDRESS Auchroisk Distillery Mulben, Banffshire, AB55 6XS
TEL 01542 885000   WEBSITE www.malts.com   VC

AUHROISK WAS CONSTRUCTED between 1972 and 1974 with the primary intention of supplying malt-spirit for blending purposes. However, the first year's production was deemed of such high quality that it was laid down for 12 years before being marketed as The Singleton, since it was thought the distillery name was too challenging for consumers. The term "singleton" is sometimes used to indicate a single cask (in this case, a sherry butt). It was therefore thought to be an appropriate substitute for the original Gaelic name, which means "ford on the red stream."

The distillery, between Rothes and Dufftown, is on a ridge by the Mulben Burn, which flows into the Spey. Nearby is a spring called Dorie's Well, which determined the site of the distillery. The soft water and large stills make whisky of a delicacy that deserves a chance to show itself without sherry, and under its own name.

Phonetic guides can always be provided, except that no one agrees. Auch Roysk, says the manager; Ach Rask (or Rusk), insist the locals. There is schism over the "ch" being pronounced as a "th." Can the foreigners cope with this? Funny how the simply delicious Singleton never hooked as many sales worldwide as some unpronounceably complex whiskies from the west.

HOUSE STYLE Very soft. Berry fruit. Aperitif. Or with fruit salad.

AUCHROISK 10-year-old, F&F, 43 vol

COLOR Soft, burnished yellow.

NOSE Pronounced fruitiness. White grapes. Gooseberry. Berry fruit.

BODY Light, soft, and seductive.

PALATE Lightly fruity, with a suggestion of figs.
Becoming nuttier and drier. Shortbread.

FINISH Faint sun-scorched grass and peat.

SCORE **78**

AULTMORE

PRODUCER John Dewar & Sons Ltd.
REGION Highlands   DISTRICT Speyside (Isla)
ADDRESS Keith, Banffshire, AB55 6QY
TEL 01542 881800   VC

A FINE MALT IN THE OAKY STYLE that seems to characterize the whiskies made near the Isla River. This distillery, which is just north of Keith, was built in 1896, and reconstructed in 1971. In 1991, United Distillers, its owners at the time, introduced a bottling in their Flora and Fauna series. They issued a Rare Malts edition in 1996, and a cask strength limited bottling in 1997–98. These and other past releases were reviewed in the fourth edition of this book. In 1998, Aultmore was acquired by Bacardi.

HOUSE STYLE Fresh, dry, herbal, spicy, oaky. Reminiscent of a fino sherry, albeit a very big one. Before dinner.

AULTMORE 1995, Connoisseurs Choice, 43 vol

COLOR Lemon yellow.

NOSE Overripe fruit bowl. A mix of juicy fruit, including lime and melon.

BODY Distinctively firm, smooth, and oily.

PALATE Soft. Melon. Sugared barley. Vanilla. Very pleasant and palatable.

FINISH Medium, rounded, and balanced.

SCORE **86**

AULTMORE 12-year-old, Old Malt Cask, 50 vol

COLOR Rich gold.

NOSE Light. Floral. Vanilla. Rose petal.

BODY Medium and pleasant.

PALATE Nicely balanced. Quite minty. Mixed fruit. Nice balance of sweetness and spice.

FINISH Quite short but very sweet and pleasant.

SCORE **79**

AULTMORE 12-year-old, 40 vol

COLOR Very pale lemon.

NOSE Pickled lime. Freshly cut grass. Hay. Tree sap.

BODY Light, cordial-like. Refreshing.

PALATE Citrus fruit. Lime cordial. Grapefruit. Clean and refreshing.
Some late spices.

FINISH Short with modest fruit and spice.

SCORE **77**

AULTMORE 21-year-old, 46 vol

COLOR Clear honey.

NOSE Prickly pear. Lemon sherbet bonbons. Polish.
Dusty office. Lemon-puff cookies.

BODY Light, cordial-like.

PALATE Quite savory. Citrus fruit. Peach. Bitter orange.
Woody astringency.

FINISH Medium and warming, with lemon and orange lingering.

SCORE **80**

AULTMORE 25-year-old, 46 vol

COLOR Pale gold.

NOSE Fresh meadow. Zesty fruit sherbet. Pantry spices. Sawdust.

BODY Light sand refreshing.

PALATE At first clean and refreshing, with fruit sherbets. Fruit bowl.
Tangerine. Orange cordial. Late on, pepper spice and oaky tannings.

FINISH Spicy, fruity, long, and warming.

SCORE **83**

BALBLAIR

PRODUCER Inver House Distillers Ltd.
REGION Highlands   DISTRICT Northern Highlands
ADDRESS Edderton, Tain, Ross-shire, IV19 1LB
EMAIL enquiries@inverhouse.com   WEBSITE www.inverhouse.com   VC

INVER HOUSE HAS WORKED SLOWLY and surely on its distilleries since it purchased them in 2001, making gradual but distinctive improvements to both the properties and malts, expanding the portfolios, and picking up awards along the way. Then, in 2008, the company took the dramatic step of not only repackaging its Balblair range, but also changing the whisky, branding the malt by distillation year rather than age and boldly repositioning the distillery's bottles in a more premium category. None of the company's distilleries is a household name, but they are all respected and are building a growing reputation under their newish owners.

The typically spicy and fresh dryness of the Northern Highlands is now complemented by a richer fruit sweetness in the new Balblairs and the relatively older expressions are a real and welcome surprise. They are made using water that has flowed from the piney hillsides of Ben Dearg and over dry, crumbly peat toward the river Carron and the Dornoch firth. A burn near the distillery feeds Balblair, which is amid fields at Edderton, close to the firth and the sea. There is said to have been brewing and distilling in the vicinity in the mid-1700s. Balblair is among Scotland's oldest distilleries. It began in 1790, and the present building dates from the 1870s. In 2012 a visitor center opened, providing yet another whisky venue for the public in this area, less than five miles from Glenmorangie.

HOUSE STYLE Light, firm, dry. Aperitif when young.
Can be woody when older.

BALBLAIR 1983, 46 vol

COLOR Full gold.

NOSE Pineapple, honey, and vanilla.

BODY Quite full.

PALATE Tropical fruit, malt, vanilla, and cinnamon.

FINISH Lengthy, with allspice, caramel, and green apples.

SCORE **85**

BALBLAIR 1990, 43 vol

COLOR Rich gold.

NOSE Pineapple, green fruit, and vanilla. Sweet.

BODY Sweet and thin syrup.

PALATE Canned pears, lots of clean fruit, and sugary spices. Very pleasant.

FINISH A mix of fruit and sweet spice, with the slightest hint of oak.

SCORE **72**

BALBLAIR 1997, 43 vol

COLOR Rich gold.

NOSE Fresh, lime, kumquat, and orange peel.

BODY Full, fresh, and mouth coating.

PALATE Rich ginger barley, lime citrus, then later, sweet pepper
and lime cordial.

FINISH Medium and sweet.

SCORE **76**

BALBLAIR 2003, 46 vol

COLOR Pale gold.

NOSE Canned peaches and apricot jam, with underlying
honey and caramel.

BODY Supple.

PALATE Early malt, then zesty lemon notes, along with freshly
cut grass and hazelnuts.

FINISH Medium in length, with white pepper and cocoa powder.

SCORE **78**

BALBLAIR 1969, 41.4 vol

999 bottles.

COLOR Rich gold.

NOSE Slight saltiness on the nose, almost ozone, then lemons
and pine, and finally, vanilla fudge.

BODY Medium.

PALATE Overt citrus notes, with aniseed, some oak, brittle toffee,
and a subtle smokiness.

FINISH Long and discreetly spicy, notably cinnamon and black pepper.

SCORE **85**

BALBLAIR 1990, Islay Cask No. 1466, 50.4 vol

COLOR Light gold.

NOSE Malt and vanilla merge with black pepper and peat.

BODY Oily.

PALATE Malt, vanilla, spicy citrus fruit, black pepper, and bonfire smoke.

FINISH Long and spicy, with discreet smoke.

SCORE **87**

TRAVEL RETAIL

BALBLAIR 2004, Bourbon Cask Matured, 46 vol

COLOR Gold.

NOSE Malt, ginger, vanilla fudge, and pineapple.

BODY Smooth.

PALATE Spicy, with apples, honey, vanilla, and nutmeg.

FINISH Spicy, with fresh citrus fruit and lingering vanilla.

SCORE **84**

BALBLAIR 2004, Sherry Cask Matured, 46 vol

COLOR Amber, with bronze highlights.

NOSE Savory and spicy, with big sherry and old leather notes.

BODY Voluptuous.

PALATE Spicy sherry, molasses, coconut, and cloves.

FINISH Medium in length, with licorice and tingling spices.

SCORE **83**

BALMENACH

PRODUCER Inver House Distillers Ltd.
REGION Highlands   DISTRICT Speyside
ADDRESS Cromdale, Grantown-on-Spey, Morayshire, PH26 3PF
EMAIL enquiries@inverhouse.com   WEBSITE www.inverhouse.com

O F THE FOUR DISTILLERIES that Inver House acquired in the 1990s, Balmenach is the one that has received the least attention, despite early mutterings that it was to be the group's flagship. Traditionally its distillate has the most powerful aromas and flavors but it has become something of a remote distillery. In the upper reaches of Speyside, beyond the Livet and Avon, the bowl known as Cromdale ("crooked plain") was once alive with illicit distillers. When Balmenach emerged there as a legal distillery in 1824, it was in the heart of whisky country.

The family that founded Balmenach, in 1824, also produced two appropriately distinguished authors: Sir Compton Mackenzie (*Whisky Galore*) and Sir Robert Bruce Lockhart (*Scotch: The Whisky of Scotland in Fact and Story*, and other books on soldiering, espionage, and travel). Balmenach later had its own spur on the Strathspey railroad. The distillery contributed malt whisky to many blends, especially Crabbie's and Johnnie Walker.

In 1991 a bottled single malt was issued at 43 vol in the flora and fauna series. A review appeared in subsequent editions of this book, praising the whisky for its depth of heather-honey flavors, herbal dryness, and sherry (SCORE 77). Two years later, United Distillers announced that Balmenach was to be mothballed. Four years later, it passed to Inver House, and the whisky has been bottled at 12 and 18 years of age under the independent Deerstalker label.

HOUSE STYLE Big, herbal, savory. Hints of peat. Surprisingly food-friendly.

BALMENACH 12-year-old, Deerstalker, 46 vol
COLOR Chardonnay.
NOSE Sweet and fruity, with sherry and chili. Faintly savory.
BODY Supple.
PALATE Fruity and very spicy, with black pepper and hints of sherry.
FINISH More chili, plus dark chocolate-covered raisins.

SCORE **78**

BALMENACH 18-year-old, Deerstalker, 46 vol

COLOR Amber.

NOSE Herbal notes, plus eucalyptus, heather, and hints
of well-mannered sherry.

BODY Full and rich.

PALATE Malt and sherry, dried fruit, and rolling tobacco.

FINISH Long and malty.

SCORE 80

SPEYSIDE SINGLE MALT SCOTCH WHISKY

DISTILLED AT
BALMENACH DISTILLERY
DISTILLED SEPTEMBER 1983 - BOTTLED DECEMBER 2013

AGED
30
YEARS

CASK - REFILL HOGSHEAD
DL REF: 10162
ONE OF 111 BOTTLES

NOSE: STILL FRESH, CLEAN & BARLEY'D AFTER SO LONG! DETECT THEN BREAD, CREAM & SUGAR.
PALATE: LIGHTLY PEPPERED - THEN OAK/VANILLA/MOCHA APPEAR + SPICY, MALTY FLAVOURS.
FINISH: WARMLY SPICED NOW + MORE RICH MALT - MORE DISTINCT SPICES & BURNT TOAST. (F)

DISTILLED, MATURED & BOTTLED IN SCOTLAND
DOUGLAS LAING & CO.LTD., GLASGOW G3 6EQ
700ml
52.8%
ALC./VOL.

BALMENACH 1983, 30-year-old, Director's Cut series (Douglas Laing), 52.8 vol

COLOR Pale gold.

NOSE Pear-flavored hard candy, ginger, butterscotch,
baked apple, and cinnamon.

BODY Supple.

PALATE Zesty fruit notes, nutty ginger, and malt.

FINISH Long and nutty, with spicy malt.

SCORE 81

BALMENACH 2004, Connoisseurs Choice (Gordon & MacPhail), 46 vol

Bottled in 2012.

COLOR Pale gold.

NOSE Initially earthy, with malt, gingersnaps, and vanilla.

BODY Light to medium.

PALATE Fresh and fruity, with vanilla fudge and graham crackers.

FINISH Medium in length, nutty with caramel.

SCORE 78

THE BALVENIE

PRODUCER William Grant & Sons Ltd.
REGION Highlands   DISTRICT Speyside (Dufftown)
ADDRESS Dufftown, Banffshire, AB55 4BB
TEL 01340 820373   WEBSITE www.thebalvenie.com

A s seductively honeyed as a speysider can be; ever more aristocratic, in recent years introducing vintages as though they were eligible offspring, The Balvenie is increasingly recognized far from her domain. Her tendency toward voluptuousness, and her ready charm, win friends easily. A dalliance by the sea resulted in the birth, in 2001, of The Balvenie Islay Cask. Fellow Speysiders resented the notion of a whisky from their elevated territory even contemplating the addition of "Islay" to its name. Meanwhile, Islanders complained that The Balvenie was merely courting popularity. There have been no more Islay Casks. It was a holiday romance.

She may be a notably rich spirit, but Bad Penny offers the easiest mnemonic for Balvenie's vowel sounds. The Balvenie distillery was built in 1892 by the Grant family, who had already established Glenfiddich in 1886. It is highly unusual for a distillery to remain in the same ownership throughout its history, but both Glenfiddich and Balvenie have done so, on their original sites, which adjoin one another. One became the world's biggest selling malt and the other the epitome of luxury, but both were established, thriftily, with second-hand stills. Balvenie's are more bulbous, and that feature no doubt contributes to the distinct character of the whisky. The distillery also has its own small floor maltings, using barley from the family farm.

In 1990, Grant's added to the site a third distillery, Kininvie. This also produces a creamy spirit, but Kininvie is rarely bottled as a single malt. Adjoining the site is the silent Convalmore distillery, acquired by Grant's in 1992 to augment warehousing capacity.

Grant's site is at Dufftown, where the rivers Fiddich and Dullan meet on their way to the Spey. The Balvenie distillery is near the castle of the same name, which dates at least from the 1200s. The castle was at one stage known as Mortlach and was at another stage occupied by the Duff family, and is now owned by the nation of Scotland.

HOUSE STYLE The most honeyish of malts, with a distinctively orangey note. Luxurious. After dinner. Ages well.

THE BALVENIE 12-year-old, Single Barrel (First-fill), 48 vol

COLOR Gold.

NOSE Powdered sugar, honey, bubblegum, and nectarines.

BODY Full.

PALATE Vanilla, honey, and spice, with baked apple and caramel.

FINISH Lengthy, with spicy honey.

SCORE **88**

THE BALVENIE 12-year-old, Double Wood, 40 vol

First- and second-fill bourbon casks, then six to 12 months in sweet oloroso casks.

COLOR Amber.

NOSE Sherry and orange skins.

BODY Medium, rich.

PALATE Beautifully combined mellow flavors: nutty, sweet, and sherried. A very orangey fruitiness. Heather. Cinnamon spiciness.

FINISH Long, tingling. Very warming.

SCORE **87**

THE BALVENIE 14-year-old, Caribbean Cask, 43 vol

COLOR Honey.

NOSE Creamy, honey, vanilla, white rum, and tropical fruit.

BODY Viscous.

PALATE Malty, with thick, heavy cream. Developing fruitiness remains muted.

FINISH Spicy, with oak and a hint of molasses.

SCORE 86

THE BALVENIE 15-year-old, Single Barrel, 47.8 vol

COLOR Lemony gold.

NOSE Fresh and clean. Starburst. Tutti-frutti ice cream. Perfumed.

BODY Full, rich, and fruity.

PALATE Massive burst of lemon and lime, clean and sweet barley,
and vanilla. Then some late powdered sugar and spice. Very summery,
very refreshing, and very addictive.

FINISH Sublime. Long, sweet, and fruity, with a late burst of spice.

SCORE 90

THE BALVENIE 15-year-old, Single Barrel, 50.4 vol

All first-fill bourbon casks.

COLOR Pale gold.

NOSE Assertive. Dry, fresh oak. Heather. Rooty. Coconut. Lemon pith.

BODY Firm.

PALATE Lively. Cedar. Orange skins. Pineapple-like sweetness
and acidity.

FINISH Very dry. Peppery alcohol.

SCORE 85

THE BALVENIE 17-year-old, Double Wood, 43 vol

COLOR Deep amber.

NOSE Honey, malt, vanilla, unripe bananas, and green apples.

BODY Creamy.

PALATE Dried fruit, malt, vanilla, cinnamon, and cloves.

FINISH Lengthy, with softly spiced oak.

SCORE **88**

THE BALVENIE 21-year-old, Port Wood, 40 vol

Primarily matured in bourbon casks, then a short period in first-fill port pipes.

COLOR Reddish amber.

NOSE Perfumy, fruity. Passion fruit. Raisiny. Nutty dryness. Marzipan.

BODY Rich.

PALATE Very complex. Toffee and aniseed. Creamy and winey.

FINISH Long, cedary, and dry.

SCORE **88**

THE BALVENIE 30-year-old, 2013, 47.3 vol

COLOR Full gold.

NOSE Floral, with butterscotch, honey, and ripe Jaffa oranges.

BODY Oily.

PALATE Poached pears in white wine, sherry, vanilla, and white pepper.

FINISH Medium in length, steadily drying, with spice and dark chocolate.

SCORE **90**

THE BALVENIE 50-year-old, 44.1 vol

COLOR Full amber.

NOSE Floral and citric, marzipan, raisins, honey, and oak. Complex.

BODY Full and soft.

PALATE Butterscotch and honey merge with citrus fruit and old oak.

FINISH More citrus fruit, licorice, and drying oak.

 SCORE **93**

THE BALVENIE Tun 1401, Batch 9, 49.3 vol

Exclusive to US.

COLOR Amber, with orange highlights.

NOSE Candied, with sherry, spicy oak, figs, red berries, and vanilla.

BODY Full.

PALATE Sweet and floral. Raisins and honey.

FINISH Dark chocolate, sherry, and cinnamon.

 SCORE **88**

THE BALVENIE Tun 1858, 50.4 vol

Exclusive to Asia.

COLOR Rich amber.

NOSE Dates, golden raisins, milk chocolate, sherry, and cinnamon.

BODY Rich.

PALATE Full and rounded, with sweet sherry, ripe cherries,
and gentle spice.

FINISH Spicy, with persistent cherry sweetness.

SCORE **90**

TRAVEL RETAIL

THE BALVENIE 12-year-old, Triple Cask, 40 vol

COLOR Mid-gold.

NOSE Melons, vanilla, and baked apples with golden raisins.

BODY Supple.

PALATE Sherry, cocoa, and dried fruit, all drizzled with honey.

FINISH Medium in length, with cocoa and spices.

SCORE 83

THE BALVENIE 16-year-old, Triple Cask, 40 vol

COLOR Tawny.

NOSE Zesty, with green grapes, honey, and caramel.

BODY Soft.

PALATE Spicy and nutty, with peaches, vanilla, and subtle oak.

FINISH Lingering, with citrus fruit and lively spices.

SCORE 84

THE BALVENIE 25-year-old, Triple Cask, 40 vol

COLOR Full gold.

NOSE Rich and fruity, with new leather and heather.

BODY Silky.

PALATE Vibrant fruit and spices, honey, and developing oak.

FINISH Medium to long, with aniseed and ginger.

SCORE 86

THE BALVENIE 40-year-old, 48.5 vol

Matured in a mixture of seven ex-sherry casks and refill hogsheads; 150 bottles.

COLOR Rich amber.

NOSE Rich, mellow, and balanced. Sweet, with oak, golden raisins, honey, vanilla, and worn leather.

BODY Full.

PALATE Vibrant and luscious, with ginger, stewed fruit, and developing bitter chocolate.

FINISH Slowly and elegantly drying, with aniseed and licorice sticks.

SCORE 92

BEN NEVIS

PRODUCER Ben Nevis Distillery Ltd. (Nikka)
REGION Highlands   DISTRICT West Highlands
ADDRESS Lochy Bridge, Fort William, PH33 6TJ
TEL 01397 702476   WEBSITE www.bennevisdistillery.com   VC

SOME CARE NEEDS TO BE TAKEN when looking for Ben Nevis malt, since it is one of the few whiskies to be bottled both as a single malt and as a blend bearing the same name. The distillery was established in 1825 and is now owned by Nikka of Japan. It is situated in Fort William, at the foot of Scotland's highest mountain, Ben Nevis (4409 ft / 1344 m). It is a very visible spot, on a street with heavy tourist traffic, but Ben Nevis is relatively distant from any other distilleries. Its regional appropriation to the western Highlands is supported by its being close to a sea loch. "We are a coastal distillery" insists manager Colin Ross, standing in front of the mighty mountain.

HOUSE STYLE Fragrant. Robust. Waxy fruitiness. Tropical fruit.
Oily. A touch of smoke. Restorative or book-at-bedtime.

BEN NEVIS MacDonald's Traditional Ben Nevis, 46 vol

COLOR Pale straw.

NOSE Initial starch, then buttery smoked haddock, a hint of chili, sherry, and gentle wood smoke.

BODY Oily.

PALATE Spicy, with hazelnuts and tarry peat.

FINISH Stewed fruit and lingering spicy cigarette ash.

SCORE **79**

BEN NEVIS 10-year-old

Found at both 40 vol and 43 vol, depending on the market.

COLOR Warm bronze to amber.

NOSE Perfumy, spicy, and soft. Waxed fruit. Kumquats.
Hard dark chocolate.

BODY Emphatically big, firm, and smooth.

PALATE Orange-cream pralines in dark chocolate. Belgian toffee wafers.

FINISH Orange zest. Pithy dryness. A touch of cigar smoke.

SCORE **77**

BEN NEVIS 25-year-old, 56 vol

*Distilled in December 1984, filled into ex-Bourbon barrels, and then vatted
into ex-sherry butts in October 1998; 628 bottles.*

COLOR Oloroso sherry.

NOSE Smoky sherry, printer's ink, cocoa, maraschino cherries,
and a hint of desiccated coconut.

BODY Full.

PALATE Fleshy on the palate, with plums and prunes. Steadily drying
with a hint of smoke.

FINISH Lingering in the finish, with dry Sherry, fruity oak,
and a tang of licorice.

SCORE **84**

BEN NEVIS 1998, 15-year-old, Cask No. 590, 57.3 vol

*Single cask bottling. Distilled in June 1998, matured in a fresh sherry butt,
and bottled in May 2014; 582 bottles.*

COLOR Full amber.

NOSE Raisins, prunes, old polished leather, roasted meat.

BODY Full and rounded.

PALATE Succulent dark berries, dates, raisins, dark chocolate.

FINISH Long, spicy, cloves and rum-raisin-flavored
dark chocolate.

SCORE **85**

BENRIACH

PRODUCER Benriach Distillery Company
REGION Highlands   DISTRICT Speyside (Lossie)
ADDRESS Longmorn, Elgin, Morayshire, IV30 3SJ
TEL 01343 862888   WEBSITE www.benriachdistillery.co.uk

O F ALL SCOTLAND'S DISTILLERIES, only Bruichladdich can match Benriach for the scale of transformation that has taken place in recent years. Having been mothballed by Pernod Ricard, it was bought in 2004 by a South African consortium headed by former Burn Stewart whisky maker and director Billy Walker. It is close to Longmorn distillery, and for some years it was known as Longmorn No 2. But its output was not altogether typical of the region, and its previous owners had experimented with peated distillations to make up for the fact that the company had no Islay distillery. In the last few years, Walker and his team have launched an array of different malts, including rich, heavily peated whiskies, capable of giving the islands a run for their money. As a result, Benriach has grown into one of the most fascinating distilleries in Scotland. In 2012 it even started using the floor maltings again.

HOUSE STYLE Cookielike, with touches of butterscotch. Restorative.
A mid-afternoon malt?

BENRIACH Heart of Speyside, 10 vol

COLOR Rich yellow honey.

NOSE Sweet and creamy. Vanilla, pineapple cubes, syrup, and lychee.

BODY Gentle, sweet, and medium full.

PALATE Clean barley and pineapple. Pure and clean. Grapefruit and other citrus fruit. Some late, sweet spice.

FINISH Medium, sweet, and with some spice.

SCORE **64**

BENRIACH 12-year-old, 43 vol

COLOR Gold.

NOSE A rich blend of fruit, vanilla, and honey. Classic Speyside.

BODY Medium, rich, and sweet.

PALATE Honey, ripe fruit, vanilla, and barley.
Balanced, rounded, and pleasant.

FINISH Medium, summer fruit.

SCORE **70**

BENRIACH 16-year-old, 46 vol

COLOR Amber.

NOSE Honey, vanilla, and lots of sweet fruit.

BODY Sweet, creamy, and full.

PALATE A bowl of sweet fruit. Stewed apples with vanilla ice cream—and honey in the mix. Some late tannin and spice to add balance.

FINISH Sweet, clean, fruity, and with some gentle spice.

SCORE **80**

BENRIACH 20-year-old, 43 vol

COLOR Rich bronze.

NOSE Subtle and restrained, with grape, pear, and apple.
Marzipan. Sweet.

BODY Rich and rounded, soft and clean.

PALATE Subtle, sophisticated, and balanced, with honey, vanilla, oak, and clean melon and pear.

FINISH Medium long, restrained, and with a delightful burst of oak and spice later on.

SCORE **84**

BENRIACH 25-year-old, 50 vol

COLOR Rich gold.

NOSE Tropical fruit, honey, and vanilla, with a hint of oak.

BODY Firm.

PALATE Ripe peaches, more honey and vanilla, and milk chocolate.

FINISH Eternally fruity, with drying oak.

SCORE **86**

BENRIACH 10-year-old, Curiositas, 46 vol

COLOR Rich amber.

NOSE Initially medicinal, with tarmac and overt peat. Then honey,
fruit, and oak notes emerge.

BODY Smooth.

PALATE Sweet and smoky, with a touch of iodine, nuts, dried fruit,
and lots of spicy oak.

FINISH Slightly phenolic, with wood preservative, along with
sweeter oak notes.

SCORE **82**

BENRIACH 17-year-old, Septendecim, 46 vol

COLOR Summer gold.

NOSE Honey, butter, damp earth, molasses, and sweet bonfire notes.

BODY Full.

PALATE Rich fruit and smoke notes. Violets, raisins, nuts,
and a medicinal tang.

FINISH Long, with spicy, citrus flavors behind smoky antiseptic.

SCORE 85

BENRIACH 25-year-old, Authenticus, 46 vol

COLOR Amber gold.

NOSE Very sweet, wood smoke, and geraniums, then lanoline,
brine, new leather, and Band-Aids.

BODY Rounded.

PALATE Coal smoke and aniseed, sweet oak, soft fruit,
and gentle spices.

FINISH Persistently sweet, with logs on a fire and
a hint of heather.

SCORE 91

BENRIACH 12-year-old, Sherry Matured, 46 vol

COLOR Deep gold.

NOSE Aromatic, with black coffee, Seville oranges,
ginger, and cinnamon.

BODY Supple.

PALATE Ripe cherries, nutmeg, golden raisins, and cocoa powder.

FINISH Lengthy and sweet.

SCORE 82

BENRIACH 12-year-old, Herodotus, Pedro Ximénez Cask Finish, 46 vol

COLOR Gold.

NOSE Sweet sherry and muscular peat merge, with
vanilla and dark chocolate.

BODY Full.

PALATE Vanilla, honey, and smoked haddock.

FINISH Long, with red currants, blackberries, peat,
and sweet sherry.

SCORE 86

BENRIACH 15-year-old, Pedro Ximénez Cask Finish, 46 vol

COLOR Suntan brown.

NOSE Toffee, mince pie, and some apple. Quite restrained.

BODY Full and mouth coating, but still soft, sweet,
rich, and very welcoming.

PALATE Ripe grapes, soft berries, apple pits, almonds, and
gentle tannins and spices. Sophisticated.

FINISH Full, long, very soft, sweet, and delicious.

SCORE *83*

BENRIACH 16-year-old, Sauternes Finish, 46 vol

COLOR Rich orange syrup.

NOSE Chinese food, sweet stewed bamboo shoots, musty sweetness,
root vegetables, and doughballs.

BODY Quite full and oily, coats the mouth, but has a distinctive zip.

PALATE Much better than the nose. Soft, sweet grape, berries, plum,
lots of vanilla, and a slash of spice.

FINISH Excellent mix of plummy fruit, sweet pepper, and tannins.
Long and tingling.

SCORE *86*

BENRIACH 17-year-old, Solstice (Second Edition), 50 vol

COLOR Bright copper, with rose highlights.

NOSE Peat combines with sweet berries.

BODY Rich.

PALATE Forceful peat notes, mixed nuts, vanilla, and raisins.

FINISH Long, sweet, and peaty.

SCORE *84*

BENRINNES

PRODUCER Diageo
REGION Highlands   DISTRICT Speyside
ADDRESS Aberlour, Banffshire, AB38 9WN
TEL Contact via Dailuaine 01340 872500

As a mountain, Ben Rinnes spreads itself to two words and is hard to miss; as a distillery and a whisky, Benrinnes compounds itself so neatly that it is too easily overlooked. It is no novice. Benrinnes may have been founded as early as the 1820s, and was largely rebuilt in the 1950s. The distillery had a long association with the Crawford blends. Its malt whisky did not have official bottling until 1991, in a Flora and Fauna edition. Benrinnes' system of partial triple distillation places it among the handful of quirky, individualistic distilleries in the Diageo group.

HOUSE STYLE Big, creamy, smoky, flavorful.
Restorative or after dinner.

BENRINNES Darkness!, 15-year-old, Oloroso, 52.9 vol

COLOR Rich brown.

NOSE Toffee apple. Overripe squishy fruit. Banana. Zesty.

BODY Rich, full, and fruity.

PALATE Soft fruit candy. Jell-O. Rounded. Church pew. Polish.

FINISH Long, soft, and sweet.

SCORE **90**

BENROMACH

PRODUCER Gordon & MacPhail
REGION Highlands   DISTRICT District Speyside (Findhorn)
ADDRESS Invererne Road, Forres, Moray, IV36 3EB
TEL 01309 675968   WEBSITE www.gordonandmacphail.com
EMAIL info@gordonandmacphail.com   VC

PRINCE CHARLES IS NO DOUBT among the malt lovers eager to taste this 100-year-old distillery's born-again whisky. Benromach appeared to have died while in the care of United Distillers in the mid-1980s. The distillery, the most immediately visible to travelers approaching Speyside from Inverness, was closed. Sadder still, its valuable copper stills were removed. United did subsequently issue one Rare Malts edition, at 20 years old. Except for that isolated instance, Benromach was for many years available only in independent bottlings.

A flowery 12-year-old and a more fruity 15-year-old, both popular ages, and each scoring 77, dried up after the fourth edition of this book appeared. However much inventory a distillery has, its stocks are finite. Devotees mourn, and independent bottlers lose a source. On this occasion, Gordon & MacPhail decided to try and buy the distillery. Having succeeded, they reequipped it with smaller stills. The idea was to adapt it to present demand, but also to produce a richer spirit. With its new still-house, Benromach was reopened in 1998—by Prince Charles. There have subsequently been a significant number of varied and enterprising bottlings of Benromach, breathing new life into this happily revived distillery and its single malt. After "Bottled by Gordon & MacPhail" and then "by the Proprietors," the legend now says "Distilled and bottled by Gordon & MacPhail."

HOUSE STYLE Assertive, flowery, sometimes creamy. With dessert
or after dinner.

BENROMACH Traditional, 40 vol

COLOR Straw.

NOSE Fresh, with citrus fruit, cereal, and peat smoke.

BODY Medium, rounded.

PALATE Sweet and gently spiced, with smoky malt.

FINISH Medium in length, spicy, with smoke and cocoa.

SCORE **76**

BENROMACH Organic, 43 vol

COLOR Golden brown.

NOSE Sweet oak, banana, and vanilla.

BODY Smooth.

PALATE Velvety mix of malt, soft toffee, oak, and cloves.

FINISH Drying steadily through sweet oak and fresh fruit.

SCORE **77**

BENROMACH 10-year-old, 40 vol

Introduced in 2009.

COLOR Gold.

NOSE Initially quite smoky, with wet grass, butter,
ginger, and brittle toffee.

BODY Firm.

PALATE Spicy and nutty, with developing citrus fruit.

FINISH Warming, with lingering barbecue notes.

SCORE **79**

BENROMACH 30-year-old, 43 vol

COLOR Polished brass.

NOSE Smoky, with apricots, vanilla, milk chocolate,
and white pepper.

BODY Supple.

PALATE Peaty malt, ginger, and hazelnuts.

FINISH Long and drying, with delicate spicy smoke.

SCORE **81**

BENROMACH 2005, Peat Smoke, 46 vol

COLOR Dark straw.

NOSE Leathery peat, progressively sweetening,
with vanilla and fresh ginger.

BODY Medium.

PALATE Full-fledged earthy peat, vanilla, and peppery orange.

FINISH Lengthy, with peppery peat and a final faint
Band-Aid note.

SCORE **80**

BENROMACH 2003, Cask Strength, 59.4 vol

COLOR Pale gold.

NOSE Initially lemonade, then cream soda,
cucumber skins, and new leather.

BODY Viscous.

PALATE Thick and sweet, with milk chocolate, banana split,
plus spicy wood smoke.

FINISH Long, fruity, and gently smoky.

SCORE **83**

BENROMACH 1969, 42.6 vol

COLOR Dark amber.

NOSE Earthy and spicy, with sherry, worn leather,
and furniture polish.

BODY Waxy.

PALATE Silky, with raisins, dark chocolate, sweet sherry,
pepper, and peat.

FINISH Allspice and drying oak.

SCORE **84**

BENROMACH 1976, 46 vol

COLOR Dark gold.

NOSE Marzipan, figs, and maraschino cherries.

BODY Medium.

PALATE Sweet and malty, with ripe Jaffa oranges and
fruit-and-nut chocolate.

FINISH Lengthy and drying, with green and orange wine-gum candy.

SCORE **83**

BENROMACH 10-year-old, 100 Proof, 57 vol

COLOR Dark amber.

NOSE Fragrant sherry, malt, milk chocolate, vanilla, chili,
and dried fruit.

BODY Smooth and voluptuous.

PALATE Rich malt, smoky sherry, Seville orange, and lively pepper.

FINISH Long, smoky, spicy milk chocolate, and persistent citrus fruit.

SCORE **82**

BLADNOCH

PRODUCER N/A
REGION Lowlands   DISTRICT Borders
ADDRESS Bladnoch, Wigtownshire, DG8 9AB
TEL 01988 402605   WEBSITE www.bladnoch.co.uk   VC

ULSTERMAN RAYMOND ARMSTRONG acquired the silent distillery of Bladnoch in October 1994, and after major work to recommission the plant, distilling recommenced in December 2000. Having Bladnoch operational once again helped restore pride in a remote region of the Lowlands, in the deep southwestern corner of Scotland. All the signs are encouraging, and there has been a nice mix of malts, some peated, some not, but all distinctive and impressive.

Bladnoch is the southernmost working distillery in Scotland. It takes its water from the river Bladnoch, which flows into the Solway Firth, which forms the border with England. The pretty little distillery, established between 1817 and 1825, was originally attached to a farm, and used local barley. For a time, it triple distilled. It was mothballed in 1993 by its then owner, United Distillers. The distillery gave rise to the hamlet of Bladnoch. Nearby is Wigtown, noted for its bookstores. A little farther away is Dumfries, where Robbie Burns's house can be visited.

Raymond Armstrong bought the distillery building to convert them into a vacation home, but came to feel they should be returned to their original purpose. A surveyor and builder, had no connections with the whisky industry, but had family links with Wigtownshire. very close to Northern Ireland. In 2014, the company that owned Bladnoch entered liquidation, with the subsequent closure of the distillery.

HOUSE STYLE Grassy, lemony, soft, sometimes with a suggestion of bananas. A classic Lowlander. Perhaps a dessert malt.

BLADNOCH 8-year-old, 46 vol

COLOR Light amber.

NOSE Fresh and citric, with lemon, cereal, soft toffee, and nuts.

BODY Medium.

PALATE Gingery and very lively, with vanilla, hot spices, and hazelnuts.

FINISH Persistently fruity spice.

SCORE 76

BLADNOCH 11-year-old, Lightly Peated, 43 vol

COLOR Mid-lemon.

NOSE Freshly sliced sweet apples, wood smoke, and sherry.

BODY Medium.

PALATE Smoke and sherry carry over from the nose,
with increasing spiciness.

FINISH Medium in length, and spicy.

SCORE **77**

BLADNOCH 11-year-old, 55 vol

COLOR Pale gold.

NOSE Lemon, cut grass, and apple.

BODY Firm.

PALATE Relatively dry, dried grass, and allspice.

FINISH Drying, with faint fruit notes.

SCORE **78**

BLADNOCH 12-year-old, Sherry Matured, 55 vol

COLOR Bright amber.

NOSE Old leather, sherry, caramel, and cinnamon.

BODY Oily.

PALATE Fruity, with orange, raspberries, honey, and ginger.

FINISH Spicy and drying, with faint sherry.

SCORE **79**

BLADNOCH Distillers Choice, Lightly Peated, 46 vol

COLOR Light gold.

NOSE Youthful, with cereal notes, dry peat, pineapple, and mango.

BODY Oily.

PALATE Barley, more dry peat, and oaky.

FINISH Medium in length, oak, and salt.

SCORE **75**

AN INDEPENDENT BOTTLING
BLADNOCH 1993, Gordon & MacPhail, 43 vol

COLOR Pale straw.

NOSE Light and sweet, with malt and peach.

BODY Creamy.

PALATE More peach influence, plus spice.

FINISH Nutty, with a hint of dark chocolate.

SCORE **77**

BLAIR ATHOL

PRODUCER Diageo
REGION Highlands   DISTRICT Eastern Highlands
ADDRESS Pitlochry, Perthshire, PH16 5LY
TEL 01796 482003
WEBSITE www.discovering-distilleries.com/www.malts.com   VC

B LAIR IS A SCOTTISH NAME, referring to a tract of flat land, a clearance, a battlefield, or someone who originates from such a place. Blair Castle is the home of the Duke of Atholl. The village of Blair Atholl ends with a double "l," while the distillery prefers to keep it single. The distillery is nearby at the inland resort of Pitlochry. It is well-designed, beautifully maintained, and can trace its origins to 1798.

Its malt whisky is extensively used in the Bell's blends. The whisky matures quickly, and behaves like a gentleman. It is a sturdy, well-proportioned whisky rather than a big bruiser, but it can take a lot of sherry without becoming showy or belligerent.

HOUSE STYLE Redolent of shortbread and ginger cake.
Spicy, nutty. A mid-afternoon malt?

BLAIR ATHOL 12-year-old, 43 vol

*Released in 2000 in the Single Distillery Malt series, another
development of the Flora and Fauna selections.*

COLOR Attractive dark orange. Satin sheen.

NOSE Rich, moist, and cakelike. Lemongrass. Assam tea (a hint of peat?).

BODY Silky smooth.

PALATE Spiced cake. Candied lemon peel. Lots of flavor development.

FINISH Lightly smoky. Rooty. Molasses. Impeccable sweet and dry balance.

SCORE **78**

BLAIR ATHOL 12-year-old, Commemorative
Limited Edition, 43 vol

A much more sherryish version.

COLOR Distinctively deep. Orange liqueur.

NOSE Very complex. Fragrant, candied orange peels, dried fruit,
and cinnamon.

BODY Medium, silky.

PALATE Walnuts. Sweetish. Cakey. Faint molasses.

FINISH Very smooth, round, soothing, lightly smoky.

Very sophisticated for its age. Blair Athol matures quickly, gaining perfuminess, sweetness, richness, spiciness, complexity, and length. The sherry helps emulsify the elements.

SCORE **77**

BLAIR ATHOL 18-year-old, Bicentenary Limited Edition, 56.7 vol

COLOR Full peachy amber (but less dark than the 12-year-old).

NOSE Very delicate. Finessed. Orange and cinnamon.

BODY Bigger and firm.

PALATE Dates. Raisins. Dried figs. Moist cake. Butter.

FINISH Toasty. The slightly burned crust on a cake.

SCORE **78**

BLAIR ATHOL 1981, Cask Strength Limited Bottling, 55.5 vol

Bottled in 1997, now becoming hard to find.

COLOR Deep, bright orange red.

NOSE Oakier and smokier, but appetizingly so.

BODY Medium, firm, smooth.

PALATE Delicious, clean toffee. Firm, slightly chewy. Pronounced dark molasses. Lively. Hints of banana, orange, and lemon. Faint fragrant smokiness.

FINISH Ginger. Toasty oak.

SCORE **78**

AN INDEPENDENT BOTTLING
BLAIR ATHOL 30-year-old, Cask No. 05543
(Duncan Taylor), 54.3 vol

Distilled in 1997, bottled in 2008.

COLOR Amber.

NOSE Pretty, floral aromas and fresh citrus fruit. Gentle caramel and smoke.

BODY Full and rounded.

PALATE Rich, brittle toffee, and spicy oak. Becoming fudgy.

FINISH Medium in length. Spicy, dried fruit.

SCORE **78**

BOWMORE

PRODUCER Morrison Bowmore Distillers Ltd.
REGION Islay DISTRICT Lochindaal
ADDRESS Bowmore, Islay, Argyll, PA34 7JS
TEL 01496 810441 WEBSITE www.bowmore.com VC

EVOCATIVE NAMES like Dawn, Darkest, Voyage, and Legend accentuate the dreamlike nature of the place. The village of Bowmore is the "capital" of Islay, but barely more than a hamlet, where the Laggan River flows into Lochindaal. On the edge of the boggy moor, the round church looks down the hill to the harbor.

The distillery, founded in 1779, is kept in beautiful condition—but is not to be confused with the local school, which has decorative pagodas. In both geography and palate, the whiskies of Bowmore are between the intense malts of the south shore and the gentlest extremes of the north. Their character is not a compromise but an enigma, and tasters have found it difficult to unfold its complexity. Bowmore has proved in recent years that it can do big peaty malts, too, with several outstanding special releases. The water used rises from iron-tinged rock, and picks up some peat from the earth as it flows by way of the Laggan, through moss, ferns, and rushes, to the distillery. While the peat higher on the island is rooty, that at Bowmore is sandier.

The company has its own maltings, where the peat is crumbled before it is fired to give more smoke than heat. The malt is peated for a shorter time than that used for the more intense Islay whiskies. Up to 30 percent of the whisky is aged in sherry casks. The distillery is more exposed to the westerly winds than others, so there may be more ozone in the complex of aromas and flavors.

HOUSE STYLE Smoky, with leafy notes (ferns?) and sea air.
Younger ages before dinner, older after.

BOWMORE 12-year-old, 40 vol

COLOR Mid-amber.

NOSE Lemon, honey, and gentle brine.

BODY Medium.

PALATE Smoky and citric, with developing cocoa notes.

FINISH Lengthy, with hard candy, milk chocolate, and sweet peat.

SCORE **82**

BOWMORE 17-year-old, 43 vol

Exclusive to travel retail outlets.

COLOR Warm gold.

NOSE Toffee, ripe fruit, and delicate peat.

BODY Medium to full-bodied.

PALATE Fresh fruit, creamy malt, and smoke.

FINISH Long and warming, with lingering spicy smoke.

SCORE **87**

BOWMORE 18-year-old, 43 vol

COLOR Mahogany.

NOSE Gingery fruit, malt, and subtle peat, plus muted sherry.

BODY Rounded.

PALATE Initially floral, with sherry and stewed fruit. Complex.

FINISH Long and nutty, with lingering peatiness.

SCORE **87**

BOWMORE 25-year-old, 43 vol

COLOR Deep mahogany.

NOSE Rich, with sweet sherry and just a hint of smoke.

BODY Full.

PALATE Perfumed fruit, toffee, and sherry. A suggestion of peat
and oak tannins.

FINISH Long, with dark chocolate, nuts, and gentle, smoky oak.

SCORE **88**

BOWMORE Small Batch Bourbon Cask, 40 vol

COLOR Gold.

NOSE Gooseberry. Grapefruit. Damp wood. Moss. Earthy.

BODY Rich mouthfeel.

PALATE Some peat but subdued. Banana. Some grape and melon.
Vanilla overtones. Refreshing and zippy.

FINISH Medium with peat lingering.

SCORE **82**

BOWMORE 15-year-old, Darkest, 43 vol

COLOR Deep brown.

NOSE Smoke. Seaweed. Dark berries. Rose hip. Autumnal.

BODY Rich, sweet, and full.

PALATE Peat, sherry, and oaky spiciness. Fruitcake dipped
in cigarette ash. Very balanced and pleasant.

FINISH Bold and long, with smoke and plums.

SCORE **88**

BOWMORE 15-year-old, Laimrig, 53.7 vol

COLOR Teak brown.

NOSE Red and black berries. Dark chocolate. Rich,
oily smokiness. Fruit compote. Sherry trifle.

BODY Big, full, and weighty.

PALATE Stunning. Deep, rich cocoa. Big waves of peat.
Smoked raisins. Smoky fruit rumtopf. Tangerine and mandarin.
Sherry and peat.

FINISH Rich, oily, long, and peaty. Storming.

SCORE **93**

BOWMORE Tempest, Batch No. 4, 55.1 vol

COLOR Bright gold.

NOSE Peat. Canned cream. Characteristic grapefruit.

BODY Assertive and robust.

PALATE Needs water. Sweet industrial smoke. Tangerine
and grapefruit. Some red licorice and menthol notes.
Grungy and big.

FINISH Smokiness retires gracefully. The orange and other
fruit notes hang around a bit. Very nice.

SCORE **90**

BOWMORE Tempest, Batch No. 5, 55.9 vol

COLOR Deep gold.

NOSE Sweet fruit including peach. Aniseed. Black currant.
An undercurrent of earthy peat.

BODY Full and intense.

PALATE With water, sea spray. Boathouse. Vanilla ice cream
with canned fruit. Packed with flavor.

FINISH Big, full, peaty, and fruity.

SCORE 89

BRAEVAL

PRODUCER Chivas Brothers (Pernod Ricard)
REGION Highlands DISTRICT Speyside (Livet)
ADDRESS Chapeltown, Ballindalloch, Banffshire, AB37 9JS
TEL 01542 783200

THE REOPENING OF BRAEVAL in 2008 was more good news for Scotland's whisky industry, though you suspect that they weren't celebrating at Dalwhinnie. Its claim to be Scotland's highest working distillery was firmly knocked on the head.

Originally the distillery was called Braes of Glenlivet, and this was the distillery's name when the whiskies reviewed here were distilled. This name had the merit of linking this distillery with its famous neighbor and parent—but made it difficult for the owners to dissuade other companies from treating Glenlivet as a region or style. The current name, Braeval, is an even older form. Brae is Scottish Gaelic for a "hillside" or "steep bank." Against a mountain ridge, this distillery is perched over a stream that feeds the Livet River. Despite its romantic name, and handsomely monastic appearance, it is a modern distillery, built between 1973 and 1978. It can be operated by one person, or even from its parent distillery, Glenlivet. Braeval's whisky has been a component of Chivas Regal, among other blends.

HOUSE STYLE Light, sweet, honeyish, with a zesty finish. Aperitif.

BRAEVAL 12-year-old, Provenance, 46 vol
COLOR Light bronze.
NOSE Very fruity. Orange Jell-O. Banana. Toffee. Cookie mix. Ginger.
BODY Full and sweet.
PALATE Honey. Apricot jam. Slightly nutty. Aniseed. Vanilla. Spearmint.
FINISH Long, honeyed, and sweet. Very pleasant.
SCORE **83**

BRUICHLADDICH

PRODUCER Remy Cointreau
REGION Islay   DISTRICT Loch Indaal
ADDRESS Bruichladdich, Islay, Argyll, PA49 7UN
TEL 01496 850221   WEBSITE www.bruichladdich.com
EMAIL laddie@bruichladdich.com   VC

I SLANDERS CARRIED CHILDREN on their shoulders to witness the historic moment. They lined the Islay shore to watch the reopening in 2001 of Bruichladdich. The single morning plane, bringing more guests, was running late. The people on the shore scanned the skies. They had waited ten years; what was another hour? Lovers of Bruichladdich had come from London, Seattle, and Tokyo. There were tears of joy, a ceilidh, and fireworks at midnight.

The new owners, headed by Mark Reynier, inherited plenty of maturing stock and a large mix of sherry and bourbon casks at various stages of maturation and in first-, second-, and third-fill casks. As a result, veteran Islay whisky maker Jim McEwan has spent the years since creating a broad range of different whisky styles. Some have been light and delicate, others more robust, and, although the distillery is not known for producing a typical Islay-style whisky, there have been plenty of experiments with peat, too. One of the distillery's whiskies is actually quadruple distilled.

The whisky has long combined light, firm maltiness with suggestions of passion fruit, seaweed, and salt. McEwan has coaxed out more fruitiness and some sweetness, and has given everything more life and definition. The latter qualities are heightened by the use of the distillery's own water in reduction and by the lack of chill filtration. These changes in procedure were made possible by the installation in 2003 of a bottling line. Bruichladdich thus becomes the third distillery to have its own bottling line on site. (The others are Springbank and Glenfiddich/Balvenie.)

When Bruichladdich reopened, McEwan immediately reset the stills to produce a spirit to his requirements. This was light to medium in its peating. Two new spirits were added, with a heavier peating.

Bruichladdich (pronounced "brook laddie") is on the north shore of Lochindaal. The new owners promoted the nickname "The Laddie," and introduced labels in a pale seaside blue to match the paintwork at the distillery. The distillery's water rises from iron-tinged stone, and flows lightly over peat. Unlike the other Islay distilleries, Bruichladdich is separated from the sea loch, albeit only by a quiet, coastal road.

The distillery was founded in 1881, rebuilt in 1886 and, despite an extension in 1975, remains little changed. All maturing spirit in its ownership is warehoused on the island, either at Bruichladdich or in the vestiges of the Lochindaal distillery, at Port Charlotte, the nearest village. Some independent bottlers of Bruichladdich have labeled the whisky Lochindaal.

Bruichladdich bottles some of its more heavily peated whisky under the name Port Charlotte and its most heavily peated whisky— informally known as The Beast and a remarkable whisky even by this island's high standards—is called Octomore, after another former distillery at Port Charlotte. In late 2008 the distillery was also able to bottle a malt made entirely from spirit distilled after the 2001 reopening, and three years later a 10-year-old with the same provenance was released.

In 2012 Bruichladdich lost its much-vaunted independent status when the business was acquired by the French spirits group Remy Cointreau. However, outwardly, at least, the prevailing ethos at Bruichladdich has not changed significantly.

HOUSE STYLE Light to medium, very firm, hint of passion fruit, salty, spicy (mace?). Very drinkable. Aperitif.

BRUICHLADDICH The Laddie Classic, 46 vol
COLOR Mid-gold.

NOSE Malt, powdered sugar, milk chocolate, and a hint of rock salt.

BODY Medium.

PALATE Spicy and salty, with vanilla and kiwi.

FINISH Fresh fruit lingers amid spice. A final sprinkling of black pepper.

SCORE **78**

BRUICHLADDICH The Laddie 10-year-old, 46 vol
COLOR Golden amber.

NOSE Overt ozone, lemon zest, white pepper, and emerging malt.

BODY Oily.

PALATE Clear maritime notes, vanilla, warm honey, malt, and citrus fruit.

FINISH Peppery, with a carry-over of citrus.

SCORE **80**

BRUICHLADDICH The Classic Scottish Barley, 50 vol

COLOR Mid-straw.

NOSE Mildly metallic on the early nose, then cooked apple aromas
develop, with a touch of linseed.

BODY Slightly oily.

PALATE Initially very fruity: ripe peaches and apricots, with vanilla,
brittle toffee, lots of spice and sea salt.

FINISH Drying, with breakfast tea.

SCORE **75**

BRUICHLADDICH The Organic Scottish Barley, 50 vol

COLOR Drying hay.

NOSE Sweet, with toffee, vanilla, and lemon sherbet.

BODY Creamy.

PALATE Buttery, with honey, barley sugar, and ripe pears.

FINISH Lively and medium in length.

SCORE **80**

BRUICHLADDICH Islay Barley 2007, 50 vol

COLOR Golden hay.

NOSE Earthy malt, vanilla, and honey, with ripe apples.

BODY Creamy.

PALATE Cereal, vanilla, and honey, with contrasting lemon notes;
finally ginger.

FINISH Medium in length, dried fruit, and cinnamon spiciness.

SCORE **82**

BRUICHLADDICH Bere Barley 2006, 50 vol

COLOR Straw.

NOSE Floral, malty, with vanilla and a suggestion of smoke.

BODY Waxy.

PALATE Light cereal notes, more vanilla, orchard fruit, and oak.

FINISH Drying oak.

SCORE **80**

BRUICHLADDICH Black Art 4, 49.2 vol

COLOR Burnished copper.

NOSE Oloroso, gingersnaps, vanilla, and golden raisins.

BODY Silky.

PALATE Sweet and vigorously spicy. Marzipan and maraschino cherries.

FINISH Dark chocolate in a lingering, spicy finish.

SCORE **84**

PORT CHARLOTTE AND OCTOMORE BOTTLINGS
BRUICHLADDICH Port Charlotte Scottish Barley, 50 vol

COLOR Pale straw.

NOSE Wood smoke and contrasting bonbons. Warm tarmac
develops, with white pepper. Finally, fragrant pipe tobacco.

BODY Supple.

PALATE Peppery peat and molasses toffee, with a maritime note.

FINISH Long, with black pepper and oak.

SCORE **78**

BRUICHLADDICH Port Charlotte 10-year-old, 46 vol

COLOR Dark bronze.

NOSE Earthy, with peat and sherry notes, caramel, and vanilla.

BODY Luscious.

PALATE Rich wood smoke, caramel, orange and sherry, and molasses toffee.

FINISH Spicy and cookielike, with dark chocolate.

SCORE **82**

BRUICHLADDICH Port Charlotte PC 11, 59.5 vol

COLOR Amber.

NOSE New leather, black coffee, iodine, and contrasting vanilla.
Developing sea-salt notes.

BODY Supple.

PALATE Profound peat, mildly herbal, citrus fruit, and ginger in syrup.

FINISH Chili and peat.

SCORE **83**

BRUICHLADDICH Octomore 6.1 Scottish Barley, 57 vol

COLOR Pale gold.

NOSE Sweet peat, ozone, and tide pools. Supple leather and damp tweed.

BODY Full.

PALATE Peat is held in check by allspice, vanilla, and
apple and pears fruitiness.

FINISH Very long, with dry-roasted nuts, chili, and wood smoke.

SCORE **84**

BRUICHLADDICH Octomore 6.2, 58.2 vol

COLOR Straw.

NOSE Big, earthy peat notes, barbecue sauce, then antiseptic
and a hint of pine.

BODY Full.

PALATE Citrus, aniseed, chili, vanilla, and more earthy peat.

FINISH Band-Aid, pepper, and licorice.

SCORE **82**

BRUICHLADDICH Octomore 6.3 Islay Barley, 64 vol

COLOR Bright amber.

NOSE Apricots and rich, ashy peat. Vanilla and lanolin.

BODY Supple.

PALATE Huge initial peat hit, lots of lively spices, vanilla,
cherry soda, and black pepper.

FINISH Peat embers, persistent black pepper, and licorice sticks.

SCORE **83**

BUNNAHABHAIN

PRODUCER Burn Stewart Distillers PLC
REGION Islay   DISTRICT North Shore
ADDRESS Port Askaig, Islay, Argyll, PA46 7RP
TEL 01496 840646   WEBSITE www.blackbottle.com
EMAIL enquiries@burnstewartdistillers.com   VC

A NEW LIFE for the elusive Bunnahabhain confirmed the Islay revival in the new millennium. Elusive? Bunnahabhain has the most hidden location of the Islay distilleries, the most superficially difficult name (pronounced "boona'hhavn"), and the most delicate whisky. Since 2003, Bunnahabhain has been owned, along with Tobermory and Deanston, by the Burn Stewart group, well known in the Far East for its Scottish Leader blends. With the acquisition of Bunnahabhain, Burn Stewart also gained the cult blend Black Bottle, which contains malts from all the Islay distilleries. In 2013, Burn Stewart's Trinidad based owners CL Financial sold it to the South African wine and spirits giant Distell group Ltd.

The Bunnahabhain distillery had been well maintained by its previous owners, Edrington, but both production and marketing of its products had been sporadic. Despite its delicacy, Bunnahabhain does have a touch of Islay maritime character and heavily peated variants have been marketed since 2004.

The distillery, expanded in 1963, was built in 1881. It is set around a courtyard in a remote cove. A curb has been built to stops visitors' cars from rolling into the sea. A ship's bell, salvaged from a nearby wreck, hangs from the wall. It was at one time used to summon the manager from his home if he were urgently needed. The distillery's water rises through limestone, and because it is piped to the distillery, it does not pick up peat on the way. The stills are large, in the style that the industry refers to as onion-shaped.

HOUSE STYLE Fresh, sweetish, nutty, herbal, salty. Aperitif.

BUNNAHABHAIN 12-year-old, 46.3 vol

COLOR Chardonnay.

NOSE Fresh on the nose, with light peat, leather, sherry, and a wisp of smoke.

BODY Firm.

PALATE Nutty, with toffee, white pepper, and sea salt.

FINISH Strong coffee, dark chocolate, cloves, and light smoke.

SCORE **82**

BUNNAHABHAIN 18-year-old, 46.3 vol

COLOR Rich gold.

NOSE Toffee, marshmallows, mixed nuts, old leather, and ozone.

BODY Full.

PALATE Nutty, with sherry, black pepper, and honey.

FINISH Caramelized fruit, dry sherry, and soft oak.

SCORE **84**

BUNNAHABHAIN 25-year-old, 46.3 vol

COLOR Amber gold.

NOSE Initially floral, with emerging caramel, sherry, cinnamon, and old leather.

BODY Luscious.

PALATE Sherried and rich, with baked apple and cream, plus a sprinkling of nuts.

FINISH Sherry, caramel, and spicy oak.

SCORE **85**

BUNNAHABHAIN 40-year-old, 41.7 vol

750 bottles.

COLOR Copper gold.

NOSE Apple pie with cinnamon, vanilla ice cream, salted popcorn, molasses, and sweet bonfire smoke.

BODY Rich.

PALATE Sweet and fruity, with honey and ginger.

FINISH Long and mildly tannic, with black pepper, musty oak, and a hint of salt and smoke.

SCORE **86**

BUNNAHABHAIN Toiteach, 46 vol

COLOR Light gold.

NOSE Aromatic, with burning peat, caramel, and spiky spices.

BODY Firm.

PALATE Peat looms large, with more caramel, dried fruit, and sea salt.

FINISH Long and smoky, drying oak.

SCORE **82**

BUNNAHABHAIN Cruach-Mhòna, 50 vol

COLOR Chardonnay.

NOSE Sweet peat, seaweed, and developing fruitiness.

BODY Medium.

PALATE Warm tar, tropical fruit, malt, and rock salt.

FINISH Smoky, dry, and spicy, with a maritime note.

SCORE **83**

INDEPENDENT BOTTLINGS
BUNNAHABHAIN 1987, Cask No. 2464
(Berry Bros. & Rudd), 56.2 vol

COLOR Green-tinged gold.

NOSE Winey. Smoke. Gooseberry. Damp forest.

BODY Rich and mouth coating.

PALATE Big peaty and green-apple hit, red licorice, spearmint, and date. Passion fruit.

FINISH Long, lingering smokiness and fruit.

SCORE **90**

BUNNAHABHAIN Moine 2007, Cask No. 800097
(Berry Bros. & Rudd), 60 vol

COLOR Pale lime.

NOSE Coastal. Harbor sea wall. Peat. Fish market.

BODY Big and unctuous.

PALATE A mighty wave of peat, seaweed, seafood, sweet pear, and damson. Impressive but not subtle.

FINISH Big, sweet, and peaty.

SCORE **88**

TRAVEL RETAIL
BUNNAHABHAIN Darach Ùr, 46.3 vol

Exclusive to global travel retail outlets.

COLOR Bright amber.

NOSE Fresh oak, spice, and pine nuts.

BODY Firm.

PALATE Citrus fruit, spicy vanilla, cloves, and cinnamon.

FINISH Medium. Gingery and drying.

SCORE **82**

BUNNAHABHAIN Eirigh Na Greine, 46.3 vol

COLOR Dark copper.

NOSE Spicy red wine, floral notes, honey, and caramel.

BODY Smooth.

PALATE Blackberry and raspberry sweetness, lively spices.

FINISH Warming, with fresh ginger.

SCORE **81**

CAOL ILA

PRODUCER Diageo
REGION Islay DISTRICT North shore
ADDRESS Port Askaig, Islay, Argyll, PA46 7RL
TEL 01496 302760 Distillery has shop
WEBSITE www.discovering-distilleries.com/www.malts.com

THE ONCE ELUSIVE CAOL ILA single malt has enjoyed a growing visibility and reputation during the last decade or more, following the release in 2002 of three official bottlings, the first since the old "Flora & Fauna" expression. The range has subsequently grown from that trio of 12, 18-year-old, and Cask Strength variants, while unpeated bottlings have regularly appeared in the annual Special Releases series.

The name, pronounced "cull-eela," means "Sound of Islay." The Gaelic word "caol" is more familiar as "kyle." The distillery is in a cove near Port Askaig. The large windows of the still-house overlook the Sound of Islay, across which the ferry chugs to the nearby island of Jura. The best view of the distillery is from the ferry.

Its 1970s façade is beginning to be accepted as a classic of the period. Inside, the distillery is both functional and attractive: a copper hood on the lauter tun; brass trim; wash stills like flat onions, spirit stills more pear shaped; Oregon pine washbacks. Some of the structure dates from 1879, and the distillery was founded in 1846. In 2011 around $5.25 (£3.5) million was spent, increasing the capacity of Caol Ila, already Islay's largest distillery.

Behind the distillery, a hillside covered in fuchsias, foxgloves, and wild roses rises toward the peaty loch where the water gathers. It is quite salty and minerally, having risen from limestone. As a modern, well-engineered distillery, making whisky for several blends, Caol Ila has over the years used different levels of peating. This is apparent in the independent bottlings.

HOUSE STYLE Oily, olivelike. Junipery, fruity, esterlike.
A wonderful aperitif.

CAOL ILA 12-year-old, 43 vol

COLOR Vinho verde.

NOSE Soft. Juniper. Garden mint. Grass. Burned grass.

BODY Lightly oily. Simultaneously soothing and appetizing.

PALATE Lots of flavor development. Becoming spicy. Vanilla, nutmeg, and mustard seed. Complex. Flavors combine with great delicacy.

FINISH Very long.

SCORE **83**

CAOL ILA 18-year-old, 43 vol

COLOR Fino sherry on a sunny day.

NOSE Fragrant. Menthol. Markedly vegetal. Nutty vanilla pod.

BODY Firmer. Much bigger.

PALATE More assertively expressive. Sweeter. Leafy sweetness. Spring greens. Crushed almonds. Rooty and cedary.

FINISH Powerful reverberations of a remarkable whisky.

SCORE **86**

CAOL ILA 25-year-old, Distilled 1979, Cask Strength, 58.4 vol

COLOR Mid-gold.

NOSE Sweet, spicy, and peaty, with warm soil.

BODY Medium and oily.

PALATE Sweetness is balanced by lemon, pepper, and olives.

FINISH Lengthy and drying, with bonfire embers, gauze dressings, and shellfish.

SCORE **84**

CAOL ILA Cask Strength, 55 vol

COLOR Remarkably pale. White wine.

NOSE Intense. Sweetish smokiness. Coconut. Grapefruit.

PALATE A very lively interplay of flavors, with malty sweetness, fruity esteriness, and peppery dryness. Perfumy, with suggestions of thyme.

FINISH The flavors come together in a rousing finale, with the alcohol providing a backbeat.

SCORE 85

CAOL ILA 2001, Moscatel Finish (Distillers Edition), 43 vol

Bottled 2013; finished in Muscatel casks.

COLOR Pale straw.

NOSE Sweet and gummy, cloves, and a hint of smoke.

BODY Rounded.

PALATE Cloves, followed by sweet, fruitier notes and developing peat.

FINISH Long, drying, and peppery, with a final hint of peat.

SCORE 83

CAOL ILA 1997, Managers' Choice, 58 vol

Matured in a European oak bodega sherry cask; 366 bottles.

COLOR Bright amber.

NOSE Smoked fish cooked in butter, a whiff of chlorine, with contrasting sherry and Turkish delight.

BODY Full.

PALATE Phenolic, with pine, citrus fruit, and nutty peat.

FINISH Long and slightly earthy, with sweet peat, pepper, and spice.

SCORE 85

CAOL ILA 14-year-old,
Special Releases 2012, 59.3 vol

Unpeated.

COLOR Pale gold.

NOSE Zesty lemon and wet grass, becoming salted popcorn and ultimately caramel.

BODY Oily and full.

PALATE Initially fresh fruit, notably peaches and apricots, with malt and honey, followed by drier, saltier notes.

FINISH Drying, lengthy, and briny fruity to the end.

SCORE 84

CAOL ILA Stitchell Reserve, Special Releases 2013, 50 vol

Unpeated.

COLOR Clear gold.

NOSE Sweet and grassy, with cereal and vanilla notes.

BODY Oily.

PALATE Sweet and grassy notes carry over from the nose.
Licorice and freshly planed lumber.

FINISH Relatively long, with lively spices and a squeeze of lemon.

SCORE **83**

CAOL ILA Moch, 43 vol

COLOR Pale gold.

NOSE Initially a little mashy on the nose; inky, with brine, peat,
and a hint of peanut brittle.

BODY Medium and oily.

PALATE Soft and sweet, with developing notes of caramel and bonfire smoke.

FINISH Medium in length, drying with more smoke and ginger.

SCORE **82**

CAOL ILA 15-year-old, Special Releases 2014, 60.39 vol

COLOR Straw lemon.

NOSE Playful and tantalizing, with sherbet, graham crackers, vanilla
ice cream, bitter orange marmalade, and sweet berry fruit.

BODY Rich and full.

PALATE Bitter lemon and orange, sharp chili spice, and dark chocolate.
But with time, licorice and menthol make an appearance and
berry fruits add a further level.

FINISH Quite short, sweet, fruity, and spicy.

SCORE **84**

CAOL ILA 30-year-old, Special Releases 2014, 55.1 vol

COLOR Golden tobacco.

NOSE Big smoke, both industrial and wood. But with water
there are toffee notes and some honey sweetness. Then more smoke.

BODY Full, rich, and oily.

PALATE Punchy peat and herbal savory notes. Gives way to a much sweeter
core but the savory sweet combination dominates. Dark chili chocolate,
candied cherries, and bonfire combo. Some oaky tannins but peat dominates.

FINISH Long and smoky, with some herbal notes.

SCORE **92**

CARDHU/CARDOW

PRODUCER Diageo
REGION Highlands DISTRICT Speyside
ADDRESS Aberlour, Banffshire, AB38 7RY
TEL 01340 872555 WEBSITE www.discovering-distilleries.com VC

A FEW YEARS AGO Cardhu became famous for all the wrong reasons when Diageo added two other malts from its portfolio to Cardhu Single Malt and renamed it Cardhu Pure in a bid to stretch supplies further to slake the thirst of drinkers in Spain, where it enjoys enormous popularity. The move caused outrage and Diageo backed down, but the furor led to a change in rules by the Scotch Whisky Association.

Cardow has several claims to renown. It provided the industry with a dynastic family, the Cummings, and contributed twice to the tradition of strong women running distilleries. Helen Cummings distilled illegally on the family farm. Her daughter-in-law, Elizabeth, developed the legal distillery, which produced malt whisky as a substantial component of the Johnnie Walker blends.

The distillery was founded as Cardow (Gaelic for "black rock," after a nearby point on the river Spey). An alternative spelling, "Cardhu," better reflecting the pronunciation, was adopted when the distillery began to promote a bottled single malt. This mild, easily drinkable whisky was launched to compete with the popular malts in the early days of consumer interest.

It was a modest success in the United Kingdom, but enjoyed far greater sales in new markets for malts, such as France and Spain. In the latter country, the distinction between malts and blends seems to engage the consumer less than the age statement. Cardhu found itself head to head with the blend Chivas Regal, both being 12 years old. The Spaniards' taste for Scotch whisky is so great that the success of Cardhu in that market rendered it the world's fastest growing malt, outstripping the capacity of the distillery.

HOUSE STYLE In the original form: light, smooth, delicate;
an easy-drinking malt. Greater ages are richer, more toffeeish,
and often work well with desserts.

CARDHU 18-year-old, 40 vol

COLOR Clear honey.

NOSE Honey. Macadam nuts in soft toffee. Orange blossom. Citrus.

BODY Medium, clean, and refreshing.

PALATE Balanced and rounded. Fruit. Dried apple. Fig and date.
Raisin. Some late astringency from the oak.

FINISH Short, fruity, and with some spice.

SCORE **83**

CARDHU 21-year-old, 54.2 vol

COLOR Gold.

NOSE Summer orchard. Melon. Pineapple. Grapefruit. Clean and fresh.

BODY Medium and rounded.

PALATE Soft and sweet. Very little oak. Peach. Apple Danish.
Lemon cake. Puréed pear.

FINISH Big fruit notes. Late chili spice. Spice and fruit battle
it out in a long finish.

SCORE **86**

CLYNELISH

PRODUCER Diageo
REGION Highlands   DISTRICT Northern Highlands
ADDRESS Brora, Sutherland, KW9 6LR
TEL 01408 623003
WEBSITE www.discovering-distilleries.com/www.malts.com   VC

CULT STATUS SEEMS TO have been conferred in recent years on the Clynelish distillery and its adjoining predecessor, Brora, which command the middle stretch of the northern Highlands.

The appeal of their malts lies partly in their coastal aromas and flavors. Sceptics may question the brinyness of coastal malts, but some bottlings of Brora and Clynelish make that characteristic hard to deny. They are the most maritime of the East Coast malts, and on the Western mainland are challenged only by Springbank.

For a time, the big flavors of Clynelish and Brora were heightened by the use of well-peated malts. Clynelish cultists are always eager to identify distillates from this period. A similar preoccupation is to distinguish malts made at the Brora distillery from those that were distilled at Clynelish.

The two distilleries stand next door to each other on a landscaped hillside near the fishing and golfing resort of Brora. They overlook the coastal road as it heads toward the northernmost tip of the Scottish mainland.

The older of the two distilleries was built in 1819 by the Duke of Sutherland to use grain grown by his tenants. This distillery was originally known as Clynelish: the first syllable rhymes with "wine," the second with "leash." The name means "slope of the garden." After a century and half, a new Clynelish was built in 1967–68, but demand was sufficient for the two distilleries to operate in tandem for a time. They were initially known as Clynelish 1 and 2. Eventually, the older distillery was renamed Brora. It worked sporadically until 1983.

Brora is a traditional 19th-century distillery, in local stone (now overgrown), with a pagoda. Clynelish's stills greet the world through the floor-to-ceiling windows, in the classic design of the period, with a fountain to soften the façade.

Inside, the still-house has its own peculiarities, in which the deposits in the low wines and feints receivers play a part. The result is an oily, beeswax background flavor—another distinctive feature.

For years, this robustly distinctive malt was available only as a 12-year-old, bearing a charmingly amateurish label, from Ainslie and Heilbron, a DCL subsidiary, whose blends were given brand names of equal charm. The Real McTavish was a good example. Since the United Distillers and Diageo eras, Brora and Clynelish have been positively anthology-like. Editions have been issues by Flora and Fauna, The Rare Malts, Cask Strength Limited Editions, Hidden Malts, as well as Special Releases.

HOUSE STYLE Seaweedy, spicy. Mustard-and-oil.
With a roast-beef sandwich.

CLYNELISH Select Reserve, Special Releases 2014, 54.9 vol

COLOR Green-tinged gold.

NOSE Spiky. Lemon curd. Blood orange. Dark chocolate. Citrus.

BODY Spicy, oily, and mouth coating.

PALATE Spicy. With water, licorice with traces of delightful rancio. Menthol. Aggressive peat. Canned pears and peaches.

FINISH Peaty, peachy, and long.

SCORE **90**

CLYNELISH 1977, Cask No. 4043 (Berry Bros. & Rudd), 46 vol

COLOR Pale straw.

NOSE Tight and dusty, with some vanilla, prickly pear, and soft apple.

BODY Rich and syrupy.

PALATE Sweet fruit, with a touch of smokiness. Honeysuckle. Vanilla. Honey. Canned pears.

FINISH Long, sweet, and peaty.

SCORE **85**

CLYNELISH 1997, Cask No. 6871 (Berry Bros. & Rudd), 55.4 vol

COLOR Light gold.

NOSE Toffee. Crushed hazelnuts on vanilla ice cream.

BODY Soft and rounded.

PALATE Puréed fruit, peach melba, gentle peat, sweet grapefruit, and pineapple.

FINISH Medium long, sweet, and smoky.

SCORE **86**

CLYNELISH 1997, Cask No. 6873 (Berry Bros. & Rudd), 57.3 vol

COLOR Clear honey.

NOSE Squeezed lemon juice. Dusty. Old parchment. Hazelnut. Kumquat.

BODY Light, fresh, and easy drinking.

PALATE Citrus and smoke, trade-off between peat and sweet. Light easy drinking and refreshing.

FINISH Long, sweet, and teasingly pleasant.

SCORE **91**

BRORA 35-year-old, Special Releases 2014, 56.3 vol

COLOR Clear honey.

NOSE Stewed lemon. Pear hard candy. Meaty. Beeswax. Honey. Dusty smoke.

BODY Smooth, gentle, rounded, and mouth coating.

PALATE Honeyed. Sweet tangerine. Maple syrup. Lychees. Sweet pears. Base of earthy peat and gentle paprika. Soft apple. Trace of marzipan.

FINISH Very long and warming. Traces of menthol.

SCORE **94**

CRAGGANMORE

PRODUCER Diageo
REGION Highlands   DISTRICT Speyside
ADDRESS Ballindalloch, Banffshire, AB37 9AB   TEL 01479 8747000
WEBSITE www.discovering-distilleries.com/www.malts.com

SPECIAL RELEASES IN RECENT YEARS have demonstrated just what a complex and special malt this is. Despite being one of the original six Classic Malt selections, this Speyside great still isn't as well known as it could be. The distillery, founded in 1869–70, is very pretty, hidden in a hollow high on the Spey. Its water, from nearby springs, is relatively hard, and its spirit stills have an unusual, flat-topped shape. These two elements may be factors in the complexity of the malt. The usual version from refill sherry casks, some more sherried independent bottlings, and the port finish, are each, in their own ways, almost equal delights. Cragganmore is a component of the Old Parr blends.

HOUSE STYLE Austere, stonily dry, aromatic.
After dinner.

CRAGGANMORE 12-year-old, 40 vol

COLOR Golden.

NOSE The most complex of any malt. Astonishingly fragrant and delicate, with sweetish notes of cut grass and herbs (thyme perhaps?).

BODY Light to medium, but very firm and smooth.

PALATE Delicate, clean, restrained; a huge range of herbal, flowery notes.

FINISH Long.

SCORE 90

CRAGGANMORE 1997, Managers' Choice, 59.7 vol

Matured in a Bodega Sherry European oak cask; 246 bottles.

COLOR Gold.

NOSE Fruity and mildly smoky, with hints of vanilla, soy sauce, and sherry.

BODY Rich.

PALATE Lively spices, white pepper, and Jaffa orange.

FINISH Drying slowly, with a whiff of smoke.

SCORE 93

CRAGGANMORE 2000, Bottled 2013, Port Wood Finish, Distillers Edition, 40 vol

COLOR Warm gold.

NOSE Orchard fruit, malt, and a wisp of smoke.

BODY Medium.

PALATE Cherries and oranges, toffee, and smoky red wine.

FINISH Relatively long, with fudge and drying smoke.

SCORE **90**

CRAGGANMORE 21-year-old, Special Releases 2010, 56 vol

Filled into refill American oak casks in 1989; 5,856 bottles.

COLOR Chardonnay.

NOSE Orange fondant cream, with marzipan and malt, deepening to molasses.

BODY Medium.

PALATE Fresh citrus fruit; lively and spicy, becoming drier and more oaky.

FINISH Ginger and licorice, lengthy, and slightly bitter.

SCORE **92**

CRAGGANMORE 25-year-old, Special Releases 2014, 51.4 vol

COLOR Golden brown.

NOSE Banana toffee. Cooking apples. Apple pit. Sweet and clean.

BODY Medium, fluttery, and sweet.

PALATE Ripe fruit bowl, puréed and sweet. With water, some berry fruit. Sweet barley. Milk chocolate. Traces of oak and tannins.

FINISH Medium, fruity, nutty, sweet, and balanced.

SCORE **90**

CRAIGELLACHIE

PRODUCER John Dewar & Sons Ltd. (Bacardi)
REGION Highlands   DISTRICT Speyside
ADDRESS Craigellachie, Banffshire, AB38 9ST
TEL 01340 872971

I N MANY WAYS THE MALT WHISKIES of John Dewar & Sons, including those of Craigellachie, are the star performers of this new edition of the *Malt Whisky Companion*, the rising stars at a time when many malts are increasingly being directed into the blended whisky market.

If you have a copy of the last edition of this book you'll find a succinct entry for Craigelllachie, with one entry and a somewhat prophetic last couple of lines where the authors almost wistfully hope for a resurrection of the distillery as a provider of single malt whiskies.

Well, here we are. Along with Aultmore, Royal Brackla, and MacDuff, Craigellachie has been relaunched in various expressions as part of Dewars' Last Great Malts range. It may be that of all the new releases from the company, these are the most important, because they are highly unusual and challenging, and will divide the room. But they offer something genuinely different, and that's to be applauded. After all, isn't it said that the great smoky, peaty whiskies of Islay are challenging and can divide the room?

The village of Craigellachie—between Dufftown, Aberlour, and Rothes—is at the very heart of Speyside distillery country. It also has the Speyside Cooperage. Here, the Fiddich meets the Spey, and the latter is crossed by a bridge designed by the great Scottish engineer Thomas Telford. Craigellachie, founded in 1891 and remodeled in 1965, is pronounced "Craig-ella-ki"—the "I" is short.

The distillery has kept a low profile and its output has almost exclusively gone into blends. But now that it is being bottled as a single malt, its owners aren't holding back and have taken steps to be different. Just look at the ages of the whiskies—aged and bottled at cardinal number years for heaven knows what reason.

But it is the spirit that really makes an impact. Craigelllachie provides Dewars with an important "meaty" and "sulfury" characteristic. This is not just obtained by using the traditional slow condensing worm tubs that snake through a pond of cool water on the roof of the distillery, but by actually burning sulfur to flavor the barley. This is fascinating given that sulfur is seen as such a negative by many whisky lovers, but nobody can deny that it makes for a very different style of malt whisky.

HOUSE STYLE Sweet, malty-nutty, fruity. After dinner.

CRAIGELLACHIE 13-year-old, 40 vol

COLOR Orange.

NOSE Orange zest. Apple. Grapefruit. Bread dough. Light peppery notes.

BODY Full, earthy mouthfeel.

PALATE Malty, earthy, and rustic. Some sulfury "meaty" notes. Industrial. Some citrus fruit. Dusty spices.

FINISH Medium and warming.

SCORE **78**

CRAIGELLACHIE 17-year-old, 43 vol

COLOR Rich orange.

NOSE Sweet. Vanilla and honey. Pineapple. Canned fruit in cream.

BODY Smooth, sweet, and rounded.

PALATE Canned pear and peach. Wispy smoke. Vanilla. Toffee.

FINISH Medium, sweet, and fruity.

SCORE **80**

CRAIGELLACHIE 23-year-old, 46 vol

COLOR Gold.

NOSE Rustic. Earthy. Trace of sulfur. Tangy.

BODY Big, rich, and mouth coating.

PALATE Meaty, big, and bouncy. Earthy sulfur. Savory green fruit. Vanilla. Rural with traces of oaky tannin. Mint.

FINISH Medium long and spicy.

SCORE **84**

DAILUAINE

PRODUCER Diageo
REGION Highlands   DISTRICT Speyside
ADDRESS Carron, Aberlour, Banffshire, AB38 7RE
TEL 01340 872500

ETWEEN THE MOUNTAIN BEN RINNES and the Spey River, at the hamlet of Carron, not far from Aberlour, the Dailuaine ("Dal-oo-ayn") distillery is hidden in a hollow. The name means "green vale," and that accurately describes the setting. It was founded in 1852, and has been rebuilt several times since.

It is one of several distilleries along the Spey valley that once had its own railroad flag stop for workers and visitors—and as a means of shipping in barley or malt and despatching the whisky. A small part of the Speyside line still runs trains for hobbyists and visitors, at the Aviemore ski resort, and Dailuaine's own shunting locomotive has appeared there under steam, but is now preserved at Aberfeldy, a distillery formerly in the same group. Most of the route from the mountains to the sea is now preserved for walkers, as the Speyside Way. Dailuaine's whisky has long been a component of the Johnnie Walker blends. It was made available as a single malt in the Flora and Fauna series in 1991, and later in a Cask Strength Limited Edition.

HOUSE STYLE Firmly malty, fruity, fragrant.
After dinner.

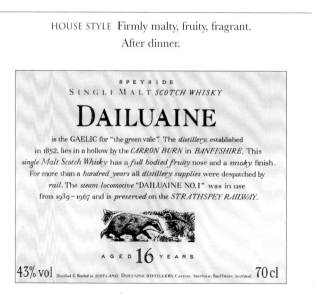

SPEYSIDE
SINGLE MALT *SCOTCH WHISKY*

DAILUAINE

is the GAELIC for "the green vale". The *distillery*, established
in 1852, lies in a hollow by the *CARRON BURN* in *BANFFSHIRE*. This
single *Malt Scotch Whisky* has a *full bodied fruity* nose and a *smoky* finish.
For more than a *hundred years* all *distillery supplies* were despatched by
rail. The *steam locomotive* "DAILUAINE NO.1" was in use
from 1939~1967 and is preserved on the *STRATHSPEY RAILWAY*.

AGED **16** YEARS

43% vol   Distilled & Bottled in *SCOTLAND*. DAILUAINE DISTILLERY, Carron, Aberlour, Banffshire, *Scotland*.   70 cl

DAILUAINE 16-year-old, Flora and Fauna, 43 vol

COLOR Emphatically reddish amber.

NOSE Sherryish but dry. Perfumy.

BODY Medium to full; smooth.

PALATE Sherryish, with barley-sugar maltiness, but balanced
by a dry cedar or oak background.

FINISH Sherryish, smooth, and very warming. Long.

SCORE 76

SOME INDEPENDENT BOTTLINGS
DAILUAINE 9-year-old, Provenance, 46 vol

COLOR Rich gold.

NOSE Soft caramel. Banana toffee.

BODY Full, creamy, and pleasant.

PALATE Sweet banana toffee at first. Then chunky
and chewy malt. Finally powdered sugar.

FINISH Long. Like licking the cake-icing bowl.

SCORE 77

DAILUAINE 1993, 13-year-old,
Connoisseurs Choice, 43 vol

COLOR Pale gold.

NOSE Restrained. Subtle. Flowery. Perfumy.

BODY Medium full, sweet, and quite oily.

PALATE Sweet and clean barley. Green fruit.
Gooseberry. Some spice.

FINISH Quite short and spicy.

SCORE 73

DAILUAINE 14-year-old, Duncan Taylor, N.C.2, 46 vol

COLOR Straw yellow.

NOSE Spring meadow. Floral. Lemon.

BODY Melon. Rich and sweet.

PALATE Lemon sherbet. Grapefruit soda. Refreshing.

FINISH Short and spicy.

SCORE 70

THE DALMORE

PRODUCER Whyte and Mackay Ltd.
REGION Highlands   DISTRICT Northern Highlands
ADDRESS Alness, Morayshire, IV17 0UT
TEL 01349 882362   WEBSITE www.dalmoredistillery.co.uk   VC

During the past few years, The Dalmore has stealthily taken a place at the top table of single malts in terms of its collectability and the profusion of highly priced limited editions that have been released. This culminated during 2013 in The Paterson Collection, one-off set of 12 unique bottles, created by third-generation Master Blender Richard Paterson and produced in association with Harrods in London. One of the industry's great extroverts, Paterson wanted it to grab headlines as the first "million pound whisky," but Harrods thought that was too vulgar, hence an asking price of £987,500 ($1.5 million)!

Along with its new-found status as one of the whiskies craved by Russian oligarchs and Asian grandees, Dalmore distillery has developed sumptuous visitor facilities to match. In 2014 the distillery and brand, along with the rest of parent company Whyte and Mackay, was taken over from Indian owners United Spirits Ltd. by Philippines-based brandy producer Emperador for $645 million (£430 million).

Dalmore, said to have been founded in 1839, was once owned by a distinguished local family, the Mackenzies, friends of James Whyte and Charles Mackay, who created a famous name in blended Scotch. Later, the proprietor was Jim Beam, of Kentucky. The management buy out of Jim Beam's Scottish distilleries led to the restoration of the Whyte and Mackay name, and in 2007 the company was acquired by the Indian-based UB Group.

Dalmore has an unusual still-house. The wash stills have a conical upper chamber and the spirit stills are cooled with a water jacket—another distinctive feature. There are two pairs of stills, identical in shape but different sizes. The warehouses are by the waters of the Cromarty Firth. About 85 percent of the whisky is matured in bourbon casks, mainly first-fill, the rest in sweet oloroso and amontillado, but it is all married in sherry butts.

HOUSE STYLE Rich, flavorful, orange marmalade. After dinner.

THE DALMORE 12-year-old, 40 vol

COLOR Antique gold.

NOSE Vanilla fudge, thick-cut orange marmalade, sherry, and a whiff of leather.

BODY Velvety smooth.

PALATE Sherry and spice, plus delicate citrus notes.

FINISH Medium, with ginger, Seville oranges, and a hint of vanilla.

SCORE **81**

THE DALMORE 15-year-old, 40 vol

COLOR Fresh copper.

NOSE Generous. Sweet. Toffee, medium sherry, and ripe oranges.

BODY Medium and firm. Lush malt and a drier, gingery nuttiness.

PALATE Sherry and Christmas spices.

FINISH Quite long and nutty, with a final note of vanilla.

SCORE **83**

THE DALMORE 18-year-old, 43 vol

COLOR Walnut.

NOSE Sweet and Sherried, with spicy orange peel, brittle toffee, and a hint of background soot.

BODY Voluptuous.

PALATE Lots of citrus fruit, mild oak, plus developing marzipan and sherry.

FINISH Lengthy, with lingering marzipan, coffee, and dark-chocolate notes.

SCORE **85**

THE DALMORE 25-year-old, 42 vol

COLOR Soft gold, with amber highlights.

NOSE Toffee, vanilla, figs, and Jaffa oranges.

BODY Smooth.

PALATE More oranges, with canned peaches, milk chocolate,
and silky sherry.

FINISH Long, with allspice, licorice, and dark chocolate notes.

SCORE **86**

THE DALMORE 30-year-old, Ceti, 40 vol

COLOR Full amber.

NOSE Ripe oranges, dark chocolate, vanilla, worn leather,
and sandalwood.

BODY Full.

PALATE Sticky-toffee-pudding, burned orange, and ripe pineapple.

FINISH Ginger, oak, and orange wine-gum candies.

SCORE **88**

THE DALMORE 40-year-old, Astrum, 40 vol

COLOR Rich amber.

NOSE Classic Dalmore: orange, rich fruit-cake notes, background oak.

BODY Big and rounded.

PALATE Brittle toffee and bitter chocolate combine with
spicy orange and almonds.

FINISH Long and quite sweet. A touch of licorice.

SCORE **84**

THE DALMORE 64-year-old, Trinitas, 40 vol

*Trinitas comprises whisky dating from 1868, 1878, 1926, and 1939.
Just three bottles were released.*

COLOR Deep amber.

NOSE Luscious and complex, with figs, dates, mandarin oranges,
vanilla, baked apple and cinnamon, and warm leather.

BODY Full and supple.

PALATE Seville oranges, molasses toffee, dark chocolate, and licorice.

FINISH Extremely long, with lingering orange and black coffee,
plus developing mahogany and char.

SCORE **94**

THE DALMORE Cigar Malt Reserve, 44 vol

COLOR Golden amber.

NOSE Rich sherry and freshly baked rich fruit cake,
figs, and Jaffa oranges.

BODY Luscious.

PALATE Oloroso sherry, rich toffee, vanilla, and ginger.

FINISH Medium to long, more ginger, plus licorice and molasses toffee.

SCORE **83**

THE DALMORE 1263 King Alexander III, 40 vol

Matured in vintage oloroso and Madeira butts,
vintage bourbon barrels, and Cabernet Sauvignon barriques.

COLOR Warm amber.

NOSE Almonds, hedgerow berries, plums, brittle toffee,
and a faint whiff of molasses.

BODY Firm.

PALATE Complex, with sherry and fresh berries,
plums, vanilla, and toffee.

FINISH Black currants and a tang of molasses. Lingering.

SCORE **83**

THE RIVERS COLLECTION
THE DALMORE Spey Dram, 40 vol

COLOR Walnut.

NOSE Brittle toffee, heavy cream, ginger, and freshly squeezed
orange juice.

BODY Medium.

PALATE Nutty, with orchard fruit, ginger, and chili.

FINISH Lengthy, spicy, and a hint of molasses.

SCORE **82**

THE DALMORE Dee Dram, 40 vol

COLOR Rich mahogany.

NOSE Seville oranges, cocoa, golden raisins, and malt.

BODY Medium to full.

PALATE Dark chocolate, sherry, cinnamon, walnuts, and raisins.

FINISH Long, with black coffee, plums, and light licorice.

SCORE **83**

THE DALMORE **Tay Dram, 40 vol**

COLOR Deep amber.

NOSE Vibrant, with stewed fruit and brittle toffee.

BODY Relatively full.

PALATE Overt sherry, honey, almonds, and milky coffee.

FINISH Orange-flavored chocolate.

SCORE **84**

THE DALMORE **Tweed Dram, 40 vol**

COLOR Honey gold.

NOSE Juicy orange and lemon notes, powdered sugar, and vanilla fudge.

BODY Medium.

PALATE Ripe Jaffa oranges, malt, and lively spices.

FINISH Spicy oak, nutmeg, and dark chocolate.

SCORE **83**

THE DALMORE **1996, Cromartie, 45 vol**

COLOR Golden amber.

NOSE Fragrant and floral, with new leather, cocoa powder,
sweet tobacco, and dried fruit.

BODY Full.

PALATE Orange marmalade, more dried fruit, rich sherry, and
peppery dark chocolate.

FINISH Lengthy, spicy, dark chocolate, orange, and licorice.

SCORE **85**

TRAVEL RETAIL
THE DALMORE **Valour, 40 vol**

COLOR Bright amber.

NOSE Floral, with sherry, oranges, and marzipan.

BODY Medium.

PALATE Dark sherry notes, with bitter orange and gingersnaps.

FINISH Medium to long, lively spices and raisins.

SCORE **83**

DALWHINNIE

PRODUCER Diageo
REGION Highlands   DISTRICT Speyside
ADDRESS Dalwhinnie, Inverness-shire, PH19 1AB
TEL 01540 672219   VC
WEBSITE www.discovering-distilleries.com/www.malts.com

ONE OF THE HIGHEST DISTILLERIES in Scotland, at 1073 feet (326 meters), Dalwhinnie has the Monadhlaith Mountains on one side, and the Forest of Atholl, the Cairngorms, and the Grampians on the other. Its name is Gaelic for "meeting place." The village of the same name stands at the junction of old cattle-driving routes from the west and north down to the central Lowlands. Much whisky smuggling went on along this route. The distillery was called Strathspey when it opened in 1897.

HOUSE STYLE Lightly peaty. Cut grass and heather honey. Clear flavors against a very clean background. Aperitif.

DALWHINNIE 25-year-old, Special Release, 52.1 vol

COLOR Rich chestnut.

NOSE Apple. Sawdust. Dark chocolate. Honey. Allspice.

BODY Rich and waxy.

PALATE Young, given its age. Mint. Honey. Barley. Pepper. Some citrus. Surprisingly delicate.

FINISH Oak, pepper, and other spices. Medium long.

SCORE **85**

DALWHINNIE 12-year-old, The Manager's Dram, 57.5 vol

COLOR Rich straw.

NOSE Vanilla. Sweet cask mix. Spring meadow. Perfumed. Distinctively honey.

BODY Medium, mouth coating, and sweet.

PALATE Sweet, honeyed, vanilla, light, and easy. Sweet citrus, fresh ginger, and barley. Stewed apples.

FINISH Short and sweet.

SCORE **83**

DEANSTON

PRODUCER Burn Stewart Distillers PLC
REGION Highlands DISTRICT Eastern Highlands
ADDRESS Deanston, near Doune, Perthshire, FK16 6AG
TEL 01786 841422 WEBSITE www.burnstewartdistillers.com
enquiries@burnstewartdistillers.com VC

THE TOWN OF DOUNE was known in the 17th century for the manufacture of pistols, some of which may have seen service on the pirate-infested Caribbean Sea. Now the old empire strikes back. The Trinidadian drinks company, Angostura, has acquired Burn Stewart, owners of the town's Deanston distillery. That enterprise itself has an interesting history. It is housed in a cotton mill, designed in 1785 by Richard Arkwright and extended in 1836. The mill was driven by the waters of the Teith River The supply of good water apparently contributed to the decision to turn the building into a distillery at a time when the whisky industry was doing very well.

It opened as the Deanston distillery in 1965–66, with the vaulted weaving shed serving as a warehouse. The distillery prospered during the 1970s, but closed during the difficult mid-1980s. At the time it was owned by Invergordon. With the growth of interest in single malts in the late 1980s and early 1990s, Deanston was bought by the blenders, Burn Stewart, and more versions of this pleasant whisky became available. In 2012 an attractive visitor center was opened, allowing the general public access to this unique distillery for the first time.

HOUSE STYLE Light, slightly oily, nutty, accented toward a notably clean, malty sweetness. Restorative.

DEANSTON 12-year-old, 46.3 vol

COLOR Antique gold.

NOSE Fresh and fruity, with malt and honey.

BODY Medium.

PALATE Cloves, ginger, honey, and malt.

FINISH Long, quite dry, and pleasantly herbal.

SCORE 75

DEANSTON Virgin Oak Finish, 46.3 vol

COLOR Amber.

NOSE Tropical fruit, lively spices, and vanilla.

BODY Light and creamy.

PALATE Bananas and custard. Spicy oak.

FINISH Malty, but soon drying.

SCORE **80**

DEANSTON Spanish Oak Finish, 57.4 vol

Exclusive to distillery visitor center; 784 bottles.

COLOR Sparkling copper.

NOSE Rich, with toffee, honey, and cocoa powder.

BODY Rounded.

PALATE Warm fruit cake, hazelnuts, and Jaffa oranges.

FINISH Zesty spice and citrus fruit.

SCORE **84**

DEANSTON 11-year-old, Marsala Cask Finish, 2014 Festival Edition, 57.2 vol

Exclusive to distillery visitor center; 130 bottles.

COLOR Ruby-tinged amber.

NOSE Musty fruit, toffee, and ripe red grapes.

BODY Voluptuous.

PALATE Sweet, rich, and malty, with red berries and spice.

FINISH Long, with sweet chili.

SCORE **82**

DEANSTON 16-year-old, Toasted Oak Finish, 55.3 vol

Exclusive to distillery visitor center.

COLOR Dark amber.

NOSE Dark chocolate, raisins, ginger, then ultimately a big hit
of vanilla and powdered sugar.

BODY Luxurious.

PALATE Big fruit notes, bourbonlike, and sweet spices.

FINISH Lengthy, with persistent spice and drying oak.

SCORE **82**

DEANSTON 18-year-old, Cognac Finish, 46.3 vol

US exclusive.

COLOR Full gold.

NOSE Floral, with a pinch of cayenne pepper. Dark chocolate
and black cherries.

BODY Smooth.

PALATE Spicy green grapes and black pepper.

FINISH Medium in length, lots of spice, plus notes of licorice and char.

SCORE **80**

DUFFTOWN

PRODUCER Diageo
REGION Highlands   DISTRICT Speyside (Dufftown)
ADDRESS Dufftown, Keith, Banffshire, AB55 4BR
TEL 01340 822100   WEBSITE www.malts.com

THE EARL OF FIFE, James Duff, laid out this handsome, hilly little town of stone buildings in 1817. The town's name is pronounced "duff-ton." Dufftown lies at the confluence of the Fiddich and Dullan rivers on their way to the Spey. There are six active malt distilleries in the town; another two survive as buildings but are highly unlikely ever to operate again. A ninth, Pittyvaich, was demolished in 2002.

Only one of the distilleries appropriates Dufftown as its name. This distillery and Pittyvaich, its erstwhile next-door neighbor, were both owned by Bell's until that company was acquired by United Distillers, now Diageo. Dufftown's stone-built premises were a grain mill until 1896, but they have since sprouted a pagoda, and were twice expanded in the 1970s. They now comprise one of Diageo's larger distilleries, but most of its output goes into Bell's, though the Singleton expression, launched in 2006, has raised the profile of the Dufftown brand significantly.

HOUSE STYLE Aromatic, dry, malty. Aperitif.

SINGLETON OF DUFFTOWN 12-year-old, 40 vol
COLOR Golden honey.
NOSE Sweet and almost violetlike, with underlying malt.
BODY Supple.
PALATE Rich, with orchard fruit, malt, and spice.
FINISH Medium to long, warming and spicy, with slowly fading notes of sherry, soft fruit, and fudge.
SCORE **77**

SINGLETON OF DUFFTOWN 15-year-old, 40 vol
COLOR Deep amber.
NOSE Baked apples with cinnamon, orange blossom, and honey.
BODY Smooth.
PALATE Nutty, fruity, and softly spiced, with honey.
FINISH Lengthy, with warm pastry, milky coffee, and malt.
SCORE **78**

SINGLETON OF DUFFTOWN 18-year-old, 40 vol

COLOR Rich amber.

NOSE Quite dry sherry combines with beeswax, vanilla, and brittle toffee.

BODY Supple.

PALATE Sweet, stewed fruit, contrasting dark berry notes, becoming nuttier.

FINISH Medium to long, toasted oak.

SCORE **78**

SINGLETON OF DUFFTOWN Tailfire, 40 vol

COLOR Full amber.

NOSE Autumn berries, sherry, slightly earthy, and mild oak.

BODY Medium.

PALATE Spicy, with overripe black currants, malt, and slightly bitter oak.

FINISH Drying sherry.

SCORE **75**

SINGLETON OF DUFFTOWN Sunray, 40 vol

COLOR Medium amber.

NOSE Honey, canned pineapple, and sweet apples.

BODY Medium and smooth.

PALATE More sweet fruit notes, with soft spices.

FINISH Honey and vanilla, with a hint of ginger.

SCORE **76**

EDRADOUR

PRODUCER Signatory Vintage Scotch Whisky Co. Ltd.
REGION Highlands   DISTRICT Eastern Highlands
ADDRESS Pitlochry, Perthshire, PH16 5JP   TEL 01796 472095
WEBSITE www.edradour.co.uk   EMAIL info@edradour.fsbusiness.co.uk   VC

THE COUNTRY'S SMALLEST DISTILLERY was returned to Scottish—and independent—ownership in 2002. Edradour is a working commercial distillery on a farmhouse scale, using very old, open equipment, the function of which is easy to understand—a bonus for the visitor. It is near the inland resort of Pitlochry, and within easy reach of Edinburgh and Glasgow. The change in the ownership of Edradour was greeted with widespread goodwill.

With the much bigger Speyside distillery, Aberlour, it had for some years been a Scottish outpost of Pernod Ricard. With the acquisition of Chivas Brothers' ten distilleries, the French found their hands full. They took care of Edradour well, but such a small distillery might benefit from ownership by an individual. It was sold to Andrew Symington, the enterprising founder of the independent bottler Signatory. A wide range of diverse Edradour bottlings have subsequently appeared, including single cask, cask strength variants, and numerous "finished" expressions, while heavily peated Edradour spirit has been distilled under the name Ballechin.

Edradour likes to trace its history back to the beginning of legal whisky production in the Highlands in 1825, although the present distillery is believed to have been founded in 1837. The distillery, at the hamlet of Balnauld, above Pitlochry, is secreted by the hills.

HOUSE STYLE Spicy. Minty. Creamy. After dinner.

EDRADOUR 10-year-old, 40 vol

COLOR Antique gold.

NOSE Floral, with vanilla, caramel, and faintly earthy notes.

BODY Smooth.

PALATE Rich, sweet, spicy, and fruity.

FINISH Lengthy and sweet.

SCORE **81**

EDRADOUR 1998, 10-year-old, Un-chillfiltered, 46 vol

COLOR Gold with amber highlights.

NOSE Sweet orange marmalade. Fresh cut flowers. Caramel. Mild licorice.

BODY Smooth and rounded.

PALATE Butterscotch, spice, and mild pepper.

FINISH Medium to long; spicy.

SCORE **83**

EDRADOUR 1995, 12-year-old, Cask No. 460, 57.2 vol

COLOR Mid-amber.

NOSE Nougat, ripe oranges, and golden raisins.

BODY Slightly oily and full.

PALATE Spicy malt, dried fruit, and a hint of warm leather.

FINISH Long and mildly gingery.

SCORE **84**

EDRADOUR 2003, Port Cask Matured, Cask No. 378, 46 vol

Released August 2008

COLOR Bronze with pink highlights.

NOSE Clean and fragrant, with cherries and summer berries.

BODY Medium.

PALATE Fruity, with pineapples and red wine.

FINISH Lengthy, with slightly smoky raspberry jam.

SCORE **83**

EDRADOUR 1997, 10-year-old, Straight from the Cask, D'Yquem Finish, 57.7 vol

COLOR Pale gold.

NOSE Medium-sweet, with apricots and nougat.

BODY Rounded.

PALATE Sweet, with orange chocolate, almonds, and instant coffee.

FINISH Long, spicy, and nutty.

SCORE **83**

EDRADOUR 1998, 10-year-old, Straight from the Cask, Sherry Finish, Cask No. 325, 58.1 vol

COLOR Bright amber.

NOSE Slightly menthol; medium sherry.

BODY Rich.

PALATE Full and rounded. Big, leathery, fruity sherry flavors.

FINISH Medium to long. Golden raisins, leather, and spice.

SCORE **84**

EDRADOUR 1998, 10-year-old, Straight from the Cask, Sassicaia Finish, 58.1 vol

COLOR Rosé.

NOSE Rich, scented, and creamy.

BODY Medium.

PALATE Mellow, with summer berries, custard, and milk-chocolate notes.

FINISH The chocolate darkens slightly and spices develop.

SCORE **83**

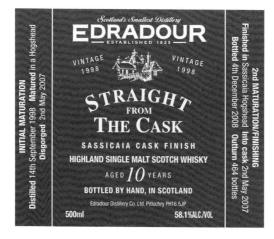

EDRADOUR 1997, 11-year-old, Straight from the Cask, Moscatel Finish, 58.3 vol

COLOR Amber with golden highlights.

NOSE Aerosol furniture polish, candied lemon, and pepper.

BODY Soft and rounded.

PALATE Quite dry. Fruit notes. Slightly herbal.

FINISH Medium, drying.

SCORE **81**

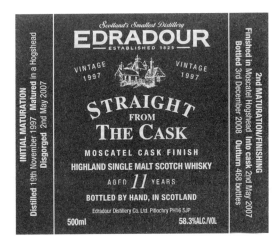

EDRADOUR 1996, 12-year-old, Straight from the Cask, Madeira Finish, 56.7 vol

COLOR Pale gold.

NOSE Raisins, wax, and citrus fruit.

BODY Lush.

PALATE Soft toffee and cinnamon.

FINISH Lengthy, with intensifying ginger and pepper notes.

SCORE **82**

EDRADOUR 1995, 12-year-old, Straight from the Cask, Chardonnay Finish, 56.9 vol

COLOR Amber.

NOSE Dense and aromatic. Prunes, new leather, and mild smoke.

BODY Medium to full.

PALATE Very focused fruitiness; developing spiciness.

FINISH Long, with slightly rubbery spice.

SCORE **81**

EDRADOUR 1996, 12-year-old, Straight from the Cask, Port Wood Finish, 57 vol

COLOR Pale gold with copper highlights.

NOSE Very fruity, with sweet, musky wine.

BODY Syrupy.

PALATE Rich and gingery, with developing confectionery notes.

FINISH Long and peppery.

SCORE **82**

EDRADOUR 1983, 25-year-old, Port Wood Finish, 52.5 vol

COLOR Bright copper.

NOSE Soft and mature. Cherries, golden raisins, and a whiff of smoke.

BODY Quite full.

PALATE Fruity and intense, with emerging mild licorice.

FINISH Raisins and slightly bitter oak.

SCORE **82**

EDRADOUR 2006, Ballechin, Discovery Series, Burgundy, 46 vol

COLOR Antique gold.

NOSE Soft peat and strawberries. Developing nut and coal notes.

BODY Rounded.

PALATE Very spicy peat smoke. Quite dry, with emerging
black currants and coffee.

FINISH Medium in length, with malt and lingering peat.

SCORE **81**

EDRADOUR 2007, Ballechin, Discovery Series, Madeira, 46 vol

COLOR Pale gold.

NOSE Cowsheds, dried flowers, charcoal, and background peat.

BODY Soft.

PALATE Slightly herbal, with almonds, discreet peat, and oatmeal.

FINISH Medium to long, sweetish peat, closing with paprika.

SCORE **82**

EDRADOUR 2008, Ballechin, Discovery Series, Port, 46 vol

COLOR Light gold.

NOSE Mild iodine, nutty, spicy peat, and summer fruit.

BODY Medium and silky.

PALATE Apricots and ginger, with a splash of cream.

FINISH Spicy, with developing peat.

SCORE **84**

FETTERCAIRN

PRODUCER Whyte and Mackay Ltd.
REGION Highlands   DISTRICT Eastern Highlands
ADDRESS Distillery Road, Fettercairn, near Laurencekirk,
Kincardineshire, AB30 1YE   TEL 01561 340244   VC

THE ESTATE OF THE GLADSTONE FAMILY, who provided Queen Victoria with a famous prime minister, accommodates Fettercairn. This pretty, cream-painted distillery is amid farmers' fields on the edge of the village of attractive Georgian cottages from which it takes its name. The distillery was founded in 1824, and that date was incorporated in the name of the 12-year-old core expression, as Fettercairn 1824, until the range was given a major makeover in 2009–10. The 24, 30, and 40-year-old vintages were introduced, followed by Fettercairn Fior (Gaelic for "pure" or "true"). Fior comprises a considerable amount of 14 and 15-year-old spirit, along with 15 percent heavily peated five-year-old whisky, which was matured in first-fill bourbon barrels.

HOUSE STYLE Lightly earthy, nutty. Easy drinking or aperitif.

FETTERCAIRN Fior, 42 vol

COLOR Full gold.

NOSE Bold, with sherry, wood smoke, toffee, and orange.

BODY Medium to full.

PALATE Autumn berries, spice, and smoky toffee.

FINISH Slightly musty, with spicy oak. Quite lengthy.

SCORE **86**

FETTERCAIRN Fasque, 42 vol

COLOR Honey gold.

NOSE Fragrant, with molasses toffee, cherries, and vanilla.

BODY Medium.

PALATE Rich and spicy. Jaffa oranges and dark chocolate.
Drying quite quickly.

FINISH Black coffee and spicy licorice.

SCORE **84**

FETTERCAIRN 24-year-old, 44.4 vol

COLOR Mahogany gold.

NOSE Cereal, caramel, and citrus fruit, plus a slightly savory note and coal embers.

BODY Smooth.

PALATE Fresh fruit, especially apples. Aniseed and a subtle note of peat.

FINISH Lingering, with smoke, spice, black coffee, and molasses.

SCORE **86**

FETTERCAIRN 30-year-old, 43.3 vol

COLOR Honey gold.

NOSE Vibrant for its age, with marmalade, plum jam, and toffee notes, plus hints of sherry.

BODY Rich.

PALATE Pineapple, marzipan, and soft fudge.

FINISH Long, with molasses toffee, licorice, and peat smoke.

SCORE **88**

FETTERCAIRN 40-year-old, 40 vol

COLOR Mahogany, with cherry highlights.

NOSE Confident and full, with sherry, orange, dark chocolate, coffee, ginger, and spices.

BODY Full.

PALATE More dark chocolate and spices, along with marzipan and orange marmalade notes.

FINISH Raisins, licorice, and dry smoke.

SCORE **89**

GLEN ELGIN

PRODUCER Diageo
REGION Highlands   DISTRICT Speyside (Lossie)
ADDRESS Longmorn, Elgin, Morayshire, IV30 3SL
TEL 01343 862000

GLEN ELGIN HAS A SMALL but passionate fan base and there are plenty who believe its whisky deserves more prominence as a single malt. The principal "house" expressions currently available are a 12-year-old and a 32-year-old, with the latter appearing as part of Diageo's annual "Special Releases" program in 2003. It follows a well-liked and respected "hidden malts" bottling that was released a few years ago.

The distillery itself has never been hidden, but it was for some years heavily branded with the name White Horse, in recognition of its contribution to that blend. The Glen Elgin distillery is very visible on one of the main roads into the town whose name it bears. Although it is just over a hundred years old, its façade dates from 1964, and reflects the classic DCL still-house design of the period.

Where the Lossie River approaches the town of Elgin, there are no fewer than eight distilleries within a few miles. Elgin is also worth a visit for Gordon & MacPhail's whisky store as well as 13th-century cathedral ruins.

HOUSE STYLE Honey and tangerines.
Restorative or after dinner.

GLEN ELGIN Managers' Choice, Distilled 1998, Bottled 2009, 61.1 vol

Matured in a rejuvenated European oak cask.

COLOR Autumn gold, with copper highlights.

NOSE Furniture polish and brittle toffee. Raisins, prunes, and spice.

BODY Smooth.

PALATE Oranges and peaches, then fresh ginger and black pepper.

FINISH Drying to licorice.

SCORE 79

GLEN ELGIN 12 year-old, 43 vol

COLOR Deep gold.

NOSE Fruity and flowery. Heather honey.
Pears poached in spices. Hint of coffee beans.

BODY Light but firm.

PALATE Fresh and crisp, flowery, and gingery. A touch of mandarin.

FINISH Dry and spicy.

SCORE **77**

GLEN ELGIN 32-year-old, Distilled 1971,
Special Release 2003, 42.3 vol

COLOR Full gold.

NOSE Fragrant. Cedary. Honeyed. Seductive.

BODY Soft, rich, and tongue coating.

PALATE Clean and sweet. A hint of Seville orange. Intense heather
honey. Cereal grain. Crunchy. A lovely whisky.

FINISH Gently drying. Shortbread.

SCORE **81**

INDEPENDENT BOTTLINGS
GLEN ELGIN 1992, 21-year-old, Old Particular
(Douglas Laing), 51.5 vol

COLOR Mid-gold.

NOSE Jaffa oranges, honey, almonds, and cereal notes

BODY Supple.

PALATE Ripe orchard fruit, milky coffee, and developing dark chocolate.

FINISH Herbal, with freshly sawed wood.

SCORE 84

GLEN ELGIN 1995, 18-year-old, Eastern Promise
(Wemyss Malts), 46 vol

COLOR Straw.

NOSE Initially grassy, with toffee and malt.

BODY Oily.

PALATE Floral, with citrus fruit, spices, and vanilla.

FINISH Lengthy, with softly spiced malt.

SCORE 82

GLEN ELGIN 1996, Connoisseurs Choice
(Gordon & MacPhail), 46 vol

COLOR Pale gold.

NOSE Sherry and malt balanced by lemon juice.

BODY Medium.

PALATE Lively spices, white pepper, and citrus fruit.

FINISH Fruity and spicy, with vanilla and sherry.

SCORE 82

GLEN GARIOCH

PRODUCER Morrison Bowmore Distillers Ltd.
REGION Highlands   DISTRICT Eastern Highlands
ADDRESS Oldmeldrum, Inverurie, Aberdeenshire, AB51 0ES
TEL 01651 873450   WEBSITE www.glengarioch.com   VC

GLEN GARIOCH—PRONOUNCED "GLEN GEER-Y-OCH"—has been described as one of Scotland's hidden, or even forgotten, gems. It is owned by Morrison Bowmore, whose focus was first on Bowmore and then Auchentoshan. But it seems that Glen Garioch is now having its time in the sun, with a flurry of new expressions, some stylish repackaging, and a dedicated media campaign to raise awareness of the distillery. The distillery is situated at Old Meldrum, which lies off the road from Aberdeen going into the heart of Speyside. The building's stonework, decorated with a clock, faces the small town, which is on the road from Aberdeen to Banff. A visitor center was built here a few years back, and there are other reasons to visit.

First, there is the distillery's antiquity. An announcement in *The Aberdeen Journal* in 1785 refers to a licensed distillery on the same site. This makes it Scotland's oldest licence holder. Second, there is the old distillery itself—a labor-intensive traditional affair packed with old equipment and tastefully decorated to reflect the region's strong Doric links. And finally, there is the location itself. The glen grows some of Scotland's finest barley—and here is one of the few distilleries with its own malting floors.

Taste-wise Glen Garioch is confusing. When the distillery was acquired by its present owners in 1970, their maltster, trained on Islay, was relatively heavy-handed with the peat. The result was a whisky with the "old-fashioned," smoky flavor that the Highland/Speyside region had largely forgotten. In recent years, peat has been reduced and then removed altogether. Peated Glen Garioch bottlings can be found but these days the distillery produces a range of styles including some highly enjoyable ones dominated by citrus and vanilla.

HOUSE STYLE Lightly peaty, flowery, fragrant, spicy.
Aperitif in younger ages. Digestif when older.

GLEN GARIOCH Virgin Oak, 43 vol

COLOR Orange marmalade.

NOSE Honey, peach, and mango.

BODY Sweet, medium full, and smooth.

PALATE Sweet. Honey. Sweet peach and mango.
Very pleasant and fruity, with light spice.

FINISH Outstanding, sweet, fruit, and spice.

SCORE **93**

GLEN GARIOCH Founder's Reserve, 48 vol

COLOR Bright orange.

NOSE Dusty. Spiky. Orange soda. Musk. Musty. Polished oak.

BODY Medium. Spicy. Assertive.

PALATE Clean and sharp. Complex. Rooty. Quite savory.
Grapefruit. Big chili and cumin hit. Occasional sappy note.

FINISH Quite long and very spicy.

SCORE **82**

GLEN GARIOCH 1999, 56.3 vol

COLOR Chestnut.

NOSE Autumn forest. Damp leaves. Chestnuts. Nutty.

BODY Full and mouth coating.

PALATE Big, sweet, and sherries. Juicy raisins. Macaroon.
Currants. Some meatiness to provide depth.

FINISH Long, sweet, and spicy.

SCORE **89**

GLEN GARIOCH 1997, 56.7 vol

COLOR Bronze.

NOSE Some smoke. Spring meadow. Lemon. Sweet nuttiness.

BODY Medium and sweet.

PALATE Sweet citrus and honey. Delightfully balanced—rounded
and sweet with a peatier, earthier base. Clean, with gentle spice
and some nuttiness.

FINISH Medium, with peat and sweet notes.

SCORE **90**

GLEN GARIOCH 1995, 55.5 vol

COLOR Light honey.

NOSE Light citrus. Banana toffee. Trace of lime and spearmint.

BODY Refreshing, cordial-like, and clean.

PALATE Candied fruit. Peach rumtopf. Dessert whisky.
Canned pears and apricots. Sweet, soft, and rounded.

FINISH Rich and sweet, with a trace of paprika.

SCORE **91**

GLEN GARIOCH 1994, 53.9 vol

COLOR Pale honey.

NOSE Citrus bath salts. Dusty. With water, medicine cabinet. Sherbet.

BODY Very full and rich. Benefits from water.

PALATE Spicy, sherbety, and zingy. Sour-apple candy. Clementine.
Tangy fruit.

FINISH Medium, clean, fresh, and spicy.

SCORE **80**

GLEN GARIOCH 1991, 54.7 vol

COLOR Deep lemon.

NOSE Crab apple. Grape. Wood shavings. Gooseberry.

BODY Rich and mouth coating. A little oily.

PALATE With water, gooseberry. Honey. Toffee. Crushed nuts.
Some smoke.

FINISH Soft, sweet, and tangy.

SCORE **84**

GLEN GARIOCH 1986, 54.6 vol

COLOR Liquid honey.

NOSE Lemon. Peaches in cream. Cigarette smoke.

BODY Big, full-bodied, and mouth coating. Demands attention.

PALATE Big, sweet, and rich, with tangy peaches and rich cream.
Tangy, very fruity—like alcoholic sherbet. Absolutely excellent whisky.

FINISH Continues where the palate left off... and continues...
and continues. Exquisite.

SCORE **94**

GLEN GARIOCH 1990, Cask No. 7940
(Berry Bros. & Rudd), 54.6 vol

COLOR Bronze.

NOSE Deep. Autumnal. Plums. Sooty. Dark berries.

BODY Intense and full.

PALATE More plums and berries. Intense peaty notes. Nutty. Dates.

FINISH Sweet and medium long.

SCORE **83**

GLEN GARIOCH 1989, Cask No. 7856
(Berry Bros. & Rudd), 54.8 vol

COLOR Pale straw.

NOSE Lemon dish-soap. Summer meadow. Floral. Sweet.

BODY Soft and sweet.

PALATE Dusty, almost sherbet, with kiwi fruit, mango, and vanilla.

FINISH Medium long, but very sweet.

SCORE **83**

GLEN GRANT

PRODUCER Campari Group
REGION Highlands   DISTRICT Speyside (Rothes)
ADDRESS Rothes, Morayshire, AB38 7BS   TEL 01340 832118   VC

A CHIC SUCCESS IN ITALY, and a Victorian classic in Scotland. Glen Grant was the lone single malt in many a bar from Glasgow to Genoa in the days when this form of whisky was scarcely known outside the Highlands. The distillery, founded in 1840 by John and James Grant, quickly gained a reputation for the quality of its whisky. James Grant, who was a prominent local politician, played a big part in bringing railroads to the area, and they in turn distributed his product. The turreted and gabled offices in the "Scottish baronial" style, and the distillery, are set around a small courtyard. James Grant's son, a military major, brought plants from his travels in India and Africa, and created a garden in the glen behind the distillery. In 1995, the garden was restored and is open to visitors.

For the greater part of its history, Glen Grant won its renown as a single malt in versions bottled by merchants. Older vintages can still be found bearing in small type the name of bottlers Gordon & MacPhail. Glen Grant is highly regarded by blenders and has long been a contributor to Chivas Regal. Indeed, the distillery and its brand were formerly owned by Chivas, but in 2006 the Italian-based company Campari acquired them, and instigated a welcome program of occasional single cask, vintage, and other limited edition releases. During 2013 an on-site bottling hall was developed. It is capable of handling 2,000 bottles per hour, with most of the output destined for mainland Europe and Asia.

HOUSE STYLE Herbal, with notes of hazelnut.
In younger ages, it works as an aperitif; with greater
age and sherry influence, it becomes an after-dinner malt.

GLEN GRANT The Major's Reserve, 40 vol

COLOR Gold.

NOSE Delicate, with vanilla, malt, lemon, and damp leaves.

BODY Light but firm.

PALATE Malt and vanilla, citrus fruit, and hazelnuts.

FINISH Brisk.

SCORE **74**

GLEN GRANT 10-year-old, 43 vol

COLOR Full gold.

NOSE Still dry, but much softer, with some sweetness.

BODY Light to medium, with no obvious intervention of sherry.

PALATE Lightly sweet start, quickly becoming nutty and very dry.

FINISH Very dry, with herbal notes.

SCORE **76**

GLEN GRANT 16-year-old, 43 vol

COLOR Full gold.

NOSE Delicate, with pears and brittle toffee.

BODY Medium.

PALATE Sweet, with orchard fruit and vanilla.

FINISH Very fruity and softly spiced.

SCORE **80**

GLEN GRANT 25-year-old, 43 vol

COLOR Amber.

NOSE Sherry, peaches, toffee, and worn leather.

BODY Supple.

PALATE Golden raisins and figs, oloroso sherry, and honey.

FINISH Medium to long, ginger, and gentle oak.

SCORE **83**

GLEN GRANT 50-year-old, 54.4 vol

COLOR Dark amber.

NOSE Rich, sweet sherry, soft fruit candy, toffee, and finally dark chocolate.

BODY Voluptuous.

PALATE Full-fledged sherry, ripe cherries, baked orange, and abundant Christmas spices.

FINISH Long, slightly musty, and mouth drying.

SCORE **86**

GLEN GRANT 1992, Cellar Reserve, 46 vol

COLOR Pale gold.

NOSE Medium sweet, with ripening pears. Slightly heathery.

BODY Rounded.

PALATE Fresh fruit and malt, with developing nuttiness.

FINISH Medium in length, with hazelnuts and ginger.

SCORE 81

GLEN GRANT Five Decades, 46 vol

COLOR Bright gold.

NOSE Floral, with orange blossom, peaches, and caramel.

BODY Smooth.

PALATE Softly spiced, with sherry, golden raisins, salted caramels,
and ripe pears.

FINISH Relatively long and sweet, with vanilla and
a hint of cinnamon.

SCORE 82

GLEN GRANT 170th Anniversary Edition, 46 vol

COLOR Light gold.

NOSE Floral, with marzipan, caramel, honey, and Jaffa orange.

BODY Silky.

PALATE Early fino-style sherry, then stewed fruit and
a suggestion of smoke.

FINISH Gentle spices and raisins.

SCORE 83

GLEN MORAY

PRODUCER La Martiniquaise
REGION Highlands DISTRICT Speyside (Lossie)
ADDRESS Bruceland Road, Elgin, Morayshire, IV30 1YE
TEL 01343 542577 WEBSITE www.glenmoray.com

THE GRAPEY NOTE that some find in Glen Moray is a house characteristic that preceded the distillery's enthusiasm for wine finishes, such as Vallée du Rhône. The earlier Chardonnay and Chenin Blanc finishes, launched in 1999, seemed to be aimed at ladies who lunch. The use of whites was an innovation in the industry. Until its purchase in 2008 by French-based La Martiniquaise, Glen Moray shared owners with the more northerly Glenmorangie distillery, which pioneered the notion of "wine" finishes, but with reds, port, and Madeira.

The two distilleries' similar names predate their common ownership. It is a second coincidence that both were formerly breweries. Glen Moray was converted into a distillery in 1897, acquired by Macdonald & Muir (which later became Glenmorangie PLC) in the 1920s, and extended in 1958. Its whiskies are admired, but have never enjoyed great glamour. The distillery previously favored gift tins decorated with the insignia of Highland regiments. The smartly kept distillery is on boggy land near the Lossie River, just outside Elgin.

HOUSE STYLE Grassy, with barley notes. Aperitif.

GLEN MORAY Classic, 40 vol
COLOR Light gold.
NOSE Floral and fragrant, with banana and malt, plus lemongrass.
BODY Smooth.
PALATE Fudge, honey, cereal, soft spices, and lemon.
FINISH Relatively short, with ginger and citrus notes.
SCORE **78**

GLEN MORAY Classic Port Finish, 40 vol

COLOR Light gold, with tinges of pink.

NOSE Vanilla, bubblegum, dried fruit, and dark chocolate.

BODY Viscous.

PALATE Spices, caramel, and citrus fruit.

FINISH Spicy and fruity, with dark chocolate and oak.

SCORE **78**

GLEN MORAY 10 year-old, Chardonnay Cask, 40 vol

COLOR Old gold.

NOSE Fresh and approachable, with apples, pears, subtle spice, and warm sugar.

BODY Medium.

PALATE A hint of dry white wine, then butterscotch, vanilla,
with sweeter wine notes emerging.

FINISH Hot buttered toast, cinnamon, and drying oak.

SCORE **79**

GLEN MORAY 12-year-old, 40 vol

"Mellowed" in Chenin Blanc casks.

COLOR Softer, more yellowy.

NOSE Pears. Walnuts. Fresh oak.

BODY Smooth and oily. Beeswax. Honeyed.

PALATE Pears in cream. Late, lively, peachy fruitiness. Fresh mint.

FINISH Raisiny. Also resiny. Fresh oak. Soothing warmth.

SCORE **76**

GLEN MORAY 16-year-old, 40 vol

COLOR Old gold.

NOSE Very aromatic. Hint of cloves. Apples. Tannin.

BODY Smooth and very firm.

PALATE More assertive. Toffee, apple, and oak.

FINISH Long. Hints of peat. Grassy. Leafy. Resiny. Peppery.

SCORE **76**

GLEN MORAY 25-year-old, Portwood Finish, 43 vol

COLOR Gold with orange facets.

NOSE Fresh and sweet, with red berries and bourbon vanilla notes.

BODY Relatively full.

PALATE More red berries. Spun sugar. Gentle spices.

FINISH Long and fruity.

SCORE **84**

GLEN MORAY 30-year-old, 43 vol

COLOR Bright gold.

NOSE Floral and elegant, with vanilla, nutmeg, and a whiff
of background smoke.

BODY Medium, oily.

PALATE Fruity and spicy, with lavender, eucalyptus, and nutty vanilla.

FINISH Medium to long. Elegant, with gentle oak, dates,
and creamy vanilla.

SCORE **79**

GLEN MORAY Mountain Oak Malt,
The Final Release (1991), 58.6 vol

*Matured in "a unique selection of toasted and charred mountain
oak casks from North America."*

COLOR Deep amber.

NOSE Chewy toffee, orange fruit pastilles, nutmeg,
and vanilla. A hint of mint.

BODY Firm.

PALATE Pears, pineapples, and soft fudge. Developing
hazelnuts, molasses, and ginger.

FINISH Lengthy, with tobacco, ginger, and a touch of pepper.

SCORE **80**

GLEN ORD

PRODUCER Diageo
REGION Highlands DISTRICT Northern Highlands
ADDRESS Muir of Ord, Ross-shire, IV6 7UJ TEL 01463 872004
WEBSITE www.discovering-distilleries.com/www.malts.com VC

THE LAUNCH IN 2003 of a 12-year-old "Hidden Malt" from Glen Ord was very welcome, but begged a question. Why was it hidden in the first place? Why has this distillery been obliged to play hide-and-seek over the years? Under different managements, its whisky has occupied endless different positions in the marketing portfolio. It has even sported different names: Glenordie, Ordie, Ord, Muir of Ord. The latest addition to the list is the Singleton of Glen Ord, a version containing more sherry casks than normal and targeted at the Asian market, and particularly Taiwan, where sherry seems to appeal to the palate. The original 12-year-old is becoming increasingly hard to find in the European market.

It is at a village called Muir of Ord ("the moor by the hill"), just to the west and north of Inverness. This is the region where Ferintosh, the first famous whisky, was made. Glen Ord also has a maltings (of the drum type). The distillery and maltings look over the barley-growing country of the Black Isle.

HOUSE STYLE Flavorful, roselike, spicy (cinnamon?),
and malty, with a dry finish. After dinner.

THE SINGLETON OF GLEN ORD 12-year-old, 40 vol
Matured in sherry and bourbon casks.

COLOR Rich gold.

NOSE Floral, sweet sherry, marzipan, ripe plums, and peaches.

BODY Soft and rounded.

PALATE Full, malty, and approachable, with sherry, cinnamon, and hazelnuts.

FINISH Initial cough lozenges, followed by soft fruit, rose petals, and mild oak tannins.

SCORE **82**

THE SINGLETON OF GLEN ORD 15-year-old, 40 vol

COLOR Golden amber.

NOSE Sweet and malty. Tangy fruit. A suggestion of new
leather and nutmeg.

BODY Soft.

PALATE Golden raisins, figs, honey, malt, cinnamon, and subtle wood smoke.

FINISH Medium in length, citrus fruit, and wood spices.

SCORE **84**

THE SINGLETON OF GLEN ORD 18-year-old, 40 vol

COLOR Deep amber.

NOSE Stewed fruit, soft spices, and malt.

BODY Quite full.

PALATE Figs and peaches, with cinnamon.

FINISH Medium to long, warming.

SCORE **85**

GLEN ORD 1997, Manager's Choice, 59.2 vol

Matured in an ex-bourbon cask; 204 bottles.

COLOR Gold, with orange facets.

NOSE Quite sweet, with vanilla and lemonade notes.
Sticky fruit cake and faint aniseed develop.

BODY Mouth coating.

PALATE Rich, with golden raisins, white chocolate, fruit pastilles,
and a hint of leather.

FINISH Long and sophisticated.

SCORE **87**

GLEN SCOTIA

PRODUCER Loch Lomond Distillery Co. Ltd.
REGION Campbeltown
ADDRESS 12 High Street, Campbeltown, Argyll, PA28 6DS
TEL 01586 552288 *Visits by appointment only*
EMAIL mail@lochlomonddistillery.com

ALONG WITH GLENGYLE AND SPRINGBANK, Glen Scotia is one of the last survivors in the Campbeltown malt whisky region, and the distillery has suffered during the past few decades from periods of silence and lack of investment.

A major renovation program took place between 1979 and 1982, but production thereafter was comparatively sporadic. However, during the past few years the distillery has benefited from significant spending by owners The Loch Lomond Distillery Co. Ltd., resulting in a much more pleasing external appearance and internal upgrading. The distillery currently produces between 120–130,000 liters of spirit per year, from three mashes per week, but given additional production staff that figure could reportedly rise to 480,000 liters from 10 weekly mashes.

The investment in Glen Scotia's fabric was matched by the release of an entirely new range of single malts during 2012. Five aged expressions dating from 10 to 21 years old were introduced in striking new packaging. They are offered at 92 proof (46% ABV) and not chill filtered.

Founded around 1832, Glen Scotia is known for more than one manifestation of spirit: it is said to be haunted by the ghost of a former proprietor who drowned himself in Campbeltown Loch.

HOUSE STYLE Fresh, salty. Aperitif, or with salty foods.

GLEN SCOTIA 10-year-old, 46 vol

COLOR Chamomile tea.

NOSE Lemonade, hints of aniseed, and putty.

BODY Medium.

PALATE Tropical fruit, spice, and milk chocolate.

FINISH Medium in length and spicy, with a hint of licorice.

SCORE **82**

GLEN SCOTIA 12-year-old, 46 vol

COLOR Barley sugar.

NOSE Nougat and a suggestion of fresh newsprint.

BODY Relatively full.

PALATE Mixed nuts and peaches in brandy.

FINISH Slightly waxy, with fruit-and-nut chocolate.

SCORE **83**

GLEN SCOTIA 16-year-old, 46 vol

COLOR Lemon tea.

NOSE Vanilla fudge, then black pepper, sea salt,
and a savory note develops.

BODY Lush and slightly oily.

PALATE Maritime-tinged candied fruit and wood smoke.

FINISH Slightly tarry. Medium in length.

SCORE **84**

GLEN SCOTIA 18-year-old, 46 vol

COLOR Honey.

NOSE Lemons, salt, then emerging malt.

BODY Smooth. A little oily.

PALATE Carbonated fruit, with a hint of vanilla and slight brininess.

FINISH Spicy soft fruit.

SCORE **83**

GLEN SCOTIA 21-year-old, 46 vol

COLOR Earl Grey tea.

NOSE Canned peaches, fresh ginger, and a slightly herbal note.

BODY Voluptuous.

PALATE Vanilla, malt, vigorous spices, and white chocolate.

FINISH Lingering coffee and gingery oak.

SCORE **86**

GLEN SPEY

PRODUCER Diageo
REGION Highlands   DISTRICT Speyside (Rothes)
ADDRESS Rothes, Aberlour, Banffshire, AB38 7AU
TEL 01340 882000

Dating from the 1880s, Glen Spey is in Rothes. Much of its whisky is destined for the house blend of an aristocratic wine and spirits merchant in St. James's, London. (It is coincidence that neighbor Glenrothes follows a parallel path.) In the case of Glen Spey, the merchant is Justerini & Brooks, whose house blend is J&B.

Giacomo Justerini was an Italian, from Bologna. He emigrated to Britain in pursuit of an opera singer, Margherita Bellion, in 1749. The romance does not seem to have come to fruition, but Justerini meanwhile worked in Britain as a maker of liqueurs. By 1779, he was already selling Scotch whisky. Brooks was a later partner in the firm. The business was for a time part of Gilbeys, at which point there was for a time a nutty, grassy eight-year-old Glen Spey.

HOUSE STYLE Light, grassy, nutty. Aperitif.

GLEN SPEY 12 year-old, Flora and Fauna, 43 vol

COLOR Full gold.

NOSE Maltiness (rich, tea cookie). Dusty. Kumquat. Leafy. Mint.

BODY Medium. Oily.

PALATE Vivacious. Starts intensely sweet, with light citrus notes, then becomes dramatically drier.

FINISH Crisp. Lemon zest. Pith.

SCORE 75

GLEN SPEY 17-year-old, Old Malt Cask, 50 vol

COLOR Yellowy green.

NOSE Sweet. Toffee. Bourbon. Vanilla. Spearmint chewing gum.

BODY Soft and mouth filling.

PALATE Lively. Red licorice. Peach. Soft fruit. Banana. Some spearmint. Later, tannins.

FINISH Full, firm, and sweet, with some woody and spicy notes.

SCORE 69

GLENALLACHIE

PRODUCER Chivas Brothers (Pernod Ricard)
REGION Highlands   DISTRICT Speyside
ADDRESS Aberlour, Banffshire, AB38 9LR   TEL 01340 871315

TRUE WHISKY LOVERS LIKE TO SAMPLE EVERYTHING, and, although Glenallachie (pronounced "glen-alec-y") has only a modest reputation, it is a good example of a subtle, delicate, flowery Speysider.

The distillery was built in 1967 primarily to contribute malt to the Mackinlay blends. It was temporarily closed in the late 1980s, then acquired and reopened by Campbell Distillers at the end of the decade.

It takes its water from a spring on Ben Rinnes, just over the hill from its senior partner, Aberlour. Despite their proximity, their water is different, and so is their whisky: Glenallachie lighter, more acidic, drier, more delicate; Aberlour richer, more luscious, sweeter, maltier.

HOUSE STYLE Clean, subtle, delicate. Aperitif.

GLENALLACHIE 12-year-old, 40 vol
A Mackinlay bottling that is now difficult to find.

COLOR Very pale.

NOSE Hint of peat. Fragrant. Lightly malty.

BODY Light but firm.

PALATE Beautifully clean, smooth, and delicate.

FINISH Starts sweet and develops toward a long, perfumy finish. A graceful predinner companion.

SCORE **75**

GLENALLACHIE 12-year-old, Provenance, 46 vol

COLOR Light lemon.

NOSE Clean. Sweet Starburst fruit. Lime?

BODY Pleasant. Medium and unassertive.

PALATE Yellow fruit. Mild vanilla. Sweet and fresh.

FINISH Medium and sweet. A touch of nutmeg. Pleasant.

SCORE **69**

GLENALLACHIE 18-year-old, Cask Strength Edition, Distilled 1989, Bottled 2008, Batch GA 18 005, 57.1 vol

COLOR Deep mahogany, with reddish hues.

NOSE Cloves, cardamom, and leather.

BODY Full and chewy.

PALATE Rich sherry, with cloves, a rich fruit cake with a vast array of spices, raisins, and dates; water opens up and accents the cloves.

FINISH Long. Cloves with leather, hints of tobacco, and a not unpleasant trace of sulfur.

COMMENT Aged in first-fill sherry butts, this is a wonderful dram for sherry lovers, though it does mask many of the distillery's subtle qualities.

SCORE **85**

GLENALLACHIE 1992, Connoisseurs Choice, 43 vol

COLOR Pale gold.

NOSE Buttery lemon. Very peaty undertow.

BODY Medium full.

PALATE Limp. Clean and gingery barley. Some green apple. Traces of tannin. Little depth.

FINISH Medium long, with fluffy apple and a hint of pepper.

SCORE **63**

GLENBURGIE

PRODUCER Chivas Brothers (Pernod Ricard)
REGION Highlands   DISTRICT Speyside (Findhorn)
ADDRESS Forres, Morayshire, IV36 0QX   TEL 01343 850258

G LENBURGIE ISN'T WELL KNOWN for its whiskies and its malts rarely make it to the bottle. But the distillery has grown over the last few years and is now a sizeable powerhouse, creating whisky that is mainly destined for Ballantine's, a blend enjoying considerable success under owners Pernod Ricard. Glenburgie is a cutting edge distillery producing more than four million liters of spirit a year. A noted admirer of Glenburgie's herbal, fruity whisky was writer Maurice Walsh, whose story *The Quiet Man* was made into a movie starring John Wayne and Maureen O'Hara. Like Robert Burns and Neil Gunn, writer Walsh had a "day job" as an excise man, in his case at Glenburgie. A less romantic, more technical claim to the noteworthiness of this distillery is its second malt whisky.

The distillery traces its history to 1810, and on its present site to 1829. It is in the watershed of the Findhorn, at Alves, between Forres and Elgin. Glenburgie was extended after World War II, at a time when many whiskies were in short supply. At that time, some Allied distilleries were being given additional stills of a different design, to extend their range. These "Lomond" stills, with a column-shaped neck, produced an oilier, fruitier malt. The whisky from Glenburgie's Lomond stills was named after Willie Craig, one of the company's senior managers. Those stills were removed in the early 1980s, but Glencraig can still be found in independent bottlings.

HOUSE STYLE Oily, fruity, herbal. Aperitif.

GLENBURGIE 15 year-old, 46 vol

COLOR Bright gold.

NOSE Attractive sweetness. Fragrant. Praline. A touch of orange peel.

BODY Medium and firm.

PALATE Round and velvety. Assertive. Fruity and toffeeish.

FINISH Dry and leafy. Hint of licorice.

SCORE **76**

GLENBURGIE 15-year-old, Cask Strength Edition,
Distilled 1992, Bottled 2007, Batch GB 15 001, 58.8 vol

COLOR Dusty, antique gold.

NOSE Sweet and tangy. Allspice and pecans, with a hint of orange peel.
Trace of eucalyptus, coaxed out with a few drops of water. Wax beans?

BODY Chewy and mouth coating.

PALATE Vegetation. Spices. Pine.

FINISH Long and dry, with notes of orange.

SCORE **84**

AN INDEPENDENT BOTTLING OF GLENCRAIG
GLENCRAIG 1974, 34-year-old, Rarest of the Rare, 40.3 vol

COLOR Yellow with greenish hue.

NOSE Traces of mint. Pencil eraser. Fruity Jell-O. Sweet. Clean.

BODY Quite light and soft.

PALATE Very clean. No blemishes or cask imperfections.
Sugared barley. Traces of lemon and grapefruit.

FINISH Medium sweet and fruity.

SCORE **82**

GLENCADAM

PRODUCER Angus Dundee Distillers PLC
REGION Highlands   DISTRICT Eastern Highlands
ADDRESS Brechin, Angus, DD9 7PA   TEL 01356 622217

GLENCADAM IS A NOTABLY CREAMY MALT, using unpeated malt. Appropriately, much of the distillery's output has, over the years, gone into "Cream of the Barley," originally blended in Dundee and now popular in Belfast.

The neat little distillery, at Brechin, was founded in 1825 and modernized in 1959. The very soft water is piped an astonishing 30 miles (48 km) from Loch Lee, at the head of Glen Esk. With neighbor North Port now gone, Glencadam is a lonely survivor on this stretch of coastline. The distillery was acquired by Angus Dundee from Allied Domecq in 2003.

Glencadam uses mostly first-fill bourbon casks, and fills only a handful of sherry butts each year. This makes the new 25-year-old release an extra special bottling.

HOUSE STYLE Creamy, with a suggestion of berry fruit.
With dessert, or after dinner.

GLENCADAM 10-year-old, 46 vol
COLOR Pale gold.

NOSE Strawberries and vanilla.

BODY Moderately robust.

PALATE Creamy, with a hint of berries; perhaps cassis.

FINISH Dusting of spice.

SCORE **73**

GLENCADAM 12-year-old, The Rather Refined Port Wood Finish, 46 vol
COLOR Pale rosé, with copper highlights.

NOSE Sweet red wine, roses in bloom, milk chocolate,
stewed rhubarb, and black pepper.

BODY Viscous.

PALATE Initially strawberries, then spicy milk chocolate, caramel,
and candied cherries.

FINISH Remaining sweet, with nutmeg and darker chocolate notes.

SCORE **77**

GLENCADAM 14-year-old, The Rather Enriched Oloroso Finish, 46 vol

COLOR Orange gold.

NOSE Sweetness, with vanilla, dates, apples, and cinnamon.

BODY Rich.

PALATE Floral and spicy notes, with toffee, ginger, and sweet sherry.

FINISH Fruity and spicy.

SCORE **78**

GLENCADAM 15-year-old, 46 vol

COLOR Golden.

NOSE Spicy, with hints of berries.

BODY Moderately full and smooth.

PALATE Oak and berries, with a note of coarse salt. Rich oak. Strawberries, with traces of vanilla and spice.

FINISH Long oak with spice.

SCORE **76**

GLENCADAM 21-year-old, The Exceptional, 46 vol

COLOR Pale gold.

NOSE Floral, with ripe oranges, pineapple, and a herbal note.

BODY Medium.

PALATE Elegant and complex, with orange, vanilla, and contrasting dark berries and pepper.

FINISH Lengthy, a little oily.

SCORE **83**

GLENCADAM 30-year-old, Single Cask, 46 vol

A single cask (No. 729) bottling, distilled in 1982; 260 bottles.

COLOR Rich amber.

NOSE Soft and waxy, with worn leather, Jaffa oranges, and malt.

BODY Full.

PALATE Hard toffee, orange creams, and a slightly musty note.

FINISH Long and mouth-drying, but tannins held well in check.

SCORE **87**

GLENDRONACH

PRODUCER The Benriach Distillery Company
REGION Highlands DISTRICT Speyside (Deveron)
ADDRESS Forgue, by Huntly, Aberdeenshire, AB54 6DB
TEL 01466 730202 VC

THE RECENT WHISKY BOOM has ensured that the potential sale of any distillery will attract a line of possible suitors, and so it proved when Glendronach was put on the market by owners Pernod Ricard, who had inherited it after the breakup of Allied and couldn't seem to find a place for it in the company portfolio.

The new owners are the same team that has so magnificently restored the fortunes and offerings of Benriach. Fronted by the irrepressible Billy Walker, they look set to restore this distillery to all its magnificent sherried glory.

Production at Glendronach restarted in 2002 and the owners at the time announced plans for a new-style 12-year-old. Whether that will now appear in four or five years' time remains to be seen, but if it does it will add to a list of bottlings from the distillery at that age.

Over the years, Glendronach 12 has appeared in a confusion of styles. At one stage, there was a welcome choice between "The Original" (second-fill, mainly bourbon) and a version labeled "100 percent matured in sherry casks." These two were then replaced by "Traditional," which attempted to marry their virtues.

The distillery has good stocks and Walker has successfully traded to bring in even more. His stated intent to restore Glendronach's reputation for bold, sherried whiskies has certainly been borne out by the first releases under the new regime. He plans to recask some stock from bourbon casks to sherry ones, too. In addition to a comprehensive aged range, Walker and associates have also followed their BenRiach model by releasing an ongoing series of single cask bottlings.

The whiskies are greatly appreciated by malt lovers, but much affection is also felt for the place itself. Deep in Aberdeenshire's fertile barley-growing country, the glen of the Dronac Burn almost entirely hides the cluster of buildings that make up the distillery—though a pagoda is hard to conceal. The floor maltings have not been restarted yet, but there have been suggestions that they might.

The distillery has its own small mansion house, flower beds, and kitchen garden, as though it were a small estate. (Domaine Dronac?)

The fifth Duke of Gordon, the man behind the legalization of distilling in the Highlands in the 1820s, is credited with having encouraged local farmers to establish this distillery. It was later run by a member of the William Grant family (owners of Glenfiddich), and in 1960 was acquired to help provide the malty background to the well-known blend Teacher's.

HOUSE STYLE Smooth and big, with a teasing sweet-and-dry maltiness. Sherry-friendly. After dinner.

GLENDRONACH 12-year-old, 40 vol

COLOR Deep tan.

NOSE Mint-flavored toffee. Vanilla. Sherry, winey notes, and berries.

BODY Medium.

PALATE Fresh cranberry and blueberry juice. Peppery. No cloying sweetness, Highland peat carpet.

FINISH Medium, savory, and peaty.

SCORE **70**

GLENDRONACH 15-year-old, 46 vol

COLOR Horse-chestnut brown.

NOSE Big. Sherry, chicory coffee, fresh figs, and floral notes.
Magnificent, with wisps of sulfur.

BODY Sweet, bold, and full.

PALATE Sweet, fruitcake, followed by a pepper surge, drying tannins,
and plummy smoke. Complex and intense. Evolving.

FINISH Plummy, with pepper and peat. Long.

SCORE **90**

GLENDRONACH 18-year-old, 46 vol

2009 Release.

COLOR Deep bronze.

NOSE Earthy and rooty. Sulfur. Old pantry.

BODY Creamy and soft.

PALATE Rich, deep red fruit, particularly plum. Some tannin astringency,
wisps of peat, and menthol. Bold.

FINISH Sherry and a peat underlay, with gentle spice. Long and lingering.

SCORE **84**

GLENDRONACH 21-year-old, Parliament, 48 vol

COLOR Deep amber.

NOSE Sweet sherry, soy sauce, molasses, and new leather.

BODY Full and rich.

PALATE Fruity, with caramel and lots of spicy leather,
then late-developing cloves.

FINISH Lingering, with licorice, dark chocolate, more spice
and oak tannins.

SCORE **86**

GLENDRONACH Cask Strength (Batch 3), 54.9 vol

COLOR Golden amber.

NOSE Overripe oranges, dates, and hot cocoa.

BODY Full.

PALATE Dried fruit, zesty oak, and more chocolate.

FINISH Long and rich.

SCORE **85**

GLENDRONACH 31-year-old, Grandeur, 45.8 vol

COLOR Autumn gold.

NOSE Pipe tobacco and old polished oak. Sweet sherry, figs, and dates.

BODY Full.

PALATE Jaffa oranges, molasses toffee, oloroso sherry, and milky coffee.

FINISH Sherry, ginger, tobacco, and dark chocolate.

SCORE **89**

GLENDRONACH 14-year-old, Sauternes Finish, 46 vol

COLOR Bright straw.

NOSE Strawberries and cream. Rose wine.

BODY Supple.

PALATE Heavy cream over apple pie. More sweet wine.

FINISH Medium in length, sweet, and fruity.

SCORE **82**

GLENDRONACH 18-year-old, Tawny Port Finish, 46 vol

COLOR Bright amber.

NOSE Red currants, soft fudge, and a sprinkling of cinnamon.

BODY Medium.

PALATE Cedar spice. More red berry fruit.

FINISH Long, with lots of oaky spice.

SCORE **79**

GLENDULLAN

PRODUCER Diageo
REGION Highland   DISTRICT Speyside (Dufftown)
ADDRESS Dufftown, Banffshire, AB55 4DJ
TEL 01340 822100

THIS DISTILLERY, ESTABLISHED IN 1897–98, has had its moments of glory, notably the supply of its whisky in the early 1900s to King Edward VII, an honor that was for some years proclaimed on its casks. This is a large producer of malt whisky, but most of it goes into Diageo's blends, and into the Singleton of Glendullan, which is sold in the United States.

HOUSE STYLE Perfumy, fruity, dry, chili-like, oily, big. Put it in a hip flask.

SINGLETON OF GLENDULLAN 12-year-old, 40 vol
COLOR Amber, with gold highlights.
NOSE Fragrant sherry, underlying cereal, apple, and subtle spice.
BODY Quite full.
PALATE Sherried and rich. Caramel, brittle toffee, and hazelnuts.
FINISH Medium in length. Spice and raisins.
SCORE **77**

GLENDULLAN 12-year-old, Flora and Fauna, 43 vol
COLOR Almost white, with just a tinge of gold.
NOSE Light, dry maltiness. Hint of fruit.
BODY A hard edge, then silky.
PALATE Dry start, becoming buttery, malty, nutty, perfumy, and lightly fruity.
FINISH Extraordinarily perfumy and long.
SCORE **75**

SINGLETON OF GLENDULLAN 38-year-old, 59.8 vol
COLOR Golden brown.
NOSE Rich citrus, clementine, oak, burned toffee, and spice.
BODY Rich, full, and waxy.
PALATE Not as intense as you might expect. Melon. Berry fruit. Vanilla. Oak spice. Some astringency.
FINISH Long and woody.
SCORE **83**

GLENFARCLAS

PRODUCER J. & G. Grant
REGION Highlands   DISTRICT Speyside
ADDRESS Ballindalloch, Banffshire, AB37 9BD   TEL 01807 500257
WEBSITE www.glenfarclas.co.uk   EMAIL enquiries@glenfarclas.co.uk   VC

WITH A SIXTH GENERATION of the family now active in the business, prospects look good for this most independent of distilleries. Glenfarclas whiskies are in the top flight among Speysiders, though they are not as widely known as some similar examples from this region. From the Spey River, it is about a mile to Glenfarclas ("valley of the green grass"). The distillery is near the village of Marypark. Behind it, heather-covered hills rise toward Ben Rinnes, from which the distillery's water flows. Barley is grown in the surrounding area.

The distillery belongs to a private, family-owned company, J & G. Grant. The family is not connected (except perhaps distantly) to any of the other whisky-making Grants, and does not own any other distilleries or bottlers. Glenfarclas traces its history to 1836, and has been in the family since 1865. Although some of the buildings date from that period, and the reception room has paneling from an ocean liner, the equipment is modern, and its stills are the biggest in Speyside.

HOUSE STYLE Big, complex, malty, sherryish. After dinner.

GLENFARCLAS 8-year-old, 40 vol
COLOR Mid-bronze.
NOSE Malted milk balls, Turkish delight, peaches, golden raisins, and sweet sherry.
BODY Firm.
PALATE Light malt, nutmeg, sherry, and baked apple.
FINISH Spicy dark chocolate—medium in length.
SCORE **83**

GLENFARCLAS 10-year-old, 40 vol

Elegant and quite dry for a Glenfarclas.

COLOR Full gold.

NOSE Big, with some sherry sweetness and nuttiness,

but also smokiness at the back of the nose.

BODY Characteristically firm.

PALATE Crisp and dry at first, with the flavor filling out as it develops.

FINISH Sweet and long.

SCORE **86**

GLENFARCLAS 12-year-old, 43 vol

For many devotees, the most familiar face of Glenfarclas.

COLOR Bronze.

NOSE Drier than the 10-year-old, with a quick, big attack.

BODY Firm and slightly oily.

PALATE Plenty of flavor, with notes of peat smoke.

FINISH Long, with oaky notes, even at this relatively young age.

SCORE **87**

GLENFARCLAS 15-year-old, 46 vol

Many enthusiasts feel that this age most deftly demonstrates the complexity of this malt. Certainly the best-balanced Glenfarclas.

COLOR Amber.

NOSE Plenty of sherry, oak, maltiness, and a hint of smokiness— all the elements of a lovely, mixed bouquet.

BODY Firm and rounded.

PALATE Assertive, again with all the elements beautifully melded.

FINISH Long and smooth.

SCORE **88**

GLENFARCLAS 17-year-old, 43 vol

COLOR Full amber.

NOSE Sweet sherry, vanilla fudge, stewed fruit, and light peat.

BODY Full.

PALATE More sherry, malt, and peat smoke, with an elusive herbal note.

FINISH Long, sweet, and spicy, with delicate oak.

SCORE **88**

GLENFARCLAS 18-year-old, 43 vol

COLOR Ripe straw.

NOSE Cereal, succulent orchard fruit, honey, and vanilla.

BODY Full.

PALATE Milk chocolate, mandarin oranges, soft toffee, and rosewater.

FINISH Medium and silky, with Bing cherries.

SCORE **87**

GLENFARCLAS 21-year-old, 43 vol

COLOR Amber.

NOSE More sherry. Butter. Golden raisinlike fruitiness.
Sweet lemon juice on a crêpe. Greater smokiness,
as well as a dash of oak. All slowly emerge.

BODY Big. Firm.

PALATE Immense flavor development. Raisiny, spicy, and gingery.

FINISH Remarkably long, with lots of sherry, becoming
sweetish and perfumy.

SCORE **89**

GLENFARCLAS 25-year-old, 43 vol

More of everything. Perhaps a touch woody for purists,
but a remorselessly serious after-dinner malt for others.

COLOR Dark amber.

NOSE Pungent and sappy.

BODY Big, with some dryness of texture.

PALATE The flavors are tightly interlocked and the whisky appears
reluctant to give up its secrets at first. Very slow, insistent flavor development.
All the components gradually emerge, but in a drier mood.

FINISH Long, oaky, and sappy. Extra points out of respect
for idiosyncratic age.

SCORE **88**

GLENFARCLAS 30-year-old, 43 vol

COLOR Refractive, bright amber.

NOSE Oaky and slightly woody.

BODY Very firm.

PALATE Nutty and oaky.

FINISH Oaky, sappy, and peaty.

SCORE **87**

GLENFARCLAS 40-year-old, 46 vol

COLOR Rich gold.

NOSE Fino sherry, new leather, cut grass, slight smoke, and cloves.

BODY Medium to full.

PALATE Relatively sweet, with allspice, Jaffa oranges, cherries, and developing oak.

FINISH Lengthy, with oak tannins and black coffee.

SCORE **90**

GLENFARCLAS 105, 40-year-old, 60 vol

COLOR Deep amber.

NOSE Big. Sherry and marzipan, with developing floral and caramel notes.

BODY Rounded.

PALATE Dry sherry, raisins, walnuts, and allspice.

FINISH Steadily drying, with spice, licorice, and hints of pipe tobacco.

SCORE **89**

GLENFARCLAS 175th Anniversary Chairman's Reserve, 43 vol

COLOR Mahogany.

NOSE Spicy, sweet sherry, malt, dried fruit, Seville oranges, and mild oak.

BODY Voluptuous.

PALATE Coffee, orange, cinnamon, dark chocolate, vanilla, and caramel.

FINISH Long, with dark chocolate, cocoa, and drying sherry.

SCORE **91**

FAMILY CASK RELEASES

In 2007 Glenfarclas released an unprecedented 43 consecutive single cask vintages, dating from 1952 to 1994, under the "Family Cask" banner. Additional bottlings have subsequently been released since initial casks from specific years sold out. Indeed, the range now encompasses vintages from 1954 to 1999. Below are sampling notes for a representative selection of Family Cask releases.

GLENFARCLAS 1954, Release A13, Cask No. 1253, 46.3 vol

Sherry butt; 424 bottles.

COLOR Full amber.

NOSE Linseed, burlap, fudge, and sherry.

BODY Medium.

PALATE Dark chocolate and licorice.

FINISH Dries quite rapidly to peaty tannins.

SCORE **85**

GLENFARCLAS 1955, Release A13, Cask No. 2217, 43.3 vol

Sherry butt; 507 bottles.

COLOR Rich amber.

NOSE Grassy, with developing cherry, coffee, and milk-chocolate notes. A touch of tweed.

BODY Supple.

PALATE Dark berries and drying sherry.

FINISH Spicy, with aniseed, licorice, and raisins.

SCORE **86**

GLENFARCLAS 1958, Release A13, Cask No. 2064, 44.2 vol

Sherry hogshead; 185 bottles.

COLOR Bright mahogany.

NOSE Marzipan, spice, and medium-sweet sherry. Musty milk chocolate.

BODY Smooth and rounded.

PALATE Rich orchard fruit, old leather, and soft spices.

FINISH Dries slowly and elegantly to dark chocolate.

SCORE **89**

GLENFARCLAS 1960, Release A13, Cask No. 1770, 42.3 vol
Sherry hogshead; 166 bottles.

COLOR Dark mahogany.

NOSE Initially reticent, then sweet floral notes, fragrant sherry, and polished wood.

BODY Medium.

PALATE Stewed fruit, licorice sticks, and cocktail cherries.

FINISH Long, mouth drying, and tannic. Espresso.

SCORE **84**

GLENFARCLAS 1962, Release A13, Cask No. 3245, 45.3 vol
Sherry hogshead; 169 bottles.

COLOR Mahogany, with ruby facets.

NOSE Shy, then candy-store aromas, marzipan, and medium sherry.

BODY Rich.

PALATE Confident, with pipe tobacco, golden raisins, and dates; dark chocolate slowly develops.

FINISH Slow to dry, mildly tannic.

SCORE **86**

GLENFARCLAS 1969, Release A13, Cask No. 63, 48.9 vol
Plain hogshead; 106 bottles.

COLOR Bright amber.

NOSE Fragrant, with vanilla, ginger, and marzipan.

BODY Smooth.

PALATE Smoky citrus fruit with cream. Lively spices.

FINISH Spicy, with cocoa.

SCORE **86**

GLENFARCLAS 1974, Release A13, Cask No. 5785, 53.3 vol
Sherry butt; 240 bottles.

COLOR Dark gold.

NOSE Rich, nutty, leathery malt, and vanilla.

BODY Medium.

PALATE Big musky fruit notes, raisins, and figs.

FINISH Steadily drying, malty, with developing oak tannins.

SCORE **85**

GLENFARCLAS 1977, Release A13, Cask No. 6514, 50 vol

Plain hogshead; 232 bottles.

COLOR Bright gold.

NOSE Soft fruit, honey, and fudge.

BODY Smooth.

PALATE Sweet orchard fruit, toffee, and nutmeg.

FINISH Drying slightly, with ginger and citrus fruit.

SCORE **87**

GLENFARCLAS 1979, Release A13, Cask No. 8074, 42.7 vol

Plain butt; 591 bottles.

COLOR Light bronze.

NOSE Freshly mown grass, vanilla, and herbal notes.

BODY Supple.

PALATE Soft sweet fruit, toffee, caramel, and popcorn.

FINISH Menthol and herbal. Medium in length.

SCORE **86**

GLENFARCLAS 1982, Release A13, Cask No. 635, 54.9 vol

Plain hogshead; 239 bottles.

COLOR Straw gold.

NOSE Vanilla fudge and crème brûlée.

BODY Medium to full.

PALATE Rich and peppery. Berry fruit and ginger; fudge emerges.

FINISH Soft fudge sprinkled with black pepper.

SCORE **87**

GLENFARCLAS 1984, Release A13, Cask No. 6031, 47.1 vol

Plain hogshead; 211 bottles.

COLOR Light gold.

NOSE Orange zest, ginger, and malt.

BODY Smooth.

PALATE Spicy fresh fruit and developing oak.

FINISH Medium in length; nutmeg and ginger.

SCORE **87**

GLENFARCLAS 1986, Release IX, Cask No. 4336, 58.4 vol

Refill sherry butt; 270 bottles.

COLOR Rich amber.

NOSE Struck matches, a hint of warm leather, and developing vanilla.

BODY Silky.

PALATE Sherried and malty—rich fruit cake fresh from the oven.

FINISH Medium to long, soft spices, and gently drying oak.

SCORE **89**

GLENFARCLAS 1992, Release X, Cask No. 1710, 59.5 vol

Sherry butt; 654 bottles.

COLOR Gold.

NOSE Putty and resin. More floral, nutty, and sherried in time.

BODY Relatively full.

PALATE Spicy sweet sherry, ripe apples, and milk chocolate.

FINISH Sweet and fruity, with vanilla fudge, aniseed, and ginger.

SCORE **90**

GLENFARCLAS 1996, Release X, Cask No. 5979, 58.8 vol

Refill sherry hogshead; 282 bottles.

COLOR Polished bronze.

NOSE Warm plastic, then freshly mown hay, sweet sherry, toffee,
and a mildly herbal note.

BODY Silky and rounded.

PALATE A big, sweet sherry hit, soft spices, Jaffa oranges,
and ripe cherries.

FINISH Long and sweet, with cinnamon spice.

SCORE **89**

GLENFARCLAS 1998, Release A13, Cask 8976, 58 vol

Refill sherry hogshead; 190 bottles.

COLOR Bright amber.

NOSE Quite light; malt and subtle sherry.

BODY Viscous.

PALATE Well-mannered sherry, caramel, and allspice.

FINISH Lengthy and sweet; soft spices.

SCORE **88**

GLENFIDDICH

PRODUCER William Grant & Sons Ltd.
REGION Highlands   DISTRICT Speyside (Dufftown)
ADDRESS Dufftown, Banffshire, AB55 4DH
TEL 01340 820373   WEBSITE www.glenfiddich.com   VC

WOE BETIDE YOU IF YOU TAKE the world's best malt distillery and its owners William Grant for (excuse the pun) granted. It's widely accepted that the quality of the whisky from this distillery has been getting better and better, and a series of vintage releases has amply demonstrated that Glenfiddich can hold its own with the very best that Scotland has to offer. Innovations such as the quite wonderful blended malt Monkey Shoulder show that the family isn't necessarily standing on tradition either.

The Glenfiddich distillery lies on the small river whose name it bears, in Dufftown. The name Fiddich indicates that the river runs through the valley of the deer. Hence the company's stag emblem.

This justifiably famous distillery was founded in 1886–87, and is still controlled by the original family. As a relatively small enterprise, it faced intense competition from bigger companies during the big economic boom after World War II. Rather than relying on supplying whisky to blenders owned by the giants, it decided in 1963 to widen the availability of its whisky as a bottled single malt. An industry dominated at the time by blended Scotches regarded this as foolishness. The widely held view was that single malts were too intense, flavorful, or complex for the English and other foreigners.

This independent spirit was an example without which few of its rivals would have been emboldened to offer themselves as bottled single malts. Devotees of the genre owe a debt of gratitude to Glenfiddich. The early start laid the foundations for the success of Glenfiddich. Its fortunes were no doubt further assisted by its being, among malts, very easily drinkable.

Devotees of malts who are ready for a greater challenge will find much more complexity in the longer matured versions, including the one that is aged for 15 years then vatted in a solera system.

The Glenfiddich distillery is full of character. Much of the original structure, in honey-and-gray stone, remains beautifully maintained, and the style has been followed in considerable new construction.

Glenfiddich also led the way in the industry by being the first to have a visitor center. Some may argue that this is for tourists rather than purists, but no visitor to this part of the Highlands should miss it. and in recent years a range of new tours, aimed at the connoisseur, have been introduced. The stills are small, and the whisky is principally aged in "plain oak" (refill bourbon), although about 10 percent goes into sherry casks. Whisky aged in different woods is married in plain oak.

Adjoining the Glenfiddich site, William Grant also owns The Balvenie (established 1892), with a small floor maltings, and the (1990) Kininvie malt distilleries. Kininvie is little more than a basic still-house. Its rich, creamy malt goes into the Grant's blends, but has rarely been bottled as a single. Elsewhere in Scotland, it has the Girvan grain distillery and the adjacent Ailsa Bay malt distillery, which opened in late 2008.

HOUSE STYLE When young, a dry, fruity aperitif;
when more mature, a raisiny, chocolatey, after-dinner malt.

GLENFIDDICH Malt Master's Edition, 43 vol

COLOR Deep ruby.

NOSE Sharply focused nectarines, with dates, caramel,
cocoa powder, and vanilla.

BODY Rounded.

PALATE Toffee, apples, almonds, and allspice.

FINISH Lingering spice, walnuts, and mild oak.

SCORE **82**

GLENFIDDICH 12-year-old, 40 vol

COLOR Slightly fuller gold than it used to be. Faint green tinge.

NOSE Fresh but sweet. Appetizing, fruity, and pearlike. Juicy grass.

BODY Lean. Smooth. Oily maltiness.

PALATE Malty sweetness. White chocolate. Good flavor
development. Toasted hazelnuts.

FINISH Fragrant suggestion of peat smoke.

SCORE **77**

GLENFIDDICH 14-year-old, Rich Oak, 40 vol

COLOR Rich gold.

NOSE Initially herbal, with cloves, then jammy, fruit notes
emerge along with newly sawed logs.

BODY Medium.

PALATE Very lively, with vibrant oak and lots of herbs.
Cloves remain to the fore, as on the nose.

FINISH Medium in length, ultimately quite dry,
with oak and spices lingering.

SCORE **79**

GLENFIDDICH 15-year-old, 40 vol

COLOR Bright gold.

NOSE Chocolate. Toast. Hint of peat.

BODY Light, but very smooth indeed.

PALATE Suave. Silky. White chocolate. Pears in cream. Cardamom.

FINISH Cream. A hint of ginger.

SCORE **81**

GLENFIDDICH 15-year-old, Distillery Edition, 51 vol

COLOR Deep gold.

NOSE Rich, floral, and malty, with a suggestion of pepper.

BODY Supple.

PALATE Lively and spicy, with ripe fruit and a tang of sherry.

FINISH Sweet and lengthy, with a hint of cloves.

SCORE **82**

GLENFIDDICH 18-year-old, 40 vol

A proportion of the whisky in this version is older than the age on the label, with a slight accent toward first-fill sherry (butts, rather than hogsheads, and made from Spanish oak rather than American), and earth-floored, traditional warehouses.

COLOR Old gold.

NOSE Rich.

BODY Soft.

PALATE Mellow and rounded, soft, and restrained.
Scores points for sophistication and sherry character.

FINISH Nutty. A flowery hint of peat.

SCORE **78**

GLENFIDDICH 21-year-old, Gran Reserva, 40 vol

COLOR Apricot.

NOSE Toasty. Cookielike. Petit fours. The aroma when
a box of chocolates is opened.

BODY Soft. Lightly creamy.

PALATE Vanilla flan. Sweet Cuban coffee.

FINISH Juicy. A hint of dried tropical fruit.

SCORE **86**

GLENFIDDICH 19-year-old, Age of Discovery, Madeira Cask Finish, 40 vol

COLOR Antique gold.

NOSE Sweet, with figs, peaches, fresh pineapple,
and gingerbread. Notably spicy.

BODY Medium to full.

PALATE More spice, cinnamon, ginger, and pepper,
with candied peel and developing vanilla.

FINISH Creamy, with cocoa.

SCORE **80**

GLENFIDDICH 19-year-old, Age of Discovery, Bourbon Cask Reserve, 40 vol

COLOR Ripe barley.

NOSE Buttery and floral, with chrysanthemums, apricots,
oranges, and vanilla. Finally green apples.

BODY Voluptuous.

PALATE Soft spice, vanilla, and quite oaky bourbon notes.

FINISH Drying. Slightly charred oak.

SCORE **79**

GLENFIDDICH 19-year-old, Age of Discovery, Red Wine Cask Finish, 40 vol

COLOR Rich gold, with red highlights.

NOSE Fragrant, with soft toffee. Red berries. Developing caramel and oak.

BODY Luscious.

PALATE Red berries, spice, and tannins.

FINISH Tannic, with dark chocolate and lively spices.

SCORE **78**

GLENFIDDICH 26-year-old, Excellence, 43.2 vol

COLOR Rich gold.

NOSE Fruity and spicy, pineapple, graham crackers, and developing malt.

BODY Smooth.

PALATE Spicy fresh fruit, notably peaches and apples,
then dark chocolate and tannins.

FINISH Dries steadily, with aniseed and oak char.

SCORE **88**

GLENFIDDICH 30-year-old, 43 vol

COLOR Full gold, fractionally darker still.

NOSE Notes of sherry, fruit, chocolate, and ginger.

BODY Soft. Full. Some viscosity.

PALATE More sherry, raisins, chocolate, and ginger. Luxurious.

FINISH Unhurried, with chocolatey notes and gingery dryness.

SCORE **86**

GLENFIDDICH 38-year-old, Ultimate, 40 vol

Exclusive to China.

COLOR Rich gold.

NOSE Vanilla, new leather, raspberries, and blueberries.

BODY Soft and oily.

PALATE Spicy sherry notes, vanilla, and soft fruit.

FINISH Chili notes linger in a long finish, which dries only slightly.

SCORE **89**

GLENFIDDICH 40-year-old, Rare Collection, 43.6 vol

COLOR Chestnut with a green tinge.

NOSE Reticent. Chestnut. Old fruit. Damp.

BODY Soft, creamy, and gentle.

PALATE Soft and subtle, with a big dose of aniseed, honey, and melon.

No astringency. Incredibly dainty and polished, like a dapper old man.

FINISH Medium, but very soft, rounded, and balanced. Quite a work of art.

SCORE **92**

GLENFIDDICH 50-year-old, 43 vol

COLOR Golden amber.

NOSE Surprisingly spritely. Grapefruit marmalade. Melon. Lemon.

BODY Light and delicate.

PALATE Rich orange marmalade at first, then a wave of other citrus fruit.
Clean and fresh. Sweet. Creamy vanilla. Traces of oak and peat.

FINISH Long, clean, and fruity, with a healthy dash of oak and spice.

SCORE **88**

GLENFIDDICH 55-year-old, Janet Sheed
Roberts Reserve, 44.4 vol

11 bottles released.

COLOR Very pale gold.

NOSE Complex; initially floral, then herbal notes emerge,
with damp blackberry bushes, lemon, bergamot, and a wisp of smoke.

BODY Creamy.

PALATE Vanilla and spicy orange. Light wood smoke.

FINISH Long, sweet, and vibrant for its age.

SCORE **93**

TRAVEL RETAIL
GLENFIDDICH Select Cask, 40 vol

COLOR Ripe barley.

NOSE Baked apple, brittle toffee, golden raisins, and malt.

BODY Smooth.

PALATE Fruity, with more toffee, allspice, and a hint of cloves.

FINISH Caramel and a hint of black pepper.

SCORE **78**

GLENFIDDICH Reserve Cask, 40 vol

COLOR Dark gold.

NOSE Fragrant, with soft peaches, milk chocolate, figs, and oak.

BODY Medium.

PALATE Spicy, with citrus fruit and fudge.

FINISH Lengthy and sweet.

SCORE **79**

GLENFIDDICH Vintage Cask, 40 vol

COLOR Golden barley.

NOSE Maritime. Brine and smoke, with hay and Jaffa oranges.

BODY Smooth.

PALATE Vanilla and smoky summer fruit.

FINISH Lingering sweet wood smoke.

SCORE **82**

GLENGLASSAUGH

PRODUCER Benriach Distillery Company
REGION Highlands DISTRICT Speyside (Deveron)
ADDRESS Portsoy, Banffshire, AB45 2SQ   VC

AFTER 22 YEARS IN MOTHBALLS, it came as a surprise to most observers when Glenglassaugh distillery was purchased in 2008 by the Scaent Group, which has global energy interests and was eager to expand into Scotch whisky. Scaent formed the Glenglassaugh Distillery Co Ltd., and as thieves, neglect, and inclement weather had taken their toll on this Moray Firth distillery over the years, around $1.5 million (£1 million) needed to be spent refurbishing the plant before spirit flowed once more on December 4, 2008.

Stocks of old Glenglassaugh were low, but the Scaent Group proceeded to release 21, 30, and 40-year-old bottlings, along with new-make spirit and spirit aged for six months, with 26 and 35-year-olds following, along with a three-year-old and several limited edition expressions. In 2012 a visitor center opened, and Revival was released. It is a three-year-old whisky that has been finished for six months in oloroso sherry casks.

In 2013 the Benriach Distillery Company bought Glenglassaugh from Scaent, adding it to their existing portfolio of Benriach and Glendronach distilleries. Subsequent bottlings were of 30 and 40-year-olds, along with Evolution, matured for over three years in American oak barrels. True to company form, eight single cask bottlings appeared in 2014, and this is destined to be an ongoing feature of the operation.

Glenglassaugh is a coastal malt, produced near Portsoy, between the mouths of the rivers Spey and Deveron. The whisky has a distinctive taste and has contributed to highly respected blends such as The Famous Grouse and Cutty Sark in the past.

The future should be a bright and happy one. Let's hope that the new owners will use the distillery's little beach for fun events and barbecues, to fully bring this wonderful location back to life.

HOUSE STYLE Grassy maltiness. Restorative or refresher.

GLENGLASSAUGH Revival, 46 vol

COLOR Copper.

NOSE Initially a little mashy; sweet and mildly sherried, with roasted malt, ginger and caramel.

BODY Medium.

PALATE New leather and lots of spice, principally nutmeg and cinnamon.

FINISH Medium in length, spicy, and fruity.

SCORE 76

GLENGLASSAUGH Evolution, 57.2 vol

COLOR Pale lemon.

NOSE Brittle toffee, warm gingerbread, canned peaches, and vanilla.

BODY Medium.

PALATE Caramel-coated soft fruit, with coconut and discreet ginger.

FINISH Spicy toffee.

SCORE 80

GLENGLASSAUGH Torfa, 40 vol

COLOR Straw.

NOSE Early heather and light peatiness, then malt, cream soda, and dried fruit. Wood smoke.

BODY Supple.

PALATE A dash of coal soot, then ripe peaches, chili, and ginger. Finally, peat and ozone. Lively.

FINISH Long and fruity, with spicy peat smoke.

SCORE 82

GLENGLASSAUGH 30-year-old, 44.8 vol

COLOR Amber.

NOSE Early moss and cedar, followed by golden raisins, candied orange, and sherry. Ultimately, molasses.

BODY Full and mellow.

PALATE Sherry, hard toffee, ginger, figs, and orchard fruit.

FINISH Medium to long, spicy oak. Finally, a wisp of smoke.

SCORE 91

GLENGLASSAUGH 40-year-old, 42.5 vol

COLOR Deep gold.

NOSE Complex, with new leather, milk chocolate, ginger,
sherry, and ripe plums.

BODY Relatively full.

PALATE Early resin notes, then toffee, pineapple, spicy oak, and black coffee.

FINISH Quite long, drying, licorice, and tannins.

SCORE **89**

GLENGLASSAUGH Massandra Connection, 1973, 41-year-old, Sherry Wood Finish, 44.5 vol

COLOR Warm gold.

NOSE Complex, with golden raisins, cinnamon, hay, and a mildly herbal
note. Bung cloth and a hint of char.

BODY Full and rounded.

PALATE Spicy tropical fruit notes and oloroso sherry.

FINISH Slowly drying, with Seville orange and oak tannins.

SCORE **88**

GLENGLASSAUGH Massandra Connection, 1978, 35-year-old, Madeira Wood Finish, 41.7 vol

COLOR Dark oak.

NOSE Stewed fruit, golden raisins, caramel, a hint of ozone, and spices.

BODY Smooth and full.

PALATE Cocoa, apricots, sweet oak, and lots of spice development.

FINISH Long, citric, spicy, with reserved oak.

SCORE **87**

GLENGOYNE

PRODUCER Ian Macleod Distillers Ltd.
REGION Highlands   DISTRICT Highlands (Southwest)
ADDRESS Dumgoyne (by Glasgow), Stirlingshire, G63 9LV
TEL 01360 550254 WEBSITE www.glengoyne.com
EMAIL reception@glengoyne.com   VC

GLENGOYNE HAS BEEN ESTABLISHING itself as Glasgow's other distillery in recent years. Its marketing efforts have highlighted its proximity to the city, and it has made great strides in offering visitors a wide range of experiences and a growing and eclectic mix of malts. It has never been an especially well-known distillery, but it has one of the prettiest locations (complete with waterfall), and it is only a dozen miles from the center of Glasgow. The distillery is said to have been established in 1833.

Glengoyne has long used as a cornerstone of its marketing the fact that the malt employed in its whisky-making process is unpeated. It is explained that the delicate flavors of Glengoyne would be overwhelmed by the heavy smoke of peat. More recently, another factor in the distillation regimen has been highlighted, namely the fact that the stills are run more slowly than any other in Scotland, allowing for the favorable effects of greater copper contact on the spirit ultimately produced.

HOUSE STYLE Easily drinkable, but full of malty flavor. Restorative, with dessert, or after dinner.

GLENGOYNE Teapot dram (Batch 3), 59.4 vol
Distillery-exclusive bottling
COLOR Dark amber.
NOSE Fruity and fragrant, with profound spicy sherry notes.
BODY Mouth coating.
PALATE Sherry, prunes, hot cocoa, and a little oak.
FINISH Lingering, with drying sherry, light spice, and dark chocolate.

SCORE **82**

GLENGOYNE 10-year-old, 40 vol

COLOR Yellowy gold.

NOSE A fresh but very soft, warm fruitiness (Cox's apples?), with rich
malty dryness, very light sherry, and a touch of juicy oak.

BODY Light to medium. Smooth and rounded.

PALATE Clean, grassy, and fruity, with more apple notes.
Tasty and very pleasant.

FINISH Still sweet, but drying slightly. Clean and appetizing.

SCORE **74**

A Glengoyne 12-year-old, at 43 vol, now hard to find is very similar
to the 10-year-old. A dash more of everything. SCORE 75

GLENGOYNE 12-year-old, Cask Strength, 57.2 vol

COLOR Soft yellowy gold.

NOSE Green apples. A touch of sulfur. Barley, a trace of almonds.

BODY Medium and oily.

PALATE Sharp spice and pepper. Abrasive but clean, with crystal barley
breaking through and some sour fruit.

FINISH Medium, savory, and spicy.

SCORE **68**

GLENGOYNE 15-year-old, Scottish Oak, 43 vol

COLOR Rich orange.

NOSE Tingling spices and zippy black currant. Earthy and savory.

BODY Full, rich, and savory.

PALATE Sweet barley, rooty, and reedy. Unripe plum and some strong spice notes.

FINISH Medium long. Sugar and spice. Savory.

SCORE **74**

GLENGOYNE 15-year-old, 43 vol

COLOR Bright gold.

NOSE Old leather, sweet fresh fruit, vanilla, toffee, and ginger.

BODY Oily.

PALATE Tingling spices, oak, raisins, and hazelnuts.

FINISH Relatively lengthy, with latte coffee.

SCORE **78**

GLENGOYNE 18-year-old, 43 vol

COLOR Light amber.

NOSE Dry sherry, warm fruitcake on the nose, with milk chocolate, vanilla, and ripe grapefruit.

BODY Rounded.

PALATE The sherry is sweeter here, with caramel, orange marmalade, and cinnamon.

FINISH Medium to long, spicy, with gentle oak.

SCORE **81**

GLENGOYNE 18-year-old, Robbie's Choice, Ruby Port Hogshead, No. 328, 55.1 vol

COLOR Rich sunset orangey brown.

NOSE Chestnut, moist bark, mushrooms, dates, and damp leather.

BODY Rounded, full, and mouth coating.

PALATE Soft overripe fruit, some citrus, then wood, dark chocolate, and pepper.

FINISH Long, with chili, oak, plummy fruit residue, and astringency.

SCORE **79**

GLENGOYNE 21-year-old, 43 vol

COLOR Full copper.

NOSE Raisins, cherries, honey, dark chocolate, and a hint
of spicy marzipan.

BODY Silky.

PALATE Rich and sherried, with overbaked fruitcake, vanilla,
and cinnamon sticks.

FINISH Medium to long, with dry sherry, black pepper, and licorice.

SCORE **83**

GLENGOYNE 24-year-old Single Cask No. 354, Distilled 1987, 54.8 vol

European oak sherry butt

COLOR Black coffee.

NOSE Dark chocolate, rum and raisin fudge, and musty oloroso,
backed by pepper.

BODY Luscious.

PALATE Full and initially sweet, with dates, prune juice,
barbecue sauce, and lots of spice.

FINISH Dries slowly, with ever-present spice, and a suggestion of mint.

SCORE **87**

GLENGOYNE 25-year-old, 48 vol

COLOR Bright amber.

NOSE Sweet, with oranges, toffee, ginger, and milk chocolate.

BODY Smooth and rounded.

PALATE Oloroso sherry, golden raisins, and well-mannered spice.

FINISH Relatively lengthy, worn leather, soft oak, cloves.

SCORE **84**

GLENGOYNE 26-year-old Single Cask No. 384, Distilled 1987, 54.6 vol

First-fill European oak sherry butt

COLOR Bright gold.

NOSE Golden raisins, figs, and vanilla, plus white pepper and a hint
of linseed.

BODY Succulent.

PALATE Honey and contrasting lemon juice, and pepper.

FINISH Lengthy, but dries rapidly, with lively pepper, oak tannins,
and a final fatty note.

SCORE **85**

GLENGOYNE 32-year-old, White Rioja, 48.7 vol

Distilled 1972, bottled 2005, cask no. 985, 328 bottles)

COLOR Bright gold.

NOSE Floral, with caramel, honey and Jaffa oranges.

BODY Slick.

PALATE Poached pears with cream, cinnamon, and ginger.

FINISH Medium in length, resolutely sweet.

SCORE **88**

GLENGOYNE 35-year-old, 46.8 vol

500 bottles

COLOR Full gold.

NOSE Sweet sherry, old leather, fudge, candied cherries, and honey.

BODY Rounded.

PALATE Spicy, dried fruit, marzipan, and cherries.

FINISH Long, with dark chocolate, spice, and cherry liqueur.

SCORE **87**

GLENGOYNE 40-year-old, 45.9 vol

*Distilled in 1969 and filled into second-fill hogsheads. Twenty-eight years later
it was reracked into first-fill sherry butts. 250 bottles*

COLOR Old copper.

NOSE Figs, dates, medium sherry, wood polish, and crème brûlée.

BODY Rich.

PALATE Apples and apricots, honey and cinnamon, with developing oak.

FINISH Drying, with cocoa powder and tannins,
but the oak always held in check.

SCORE **90**

GLENGYLE

PRODUCER Mitchell's Glengyle Ltd.
REGION Campbeltown
ADDRESS Glengyle Street, Campbeltown, Argyll PA28 6EX
TEL 01586 552009   WEBSITE www.kilkerran.com
EMAIL info@kilkerran.com

THE ORIGINAL GLENGYLE DISTILLERY was established in 1872/73 by William Mitchell, previously co-owner of Springbank with his brother, John. However, the recessionary years following World War I were particularly severe for the Campbeltown distilling industry, and Glengyle closed in 1925, having changed hands six years previously.

The distillery buildings were subsequently used by Campbeltown Miniature Rifle Club, before the Bloch brothers, who owned Glen Scotia distillery, acquired the site in 1941, intending to recommence distilling. World War II prevented that from happening. In 1951, Campbell Henderson applied for planning permission to restore and reopen Glengyle as a distillery, but those plans also came to nothing.

Then, in 2000, Springbank head honcho Hedley Wright—a descendant of the Mitchell family who had originally built both Springbank and Glengyle—formed Mitchell's Glengyle Ltd. to purchase the distillery site and restore it to its former glory. New equipment was commissioned, though the two stills that were adapted and installed had formerly been part of Ben Wyvis malt distillery, located within the Invergordon grain distilling complex.

Production began at Glengyle in March 2004, making it the first new distillery of the millennium and the first in Campbeltown for 125 years. The single malt produced there is bottled as Kilkerran, since the name Glengyle is already registered for a blended malt.

HOUSE STYLE Fruity, increasingly robust, mildly coastal.

KILKERRAN Work in Progress 5 Sherry Wood, 46 vol
Released 2013; 9,000 bottles.

COLOR Amber.

NOSE Overripe green grapes and figs, followed by honey and dark chocolate.

BODY Soft.

PALATE Gentle fresh fruit notes, with soft toffee and a hint of brine.

FINISH Drying significantly, with cocoa powder, licorice, and lots of spice.

SCORE **88**

KILKERRAN Work In Progress 5 Bourbon Wood, 46 vol
Released 2013; 9,000 bottles.

COLOR Hay.

NOSE Vanilla, cinnamon, milk chocolate, ripe apples, and ultimately, slightly smoky mango notes.

BODY Supple.

PALATE Spicy, with blood orange and a hint of peat smoke.

FINISH Medium-long and drying, with a wisp of smoke.

SCORE **87**

KILKERRAN Work in Progress 6 Sherry Wood, 46 vol
Released 2014; 9,000 bottles.

COLOR Mid-gold.

NOSE Initially savory, slightly earthy, with new leather, lemonade, and a hint of ozone.

BODY Medium.

PALATE Spicy, sherried, with dates and dark chocolate.

FINISH Long and persistently spicy, with quite dry sherry notes.

SCORE **88**

KILKERRAN Work in Progress 6 Bourbon Wood, 46 vol
Released 2014; 9,000 bottles.

COLOR Pale gold.

NOSE Lemongrass, a pinch of salt, wood smoke, and gingersnaps.

BODY Soft.

PALATE Nutty, with tropical fruit, plus a slight underpinning of spicy smoke.

FINISH Drying, with mellow spice.

SCORE **89**

GLENKINCHIE

PRODUCER Diageo
REGION Lowlands   DISTRICT Eastern Lowlands
ADDRESS Pencaitland, Tranent, East Lothian, EH34 5ET
TEL 01875 342005
WEBSITE www.discovering-distilleries.com/www.malts.com   VC

ACCORDING TO ITS LABEL, "The Edinburgh Malt." This is an eminently visitable distillery, about 15 miles (25 kilometers) from the capital, and near the village of Pencaitland. It traces its origins to at least the 1820s and 1830s, to a farm in barley-growing country in the glen of the Kinchie burn. This rises in the green Lammermuir hills, which provide medium-hard water, and flows toward the small coastal resorts where the Firth of Forth meets the sea.

In the 1940s and 1950s, the distillery manager bred prize-winning cattle, feeding them on the spent grain. Delphiniums and roses grow outside the manager's office, and the distillery has its own bowling green. The buildings resemble those of a Borders wool mill. For much of the distillery's history, the whisky was largely used in the Haig blends. In 1988–89, it was launched as a single in the Classic Malts range, and in 1997 an amontillado finish was added. In the same year a new visitor center was opened. Among the exhibits is a 75-year-old model of the distillery, which was built by the firm of Basset-Lowke, better known for their miniature steam engines.

HOUSE STYLE Flowery start, complex flavors, and a dry finish.
A restorative, especially after a walk in the hills.

GLENKINCHIE 12-year-old, 43 vol

The new standard Glenkinchie bottling.

COLOR Pale gold.

NOSE Grassy and grainy, sustained by a discreet but present oakiness. Picks up steam with time: delicate notes of walnuts and almonds, and a whiff of wild flowers. A little honey and notes of oranges, as well as oatmeal. A breakfast malt? Very faint smokiness.

BODY Light and unassertive.

PALATE Simply sweet and fruity (apple compote) with, again, a good oakiness giving it some backbone. Balanced.

FINISH Medium long, with a bigger grassiness now.

SCORE **79**

GLENKINCHIE 2000 Distillers Edition, Amontillado Finish, Bottled 2013, 43 vol

COLOR Old gold.

NOSE Rich and floral, with honey, vanilla, mixed nuts, sherry, and new leather. Late developing caramel shortcake.

BODY Full.

PALATE Stewed fruit, molasses, and spice, contrasting with drier, slightly smoky notes.

FINISH Medium to long. Walnuts and toffee apples.

SCORE **81**

GLENKINCHIE 1992, Managers' Choice, 58.1 vol

Matured in a European oak cask; 528 bottles.

COLOR Pale gold.

NOSE Initially sweet and fruity, with toasted coconut and
sticky-fruit-cake notes developing.

BODY Smooth.

PALATE Malty in the mouth, with fresh oranges, spice, and brittle toffee.

FINISH Subtle vanilla, walnuts, and a hint of Cognac. Gently drying.

SCORE **85**

GLENKINCHIE 20-year-old, Special Releases 2010, 55.1 vol

Matured in ex-Bourbon refill casks; 6,000 bottles.

COLOR Deep gold.

NOSE Sweet, with heather, malt, vanilla, and subtle spice after
a slightly sharp opening.

BODY Smooth.

PALATE Rich, floral, and very fruity, with toffee, honey, oak,
and mild licorice.

FINISH Medium in length and steadily drying.

SCORE **86**

GLENKINCHIE Cask Strength (Distillery Exclusive), 59.1 vol

COLOR Amber.

NOSE Distinctive, with early mint and dark chocolate notes, followed
by cinnamon candy and a whiff of fresh leather.

BODY Rich.

PALATE Summer fruit and honey, with developing cloves and allspice.

FINISH Lengthy and spicy, with a suggestion of nutty oak.

SCORE **84**

THE GLENLIVET

PRODUCER Chivas Brothers (Pernod Ricard)
REGION Highlands   DISTRICT Speyside (Livet)
ADDRESS Ballindalloch, Banffshire, AB37 9DB
TEL 01340 821720   WEBSITE www.theglenlivet.com   VC

THE MOST FAMOUS WHISKY-MAKING GLEN in Scotland is that of the small Livet River, which flows into the Spey. Among the distilling districts, it is the one most deeply set into the mountains. Its water rises from granite, and frequently flows underground for many miles. The mountain setting also helps produce the weather whisky makers like. During distilling, the condensers work most effectively if cooled by very cold water, and in a climate to match. The malt whiskies made in the area are on the lighter side, very clean, flowery, subtle, and elegant.

The Livet's fame also has historical origins, in the period when Highlanders were permitted to distill only on a domestic scale. The purported justification was a shortage of grain, but there was also a question of political vindictiveness. At that time, this relatively remote mountain glen was a famous nest of illicit distillation. After legalization in 1824, the legendary spirit "from Glenlivet" was greatly in demand among merchants in the cities to the south.

Distillers absurdly far from the glen have used the geographical allusion, as if it were a synonym for Speyside in general, but this practice is now in decline as the greater interest in single malts focuses attention on the issue of origin. Braeval is the distillery highest in the glen and was previously known as Braes of Glenlivet, producing a honeyish, zesty whisky. Slightly lower is Tamnavulin, which has a notably light-bodied malt (though Tomintoul, just across the hills in adjoining Avon valley, is lighter in palate).

Only one distillery in the area is permitted to call itself The Glenlivet, however. This was the first distillery to become legal, and now possesses an international reputation. The definite article is restricted even further in that it appears on only the official distillery bottlings. These bottlings carry the legend "Distilled by George & J. G. Smith" in small type at the bottom of the label, referring to the father and son who established the original business.

The Gaelic word *gobha*, pronounced "gow" (as in typically Scottish names like McGowan) translates to Smith. It has been argued the Gow family had supported Bonnie Prince Charlie and later found it politic to change their name to Smith, but this explanation is open to question. Whatever the case, when the legalization of distillers was proposed by the Duke of Gordon, one of his tenants, George Smith, already an illicit whisky maker, was the first to apply for a license. His son, John Gordon Smith, assisted and succeeded him. After distilling on two sites nearby, in 1858 the Smiths moved to the present location, Minmore, near the point where the Livet and Avon meet. The distillery stands at a point where the grassy valley is already beginning to steepen toward the mountains. In 1880, the exclusive designation "The Glenlivet" was granted in a test case. The company remained independent until 1953, when it came under the same ownership as Glen Grant. In the 1960s, Gordon & MacPhail acquired considerable quantities of the whisky, leading to a succession of bottlings. These very old and sometimes vintage-dated expressions are identified as George & J. G. Smith's Glenlivet Whisky.

By virtue of it being the biggest-selling single malt in the large American market, The Glenlivet might be deemed commonplace, but it is a whisky of structure and complexity. It is distilled from water with a dash of hardness, and the peating of the malt is on the light side. About a third of the casks used have, at some stage, held sherry, though the proportion of first fill is considerably smaller.

HOUSE STYLE Flowery, fruity, peachy. Aperitif.

THE GLENLIVET 12-year-old, 40 vol

COLOR Pale gold.

NOSE Remarkably flowery, clean, and soft.

BODY Light to medium. Firm. Smooth.

PALATE Flowery and peachy, with notes of vanilla. A delicate balance.

FINISH Restrained, long, and gently warming.

SCORE **85**

THE GLENLIVET 16-year-old, Nadurra,
Batch No. 0606A, Bottled 2006, 57.2 vol

COLOR Deep gold.

NOSE Sweet malty lemongrass, with a hint of caramel.

BODY Moderately hot. Buttery.

PALATE Vanilla and oak, with traces of pepper and a hint of spice. Dry.

FINISH Long and dry, with a touch of vanilla. Water brings
out sweetness and nuttiness.

SCORE **88**

THE GLENLIVET 2013, 17-year-old, 55.7 vol

COLOR Pale lemon.

NOSE Lime pie. Vanilla. Tropical fruit. Pineapple.

BODY Soft, sweet, and medium full.

PALATE Banana. Tropical fruit, particularly guava and mango.
Sweet pear. Vanilla. Late sweet spice.

FINISH Quite short, but sweet, spicy, and addictive.

SCORE **92**

GLENLOSSIE

PRODUCER Diageo
REGION Highlands   DISTRICT Speyside (Lossie)
ADDRESS By Elgin, Morayshire, IV30 3SF
TEL 01343 862000

RESPECTED IN THE INDUSTRY (its whisky was once an important element in Haig blends), this distillery has a much lower profile among lovers of malts. A Flora and Fauna edition introduced in the early 1990s has made more connoisseurs aware of it, and there have since been bottlings from Signatory and Hart.

The distillery, in the valley of the Lossie, south of Elgin, was built in 1876, reconstructed 20 years later, and extended in 1962. Next door is the Mannochmore distillery, built in 1971.

HOUSE STYLE Flowery, clean, grassy, malty. Aperitif.

GLENLOSSIE 10-year-old, Flora and Fauna, 43 vol

COLOR Fino sherry.

NOSE Fresh. Grass, heather, and sandalwood.

BODY Light to medium. Soft and smooth.

PALATE Malty, dryish at first, then a range of sweeter, perfumy, spicy notes.

FINISH Spicy.

SCORE **76**

GLENMORANGIE

PRODUCER Glenmorangie PLC
REGION Highlands   DISTRICT Northern Highlands
ADDRESS Tain, Ross-shire, IV19 1PZ
TEL 01862 892477   WEBSITE www.glenmorangie.com
EMAIL visitors@glenmorangieplc.co.uk   VC

STILL THE BIGGEST SELLING MALT WHISKY in Scotland; still dividing opinion by its devotion to wood finishes (which offend some whisky conservatives); still, as a company, much respected and admired.

Glenmorangie pioneered "official" cask-strength bottlings at the beginning of the 1990s. In the middle of that decade, it began introducing wood finishes, from sherry variations such as fino to madeira, port, and French wines. Subsequently it also introduced some vattings of virgin American oak.

The company selects its own trees in the Ozark mountains of Missouri, has its wood seasoned by air drying (rather than kilning), and loans its casks for four years to the Jack Daniel's distillery in Lynchburg, Tennessee. A similar arrangement existed with Heaven Hill, in Bardstown, Kentucky, until the Bourbon distillery lost substantial amounts of wood in a fire. The wood policies at Glenmorangie are some of the most highly developed in the industry. The man who developed them is Dr. Bill Lumsden, Head of Distilling and Whisky Creation.

Since 2004 Glenmorangie has been owned by French luxury goods company LVMH, and in 2008 production capacity was increased by 50 percent with the installation of four new stills. The distillery is near the pretty sandstone town of Tain. The town and distillery are on the coast about 40 miles (65 kilometers) north of Inverness. From the A9, the short private drive passes between an assortment of trees and a dam shaped like a millpond. Beyond can be seen the waters of the Dornocsh firth.

The distilling water rises on sandstone hills and flows over heather and clover, before emerging in a sandy pond about half a mile from the distillery. The sandstone surely contributes to the whisky's firmness of body, the flowers perhaps to its famously scenty character. (A French perfume house identified 26 aromas, from almond, bergamot, and cinnamon to verbena, vanilla, and wild mint. More recently, a New York fragrance company managed only 22.)

HOUSE STYLE Creamy, leafy. Restorative or with dessert.

GLENMORANGIE 10-year-old, Original, 40 vol

Introduced in 2007, this is a replacement bottling for the previous 10-year-old.

COLOR Antique gold.

NOSE Floral, with fresh fruit, butterscotch, and toffee.

BODY Silky.

PALATE More toffee than its predecessor. Nutty,
with fresh oranges and lemons.

FINISH Medium length, progressively spicier, with ginger.

SCORE **81**

EXTRA MATURED RANGE
GLENMORANGIE Nectar d'Or, 46 vol

Replacement for the former Sauternes Wood Finish expression. Additionally matured in
French wine barriques after a minimum of 10 years in bourbon casks.

COLOR Lemony gold.

NOSE Dessert wine, honey, soft fruit, and spice.

BODY Medium.

PALATE Golden raisins and dates, gingerbread, and custard,
balanced by lemon notes.

FINISH Long and spicy, with developing citrus fruit.

SCORE **87**

GLENMORANGIE Quinta Ruban, 46 vol

Replacement for the former Port Wood Finish expression. Additionally matured in port pipes after at least 10 years in bourbon casks.

COLOR Coppery pink.

NOSE Rich and fruity. Mint chocolate and walnuts.

BODY Silky smooth.

PALATE Big and slightly peppery, with barley sugar and milk chocolate.

FINISH Long and comforting. Orange-flavored dark chocolate.

SCORE **86**

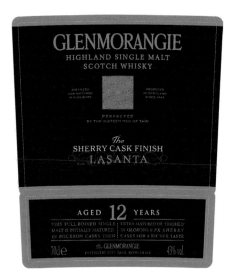

GLENMORANGIE Lasanta, 46 vol

Replacement for the former Sherry Wood Finish. Additionally matured in Spanish oloroso sherry casks after at least 10 years in bourbon casks.

COLOR Medium-dark gold.

NOSE Sweet and syrupy, with cinnamon and ginger.

BODY Medium and soft.

PALATE Malty and spicy, with vanilla fudge, walnuts, and raisins.

FINISH Slowly drying, with lingering, gingery oak, and a hint of cocoa.

SCORE **86**

GLENMORANGIE Astar, 57.3 vol

*Aged in casks sourced from the Ozark Mountains of Missouri and used to mature
Tennessee whiskey for four years prior to being filled with Glenmorangie new-make spirit.*

COLOR Gold with green highlights.

NOSE Fresh and lively. Vanilla, newly sawed lumber, and cream caramel.

BODY Rounded and smooth.

PALATE High floral, with polish notes that become richer and spicier.
Succulent peaches.

FINISH Long and creamy.

SCORE **84**

GLENMORANGIE Signet, 46 vol

*Produced using a proportion of "chocolate malt," this expression comprises whiskies that
have been matured in a variety of cask types and aged for up to 35 years.*

COLOR Copper.

NOSE Rich fruit, honey, orange marmalade, maple, sherry,
sweet oak, and spice.

BODY Silky.

PALATE Fruit and lively spice, with dark chocolate, vanilla,
and a hint of leather.

FINISH Medium in length. Vanilla and ginger.

SCORE **88**

GLENMORANGIE 18-year-old, 43 vol

COLOR Full reddish amber.

NOSE Vanilla, mint, and walnuts. Sappy and oaky.

BODY Medium, smooth, and fleshier.

PALATE Cookielike and sweet at first, more walnuts,
then the whole potpourri of spiciness.

FINISH Aromatic, nutty, and lightly oaky.

SCORE **81**

GLENMORANGIE 25-year-old, 43 vol

Mainly for the Asian/Pacific market.

COLOR Dark polished oak.

NOSE An old shop, with finishes made of polished oak, leather, and brass.

BODY Big. Slippery.

PALATE Cakey. Oily. Beeswax. A handsome whisky.

FINISH Late, gingery spiciness.

SCORE **80**

GLENMORANGIE Taghta, 46 vol

Cask Masters Selection; 12,000 bottles.

COLOR Mid-gold.

NOSE Fragrant, with dry sherry notes, sweet spices, and salted butter.

BODY Smooth.

PALATE New leather, lively spices, malt, a savory note, olives, and rock salt.

FINISH Medium in length, drying, with dates, black pepper, and licorice.

SCORE 85

LIMITED EDITION WOOD FINISHES

(Or, where indicated, wholly matured in the wood shown.)

GLENMORANGIE Tain L'Hermitage (Rhône Wine), Released 1995, 43 vol

COLOR Distinctively elegant orange.

NOSE Very fruity and sweet.

BODY Creamy.

PALATE Very clean toffee and vanilla, developing to nuttiness
and remarkably dry fruitiness. Great length.

FINISH Astonishingly lean and winey. Full of fruity, winey,
and spicy flavors. Very lively.

SCORE 88

GLENMORANGIE 25-year-old, Cote de Nuits, Wood Finish, 43 vol

COLOR Amber.

NOSE Floral, with vanilla, red berries, and smoky caramel.

BODY Full.

PALATE Rich, sweet fruit notes, more vanilla, plus almonds.

FINISH Long, drying, developing bitterness.

SCORE 86

GLENMORANGIE 1987, Margaux Cask Finish, 46 vol

After 17 years of maturation in bourbon hogsheads, this whisky was subsequently transferred into wine barriques from the House of Margaux in the French Bordeaux region.

COLOR Amber with orange highlights.

NOSE Spicy red wine and oranges, with fragrant confectionery notes.

BODY Very smooth.

PALATE Summer berries, cinnamon, and ginger, with developing nougat.

FINISH Succulent. Spicy fruit linger.

SCORE 88

TRAVEL RETAIL
GLENMORANGIE 1981, 28-year-old, Pride, 56.7 vol

Aged for 18 years in first-fill ex-bourbon barrels, then transferred to Chateau d'Yquem Sauternes casks for another 10 years.

COLOR Deep gold.

NOSE Intense, pungent, and earthy, with polished furniture, spices, oak tannins, and licorice.

BODY Full and luscious.

PALATE Waxy, with sherbet, honey, baked apple, orange marmalade, and golden raisins.

FINISH Lengthy, with hints of smoke, raisins, and oak.

SCORE 91

GLENMORANGIE Ealanta, Private Collection Range, 46 vol
19 years old, fully matured in virgin American white oak casks.

COLOR Burned ocher.

NOSE Cream soda, milk chocolate, fudge, pineapple, and honey; spicy and creamy.

BODY Silky.

PALATE Brittle toffee and orange notes; gently herbal, with cloves and newly sawed wood.

FINISH Long, with citrus fruit, oak, aniseed, and an enduring spicy creaminess.

SCORE **90**

GLENMORANGIE Artein, Private Collection Range, 46 vol
Finished in Super Tuscan wine barrels. Two parts 15-year-old and one part 21-year-old whisky.

COLOR Full copper.

NOSE Initially, pear-flavored hard candy, then vanilla, peaches, and apricots, plus gentle ginger.

BODY Viscous.

PALATE Dark fruit, spice, aniseed, black currant, cough medicine, and finally cloves.

FINISH Long, fruity, and herbal.

SCORE **88**

GLENMORANGIE Sonnalta PX, Private Collection Range, 46 vol
Finished in ex-Pedro Ximénez sherry casks.

COLOR Burnished gold.

NOSE Sweet, with apricots, peaches, vanilla, milk chocolate, dark rum, almonds, and caramel.

BODY Viscous.

PALATE Caramel, cocoa powder, stewed fruit, and pipe tobacco.

FINISH Lengthy, with black coffee and spicy oak tannins.

SCORE **90**

GLENMORANGIE Finealta, Private Collection Range, 46 vol

Lightly peated malt, aged in American oak and oloroso sherry casks.

COLOR Deep amber.

NOSE Smoky sherry, orange marmalade, vanilla, and honey.

BODY Full.

PALATE Molasses, almonds, nutmeg, and ginger.

FINISH Rounded, with aromatic wood smoke.

SCORE **89**

GLENMORANGIE Companta, Private Collection Range, 46 vol

Finished in Clos de Tart Grand Cru wine casks and
sweet fortified wine casks from Côtes du Rhône.

COLOR Cherry red.

NOSE Big fruity, leathery notes; spicy, with golden raisins, almonds, and powdered sugar.

BODY Rich.

PALATE Complex, with cocoa powder, nutmeg, more leather, and red currants.

FINISH Long and fruity, with vibrant spices and red berries.

SCORE **90**

GLENROTHES

PRODUCER The Edrington Group
REGION Highlands DISTRICT Speyside (Rothes)
ADDRESS Burnside Street, Rothes, Aberlour, AB38 7AA

THE MOST ARISTOCRATIC of London's wine and spirit merchants, Berry Brothers & Rudd, have in recent years showcased Glenrothes (rendered variously as one or two words) as their house malt. These are the principal bottlings of Glenrothes, and they are always vintage dated, with a partially "handwritten" label.

In 2002, the company also introduced its own range of bottlings from other distilleries, under the rubric "Berrys' Own Selection." This reflects the new appreciation of Scotland's finest whiskies. It also represents a return to tradition. Once, many respected wine merchants in England as well as Scotland offered their own bottlings of single malts, in addition to combined them in house blends. Glenrothes' quietly noble whisky has traditionally been a component of Berrys' internationally known Cutty Sark, and a favorite among blenders. The distillery, established in 1878, is one of five in the small town of Rothes.

The firm of Berrys' began in the 1690s, selling tea, groceries, and wine. Cutty Sark was launched in the 1920s. It is named after the famously fast tea clipper Cutty Sark, which was built in Scotland. Both Glenrothes and Cutty Sark are sold, not only in Berrys' 1730s premises in stately St. James's, London, but also in the company's stores at London's Heathrow airport.

HOUSE STYLE Perfumy, sweet, spicy-fruity, complex. After dinner.

GLENROTHES Select Reserve, 43 vol

COLOR Pale light straw, with a slight green tinge.

NOSE Light but complex. Currants, mince pie, vanilla, a hint of orange, and sherbet candies.

BODY Medium full, but pleasant.

PALATE Sherry and dried fruit, balanced with spice.

FINISH Gentle and sweet, with prunes and spices.

SCORE **75**

GLENROTHES 1998, 43 vol

COLOR Rich orange.

NOSE Toffee. Vanilla. Blood orange. Dusty lemon.

BODY Smooth and creamy.

PALATE Big orange notes. Fruit gumdrops. Traces of oak. Some late cinnamon and nutmeg.

FINISH Medium full and fruity, with a touch of tannin and spice.

SCORE **81**

GLENROTHES 1994, 43 vol

COLOR Rich gold.

NOSE Beeswax polish, lemon detergent, rich, and sweet.

BODY Rich, sweet, oily, and mouth coating.

PALATE Clean, fresh, yellow fruit, and caramel. Full.

FINISH Medium long, sweet, and fruity.

SCORE **80**

GLENROTHES 1992, 43 vol

COLOR Honey golden orange.

NOSE Light and floral, sprinkled with fruit dust.

BODY Full, oily, and sweet.

PALATE Licorice, melon, lemon, and pineapple.

FINISH Full, with lots of fruit and spice.

SCORE **76**

GLENROTHES 1991, 43 vol

COLOR Chestnut bronze.

NOSE Soft toffee, red and black currants, and vanilla ice cream.

BODY Rich, soft, and very pleasant.

PALATE Red fruit, caramel, and some sweet fruit counterbalanced by a hint of tannin.

FINISH Medium, rounded, very balanced, and pleasant.

SCORE **86**

GLENROTHES 1989, 43 vol

COLOR Old gold.

NOSE A subtle suggestion of soft licorice.

BODY Generous. Supple.

PALATE The licorice more emphatic now. Licorice root. Develops juicy,
mouthwatering flavors. Aniseed. Coconut.

FINISH Soothing and relaxing.

 SCORE 82

GLENROTHES 1988, 43 vol

COLOR Deep chestnut brown.

NOSE Oak. Apricot. Peach. Pepper spice. Rich and complex.

BODY Rich and creamy.

PALATE Orange. Tannin. Yellow fruit. Drying with traces of oak,
but nicely balanced.

FINISH Long, fruity, and oaky.

 SCORE 88

GLENROTHES 1985, 43 vol

COLOR Clear molassas brown.

NOSE Earthy, savory, chestnut, apple pit, and trace of smoke.

BODY Full, rich, and soft.

PALATE Rich, chewy honeyed fruit, soft peach, burned honey, and woody.

FINISH Beautifully delivered mix of flavors.
Soft, sweet, and rounded.

 SCORE 87

GLENROTHES 1984, 43 vol

COLOR Pale honey gold.

NOSE Wood sap, delicate fruit, and vanilla.

COLOR Pale gold.

BODY Full, rounded, and warming.

PALATE Vanilla ice cream, sugar, barley, and then some oak and spice.

FINISH Quite spicy but sweet. Medium long.

 SCORE 83

GLENROTHES 1981, 43 vol

COLOR Pale brown with a greenish hue.

NOSE Odd. Chinese food. Stewed beanshoots. Bamboo. Sugarcane. Subtle.

BODY Wispy, quite sharp, and dry.

PALATE Woody. Dried apricot. At first quite sweet but thin,
then sharp pepper.

FINISH Quite long, lots of tannins, and sharp spice.

SCORE 69

GLENROTHES 1978, 43 vol

COLOR Rich, chestnut brown.

NOSE Earthy, water chestnuts, sherbety, clean, and fresh.

BODY Full, imposing, and creamy.

PALATE Wonderfully sweet and rounded, with vanilla, aniseed, red licorice,
plum, peaches, and then a dose of oak and spice.

FINISH Very balanced, lingering, and lovely.

SCORE 90

GLENROTHES 1973, 43 vol

COLOR Amber.

NOSE Heather and sweet fruit, spice, floral, apple, prune, and nutmeg.

BODY Gentle, subtle yet rich.

PALATE Layers of orange. Vanilla, spice, and raisin flowing together.
Fine tannins.

FINISH Nutty. Everlasting. Quintessential Glenrothes.

SCORE 90

GLENROTHES 1972, 43 vol

COLOR Rich deep brown.

NOSE Rooy, earthy, and Chinese boiled vegetables.

BODY Creamy, full, and rounded.

PALATE Sweet and fruity, with licorice and vanilla. Astringent and spicy.

FINISH Long. Balanced. Lots of sweet fruit offsetting the spice and tannin.

SCORE 88

GLENROTHES 1971, 41 vol

COLOR Copper with a greeny rim.

NOSE Sweet tobacco, licorice, and chewy fruit. Berry fruit and allspice.

BODY Generous, soft. Rich, old, and elegant.

PALATE Cedar, anis, and cough lozenge. Gently warming.

FINISH Long, complex, and sophisticated.

SCORE **87**

GLENROTHES Robur Reserve, 40 vol

COLOR Pale lemon.

NOSE Bold, honey, apricot jam, sweet lemon zest, varied.

BODY Soft, rounded, and creamy.

PALATE Clean barley, melon, citrus, and a touch of spice.

FINISH Quite short, with a citrus fruit flourish.

SCORE **68**

GLENROTHES 25-year-old, 43 vol

COLOR Rich full bronze.

NOSE Candied fruit, spearmint candy, orange and lemon bits, lemonade.

BODY Full, creamy, rich, and sweet.

PALATE Intense sweet tropical fruit, mango, then sweet spice and
a delicate and attractive woody finish.

FINISH Beautifully balanced and long, sweet fruit, spice with some tannin.

SCORE **93**

GLENROTHES 30-year-old, 43 vol

COLOR Rich chestnut brown.

NOSE Mushroomy, damp leaves, then opens up slowly with sherried fruit and
citrus notes.

BODY Full, creamy, and sweet.

PALATE Intense sweet spice, lemon sherbet, aniseed, mint cake. Astringent.

FINISH Long and intense. Assertive.

SCORE **88**

GLENROTHES 1967, Berrys' Own Selection, 46.3 vol

COLOR Old gold.

NOSE Lean and light. Mushroom, dry wood, and cooked fruit. Fine ash.

BODY Big and soft.

PALATE Complex. Lots of flavor development. Flowers and spices galore.

FINISH Long and floral.

SCORE **85**

GLENROTHES 1966, Berrys' Own Selection, 52.8 vol

COLOR Mahogany.

NOSE Dark, woody, fig, and walnut. Madeira cake. Coffee bean.

BODY Dry. Drying.

PALATE Slightly tannic. Good balance between savory notes and dried fruit.

FINISH Long and drying.

SCORE **82**

GLENROTHES John Ramsay Legacy, 46.7 vol

COLOR Rich chestnut orange.

NOSE Old and venerable. Deep red berries. Dried fruit peel. Cocoa.

BODY Soft and velvety. Creamy.

PALATE Vanilla. Cocoa. Soft orange and yellow fruit. Late peppery spice
and oak. Beautifully balanced.

FINISH Long, spicy, and satisfying.

SCORE **91**

A COUPLE OF INDEPENDENT BOTTLINGS
GLENROTHES 1970, 38-year-old, Cask No. 10577,
Duncan Taylor Rare Auld Series, 42.3 vol

COLOR Deep orange.

NOSE Grapefruit. Tangerine. Honeyed melon.

BODY Medium and balanced.

PALATE Soft apple, pear, and yellow fruit, balanced by very
gentle pepper. Very fresh for its age.

FINISH Medium fruity and drying. Balanced and pleasant.

SCORE **87**

GLENROTHES 1969, 39-year-old, Lonarch, 42.7 vol

COLOR Rich orangey brown.

NOSE Stewed bobbing apples and then clean and fresh bowl
of green fruit.

BODY Big, full, and rich.

PALATE Apple. Apple pit. Touch of nutmeg and cinnamon. Finally pepper.

FINISH Rich, quite long, and a mix of fruit and pepper.

SCORE **87**

GLENTAUCHERS

PRODUCER Chivas Brothers (Pernod Ricard)
REGION Highlands   DISTRICT Speyside
ADDRESS Mulben, Keith, Banffshire, AB5 2YL
TEL 01542 860272

GLENTAUCHERS WAS FOUNDED IN 1898 and rebuilt in 1965. With no visitor center and few bottlings, it has not had the attention it merits. A neighbor to Auchroisk, it is in the countryside near the village of Mulben, between the distilling towns of Rothes and Keith.

When Pernod Ricard acquired Allied Domecq in 2005, Chivas Brothers gained control of the distillery.

HOUSE STYLE Clovey dryness and malty sweetness. Soothing at its best.

GLENTAUCHERS 18-year-old, Berry Bros. & Rudd, 46 vol

COLOR Bright yellow.

NOSE Gooseberry. Green vegetables. Stewed cabbage.

BODY Medium full and firm.

PALATE Nice. Sweet apple. Fresh sponge cake. Slight aniseed, tannin, and spice.

FINISH Sweet, syrupy, and balanced. Lingers pleasantly.

SCORE **86**

GLENTAUCHERS 24-year-old, Berry Bros. & Rudd, 46 vol

COLOR Rich yellow.

NOSE Autumnal. Stewed fruit. Damson fruit. Molasses.

BODY Rich, full, mouth coating, and assertive.

PALATE Sweet, toffee, big citrus, and green fruit. Savory tannin and spice.

FINISH A battle between sweet and spice, and quite long.

SCORE **82**

GLENTURRET

PRODUCER The Edrington Group
REGION Highlands   DISTRICT Eastern Highlands
ADDRESS Crieff, Perthshire, PH7 4HA   TEL 01764 656565
WEBSITE www.famousgrouse.co.uk   VC

A DISTILLERY OR an "experience"? Glenturret is certainly a distillery: the most visitable; one of the smallest; and a claimant to being Scotland's oldest, tucked in a pretty glen just an hour by road from Edinburgh or Glasgow. These attributes proved irresistible to its owners The Edrington Group, who have made it their principal visitor center. Since their biggest selling product is The Famous Grouse, this blend has been linked to the distillery.

A visit to Glenturret is now marketed as The Famous Grouse Experience. The visitor is presented with a very imaginative and entertaining range of experiences, by way of a variety of high-tech means, though this sits oddly in the location: one of the most rustic and traditional distilleries. A proportion of Glenturret is said to be included in the "recipe" for The Famous Grouse. Given the size of the distillery and the sales of Grouse, it must be a very small amount. Glenturret's new role has led to a rationalization in the number of bottlings, which was very extensive and idiosyncratic.

Glenturret also has a restaurant providing Scottish dishes (no reservations necessary for lunch; dinner for groups only). Although its world-famous cat Towser is now hunting mice in the heavens, he is remembered in a statue. There is no monument to his alleged 28,899 victims (who documented them so precisely on behalf of Guinness World Records?).

The distillery is on the banks of the Turret River, near Crieff, in Perthshire. There are records of whisky making in the neighborhood at least as early as 1717, and some of the buildings on the present site date from 1775. The distillery itself was dismantled in the 1920s, then revived in 1959 by a noted whisky enthusiast, James Fairlie. It was acquired in 1981 by Cointreau, the French liqueur company, and became part of Highland Distillers (now Edrington) in 1990.

HOUSE STYLE Dry, nutty, fresh, flowery. Young as an aperitif; older after dinner.

GLENTURRET 10-year-old, 40 vol

COLOR Pale greeny gold.

NOSE Nasturtiums. Heavy. Sweet.

BODY Light. Seems to vanish.

PALATE Chlorodyne. Cough lozenges. Toffee.

FINISH Minty. Soothing.

SCORE **76**

GLENTURRET 1987, 54.8 vol

COLOR Pale gold.

NOSE Beautiful. Vanilla, freesia, and fresh malt.

BODY Light.

PALATE Sweet and malty. Tangerine, cut flowers, great balance.
Wood comes through on back palate.

FINISH Clean and nutty.

SCORE **85**

AN INDEPENDENT BOTTLING
GLENTURRET 14-year-old, James MacArthur, 56.9 vol

COLOR Lemon yellow.

NOSE Pecan. Butterscotch. Overripe banana.

BODY Soft, sweet, and full. Creamy.

PALATE Clean sweet barley. Lemon bonbons.
Dash of pepper and touch of peppermint.

FINISH Medium and pleasant, with a dash of chili at the end.

SCORE **79**

HIGHLAND PARK

PRODUCER The Edrington Group
REGION Highlands ISLAND Orkney
ADDRESS Kirkwall, Orkney, KW15 1SU   TEL 01856 874619   VC
WEBSITE www.highlandpark.co.uk

IT HAS BEEN A BUSY FEW YEARS for Highland Park as its owner Edrington has dedicated time and resources into enhancing its already glittering reputation. The distillery is in the Orkney isles to the northeast of Scotland, and the location plays a huge role in the distinctive flavors that make up Highland Park. There are the high winds that carry sea salt deep into the distillery and blow away the peat smoke from the distillery's own floor maltings. There is the peat cut from the island, where few trees grow because of the winds, so that the peat is free of roots and made up of sweeter vegetation. And there is the mild climate, which ensures a maturation that would appear at odds with the northerly location.

Highland Park is the greatest all-rounder in the world of malt whisky. It is definitely in an island style, but it combines all the elements of a classic single malt: smokiness (with its own heather-honey accent), maltiness, smoothness, roundness, fullness of flavor, and length of finish.

Interest in Scotland's northernmost distillery is higher than it has ever been, no doubt driven by the number of special bottlings in recent years, which have revealed a surprisingly diverse array of whiskies from the distillery, from some heavily peated Islay-style releases to gentle citrussy ones.

HOUSE STYLE Smoky and full-flavored. At 18 or 25 years old, with dessert or a cigar. The yet older vintages with a book at bedtime.

HIGHLAND PARK 12-year-old, 43 vol

COLOR Amber.

NOSE Smoky, "garden bonfire" sweetness. Heathery,
malty, and a hint of sherry.

BODY Medium, exceptionally smooth.

PALATE Succulent. Smoky dryness, heather-honey sweetness, and maltiness.

FINISH Teasing, heathery, and delicious.

SCORE **90**

HIGHLAND PARK 15-year-old, 43 vol

COLOR Amber.

NOSE Thick and sweet. Botrytis. Squashed apricot, overripe pear,
toasted almond, and beechnut.

BODY Chewy.

PALATE Great balance between caramelized fruit, honey, and
heathery smoke. Mouth filling. Fudge. Malt.

FINISH Molasses toffee.

SCORE **87**

HIGHLAND PARK 18-year-old, 43 vol

COLOR Refractive, pale gold.

NOSE Warm, notably flowery. Heather honey, fresh oak, sap,
peat, and smoky fragrance. Very aromatic and appetizing.

BODY Remarkably smooth, firm, and rounded.

PALATE Lightly salty. Leafy (vine leaves?), pine nuts. Lots of flavor
development: nuts, honey, cinnamon, and dryish ginger.

FINISH Spicy. Very dry. Oaky, smoky, and hot.

SCORE **92**

HIGHLAND PARK 40-year-old, 48.1 vol

COLOR Dark mahogany with a green tinge.

NOSE Venerable. Soft nectar, scented wax candles, sweet citrus potpourri.

BODY Silky, soft, sweet, and full.

PALATE Stunning and complex mix of stewed, syrupy, mixed
exotic fruit with honey, lemon, and peat.

FINISH A classic Highland Park battle between peat, oak,
fruit, and spice. Long.

 SCORE **91**

HIGHLAND PARK Dark Origins, 46.8 vol

COLOR Rich dark brown.

NOSE Orange marmalade. Aromatic spices. Cigarette smoke.
Plummy fruit. Lemon. Wisps of sulfur.

BODY Quite full and punchy.

PALATE Gritty and earthy, with some sulfur in the mix. Pepper and peat.
Tangerines. Ginger in syrup. Some red-berry fruit. Apple pit.

FINISH Medium long, with lemon, grapefruit, and smoke lingering.

SCORE **82**

HIGHLAND PARK Einar, 40 vol

COLOR Orangey gold.

NOSE Dusty. Cocoa. Lemon jelly. Wispy smoke.

BODY Quite thin and youthful. Underdeveloped.

PALATE Savory and a touch meaty. Sappy. Youthful.
Some peat. Underdeveloped.

FINISH Medium and sweet, with an earthy undercarpet.

SCORE **78**

HIGHLAND PARK Ragnvald, 44.6 vol

COLOR Clear honey.

NOSE Floral, mead, and sherbety. Light and inoffensive.

BODY Quite creamy and full.

PALATE Clean and fresh. Very sweet. Honeysuckle. Jasmine.
Puréed almond. Soft and rounded.

FINISH Chocolate banana. Quite short, delightful, and addictive.

SCORE 88

HIGHLAND PARK Sigurd, 43 vol

COLOR Deep bronze.

NOSE Delicatessen. Fig. Cardamom seed. Cumin. Pepper.

BODY Quite full and balanced.

PALATE Mix of sweet and savory with honey, anchovies,
deli spices, and peat. Rounded and complex.

FINISH Quite smoky and medium long.

SCORE 89

HIGHLAND PARK Thorfinn, 45.1 vol

COLOR Rich gold.

NOSE Honey. Orange blossom. Kitchen pantry. Wispy smoke.
Apricot jam.

BODY Full, oily, and intense.

PALATE Bold and full. Intense smoke. Honey. Black pepper.
Lemon and lime pith. Balanced and complex.

FINISH Medium and peaty, with sweet fruit coming to the fore.

SCORE 90

INCHGOWER

PRODUCER Diageo
REGION Highlands DISTRICT Speyside
ADDRESS Buckie, Banffshire, AB56 2AB TEL 01542 836700

TASTES MORE LIKE A COASTAL MALT than a Speysider. It is both, the distillery being on the coast near the fishing town of Buckie, but not far from the mouth of the Spey River. To the palate expecting a more flowery, elegant Speyside style, this can seem assertive, or even astringent, in its saltiness. With familiarity, that can become addictive. The Inchgower distillery was built in 1871, and expanded in 1966. Its whisky is an important element in the Bell's blend.

HOUSE STYLE Dry, salty. Restorative or aperitif.

INCHGOWER 14-year-old, Fauna & Flora, 43 vol

COLOR Pale gold.

NOSE An almost chocolatey spiciness, then sweet notes like edible seaweed, and finally a whiff of saltier sea character. Overall, dry and complex.

BODY Light to medium. Smooth.

PALATE Starts sweet and malty, with lots of flavor developing, eventually becoming drier and salty.

FINISH Very salty, lingering appetizingly on the tongue.

SCORE 76

JURA

PRODUCER Whyte and Mackay Ltd.
REGION Highlands ISLAND Jura
ADDRESS Craighouse, Jura, Argyll, PA60 7XT
TEL 01496 820240 WEBSITE www.isleofjura.com VC

EVERY VISITOR TO ISLAY also makes the crossing to Jura. The two are so close that they tend to be seen as one. While Islay has seven working distilleries, Jura has just the one. Islay has some very assertive whiskies, yet Jura's is delicate—but gains power with age. Under the ownership of Whyte and Mackay Ltd., the distillery has been more active in introducing new products and marketing them with some vigor.

Two extraordinarily young bottlings, at three and four years old, were made for the Japanese market. Both showed considerable potential. The younger was clean, malty, and assertive, with good maritime flavors. The marginally less young version was more earthy, flowery, and fruity. In the British market, "Superstition" is a sweeter, richer, mature whisky, but seems a little confected, like its marketing story.

The first distillery on the site seems to have been founded around 1810, and rebuilt in 1876. Although a couple of buildings dating back to its early days are still in use, the present distillery was built during the late 1950s and early 1960s, and enlarged in the 1970s.

The name Jura derives from the Norse word for deer. These outnumber people, on an island 34 by 7 miles (55 by 11 kilometers). Jura has about 225 human inhabitants, among whom its most famous was George Orwell. He went there to find a healthy, peaceful place in which to write the novel *Nineteen Eighty-four*. A whisky named after him was released in 2003.

HOUSE STYLE Piney, lightly oily, soft, salty. Aperitif.

ISLE OF JURA 10-year-old, Origin, 40 vol

COLOR Bright gold.

NOSE Oily, lightly piney, earthy, salty, and dry.

BODY Light, slightly oily, and soft.

PALATE Sweetish; slowly developing a slight island
dryness and saltiness.

FINISH A little malty sweetness and some saltiness.

SCORE 72

ISLE OF JURA 12-year-old, Elixir, 46 vol

COLOR Rich gold.

NOSE Canned peaches in syrup, milky coffee, vanilla,
and a sprinkling of salt.

BODY Medium.

PALATE Zesty and fruity. Lots of spice, sherry, and some nutty oak.
A wisp of smoke.

FINISH Medium to long. Nutty and warming, with dark chocolate notes.

SCORE 76

ISLE OF JURA 16-year-old, Diurach's Own, 40 vol

COLOR Full gold to bronze.

NOSE Freshly chopped pine trees. Ferns. Forest floor.

BODY Light, firm, oily-creamy, and dryish.

PALATE Ground coriander. Orange. Rhubarb jam. Buttered scones.

FINISH Salty.

SCORE **77**

ISLE OF JURA Superstition, No Age Statement, 43 vol

COLOR Bronze satin.

NOSE Very light peat smoke, but also some sherryish sweetness. Sweet hay.

BODY Smooth. Waxy.

PALATE Piney, honeyish. Developing sweet creaminess. Opens very slowly.

FINISH Salty, with a surprising sting.

SCORE **80**

ISLE OF JURA 21-year-old, 43 vol

COLOR Pale orange.

NOSE Cedary. Then surprisingly fruity and tropical.
Canned pineapple, cooked peach, papaya, and melon.

BODY Luscious.

PALATE Oak. Fruitiness becomes more orangey. Sweet tobacco.

FINISH Soft fruit. Refreshing acidity.

SCORE **80**

ISLE OF JURA 30-year-old, Camas an Staca, 44 vol

COLOR Dark walnut.

NOSE Mellow, with figs, sherry, and orange. Vanilla emerges with malt and a hint of cinnamon and violet candies.

BODY Lightly oily and supple.

PALATE More orange, plus cocoa, golden raisins, and dates.

FINISH Lengthy, with dark chocolate, raisins, aniseed, and subtle spices.

SCORE **83**

ISLE OF JURA Prophecy, 46 vol

COLOR Amber gold.

NOSE Smoked fish, brine, and butter.

BODY Viscous.

PALATE Luscious fruit, peat smoke, spice, and licorice sticks.

FINISH Lingering peat and spice, becoming drier and more ashy.

SCORE **81**

ISLE OF JURA 1974, 44.5 vol

COLOR Copper.

NOSE Fresh, with ozone, cinnamon, and dried fruit.

BODY Medium. Smooth.

PALATE Fruity, with oranges, marzipan, honey, and lively spices.

FINISH Caramel and gentle smoke.

SCORE 81

ISLE OF JURA 1977, 34-year-old, Juar, 46 vol

COLOR Golden orange.

NOSE Vanilla, peaches, light oak, and some pepper.

BODY Oily and smooth

PALATE More peaches, plus ripe pears, ginger, almonds, and soft toffee.

FINISH Richly fruity, soft spices, and sweet oak.

SCORE 85

ISLE OF JURA 40-year-old, 45.1 vol

COLOR Full golden amber.

NOSE Fresh and vibrant, with pine air freshener, heather, hazelnuts, and developing marzipan notes.

BODY Medium.

PALATE Sherried, nutty, and spicy, with licorice and a hint of cinnamon.

FINISH Dry sherry and emerging oak.

SCORE 88

ISLE OF JURA 2013, Festival Bottling, 52.4 vol

A single cask bottling, distilled in 1999, triple matured in a first-fill bourbon barrel, a Burgundy barrique, and a 1963 oloroso sherry butt. 663 bottles.

COLOR Rich gold.

NOSE Sticky-toffee-pudding, sweet red berries, and a herbal note.

BODY Full.

PALATE Ripe oranges, walnuts, vanilla, and lively spices.

FINISH Lingering, with spicy bitter orange and dark chocolate.

SCORE 83

TRAVEL RETAIL
ISLE OF JURA Turas Mara, 42 vol

COLOR Golden amber.

NOSE Cherries, honey, nutmeg, and marzipan.

BODY Rich.

PALATE More cherries, along with malt, vanilla, and Seville oranges.

FINISH Quite long, brittle toffee, oak, and drying orange notes.

SCORE **83**

INDEPENDENT BOTTLING
ISLE OF JURA 1997, Connoisseurs Choice
(Gordon & MacPhail), 46 vol

COLOR Dark straw.

NOSE Quite light, spicy tropical fruit, and a hint of honey.

BODY Slightly oily.

PALATE Malty, nutty with honey, brittle toffee, and black pepper.

FINISH Peaches with a sprinkling of salt.

SCORE **81**

KILCHOMAN

PRODUCER Kilchoman Distillery Company
REGION Islay   DISTRICT Machir Bay
ADDRESS Rockside Farm, Bruichladdich, Islay, PA49 7UT
TEL 01496 850011   WEBSITE www.kilchomandistillery.com   VC

IN THE SAME WEEK that flooding forced hundreds of people from their homes in eastern Scotland and torrential storms and gales caused mayhem in the west, Islay was blessed with sunshine as the whisky industry turned out to welcome a new member to its fold.

It's not every day that a new distillery releases its first whisky—in the case of Islay, in fact, it's the first time it has happened in more than 120 years. In traditional style, and with a degree of emotion, the malt was piped in and offered to a large group of guests, including representatives from all of Islay's other distilleries.

Kilchoman calls itself a farm distillery, and it is now officially Scotland's most westerly whisky producer, it being just a few miles northwest of Bruichladdich. It is a small, traditional distillery and uses locally grown barley and peat dug from the area. The whisky is distinctively Islay in flavor, with rich, sweet peat notes.

KILCHOMAN 2007, 46 vol
A vatting of 6-year-old fresh bourbon barrels.

COLOR Light beech.

NOSE Initially very sweet peat, then brine and perserved herring. Freshly stubbed cigarettes butts, warm, gingery leather, and vanilla.

BODY Relatively full.

PALATE Nutty, with citrus fruit, black pepper, and spicy peat.

FINISH Long and fruity, with dark chocolate and lingering spice.

SCORE **86**

KILCHOMAN Machir Bay 2014, 46 vol

A vatting of 5 and 6-year-old ex-bourbon barrels and oloroso sherry butts.

COLOR Pale gold.

NOSE Citrus fruit, antiseptic, sweet smoke, and finally wood polish and background cigarette ash.

BODY Medium.

PALATE Initially sweet and ashy on the palate, with medicinal notes, rock salt, and black pepper.

FINISH Medium in length, with lingering cloth Band-Aids and insistent ginger.

 SCORE *86*

KILCHOMAN 100% Islay, 4th edition, 50 vol

A vatting of 32 five-year-old and 8 four-year-old first-fill bourbon barrels.

COLOR Light gold.

NOSE Figs, malt, bonfire embers, smoked haddock, and brine. Finally, vanilla, wood polish, and orchard fruit.

BODY Supple.

PALATE Soft fruit, with developing peat smoke.

FINISH Smoky, lengthy, and mellow.

 SCORE *85*

KILCHOMAN 2009 Loch Gorm, 2014 Release, 46 vol

COLOR Rich gold.

NOSE Sweet peat, old leather, and sherry.

BODY Medium.

PALATE Fruity peat, graham crackers, and allspice.

FINISH Quite lengthy. Spicy, and fruity. Peat smoke.

SCORE *83*

KININVIE

PRODUCER William Grant & Sons
REGION Highlands   DISTRICT Speyside
ADDRESS Dufftown, Banffshire, AB55 4DH
TEL 01340 820373

KININVIE IS ONE OF the lowest-profile distilleries on Speyside. Essentially just a stillhouse equipped with nine pots, it stands behind its "sister" distillery of Balvenie, and within Balvenie there is a dedicated Kinivie mash tun, and 10 Douglas fir washbacks.

Kininvie was constructed in 1990, with the principal purpose of providing malt spirit for Grant's Family Reserve blend, though it also became a key component of the blended malt Monkey Shoulder. When sold to third parties for blending purposes, Grants "teaspoon" Kininvie, that is they add a dash of one of their other whiskies to each cask so that no one can bottle it under the Kininvie name. As such it is termed Aldunie.

Once Grant's Ailsa Bay malt distillery was developed within the company's Girvan complex in Ayrshire during 2007–08, Kininvie's importance diminished, and a period of closure followed in 2010–11. However, the distillery subsequently reopened and is now fully operational once more.

Bottlings of Kininvie have been as rare as the proverbial hen's teeth, with very limited quantities of 15 and 17-year-olds being marketed under the Hazelwood name. But then a 17-year-old appeared under the Kininvie name, along with a 23-year-old expression titled Kininvie Batch Number One, which was released exclusively for the Taiwan market.

HOUSE STYLE Medium bodied and floral.

KININVIE 17-year-old, 43.6 vol

COLOR Bright gold.

NOSE Tropical fruit, coconut, vanilla custard, and a hint of cocoa powder.

BODY Voluptuous.

PALATE Pineapple and mango, with linseed oil, tingling ginger, and increasing nuttiness.

FINISH Slowly drying, with spice and soft oak, though linseed lingers.

SCORE **79**

KNOCKANDO

PRODUCER Diageo
REGION Highlands   DISTRICT Speyside
ADDRESS Knockando, Aberlour, Banffshire, AB38 7RT
TEL 01340 882000

MORE WAS HEARD OF this elegant whisky—in Britain, at least—when it was the most promoted malt in the portfolio of IDV, before the merger that created Diageo in 1997.

Knockando is among a small group of malts that are especially influential in the J&B (Justerini & Brooks) blends (*see also* Glen Spey). Knockando is a sophisticated malt, and its labeling policy is somewhat elaborate. The notion is that the malt is bottled when it is mature, rather than at a specific age, though bottles now also offer an age statement as well as a vintage.

One season does not differ dramatically from another, though there are very subtle differences. At older ages, the whisky gains greatly in complexity and sherry character.

The water with which the whisky is made rises from granite and flows over peat. The distillery's name, pronounced "knock-AN-do" (or 'du) sounds allusively comical to English speakers, but translates perfectly sensibly as "a little black hill." Knockando is hidden in a fold in the hills overlooking the Spey River at a fine spot for salmon fishing. The distillery was established in 1898.

HOUSE STYLE Elegant, with suggestions of berry fruit. Aperitif.

KNOCKANDO 1996, Managers' Choice, 58.6 vol
Matured in a European oak cask; 599 bottles.

COLOR Mahogany.

NOSE Black molasses, hazelnuts, fireworks, and a hint of fresh asphalt. Figs and wood smoke.

BODY Smooth and full.

PALATE Big sherry notes, prunes, and raisins, with honey also showing through.

FINISH Lingering, with increasing oak, ginger, and ultimately molasses toffee.

SCORE **83**

KNOCKANDO 12-year-old, 43 vol

COLOR Pale gold.

NOSE Delicate and fragrant, with hints of malt, worn leather, and hay.

BODY Relatively light.

PALATE Smooth and honeyed, with ripe apples and gingery malt.

FINISH Medium length, with cereal and more ginger.

SCORE **78**

KNOCKANDO 1985, 25-year-old, Special Releases 2011, 43 vol

COLOR Dark copper.

NOSE Wood polish, new leather, and brittle toffee, plus overripe bananas and freshly cut broccoli. Coal fires with time.

BODY Viscous.

PALATE Rich yet elegant. Viscous. Molasses and dried fruit, becoming drier in the mouth.

FINISH Long, with cocoa powder and developing tannins.

SCORE **82**

KNOCKANDO 1976, 40 vol

COLOR Amber.

NOSE Floral, with new leather, sherry, toffee, and cut grass.

BODY Light to medium.

PALATE Pineapple and mango, plus caramel.

FINISH Floral, with toffee and light spices.

SCORE **82**

KNOCKDHU

PRODUCER Inver House Distillers Ltd.
REGION Highlands   DISTRICT Speyside (Isla/Deveron)
ADDRESS Knock by Huntly, Aberdeenshire, AB5 5LJ
WEBSITE www.inverhouse.com   EMAIL enquiries@inverhouse.com

KNOCKDHU IS THE ENGLISH VERSION of the Gaelic words for Little Black Hill, *Cnoc Dubh*. But because Diageo has a distillery with the name Knockando, Inver House was encouraged to use the name An Cnoc on its bottles to avoid confusion. It is the Gaelic for The Hill. There was probably no thought of confusion when these two distilleries were established, both in the 1890s, as their original purpose was to produce whisky for blending, rather than as single malt.

Knockdhu was built in 1894 to supply malt for the Haig blends, and closed in 1983. Only after its acquisition by the present owners, and its reopening, did official bottlings, albeit on a small scale, begin to be issued in the 1990s. These have become more common in recent years, and the brand has been repackaged, new expressions released, and the name "anCnoc" used on bottlings.

HOUSE STYLE Creamy and fruity. A dessert malt?

AN CNOC 1999, 46 vol

COLOR Yellow amber.

NOSE Fruity, fragrant, and nutty, with milk chocolate and canned pears.

BODY Soft.

PALATE Fruity and mildly spicy, with lemon, ginger, and toffee.

FINISH Cocoa powder, lingering ginger, and mild oak.

SCORE **84**

AN CNOC 12-year-old, 40 vol

COLOR Yellow with a greenish hue.

NOSE Pepper. Dusty. Coal smoke. Fresh, clean, cut barley.

BODY Medium and rich.

PALATE Sweet barley. Very clean. Herbal. Then gradually spices
and fruit, which rise to a crescendo.

FINISH Quite long, with lots of spices and a soft melonlike fruitiness.

SCORE **80**

AN CNOC 16-year-old, 46 vol

COLOR Deep orangey yellow.

NOSE Pineapple candy. Crystalized barley. Fresh meadow.
Confectionery. Bourbon notes.

BODY Rich, full, and sweet.

PALATE Sweet barley. Honeyed. Rich yellow and orange fruit.
Later, a gentle and pleasant wave of oak and spice.

FINISH Long, rich, spicy, and sweet.

SCORE **85**

AN CNOC 22-year-old, 46 vol

COLOR Bright gold.

NOSE Zesty fresh fruit, apricots, and oranges; creamy, with honey.

BODY Supple.

PALATE Lively fruit notes for its age. Cloves, old leather, soft toffee,
and chocolate-covered sea-foam candy.

FINISH Lengthy, with lingering sweet spices.

SCORE **85**

AN CNOC 35-year-old, 46.3 vol

COLOR Rich amber.

NOSE Soft fruit notes, melon, and pear, plus honey, vanilla, and toffee.

BODY Mouth coating.

PALATE Malty, rich, and spicy, with ginger in syrup and light sherry.

FINISH Long and very spicy. Chili and drying tannins.

SCORE **86**

LAGAVULIN

PRODUCER Diageo
REGION Islay   DISTRICT South Shore
ADDRESS Port Ellen, Islay, Argyll, PA42 7DZ   TEL 01496 302730
WEBSITE www.discovering-distilleries.com/www.malts.com

LAGAVULIN ENJOYS ICONIC STATUS even alongside the other great distilleries of Islay, a position enhanced from a lengthy period when bottles of the 16-year-old were hard to come by, partly because the distillery was working just two days a week through much of the 1980s, and partly because of a miscalculation of stock that resulted in nearly all of the distillery's malt being used for inclusion in the six whisky Classic Malts collection. Today the distillery is as busy as all the others and the supply problems are in the past.

At 16 years old, Lagavulin has the driest and most sustained attack of any readily available whisky, though some argue that these days it is less brutal than it was. Until relatively recently it was sold just as a 16-year-old, although in the late 1990s a Distiller's Edition, which had been finished in Pedro Ximénez sherry casks, were released. Rarely has a whisky so divided opinion, with some saying the sherry influence dumbed down the peat attack, while others described the pairing as a perfect clash of two whisky heavyweights.

In recent years there has also been a succession of 12-year-old releases, some at higher strengths, and they have been a revelation, showing at times a citrussy and lighter side to the malt.

Lagavulin lies on the south shore of Islay and is a lovely distillery to visit. The distillery's water arrives by way of a fast-flowing stream. You can approach the distillery by sea, since the distillery has its own jetty, but navigating into the shallow "harbor" is not for the squeamish and demands a large glass of Lagavulin on arrival. Very little whisky is matured here and is stored in warehouses battered by the sea.

Lagavulin (pronounced "lagga-voolin") means "the hollow where the mill is," and it is said that at one time around the mid-1770s there were 10 illicit stills in the bay. Lagavulin itself can trace its history back to 1816. With 2016 at hand, a 16-year-old distilled in the year of the new millennium must be a distinct possibility.

HOUSE STYLE Dry, smoky, complex. Restorative or nightcap.

LAGAVULIN 2014, Feis Isle, Distilled 1995, 54.7 vol

COLOR Golden brown.

NOSE Vibrant with fresh fruit. Citrus. Mandarin.
Grapefruit. Smoke. Pepper.

BODY Rich, oily, waxy.

PALATE Sooty, wood smoke. Berry fruit. Tobacco pouch. Soft licorice.

FINISH Smoke, oak and sherry, medium to long.

SCORE 93

LAGAVULIN 12-year-old, Special Releases 2013, 55.1 vol

COLOR Lemon.

NOSE Sooty. Lemon. Barbecued fish. Peaty. Creamy and dairy.

BODY Rich, full, and oily.

PALATE Sweet and peaty, with chili. Very direct with waves
of smoke, and sea spray.

FINISH Medium long, sweet, and spicy.

SCORE 91

LAPHROAIG

PRODUCER Suntory Holdings Ltd.
REGION Islay   DISTRICT South Shore
ADDRESS Port Ellen, Islay, Argyll, PA42 7DU
TEL 01496 302418   WEBSITE www.laphroaig.com   VC

THIS IS THE MOST MEDICINAL of malts. "Love it or hate it," said one of Laphroaig's advertising slogans. Like hospital gauze? Reminiscent of mouthwash or antiseptic? Phenolic? That is the whole point: the iodine-like, seaweed character of Islay.

Many feel that the famous Laphroaig attack has diminished a little in recent years, unmasking more of the sweetness of the malt, but it is still an extremely characterful whisky, with a distinctively oily body. And a new version of the malt, partially matured in quarter-size casks, has restored some of the intensity that Laphroaig drinkers look for. Laphroaig has its own peat beds on Islay, its own dam on the Kilbride river, a floor maltings at the distillery, and relatively small stills. Its maturation warehouses face directly onto the sea.

The distillery was built in the 1820s by the Johnston family, whose name is still on the label. In 1847 the founder died after falling into a vat of partially made whisky. In the late 1950s and early 1960s, the distillery was owned by a woman, Miss Bessie Williamson—a glamorous lady, judging from a photograph on the wall. The romance of the place extends to occasional weddings at the distillery, part of which serves as the village hall. The distillery is now owned by Japanese distilling giant Suntory and watched over by a dedicated malt team, auguring well for its future.

HOUSE STYLE Medicinal. Nightcap.

LAPHROAIG Select, 40 vol
COLOR Pale gold.
NOSE Printer's ink, pipe tobacco, peat and, in time, cloth Band-Aids. Finally, smoky ripe peaches.
BODY Medium.
PALATE Peat, black tea, nutmeg, dark berries, and contrasting hints of vanilla.
FINISH Relatively short, herbal, drying, and slightly metallic.
SCORE **82**

LAPHROAIG Quarter Cask, 48 vol

COLOR Rich gold.

NOSE Grungy. Boathouse. Industrial smoke and tar. Lemon juice. Intense.

BODY Rich and oily. Full mouthfeel.

PALATE A smoky rainbow, from sweet barley and full fruit
through to intense peat and seaweed.

FINISH Long and perfectly weighted, with rich and intense peat and smoke.
Classic Laphroaig.

SCORE **91**

LAPHROAIG 10-year-old, 40 vol

Versions have been marketed at 40 and 43 vol. The stronger is slightly richer.

COLOR Full, refractive gold.

NOSE Medicinal, phenolic, seaweedy, with a hint of estery
(gooseberry?) sweetness.

BODY Medium and oily.

PALATE Seaweedy, salty, and oily.

FINISH Round and very dry.

SCORE **86**

LAPHROAIG 10-year-old, Cask Strength, Batch 006, 58 vol

COLOR Deep gold.

NOSE Sweet peat, anticeptic, white pepper, sea salt, honey, and almonds.

BODY Full and creamy.

PALATE Spicy peat, beach bonfires, seaweed, mandarin oranges, and ginger.

FINISH Lengthy and drying, with savory notes.

SCORE **88**

LAPHROAIG 18-year-old, 48 vol

COLOR Bright golden orange.

NOSE Brine and sea spray. Greasy rope. Hot tarmac in the rain.

BODY Full and oily.

PALATE Industrial steam engine. Red licorice. Peppered steak grilled
over hickory wood. Big and brooding.

FINISH Long, with peat coating the mouth and licorice
and hickory lingering.

SCORE **93**

LAPHROAIG 25-year-old, 50.9 vol

COLOR Honey gold.

NOSE Grapey, earthy, dairy, and laundry room.
Very unlike Laphroaig.

BODY Medium, quite thin, and savory.

PALATE Grape. Savory. Astringency from the wood,
some citrus notes, unripe green fruit, cocoa dark chocolate,
and hints of peat.

FINISH At last a distinctive peat wave comes through—
better late than never. Cocoa and fruit.

SCORE **73**

LAPHROAIG **Triple Wood, 48 vol**

COLOR Bright gold.

NOSE Brine, iodine, subtle dry peat, golden raisins, maraschino cherries, and vanilla.

BODY Full.

PALATE Initial vanilla and sherry notes give way to iodine, peat, sea salt, and black pepper.

FINISH Lengthy, with spice, autumn berries, and smoky oak.

SCORE **91**

TRAVEL RETAIL

LAPHROAIG **PX Cask, 40 vol**

COLOR Antique gold.

NOSE Rich, smoky sherry, maritime notes, dates, and licorice.

BODY Full and rounded.

PALATE Sherry combines with a big blast of peat and fresh tar.

FINISH Long, with drying sherry, coal, and oak.

SCORE **87**

LAPHROAIG **QA Cask, 40 vol**

COLOR Bright gold.

NOSE Peat fires, iodine, and brine contrast with vanilla and soft leather.

BODY Medium and rounded.

PALATE Sweet, with salted caramels, ginger, a blast of peat, then licorice.

FINISH Vanilla and coal soot, black pepper, and lively oak.

SCORE **84**

LAPHROAIG **An Cuan Mór, 48.7 vol**

COLOR Dark orange.

NOSE Sweet and fragrant, with oranges, figs, and honey, backed by iodine and leathery peat.

BODY Full.

PALATE Iodine, black pepper, dark chocolate, Seville oranges, salt, and oak.

FINISH Long and nutty, with iodine, spicy peat smoke, and gentle oak tannins.

SCORE **90**

LINKWOOD

PRODUCER Diageo
REGION Highlands   ISLAND Speyside (Lossie)
ADDRESS Elgin, Morayshire, IV30 3RD   TEL 01343 862000

A SECRET NATURE RESERVE or a distillery? Linkwood's appropriately flowery Speyside whisky is increasingly appreciated, judging from the profusion of independent bottlings.

The dam that provides the cooling water is a port of call to tufted ducks and goldeneyes—and a seasonal home to wagtails, oyster catchers, mute swans, and otters. In the 10 acres (hectares) of the site, nettles attract red admiral and small tortoiseshell butterflies; cuckoo flowers entice the orange tip variety; bluebells seduce bees.

The distillery was founded in 1821, and for many years Linkwood operated two stillhouses, with the second being installed in 1971. However, during 2013 major expansion work was undertaken, which saw the demolition of some old buildings and the development of an extension to the "new" stillhouse, which is now home to three pairs of stills.

HOUSE STYLE Floral. Rosewater? Cherries?
Delicious with a slice of fruit cake.

LINKWOOD Managers' Choice, Distilled 1996, Bottled 2009, 58.2 vol

COLOR Honey gold.

NOSE Soft fruit. Chocolate-covered sea-foam candy. Honey. Some floral notes and the slightest trace of pepper.

BODY Soft and full.

PALATE Big peach and apricot flavors. Some milk chocolate, tannin, and developing spice.

FINISH Sharper and spicier than the palate, but not unpleasant.

SCORE **82**

LINKWOOD 12-year-old, Flora and Fauna, 43 vol

COLOR Full primrose.

NOSE Remarkably flowery and petal-like. Buttercups. Grass. Fragrant.

BODY Medium, rounded, and slightly syrupy.

PALATE Starts slowly, and has a long, sustained development to marzipan, roses, and fresh sweetness. One to savor.

FINISH Perfumy and dryish. Lemon zest.

SCORE **82**

INDEPENDENT BOTTLINGS
LINKWOOD 15-year-old (Gordon & MacPhail), 43 vol

COLOR Gold.

NOSE Floral, with sherry; mildly savory, with dried fruit.

BODY Creamy.

PALATE Sweet and spicy, vanilla, and peppery oak.

FINISH Medium to long, nutty, with oak.

SCORE **80**

LINKWOOD Batch 1 (That Boutique-y Whisky Company), 51.2 vol

92 bottles.

COLOR Pale gold.

NOSE Malt, barley, and orchard fruit.

BODY Firm.

PALATE Cooking apples and more barley.

FINISH Relatively lengthy, fruity, but drying.

SCORE **81**

LOCH LOMOND

PRODUCER Loch Lomond Distillery Co. Ltd.
REGION Highlands   DISTRICT Western Highlands
ADDRESS Lomond Estate, Alexandria, Dunbartonshire, G83 0TL
TEL 01389 752781   WEBSITE www.lochlomonddistillery.com
EMAIL mail@lochlomonddistillery.com

A TRANSFORMATION HAS GRADUALLY been wrought at this extraordinary establishment. The building's industrial past (as a cotton-fabric dyeworks) is no longer evident. It has been smartly restyled as a very functional, if complex, distillery. It has three pairs of pot stills, but with a visible difference. Two of the pairs are equipped with rectification columns. By being operated in different ways, these stills can produce at least half a dozen different malts. Some of these malts are bottled as singles, but the distillery was designed to produce the components for its own blends. Loch Lomond also has a five-column continuous still. In 2008 a new still, consisting of two copper columns, encased in stainless steel, was installed to make malt spirit, though it has caused controversy with the Scotch Whisky Association, which declares that malt whisky must be made in pot stills.

The distillery is on an industrial estate by the Leven River, which links the Clyde and Loch Lomond. The name Loch Lomond is used on a single malt and a "single blend" (i.e., the grain and malts come from the one distillery). Other malts, such as Inchmurrin, are named after islands in the loch and other places of local interest.

Four of the malts are not usually bottled as singles. These include Glen Douglas, and the progressively more heavily peated Craiglodge, Inchmoan, and Croftengea. Tasted as a work in progress, at seven years old, Croftengea had a sweet, oily, smoky aroma; a bonfire-like palate; with suggestions of fruitwood, briar, and oak smoke; and a lingering length.

Loch Lomond's unusual pattern of business dates from its acquisition in 1987 by a whisky wholesaler called Glen Catrine. This grew out of a chain of stores that had their beginning as licensed grocers. The Loch Lomond distillery, previously owned by the American company, Barton Brands, was established in the mid-1960s.

HOUSE STYLE Loch Lomond: Nutty. Restorative.
Inchmurrin: Fruity. Aperitif. Old Rhosdhu: Piney. Soothing.

LOCH LOMOND Blue Label, No Age Statement, 40 vol

COLOR White wine.

NOSE Cream soda, cereal, lemonade, ginger, and a whiff of feints.

BODY Medium.

PALATE More cereal, grassy, and slight oak.

FINISH Bubblegum, oats, and yeast.

SCORE 72

LOCH LOMOND Green Label, Heavily Peated, 46 vol

COLOR Chardonnay.

NOSE A little mashy; savory notes with a hint of pear.

BODY Unctuous.

PALATE Dry peat and black pepper. Vague fruity backdrop.

FINISH Quite lengthy; persistent peat and pepper.

SCORE 72

LOCH LOMOND 18-year-old, 43 vol

COLOR Amber.

NOSE Gummy-fruit candy, vanilla, bubblegum, and lanolin.

BODY Rich.

PALATE Malt, honey, nuts, and white pepper.

FINISH Dries quite rapidly to dark, spicy oak notes.

SCORE 76

INCHMURRIN 15-year-old, 46 vol

COLOR Pale gold.

NOSE Initially reticent, slightly nutty, with developing citrus fruit and mild vanilla.

BODY Supple.

PALATE Fruity, with vanilla toffee and cinnamon.

FINISH Jaffa orange and hazelnuts.

SCORE 76

INCHMURRIN 18-year-old, 46 vol

COLOR Bright gold.

NOSE Floral, with malt and ripe peaches.

BODY Smooth.

PALATE Ginger, with a squeeze of lemon and unripe pears.

FINISH Drying, with licorice and chili to dark chocolate.

SCORE 76

INCHMURRIN 21-year-old, 46 vol

COLOR Honey.

NOSE Vanilla, citrus fruit, and lanolin.

BODY Rich.

PALATE Sharp fruit notes, with honey, cocoa powder, and spice.

FINISH Lengthy and drying, with lively spice, vanilla, and a hint of aniseed along the way.

SCORE 77

LONGMORN

PRODUCER Chivas Brothers (Pernod Ricard)
REGION Highlands   DISTRICT Speyside (Lossie)
ADDRESS Elgin, Morayshire, IV30 3SJ   TEL 01542 783042

LONGMORN IS ONE OF THE FINEST Speyside malts, cherished by connoisseurs but not widely known. It is admired for its complexity, its combination of smoothness and fullness of character, and from its big bouquet to its long finish. It is noted for its cereal-grain maltiness, beeswax flavors, and estery fruitiness.

The distillery was built in 1894–95, and has a disused waterwheel and a workable steam engine. Much of the equipment is very traditional, and imposing in its size and beautiful condition, including the Steel's mash mixer and some very impressive spirit safes. Alongside the distillery is the disused Longmorn railroad flag stop.

HOUSE STYLE Tongue coating, malty, complex.
Versatile, delightful before dinner, and especially
good with dessert.

LONGMORN 11-year-old, Douglas of Drumlanrig (Laphroaig), 50 vol

COLOR Rich gold.

NOSE A muddle of fruit including peach and strawberry.
Some mustiness. Sweet and pleasant.

BODY Full, clean, and sweet.

PALATE Melon, lots of exotic and tropical fruit, pineapple.
Some licorice late on. Very tasty.

FINISH Long, with the tropical fruit lingering and in no hurry to leave.

SCORE 92

LONGMORN 16-year-old, 48 vol

COLOR Deep gold. Slightly greenish hue.

NOSE Full, sweet, and malt-laced, with honey and hints
of fruit—perhaps red apples. Lovely.

BODY Fiery, big, and overpowering.

PALATE Big, assertive malt.

FINISH Oats, nuts, then peppery. Long.

COMMENT A benefit can be gained from a few drops of water, which
softens the nose, allowing more fruit to emerge on the nose and palate.
The body is still full, but the water releases the inner fruit and
floral notes, and brings back the tangerines on the finish.

SCORE **85**

LONGMORN 18-year-old, 53.1 vol

Distillery-only bottling.

COLOR Rich honey.

NOSE Soft toffee and hazelnut chocolate.

BODY Firm, rich, and mouth coating.

PALATE Sweet, with big puréed fruit flavors. Orange peel and citrus. Drying
toward the end as oaky tannins and some chili notes arrive.

FINISH Long, with a mix of honeyed fruit and spice. Delightful.

SCORE **93**

THE MACALLAN

PRODUCER The Edrington Group
REGION Highlands   DISTRICT Speyside
ADDRESS Aberlour, Banffshire, AB38 9RX
TEL 01340 872280   WEBSITE www.themacallan.com   VC

T O A GREAT EXTENT MACALLAN is without equal, and its position in the world of whisky, and in the minds of malt fanatics, is unique. It has been considered the most collectable of all malts, and has mined its history repetitively over the years. But at the same time it proved durably popular with regular malt drinkers, with a range of whiskies at a vast number of price points, from the mainstream upward. It has been a ubiquitous malt that has heralded its iconic expressions but reinvented itself to remain commercially viable, and affordable to the average consumer.

Traditionally the distillery was known for big, rich, sherried Speyside whiskies, but when demand in Southeast Asia particularly stretched demand for sherried malt to its limits, owner company Edrington launched a new range of Macallans under the banner Fine Oak. And in recent years there has been a series of controversies, with many malt lovers unhappy with the direction of this illustrious malt.

In 2010's sixth edition of this book we wrote the following: "For some at least, less emphasis on sherry has allowed the high quality of sherry to shine through. But the move away from sherry in some traditional markets has not been without controversy. By 2009 Edrington was increasingly moving its sherried whiskies to the newer territories, and emphasizing the Fine Oak series in Europe. It seems likely that the traditional sherries versions will be phased out of some markets altogether."

These proved to be prophetic words. Indeed, for Macallan aficionados the position today is even more disturbing. In the United Kingdom all expressions under 18 have been phased out entirely, and been replaced by four malts which bear no age statement, and are sold by color. They include whisky taken from sherry butts, but with the exception of the most expensive one, they taste very different from the Macallans of old. This move has caused a degree of disquiet among some. There are those that think that the move to non-age statement whisky, and to assessing whisky quality by color is spurious, and "dumbs down" the whiskies. Edrington isn't the only company going down this route but the high status that The Macallan is held in has singled it out for criticism, particularly since some feel that the new whiskies are of inferior quality to the old age statement bottles, and are overpriced.

Nevertheless, Macallan remains a huge force for good. To collectors, no other distillery has the same magical allure. The name derives from the Macallan church, now a ruin, on the Easter Elchies estate, which overlooks Telford's Bridge over the Spey at Craigellachie. A farmer is believed to have made whisky from his own barley in the 1700s. Macallan became a legal distillery as soon as that was possible, in 1824. In 1998 the estate farm was put back into use to grow Golden Promise barley, albeit a token amount in relation to Macallan's requirements. The manor house from the early days has been restored as a venue for the entertaining of visitors.

Macallan has long been a renowned contributor to blends, including The Famous Grouse. Macallan's oily, creamy richness is enhanced by the use of especially small stills, which look like potbellied aardvarks. When the company expanded output to cope with demand, it has added more stills rather than building bigger ones. The number grew from six to 21 between 1965 and 1975. Macallan probably has a more diverse selection of whiskies than it has ever had, and a range to suit most pockets. The whisky continues to perform very well in export markets particularly in Southeast Asia.

HOUSE STYLE Big, oaky, resiny, sherried, flowery-fruity. Spicy.
Very long. After dinner.

THE MACALLAN Gold, 1824 Series, 40 vol

COLOR Gold.

NOSE Orange. Citrus fruit. Dark chocolate. Raspberry sherbet.

BODY Light and cordial-like.

PALATE Oak. Zesty apple. More citrus fruit. Earthiness from the cask.
Exotic spices.

FINISH Medium, oaky, and spicy.

 SCORE **80**

THE MACALLAN Sienna, 1824 Series, 43 vol

COLOR Sienna.

NOSE Rich and full, with orange Jell-O. Pineapple. Tropical fruit.

BODY Rich, sweet, and full.

PALATE More big fruit flavors. Licorice, orange liqueur,
toasted oak, and apple strudel. Really nice.

FINISH Fruity, oaky, long, and spicy.

SCORE **91**

THE MACALLAN Amber, 1824 Series, 43 vol

COLOR Amber.

NOSE Cocoa. Kiwi. Drying sherry. Bread dough. Raisins.

BODY Light, oily, sharp, and earthy.

PALATE Quite dry, with rich fruitcake notes, dried lemon,
and orange peel. Touches of oak and tannin. Cinnamon.

FINISH Medium, fruity, spicy, and pleasant.

SCORE **83**

THE MACALLAN Ruby, 1824 Series, 43 vol

COLOR Ruby.

NOSE Traditional old sherry, with orange and citrus fruit,
English sherry trifle, and dark berries.

BODY Rich, full, and mouth coating.

PALATE Dried fruit. Almonds. Rum and raisin. Stewed apple stuffed with
mincemeat. Orange flavored dark chocolate. Alcoholic black-currant juice.
Spices, particularly cinnamon and nutmeg.

FINISH Big, bold, spicy, sherried, and mouth warming.

SCORE **85**

THE MACALLAN 15-year-old, Darkness, Pedro Ximénez (Master of Malt), 52.3 vol

COLOR Pale orange.

NOSE Assorted-fruit-flavored hard candy. Stewed berries.

BODY Soft. Mellow. Liqueurlike.

PALATE Soft peach. Kumquat. Orange fruits. Vanilla.
Marshmallow. Delightful. Canned fruit cocktail.

FINISH Long and fruity, with an earthy twist at the very end.

SCORE **88**

MACDUFF

PRODUCER John Dewar & Sons Ltd. (Bacardi)
REGION Highlands   DISTRICT Speyside (Deveron)
ADDRESS Macduff Distillery, Banff, Banffshire, AB45 3JT
TEL 01261 812612

ALTHOUGH THE DISTILLERY claims whisky production dating back centuries, citing "church records from the 1700s [that] describe the local whisky as excellent," Macduff was built during the optimistic 1960s, when distillers could not keep up with demand. It has a workaday appearance compared to some of the more architecturally refined distilleries built around that time. Its clean, uncluttered interior has in general been mirrored in the character of its whiskies. They, too, have been clean and uncluttered—whiskies that tasted of malt. They still do, but a 10-year-old, repackaged in 2002 and now the distillery's principal product, has a strong wood influence too.

The distillery is in the old fishing town and former spa of Macduff at a point where the glen of the Deveron reaches the sea (the reason why the whiskies are now marketed with the name Glen Deveron). On the other side of the river is the town of Banff. At a stretch, this is the western edge of Speyside. Not only is it a fringe location geographically—Macduff was for years somewhat lonely as the sole distillery of the William Lawson company. The distillery's output has largely gone into the Lawson blends. Since 1992, Macduff has been part of Bacardi, which also owns Dewars.

HOUSE STYLE Malty. Sweet limes in older versions.
Restorative or after dinner.

GLEN DEVERON 10-year-old, 40 vol

COLOR Deep gold.

NOSE Freshly cut wood. Cedarlike. Surprisingly assertive.

BODY Light to medium. Notably smooth.

PALATE Malted milk. Condensed milk. Fig toffee. Butterscotch. Thick yogurt.
Slightly sour. Lemony.

FINISH Crisp. Honeycomb toffee.

SCORE 72

GLEN DEVERON 12-year-old, 40 vol

COLOR Gold.

NOSE Faint hint of sherry. Rich, sweet, fresh maltiness.

BODY Light to medium, but notably smooth.

PALATE Full. Very clean delicious maltiness.

FINISH Malty dryness. Quick but pleasantly warming.

SCORE **75**

GLEN DEVERON 15-year old, 40 vol

COLOR Deep gold.

NOSE Sweet, butterscotch, with notes of sherry.

BODY Rich, full, spicy, and well-rounded.

PALATE Oak, with traces of cinnamon and a whisper of lemon.

FINISH Short, clean, and crisp.

SCORE **76**

SOME INDEPENDENT BOTTLINGS
MACDUFF 17-year-old, Old Malt Cask, 50 vol

COLOR Buttery yellow.

NOSE Dusty office. Polished desk. Molasses toffee.

BODY Soft, sweet, and unassuming.

PALATE Lemon. Zesty. Talcum powder. Drying. Peat bed.

FINISH Short and polite. Surprisingly gentle.

Little trace of wood.

SCORE **67**

MACDUFF 40-year-old, Old Malt Cask, 50 vol

COLOR Mahogany.

NOSE Rich sherry. Church altar wine. Red-fruit trifle.

Some oaky tannins.

BODY Full, rich, and mouth coating.

PALATE English sherry trifle. Red fruit. Honeyed. Prunes. Some astringency

from the wood. Still quite soft.

FINISH Long. Drying as tannins kick in. Soft, smooth, and fruity.

SCORE **85**

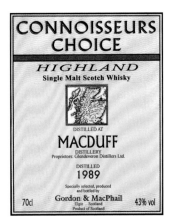

MACDUFF 1989, Connoisseurs Choice, 43 vol

COLOR Bronze.

NOSE Rooty. Green salad.

BODY Sweet, creamy, and full.

PALATE Sweet barley. Gentle spice. Unassuming. Some fruit. Pleasant.

FINISH Medium, with sugar and spice.

SCORE 73

MACDUFF 1968, 38-year-old, Duncan Taylor, 49.1 vol

COLOR Golden.

NOSE Sharp grape. Almond extract. Aniseed. Deep, vinous.
Bourbon and vanilla notes.

BODY Medium and sharp.

PALATE Old. Some citrus and barley notes, but they have to battle to
survive intense pepper and tannin.

FINISH Some fruity melon holds on, but mainly it is a medium
finish of oak and spice.

SCORE 76

MACDUFF 1969, 38-year-old, Lonarch, 40.3 vol

COLOR Gingery yellow.

NOSE Lemon cupcake. Pastry. Crème anglaise. Lime sherbet.

BODY Sweet and mouth coating. Intense.

PALATE Sugar and spice. Vanilla. Some citrus. Chili.

FINISH Medium. Lemon sherbet. Traces of almond.
Slightly bitter at the death.

SCORE 80

MANNOCHMORE

PRODUCER Diageo
REGION Highlands DISTRICT Speyside (Lossie)
ADDRESS By Elgin, Morayshire, IV30 3SF   TEL 01343 862000
WEBSITE www.malts.com

THE BLACK WHISKY Loch Dhu was produced here. This curious product was aimed at "image-conscious young men." Given the fashionability of black among young women, they may have felt excluded. Diageo insists that the color of the whisky derived from "a secret preparation, involving the double charring of selected bourbon barrels." The best guess is that the "preparation"—perhaps first a spraying and then a charring—involved caramelization.

The distillery is quite young itself, having been established in 1971–72. Its original role was to provide malt whisky as a component of the Haig blends, augmenting the production of its older neighbor, Glenlossie. The two are south of Elgin, and take their water from the Mannoch hills. With the same raw materials and location, the two make similar malts. Mannochmore's seems slightly less complex, but it is very enjoyable nonetheless.

HOUSE STYLE Fresh, flowery, dry. Aperitif.

MANNOCHMORE 12-year-old Provenance, Douglas Laing, 46 vol

COLOR Straw yellow.

NOSE Spring orchard. Grassy. Dried bark. Meadow flowers, honeysuckle. Vanilla.

BODY Light and unassertive. Quite clean. Fresh hay. Fresh ginger. Gentle spices.

FINISH Short, sweet, a touch of spice, and a trace of green fruit.

SCORE **79**

MILTONDUFF

PRODUCER Chivas Brothers (Pernod Ricard)
REGION Highlands   DISTRICT Speyside (Lossie)
ADDRESS Elgin, Morayshire, IV30 3TQ
TEL 01343 547433

THE BENEDICTINE PRIORY OF PLUSCARDEN, which still exists, was once a brewery—and provided the land on which the Miltonduff distillery stands. Although there is no other connection, the name of the Priory is invoked on the box that houses the Miltonduff bottle. The distillery, established in 1824, south of Elgin, was extensively modernized in the 1930s, and again in the 1970s. Its whisky is very important in the Ballantine blends. Formerly owned by Allied Distillers, Miltonduff was acquired by Pernod Ricard in 2005.

For a time, the company also had a Lomond still on the site. This produced a malt with similar characteristics to Miltonduff, but heavier, oilier, and smokier, identified as Mosstowie. That still has been dismantled, but the malt can occasionally be found in independent bottlings. The Miltonduff malt is well regarded by blenders, and makes a pleasant single.

HOUSE STYLE Flowery, scenty, clean, firm, elegant. Aperitif.

MILTONDUFF 7-year-old, Douglas Laing, 46 vol

COLOR Golden brown.

NOSE Lemon zest. Clementine. Barley malt. Incense notes. Honey.

BODY Medium full, rich, and pleasant.

PALATE Dark berries, dark chocolate, and raisins.
Chili-coated toffee. Traces of tannins, and gentle spices.

FINISH Long, rich, malty, and pleasant.

SCORE **80**

MORTLACH

PRODUCER Diageo
REGION Highlands   DISTRICT Speyside (Dufftown)
ADDRESS Dufftown, Banffshire, AB55 4AQ
TEL 01340 822100   WEBSITE www.malts.com

ALL THE PLEASURES OF A GOOD SPEYSIDE single malt are found in Mortlach: floweriness, peatiness, smokiness, maltiness, and fruitiness. Its complexity may well arise from its extraordinary miscellany of stills. In the course of a history stretching from the earliest days of legal distilling, successive managers seem to have been heretics: fiddling with the shape, size, and design of stills to achieve the result they desired. It seems that they strayed so far from the orthodoxies of the industry that they were never corralled, and the whisky was so good that no one wanted to risk changing it. Nor does anyone wholly understand how the combination of stills achieves its particular result. The whisky has such individuality that its character is not overwhelmed by sherry maturation. While UDV/Diageo has over the years moved away from sherry, and argued for "distillery character," Mortlach has not been bound by that orthodoxy, either. Mortlach has been sold as a 16-year-old in the past, but in 2014 Diageo replaced it with four new expressions, all of them a tribute to this excellent distillery.

HOUSE STYLE A Speyside classic: elegant and flowery
yet supple and muscular. Immensely complex, with great length.
After dinner or bedtime.

MORTLACH 18-year-old, 43.4 vol

COLOR Golden.

NOSE Tropical fruit. Overripe apples. Sweet mixed spices.
Vanilla. Hazelnut.

BODY Oily, thick, and full.

PALATE Molasses. Dark toffee. Lots of spice. More tropical fruit.
Scottish camp coffee. Chocolate. Some sweet fruit.

FINISH Superb, with chocolate-nut cookie, molasses, and earthy tannins
under a weighty fruit exit.

SCORE **94**

MORTLACH 25-year-old, 43.4 vol

COLOR Rich gold.

NOSE Floral, elegant, and with fragrant spice. Old furniture. Polished wood.

BODY Waxy, intense, and full.

PALATE Rich, waxy, complex, and full-flavored. Almond. Licorice.
Cocoa. The oak comes to the fore late with an array of spices and tannins.
Balance between sweetness, sharpness, and dryness. Works well.

FINISH Spicy, full, warming, and long.

SCORE **90**

MORTLACH **Rare Old, 43.4 vol**

COLOR Rich orange.

NOSE Fruit Jell-O. Marmalade. Sweet mango. Fresh and fruity. Very enticing.

BODY Soft, medium, and rounded.

PALATE Stewed fruit, puréed hazelnut, vanilla ice cream, and some herbs. Sherry berries are in the background. Surprisingly gentle.

FINISH Sweet and pleasant, with a touch of fruit and oak.

SCORE **85**

MORTLACH **1996, 18-year-old, Glen Mor, 52.3 Vol**

COLOR Gold.

NOSE Dusty, prickly, and with some fruit sherbet. Sooty and delicate.

BODY Medium full. Gloopy.

PALATE Very unusual. Quite perfumed. Light and floral. Rosehip. Peach. Rose water.

FINISH Light and gentle, with some lingering spice.

SCORE **81**

MORTLACH **21-year-old, Douglas of Drumlanrig, 50 vol**

COLOR Corn syrup.

NOSE Earthy, rich, and with yellow and green fruit.

BODY Full, rich, and sweet.

PALATE Given its age, surpassingly clean and fresh tasting, with lots of sweet fruit, a menthol "rancio" heart and layers of vanilla ice cream and banana.

FINISH Long and fruity.

SCORE **90**

OBAN

PRODUCER Diageo
REGION Highlands   DISTRICT Western Highlands
ADDRESS Stafford Street, Oban, Argyll, PA34 5NH
TEL 01631 572004   WEBSITE www.malts.com   VC

ENTHUSIASTS FOR THE WESTERN HIGHLAND malts sometimes dismiss Oban as being too restrained. With the 14-year-old augmented not only by the Montilla fino, but also by various limited releases, including a 21-year-old in 2013, there is now enough of an oeuvre to prove otherwise.

Oban is one of the few Western Highland distilleries on the mainland. It is a small distillery in a small town, but has a commanding position. Oban is regarded as the capital of the Western Highlands, and the distillery has a central site on the main street, facing the waterfront.

The principal expression of its whisky, the 14-year-old, has a label design incorporating a summary of the town's history: settled by Mesolithic cave dwellers before 5000BC; later by Celts, Picts, and Vikings. It was a fishing village, and in the era of trains and steamships became a gateway to the islands of the wests. Travelers following the muses of Mendelssohn, Turner, Keats, or Wordsworth to Mull, Iona, or Fingal's Cave, return to see a harbor centered on the distillery—backed by mossy, peaty hills from where its water flows.

A family of merchants in the town became brewers and distillers in 1794, though the present buildings probably date from the 1880s. The still-house was rebuilt in the late 1960s and early 1970s.

HOUSE STYLE Medium, with fresh peat and a whiff of the sea.
With seafood or game, or after dinner.

OBAN 1998 Distillers Edition, Bottled 2013, 43 vol
Finished in Montilla fino casks.

COLOR Amber, with orange facets.
NOSE Pear-flavored hard candy, orange, and bananas,
with a whiff of ozone and smoke.
BODY Rich.
PALATE Soft toffee, peaches, and almonds, sprinkled with sea salt.
FINISH Medium in length, with honey and gingery oak.

SCORE **81**

OBAN 14-year-old, 43 vol

COLOR Full gold to amber.

NOSE "Pebbles on the beach," said one taster. A whiff of the sea, but also a touch of fresh peat, and some maltiness.

BODY Firm, smooth, and slightly viscous.

PALATE Deceptively delicate at first. Perfumy. Faint hint of fruity seaweed. Then lightly waxy, becoming smoky. Dry.

FINISH Aromatic, smooth, and appetizing.

SCORE **79**

OBAN 21-year-old, Special Releases 2013, 58.5 vol

COLOR Gold, with copper highlights.

NOSE Buttery toffee balanced by brine, red apples, cinnamon, and ginger.

BODY Full and smooth.

PALATE Malt, butterscotch, ginger, and nutmeg, with a hint of sea salt.

FINISH Dark chocolate, sea spray, and wood spice.

SCORE **84**

OBAN Managers' Choice, Distilled 2000, Bottled 2009, 58.7 vol

Matured in a European oak sherry cask.

COLOR Burnished gold.

NOSE Maple syrup, toffee bonbons, spicy salt, and delicate smoke.

BODY Relatively full.

PALATE Fresh citrus fruit, hazelnuts, and a tang of sea salt.

FINISH Dries steadily to dark chocolate.

SCORE **80**

OLD PULTENEY

PRODUCER Inver House Distillers Ltd.
REGION Highlands DISTRICT Northern Highlands
ADDRESS Huddart Street, Wick, Caithness, KW1 5BD
WEBSITE www.inverhouse.com/www.oldpulteney.com
EMAIL enquiries@inverhouse.com VC

ONE OF WHISKY'S GREAT DEBATES (or was it a tempest in a copita?) began here, and went public in 2003: do coastal whiskies really taste of salt? The debate surfaced in *Whisky Magazine*, but the salty suggestion had first been made in respect to Old Pulteney 25 years earlier, in the wine magazine *Decanter*.

Not only is the Pulteney distillery on the coast, but until the opening of Wolfburn at Thurso in 2013, it was the northernmost distillery on the Scottish mainland, in the town of Wick, in the famously peaty, rock-faced county of Caithness. Part of the town was designed by Thomas Telford and built by Sir William Pulteney in 1810 as a model fishing port. The distillery, founded in 1826, is in "Pulteneytown." It is thus one of the few urban distilleries, albeit only 250 yards from the closest part of the waterfront. Even that walk can be sufficiently windy to demand a dram. "Caithness is a bare county, and needs a good whisky to warm it up," observed an early writer on the water of life, Professor R. J. S. McDowall. He was referring to Old Pulteney.

HOUSE STYLE Fresh, salty, appetizing. Predinner.

OLD PULTENEY 12-year-old, 40 vol

COLOR Deep yellow.

NOSE Dry. Peat, grass, and sweet broom.

BODY Light and oily.

PALATE Light. Still honey and nuts, but oilier.

FINISH Oily. Soothing. Very salty.

SCORE **79**

OLD PULTENEY 17-year-old, 46 vol

COLOR Rich orange.

NOSE Subtle and shy but, with time, melon, gooseberry, vanilla, and light citrus.

BODY Soft and rounded, slightly oily, and mouth coating.

PALATE Sweet, with green fruit, barley, and eventually soft spice and oakiness.

FINISH Fruit first, then pepper, spice, and some tannins. Quite long.

SCORE **82**

OLD PULTENEY 21-year-old, 46 vol

COLOR Rich orange.

NOSE Earthy, with citrus, medicinal, brine, and spice notes.

BODY Full, oily, and mouth coating.

PALATE Rich orange, salty, but at the same time creamy rich, full, and sweet.

FINISH Soft toffee, some trademark salt and pepper. Pleasantly rounded and impressive.

SCORE **85**

OLD PULTENEY 2013, 30-year-old, 40.1 vol

COLOR Rich amber.

NOSE Sweet, with zesty fruit notes, caramel apples, and banana.

BODY Full.

PALATE More apple and banana, and sweet oak.

FINISH Cereal and soft oak.

SCORE **86**

OLD PULTENEY 35-year-old, 42.5 vol

COLOR Light amber.

NOSE Light fruit notes, notably tangerines, plus vanilla, lemon, and sea salt.

BODY Silky.

PALATE Orchard fruit, spicy sherry, worn leather, and cocoa powder.

FINISH Spicy and drying, with mild oak tannins.

SCORE **87**

OLD PULTENEY 40-year-old, 51.3 vol

Four casks yielded 493 bottles. Three casks were ex-sherry hogsheads
and one was an American oak ex-bourbon barrel.

COLOR Rich amber.

NOSE Soft and fragrant, toffee and peaches in syrup.

BODY Smooth.

PALATE Early intense orchard fruit, then nutmeg, cinnamon,
and black coffee.

FINISH Long, with spicy oak tannins and Seville orange. Notably drying.

SCORE **85**

OLD PULTENEY Navigator, 46 vol

COLOR Rich gold.

NOSE Quite complex, with sherry, Cream soda,
cocoa, and orange peel.

BODY Medium to full.

PALATE Lively nutmeg and ginger, plus Jaffa oranges and milky coffee.

FINISH Slowly drying, a hint of brine and lingering citrus notes.

SCORE **79**

OLD PULTENEY 1990, 46 vol

COLOR Amber.

NOSE A whiff of ozone, lemon, vanilla, and coconut; fleeting wood smoke.

BODY Medium.

PALATE Intense, creamy tropical fruitiness merges with milk chocolate, lemon sorbet, and lively spices.

FINISH Spicy milk chocolate, with a citric and softly peaty tang.

SCORE 87

TRAVEL RETAIL

OLD PULTENEY Noss Head Lighthouse, 46 vol

COLOR Golden amber.

NOSE Fragrant, with vanilla, lemon, and ozone.

BODY Medium.

PALATE Tropical fruit, milk chocolate, and salted caramel.

FINISH Medium in length, with wood spices.

SCORE 80

OLD PULTENEY Duncansby Head Lighthouse, 46 vol

COLOR Golden amber with bronze highlights.

NOSE Initially earthy, then brine develops, along with apple pie.

BODY Smooth.

PALATE Cooked apples, golden raisins, sherry, orange, and nutmeg.

FINISH Spicy and rounded.

SCORE 83

OLD PULTENEY Pentland Skerries Lighthouse, 46 vol

COLOR Deep amber.

NOSE Fruitcake fresh from the oven, caramel, worn leather, and salted nuts.

BODY Full.

PALATE Sherry, figs, spices, and a hint of brine.

FINISH Autumn fruit, sherry, and marine notes.

SCORE 84

ROYAL LOCHNAGAR

PRODUCER Diageo
REGION Highlands   DISTRICT Eastern Highlands
ADDRESS Crathie, Ballater, Aberdeenshire, AB35 5TB
TEL 01339 742705
WEBSITE www.discovering-distilleries.com/www.malts.com   VC

QUEEN VICTORIA'S FAVORITE DISTILLERY was once on the tourist route, but has recently been used by Diageo as a place in which to educate its own staff and customers on the subject of malt whisky. The process of making whisky can best be understood in a small, traditional distillery, and Lochnagar qualifies on both counts. It is Diageo's smallest. It is also very pretty—and makes delicious whisky.

The distillery is at the foot of the mountain of Lochnagar, near the river Dee, not far from Aberdeen. A man believed originally to have been an illicit whisky maker established the first legal Lochnagar distillery in 1826, and the present premises were built in 1845. Three years later, the royal family acquired nearby Balmoral as their Scottish country home. The then owner, John Begg, wrote a note inviting Prince Albert to visit. The Prince and Queen Victoria arrived the very next day. Soon afterward, the distillery began to supply the Queen, and became known as Royal Lochnagar. Her Majesty is said to have laced her claret with the whisky, perhaps anticipating wood finishes. There is no claret finish at Lochnagar as yet. The 12-year-old is aged in second-fill casks.

HOUSE STYLE Malty, fruity, spicy, cakelike. After dinner.

ROYAL LOCHNAGAR 12-year-old, 40 vol

COLOR Full gold.

NOSE Big, with some smokiness.

BODY Medium to full. Smooth.

PALATE Light smokiness, restrained fruitiness, and malty sweetness.

FINISH Again, dry smokiness and malty sweetness. The first impression is of dryness, then comes the sweet, malty counterpoint.

SCORE 80

ROYAL LOCHNAGAR Selected Reserve, No Age Statement, 43 vol

COLOR Amber red.

NOSE Very sherryish indeed. Spices and ginger cake.

BODY Big and smooth.

PALATE Lots of sherry, malty sweetness, spiced bread, and ginger cake. Obviously contains some very well-matured whisky.

FINISH Smoky.

SCORE 83

ROYAL LOCHNAGAR 30-year-old, Rare Malts, Distilled 1974, 56.2 vol

COLOR Pale gold.

NOSE Cut grass; slightly spirity.

BODY Medium.

PALATE Apples and a sprinkling of pepper and ginger.

FINISH Long, dry, and astringent.

SCORE 80

AN INDEPENDENT BOTTLING

ROYAL LOCHNAGAR 22-year-old, Distilled 1986, Bottled 2009, Cask No. 942 (Duncan Taylor), 56.4 vol

COLOR Bright gold.

NOSE Rose petals, green wood, and gentle spices.

BODY Firm.

PALATE Nutty and spicy, fresh oak sawdust, and linseed.

FINISH Medium, with ginger, delicate smoke, and slightly assertive oak.

SCORE 79

SCAPA

PRODUCER Chivas Brothers (Pernod Ricard)
REGION Highlands   ISLAND Orkney
ADDRESS St Ola, Kirkwall, Orkney, KW15 1SE
TEL 01856 872071   WEBSITE www.scapamalt.com

FORMERLY OWNED BY ALLIED DISTILLERS, Scapa was acquired by Pernod Ricard in 2005. The distillery had been operated intermittently, and marketed sporadically, but, nearing its 120th anniversary, it underwent a complete renovation and reopened in 2004. It retains its two stills, and the restored waterwheel, which once powered the distillery in the early 19th century.

Scapa's greatest asset is its evocative location. Scapa Flow, a stretch of water linking the North Sea to the Atlantic, is famous for its role in both World Wars.

The water for the distillery's mash tun is from springs that feed a stream called the Lingro Burn. The water is very peaty, though the distillery uses wholly unpeated malt. Scapa has a Lomond wash still, which may contribute to the slight oiliness of the whisky. Maturation is in bourbon casks. Although the whisky is quite light in flavor, it has a distinctive complex of vanilla notes, sometimes suggesting very spicy chocolate, and nutty, rooty saltiness.

HOUSE STYLE Salt, hay. Oily, spicy chocolate.
After a hearty walk, before dinner.

SCAPA 12-year-old, 40 vol

COLOR Bright, full gold.

NOSE Softer. Hay. Warm.

BODY Light, smooth, and salty.

PALATE Clean and sweetish. Vanilla, nuts, and salt.

FINISH Late salt and pepper, with a hint of peat.

SCORE **76**

SCAPA 14-year-old, Cask Strength Edition,
Distilled 1992, Bottled 2006, Batch SC 14001, 60.6 vol

COLOR Deep gold.

NOSE Menthol and minty straw with a hint of grapefruit.
Chocolate-covered cherries.

BODY Sinewy, silkily smooth, mouth coating, and slightly oily.

PALATE More minty straw, with vanilla and a hint of citrus.
Water brings out oak.

FINISH Long, peppery, and dry, with a return of menthol.

SCORE **85**

SCAPA 16-year-old, 40 vol

COLOR Full gold. Brass.

NOSE Sweet and inviting. Peaches and custard, with a trace
of ocean air, as if near a beach.

BODY Slippery, slightly oily, smooth, and salty.

PALATE Clean, sweet custard with floral notes; vanilla with
a hint of coconut.

FINISH Late salt and pepper, with a hint of peat.

SCORE **79**

SPEYBURN

PRODUCER Inver House Distillers Ltd.
REGION Highlands   DISTRICT Speyside (Rothes)
ADDRESS Rothes, Aberlour, Morayshire, AB38 7AG
WEBSITE www.inverhouse.com   EMAIL enquiries@inverhouse.com

PRETTY AS A PICTURE: both the growing range of whiskies (flowery and fruity) and the distillery (a much photographed Victorian classic, masked by trees in a deep, sweeping valley). Speyburn makes a spectacular sight on the road out of Rothes, heading toward Elgin. It was built in 1897 and, despite various modernizations over the years, has not undergone dramatic change, though in 2014 capacity was more than doubled to four million liters. In the early 1990s, Speyburn was acquired by Inver House.

HOUSE STYLE Flowery, herbal, heathery. Aperitif.

SPEYBURN 10-year-old, 40 vol

COLOR Solid gold.

NOSE Flowery.

BODY Medium, gentle.

PALATE Clean. Lightly malty. Developing fresh, herbal, and heathery notes.

FINISH Fresh, very sweet, and lightly syrupy.

SCORE **71**

SPEYBURN 25-year-old, 46 vol

COLOR Golden amber.

NOSE Very floral and fragrant, with violet candy, honey, and cream.

BODY Relatively full.

PALATE Creamy, nutty, and spicy, with dried fruit and a wisp of smoke.

FINISH Long, with drying spices and oak tannins.

SCORE **81**

SPEYBURN Bradan Orach, 40 vol

COLOR Bright gold.

NOSE Raw oats, mash tuns, ripe bananas, and honey.

BODY Medium.

PALATE Malty on the palate, with brittle toffee, vanilla,
and spice on the palate.

FINISH Ginger and vanilla, medium in length.

SCORE **69**

SPEYSIDE

PRODUCER Speyside Distillers Co. Ltd.
REGION Highlands   DISTRICT Speyside
ADDRESS Tromie Mills, Glentromie, Kingussie, PH21 1HS
TEL 01540 661060
WEBSITE www.speysidedistillers.co.uk   VC By appointment

SPEYSIDE IS A SMALL DISTILLERY that made its first spirit in late 1990. In recent years, it has been developing a portfolio of more mature whiskies, initially under other names and more recently as Speyside. The handsome, gabled stone building is intended to look old and traditional. Its opening was the realization of a dream for its original owner, whisky blender George Christie, who had planned it for three or four decades. His progress on the project ebbed and flowed with the fortunes of the industry. One of his earlier essays was a vatted malt, popular in the US under the name Glentromie.

The distillery is in the hamlet of Drumguish, where the tiny river Tromie flows into the highest reaches of the Spey, and hence the name for some of the whiskies that issue from the distillery. The company, Speyside, takes its name, not only from its location but also from a distillery by that name which operated in nearby Kingussie between 1895 and 1910.

In 2012 whisky dealer John Harvey McDonough, owner of Harvey's of Edinburgh Ltd., acquired Speyside Distillers Co. Ltd. Harvey's produce a range of single malts under the "Spey" label.

HOUSE STYLE Oily, nutty, lightly peaty. Aperitif.

SPEYSIDE 12-year old, 43 vol

COLOR Orange amber.

NOSE Orange zest, touch of cloves, and oak.

BODY Moderate. Slightly oily. Chewy.

PALATE Orange oil on oak.

FINISH Dry, lingering, and warming. Orange oil polish.

SCORE 76

SPRINGBANK

PRODUCER Springbank Distillers Ltd.
REGION Campbeltown DISTRICT Argyll
ADDRESS Well Close, Campbeltown, Argyll, PA28 6ET
TEL 01586 552085 VC Summer only by appointment

WITH THE OPENING OF SPRINGBANK'S new "sister" distillery of Glengyle in 2004, Scotland's one-time whisky capital of Campbeltown gained renewed credibility as an autonomous malt whisky region. The production at Springbank, from 1997 onward, of a triple-distilled, unpeated single malt under the Hazelburn name has added even more momentum. In eight and 12-year-old expressions, Hazelburn is now a fully-fledged member of the Springbank core range of whiskies. The original Hazelburn distillery, which closed in 1925, having existed since 1796, was an immediate neighbor of Springbank.

Springbank's own whisky is made from medium-peated malt, with a trajectory that amounts to two-and-a-half times distillation. With its brininess, its oily, coconut-like flavors, and its great complexity, Springbank features in almost every whisky lover's top ten malts.

Springbank dates from the 1820s, and even earlier as an illicit still. Its present proprietor, and tireless revivalist of Campbeltown distilling, Hedley Wright, is a member of the founding Mitchell family.

In the early 1990s, Springbank revived its own floor maltings. It now uses only its own malt. (Among other distilleries with their own floor maltings, none is self-sufficient.) This has been of particular benefit in the production of another revivalist malt, Longrow, first released in 1985. Springbank first distilled Longrow in 1973–74.

Longrow is double distilled from heavily peated malt. With its own maltings, the distillery can achieve exactly the character of peatiness it requires. In their peatiness, oiliness, brininess, and sense of restrained power, the Longrows are becoming cult whiskies. The original Longrow distillery closed in 1896. It adjoined the Springbank site.

Over the centuries, the town has had about 30 distilleries, some of which ruined their reputations by producing hurried whiskies for the US during Prohibition, and closed soon afterward. Vestiges remain in a bus depot, an office park, and other manifestations. The sites were diligently mapped by former Director of Production Frank McHardy, who manages Springbank. Campbeltown was the great whisky region in the age of coastal steamers, before the railroads made Speyside more accessible.

As an isolated independent with its own underutilized bottling line, in 1969, J. & A. Mitchell bought the century-old firm of Cadenhead. This company, formerly based in Aberdeen, has always been an independent bottler. Both Springbank and Cadenhead use the same bottling line, in Campbeltown, but they are run as separate enterprises.

Neither company chill filters its whiskies, or adds caramel to balance the color. Being long-established enterprises, they have a considerable inventory of casks. Some Springbank once even found its way into a couple of casks of acacia wood. As awareness of woods has increased in the industry, Springbank has mainly acquired bourbon barrels, to highlight the character of the whisky itself, but most bottlings are vatted to give a touch of color and sweetness from sherry wood.

With a maltings, two distilleries, four single malts, an independent bottlings business, and a chain of stores (Eaglesome's in Campbeltown and Cadenhead's in Edinburgh and London), J. & A. Mitchell has ensured that Campbeltown remains a whisky center. This surge of activity was the response of Hedley Wright to a suggestion that Springbank and its local rival, Glen Scotia, were insufficient justification for the town retaining its status (along with Islay, the Highlands, and the Lowlands) as one of the whisky regions. Mr. Wright can be famously taciturn, but his actions are stentorian.

The geography itself is tenuous. Hanging from the coast by a neck of land only 1 mile (1.6 kilometers) wide, Kintyre looks like an island, but is actually a peninsula, stretching 40 miles (65 kilometers) south. Physically, either an island or a peninsula might better qualify as a region, but there are no distilleries until the town itself, which is near the southern extremity. At this point, the peninsula is at its widest, but still less than 10 miles (16 kilometers) across. Drive and climb to Crosshill Loch, and the sea is visible to both east and west, as are Islay and Arran on a clear day.

This loch has provided water for all the Campbeltown distilleries: an unusual situation that perhaps accounts for some similarities of character. To the immediate south of the town, the land narrows at the tip, or "mull" of the peninsula. This is the mull of Kintyre, where the mist rolls in from the sea just as Paul McCartney promised it would. It hangs over the back-street warehouses of the curiously urban distilleries, and entraps the ghosts of all those whiskies past. No wonder Springbank and Longrow have so much character.

HOUSE STYLE Springbank: salty, oily, coconut. Aperitif.
Longrow: piney, oily, damp earth. Nightcap.

SPRINGBANK 9-year-old, Gaja Barolo Wood Expression, 54.7 vol

COLOR Amber.

NOSE Slightly earthy, with a hint of brine, dried fruit, and nutmeg.

BODY Firm.

PALATE More dried fruit, oak tannins, sea salt, and black pepper.

FINISH Drying, with pepper and oak.

SCORE **83**

SPRINGBANK 10-year-old, 46 vol

COLOR Gold.

NOSE Light brine, spice, rounded malt, and pear. Elegant for a youngster.

BODY Rich and oily. Mouth coating.

PALATE Fantastic mix of dry and sweet. Canned pear. Citrus.

A suggestion of smoke.

FINISH Melon.

SCORE **83**

SPRINGBANK 12-year-old, Cask Strength (Batch 9), 54.3 vol

COLOR Mid-gold.

NOSE New leather, sherry, white pepper, and green olives;

becoming more floral, with wood polish.

BODY Full and rounded.

PALATE Sweet and fruity, earthy peat, barley sugar, and dark chocolate.

FINISH Peat smoke, milk chocolate, and ginger, with a shake of sea salt.

SCORE **88**

SPRINGBANK 12-year-old, Calvados Wood, 52.7 vol

COLOR Mid-gold.

NOSE Spice, vanilla, and caramel apples.

BODY Medium to full.

PALATE Red peppers, wine, cinnamon, and subtle peat.

FINISH Drying. Lime and peat.

SCORE 85

SPRINGBANK 15-year-old, 46 vol

COLOR Light amber.

NOSE Sophisticated. Dundee cake, vanilla, new leather,
pipe tobacco, dried apricot, peat, and tea.

BODY Full and rich. Mouth coating.

PALATE European oak is there, but doesn't dominate. Sweet
tobacco, nut, and smoke in the background. Complex.

FINISH Soot. Malt.

SCORE 90

SPRINGBANK 1997, 16-year-old, Single Cask, 46 vol

COLOR Mid-gold.

NOSE Rum-raisin ice cream and graham crackers.

BODY Full and rounded.

PALATE Deep fruit notes, honey, light peat, and sea salt.

FINISH Medium to long. Lingering peat, malt, and citrus fruit.

SCORE 89

SPRINGBANK 18-year-old, 46 vol

COLOR Deep gold.

NOSE Sweet sherry, hazelnuts, apricots, angelica, and malt.

BODY Full and creamy.

PALATE Fresh fruit, molasses, licorice, white pepper, sherry, and sweet smoke.

FINISH Slowly drying, with cinnamons and mild oak tannins.

SCORE 90

SPRINGBANK 2014, 21-year-old, 46 vol

COLOR Gold.

NOSE Sherry, vanilla, toffee, tropical fruit, and freshly cut peat.

BODY Rich.

PALATE Dry sherry, vanilla, figs, bonfire smoke, and brine.

FINISH Lengthy, with peat, caramel, cinnamon, and sea salt.

SCORE 91

SPRINGBANK **Rundlets and Kilderkins, 49.4 vol**

COLOR Bronze.

NOSE Rich, with caramel, sherry, new oak, cloves, and a hint of coal.

BODY Smooth and creamy.

PALATE Milk chocolate, honey, brine, and young wood.

FINISH Lengthy, caramel, and warm tar.

SCORE **88**

LONGROW

LONGROW **11-year-old, Red, Port Cask, 51.8 vol**

COLOR Reddish orange.

NOSE Sweet, with cherries, caramel, new leather,

chewing tobacco, and soft peat.

BODY Voluptuous.

PALATE Rich peat, summer berries, and caramel apples,

with growing spice notes and light oak.

FINISH Lengthy, with cinnamon, peat, sweet oak, and red berries.

SCORE **88**

LONGROW **14-year-old, 46 vol**

COLOR Straw.

NOSE Barley, fresh cream, and apples. Subdued peat.

BODY Textured and oily.

PALATE Sweet and fruity, with malt, pepper, and smoke.

FINISH Peat, pepper, and brine.

SCORE **87**

LONGROW 18-year-old, 46 vol

COLOR Mid-amber.

NOSE Initially earthy and savory, with linseed and old leather, then cloves and tide pools.

BODY Voluptuous.

PALATE Sweet and spicy. Peppery peat.

FINISH Drying steadily, with peat smoke and lively spices.

SCORE **88**

LONGROW Peated, 46 vol

COLOR Chardonnay.

NOSE Peaches and vanilla, light smoke, mild cloves, and brine.

BODY Medium and rounded.

PALATE Sweet spices and soft, fruity peat, then focused smoke.

FINISH Medium in length, with more sweet spices and a sprinkling of salt.

SCORE **82**

HAZELBURN
HAZELBURN CV, 46 vol

COLOR Straw.

NOSE Initially slightly mashy and herbal, with acetone
and cigarette packages. Citric and more malty with time.

BODY Smooth.

PALATE Spicy, with orange, ginger, vanilla, and sherbet zest.

FINISH Medium in length and spicy, with a slight suggestion of salt.

 SCORE 84

HAZELBURN Triple-distilled 8-year-old, 46 vol

COLOR Pale gold.

NOSE Light, fruity, and faintly resinous.

BODY Medium.

PALATE Lively, with malt, banana, a touch of sherry, and vanilla essence.

FINISH Caramel, pear-flavored hard candy, and spicy oak.

SCORE 85

HAZELBURN 10-year-old, 46 vol

COLOR Pale gold.

NOSE Lemon, honey, salted caramel, and white pepper.

BODY Medium.

PALATE Apricots and cream, honey, and soft spices.

FINISH Orchard fruit, soft oak, and a hint of aniseed.

 SCORE 87

Distilled Nov. 2003   Aged **10** Years   Bottled Jan. 2014
No. of Bottles 12000
70cl **RUNDLETS & KILDERKINS** 50.1%vol
J.&A. Mitchell & Co. Ltd.
Springbank Distillery · Campbeltown · Scotland

HAZELBURN 10-year-old, 3rd Release
(Rundlets and Kilderkins), 50.1 vol

COLOR Amber.

NOSE Milk chocolate, malt, and honey, with a tangy marine
note in the background.

BODY Unctuous.

PALATE Soft fruit, almonds, brittle toffee, and lots of spice.

FINISH Long and earthy. Initial caramel and vanilla notes
are replaced by oak and brine.

SCORE 88

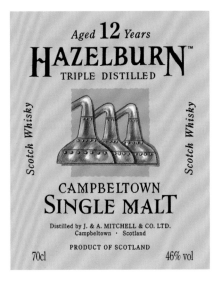

HAZELBURN Triple-distilled 12-year-old, 46 vol

COLOR Light bronze.

NOSE Rich and sherried, with milk-chocolate-coated caramels, apricots, and almonds.

BODY Relatively full.

PALATE Spice, malt, almonds, and cocoa powder.

FINISH Long and spicy. Soft fruit and milky coffee.

SCORE **88**

STRATHISLA

PRODUCER Chivas Brothers (Pernod Ricard)
REGION Highland   DISTRICT Speyside (Strathisla)
ADDRESS Seafield Avenue, Keith, Banffshire, AB55 3BS
TEL 01542 783044   VC

THE OLDEST DISTILLERY in the north of Scotland has its roots in the 13th century, when Dominican monks used a nearby spring to provide water for brewing beer. The same water, with a touch of calcium hardness and scarcely any peat character, has been used in the distillation of whisky since at least 1786.

Strathisla, which has also at times been known as Milltown, began its life as a farm distillery. It was rebuilt after a fire in 1876, and, over the years, has been restored and added to, creating a somewhat idealized traditional distillery. Chivas bought it in the 1950s.

Lightly peated malt is used, as well as wood washbacks and small stills. Although wood washbacks are by no means unusual, Strathisla believes that fermentation characteristics play a very important part in the character of its dry, fruity, oaky malt whisky.

HOUSE STYLE Dry, fruity. After dinner.

STRATHISLA 12-year-old, 43 vol

COLOR Full, deep gold.

NOSE Apricot. Cereal grains. Fresh, juicy oak.

BODY Medium, rounded.

PALATE Sherryish. Fruity. Mouth coating. Teasing sweet-and-dry character.

FINISH Smooth and soothing. Violets and vanilla.

SCORE **80**

STRATHISLA 1990, 57.8 vol

Distillery-only bottling.

COLOR Corn syrup.

NOSE Assorted jellybeans. Vanilla. British summer pudding. Bright and cheerful.

BODY Rich and mouth coating.

PALATE Sweet and very fruity. Lemon-lime sugar-coated candy. Clean and sweet early on, then late spice and tannins from the cask.

FINISH Long, with fruit, tannins, and oaky spice.

SCORE **85**

STRATHMILL

PRODUCER Diageo
REGION Highlands   DISTRICT Speyside (Strathisla)
ADDRESS Keith, Banffshire, AB55 5DQ
TEL 01542 885000   WEBSITE www.malts.com

GRAPES HAVE TO BE CRUSHED; grain has to be milled. The town of Keith must once have been a considerable grain-milling center. The Glen Keith distillery was built on the site of a grain mill. Strathmill, as its name suggests, went one better. It was rebuilt from a grain mill, in 1891, when the whisky industry was having one of its periodic upswings. Three years later, it was acquired by Gilbey, of which Justerini & Brooks became a subsidiary through IDV (Diageo). Arguably, it has been in the same ownership for more than a century. Its whisky was for many years central to the Dunhill/Old Master blends, but only became available as a single for the first time since 1909, with the release of a 1980 bottling by the wine-merchant chain Oddbins in 1993.

HOUSE STYLE The whisky world's answer to orange muscat. With dessert.

STRATHMILL 25-year-old, Special Releases 2014, 52.4 vol

COLOR Yellowy green.

NOSE Quite shy but better with water. Lime compote. Stewed orange. Fruit cordial. Chocolate-covered orange cookies

BODY Medium and unassertive.

PALATE Sweet and light. Definitely Speyside, with light fruit and berries. Menthol. Candy sticks.

FINISH Medium and sweet, with some licorice and menthol.

SCORE 82

TALISKER

PRODUCER Diageo
REGION Highlands ISLAND Skye
ADDRESS Carbost, Isle of Skye, IV47 8SR
TEL 01478 614308
WEBSITE www.discovering-distilleries.com/www.malts.com VC

ALREADY VOLCANICALLY POWERFUL, Talisker has boosted its impact in recent years by adding new expressions. However many versions there may be, it remains a singular malt. It has a distinctively peppery character, so hot as to make one taster's temples steam. The phrase "explodes on the palate" is among the descriptions used for certain whiskies by blenders at Diageo; surely they had Talisker in mind when they composed this. "The lava of the Cuillins" was another taster's response. The Cuillins are the dramatic hills of Skye, the island home of Talisker. The distillery is on the west coast of the island, on the shores of Loch Harport, in an area where Gaelic is still spoken.

After a number of false starts on other sites, the distillery was established in 1831 and expanded in 1900. For much of its life, it used triple distillation, and in those days Robert Louis Stevenson ranked Talisker as a style on its own, comparable with the Islay and Livet whiskies. It switched to double distillation in 1928, and was partly rebuilt in 1960. The distillery uses traditional cooling coils—"worm tubs"—which can make for a fuller flavor than a modern condenser.

Some malt lovers still mourn the youthfully dry assertiveness of the eight-year-old version that was replaced by the current, more rounded version a couple of summers older. For a time, this was the only expression, but official bottlings have multiplied. As if to balance an equation, independent bottlings are now extremely rare.

The island is also home to an unrelated company making a vatted malt called Poit Dubh, and a blend, Te Bheag. Both are said to contain some Talisker, and their hearty palates appear to support this. A dry, perfumy, blended whisky called Isle of Skye is made by the Ian Macleod Distillers, owners of Glengoyne and Tamdhu distilleries. The whisky liqueur represented by Drambuie is also said to have been created on the Isle of Skye, though its origins actually remain clouded in Scotch mist.

HOUSE STYLE Volcanic. A winter warmer.

TALISKER 10-year-old, 45.8 vol

COLOR Bright amber red.

NOSE Pungent, smoke-accented, and rounded.

BODY Full, slightly syrupy.

PALATE Smoky and malty sweet, with sourness and
a very big pepperiness developing.

FINISH Very peppery. Huge, long.

SCORE **90**

TALISKER 18-year-old, 45.8 vol

COLOR Rich orange.

NOSE Seaside. Peat, seaweed, rich pepper.

BODY Full, rich, and creamy.

PALATE Immense and rich. Classic Talisker, but richer than the
10-year-old. Lots of rich fruit, with oak and peat arriving later.

FINISH Perfectly balanced. Pleasant and long, with pepper
and peat in the conclusion.

SCORE **94**

TALISKER 2002, Distillers Edition, Amoroso Finish, Bottled 2013, 45.8 vol

Finished in an amoroso sherry cask.

COLOR Chestnut.

NOSE Hard candy, smoky sherry, and butterscotch.

BODY Full and rich.

PALATE Molasses, malt, and vanilla, with dry peat and mild pepperiness.

FINISH Peat, cocoa powder, and a lingering fruity sweetness.

SCORE **86**

TALISKER Port Ruighe, 45.8 vol

Finished in ex-port casks.

COLOR Antique gold.

NOSE Bacon, damp soil, ripe plums, and dark chocolate.
Sweetening, with a marine note and black pepper.

BODY Full.

PALATE Smoky peat, with a spicy, sweet red-wine edge.

FINISH Medium in length, with oak, black coffee, and dark chocolate.

SCORE **84**

TALISKER Triple Matured Edition, 48 vol

COLOR Dark gold.

NOSE Ozone, fresh asphalt, dried fruit, and old leather.

BODY Soft and full.

PALATE A blast of pepper, backed by earthy peat, wet cloth
Band-Aids, vanilla, and citrus fruit.

FINISH Drying steadily, with pepper and charcoal.

SCORE **87**

TALISKER 57 Degrees North, 57 vol

COLOR Rich orange.

NOSE Seaweed. Damp boathouse. Islay-like peat and seaweed.

BODY Mouth coating. Oily. Full.

PALATE Sweet and peaty. Very smoky, but with peach and apricot
and apple pits. Oily and spicy. Fatter and fuller than most Taliskers.
Aggressive and masculine.

FINISH Long and peaty; the trademark pepper appears at the end.

SCORE **86**

TALISKER Storm, 45.8 vol

COLOR Mid-gold.

NOSE Brine, burning wood embers, vanilla, and honey.

BODY Firm and full.

PALATE Sweet and spicy, with cranberries and black currants, ozone, peat, and black pepper.

FINISH Spicy, with walnuts and fruity peat.

SCORE **86**

TALISKER 25-year-old, 45.8 vol

COLOR Dark amber.

NOSE A sprinkling of salt, before sweet and spicy notes arrive, with summer berries, heather honey, and subtle peat.

BODY Relatively full.

PALATE Spicy and quite dry, with citrus fruit, licorice, aniseed, and smoldering peat.

FINISH Medium in length, peppery, and quite tannic.

SCORE **89**

TALISKER 30-year-old, 45.8 vol

COLOR Antique copper.

NOSE Soft fruit and fragrant malt, milk chocolate, and dry peat.

BODY Rounded and rich.

PALATE Lemon, licorice sticks, molasses toffee, black pepper,
and burning oak.

FINISH Lengthy and hot, with peat and allspice.

SCORE **91**

TALISKER 1985, 27-year-old, Special Releases 2013, 56.1 vol

COLOR Rich amber, with golden facets.

NOSE Brine, dark chocolate, new leather, savory notes, and sweet smoke.

BODY Oily.

PALATE Earthy, with ashy peat, more brine and dark chocolate,
dried fruit, and cloves.

FINISH Beach bonfires, autumn berries, and coal fires.

SCORE **91**

TALISKER 35-year-old (Special Releases 2012), 54.6 vol

COLOR Gold.

NOSE Fragrant wood smoke, nutmeg, golden raisins, and chili.

BODY Oily and full.

PALATE Fresh soil, savory notes, dried fruit, vanilla, and more chili.

FINISH Brine, orange peel, and bonfire smoke.

SCORE 92

TALISKER 1994, Managers' Choice, 58.6 vol

Matured in a bodega sherry European oak cask; 582 bottles.

COLOR Old gold.

NOSE Warm, worn leather, soft peat, and exotic spices.

BODY Full and supple.

PALATE Early citrus fruit gives way to sweeter apples;
then characteristic Talisker peat and black pepper emerge.

FINISH Lengthy, with lots of smoldering peat and insistent spices.

SCORE 89

TALISKER 175th Anniversary Edition, 45.8 vol

COLOR Amber.

NOSE Sweetness overlying smoke. Elegant heather and bourbon
notes in the background.

BODY Rounded.

PALATE Sweet and smoky, coconut, spices, and a hint of licorice.

FINISH Long and slightly salty, with insistent peat smoke.

SCORE 87

TRAVEL RETAIL
TALISKER Dark Storm, 45.8 vol

COLOR Deep amber.

NOSE Citric, with fruity spices, brine, and intensifying wood smoke.

BODY Voluptuous.

PALATE Pepper, apricot, vanilla, abundant smoke, and a hint of char.

FINISH Medium in length; ginger, Seville orange, chili,
pepper, and charcoal.

SCORE 86

TAMDHU

PRODUCER Ian Macleod Distillers Ltd.
REGION Highlands   DISTRICT Speyside
ADDRESS Knockando, Morayshire, AB38 7RP

THIS DISTILLERY IS STILL somewhat overshadowed by its charismatic neighbor, Macallan, six or seven miles downriver. Traditionally, both malts have been significant contributors to The Famous Grouse, the biggest selling blend in Scotland. As singles, their fortunes have differed. Under the ownership of Edrington, Macallan was promoted as the group's principal Speyside malt. All that has changed, however, since Ian Macleod Distillers purchased Tamdhu in 2011, two years after Edrington had mothballed it.

Like several Speyside distilleries, Tamdhu shares its name with a station on the railroad that ran up and down the valley. Tamdhu station is more elaborate than most, with two full-length platforms and a signal box. The distillery was founded in 1896, and largely rebuilt in the 1970s. Water comes from the Tamdhu burn, which flows through woodland into the Spey.

Tamdhu was notable for its rare surviving Saladin maltings, but these have now been closed due to their poor state of repair. However, Ian Macleod has breathed new life into Tamdhu single malt, reinventing it as a heavily-sherried 10-year-old in its principal "house" expression. They began marketing it enthusiastically from 2013, a year after production resumed at this impeccably well-kept distillery close to the River Spey.

HOUSE STYLE Mild, urbane. Sometimes snobbish. Versatile.

TAMDHU 10-year-old, 40 vol
COLOR Gold, with amber highlights.
NOSE Soft sherry notes, new leather, almonds, marzipan, and a hint of peat.
BODY Smooth and full.
PALATE Citrus fruit, gentle spice, and sweet sherry.
FINISH Persistent spicy leather, with a sprinkling of black pepper.

SCORE 83

TAMDHU 10-year-old, Limited Edition, 46 vol

1,000 bottles.

COLOR Mahogany.

NOSE Deep sherry notes, new leather, citrus fruit, and light spice.

BODY Full.

PALATE Sweet and richly sherried, ripe oranges, dark chocolate, and tingling spice.

FINISH Lengthy, with sherry, cinnamon, and fudge.

SCORE **84**

INDEPENDENT BOTTLINGS
TAMDHU 8-year-old, The MacPhail's Collection (Gordon & MacPhail), 43 vol

COLOR Light gold.

NOSE Resin, nougat, almonds, and a hint of sherry.

BODY Quite viscous.

PALATE Fresh orchard fruit and malt, with background sherry and ginger.

FINISH Comparatively long, citrus fruit, toffee, and oak.

SCORE **79**

TAMDHU 1998, 25-year-old, Director's Cut (Douglas Laing), 50.1 vol

COLOR Bright gold.

NOSE Raw cauliflower, instant coffee, and stewed fruit.

BODY Smooth.

PALATE Meaty sherry notes, with autumn berries and black pepper.

FINISH Very long, with dark chocolate and chili.

SCORE **80**

TAMNAVULIN

PRODUCER Whyte and Mackay Ltd.
REGION Highlands   DISTRICT Speyside (Livet)
ADDRESS Ballindalloch, Banffshire, AB37 9JA

O N THE STEEP SIDE OF THE GLEN of the Livet, the river is joined by one of its tributaries, a stream called Allt a Choire (in English, "Corrie"). This is the site of the Tamnavulin distillery, taking its name from "mill on the hill." The location is more often spelled Tomnavoulin, but such discrepancies are hardly unusual in Scotland.

Part of the premises was formerly used for the carding of wool. The distillery, built in the 1960s, has a somewhat industrial look. Tamnavulin was mothballed in 1996, but was somewhat surprisingly reopened after the UB Group bought Whyte & Mackay in 2006.

Among the malts produced in and around the glen of the Livet River, the elegant Tamnavulin is the lightest in body, although not in palate. In taste, it is a little more assertive than Tomintoul, with which it might be most closely compared.

HOUSE STYLE Aromatic, herbal. Aperitif.

TAMNAVULIN 25-year-old, Director's Cut (Douglas Laing), 48.8 vol

COLOR Pale straw.

NOSE Fragrant and floral, spicy, with vanilla and peaches.

BODY Soft.

PALATE Floral and sweet, with caramel and more peaches.

FINISH Drying, yet perpetually spicy and fruity.

SCORE **79**

TEANINICH

PRODUCER Diageo
REGION Highlands   DISTRICT Northern Highlands
ADDRESS Alness, Ross-Shire, IV17 0XB
TEL 01463 872004   WEBSITE www.malts.com

THIS LESSER-KNOWN NEIGHBOR of Glenmorangie and Dalmore is beginning to develop a following for its big, malty, fruity, spicy whisky: not before time. Teaninich was founded in 1817, as an estate distillery, and later provided whisky for such well-known blends as VAT 69 and Haig Dimple. It gained a classic DCL still-house in the 1970s. The tongue-twisting name Teaninich (usually pronounced "tee-ninick," but some say "chee-ninick") began to be heard more widely in the 1990s, when the malt was bottled in the Flora and Fauna series. Three Rare Malts bottlings followed. In 2013, it was announced that the capacity of Teaninich was to be doubled, while a new "super distillery" to match Roseisle in scale, would be built alongside.

HOUSE STYLE Robust, toffeeish, spicy, leafy. Restorative or after dinner.

TEANINICH 10-year-old, Flora and Fauna, 43 vol

COLOR Pale gold.

NOSE Big, fresh aroma. Fruity. Hints of apple. Smoky.

BODY Medium, rich.

PALATE Sweet and dry. Lime-chocolate candy. Fruity. Remarkably leafy. Lightly peaty. Gradually warms up until it almost sparks with flavor. Very appetizing.

FINISH Cilantro. Herbal. Rounded.

SCORE 74

TOBERMORY

PRODUCER Burn Stewart Distillers PLC
REGION Highlands   DISTRICT Mull
ADDRESS Tobermory, Isle of Mull, Argyllshire, PA75 6NR
TEL 01688 302645   WEBSITE www.burnstewartdistillers.com
EMAIL enquiries@burnstewartdistillers.com   VC

I F THE ART OF DISTILLATION was brought from Ireland over the
Giant's Causeway to Scotland, it must have arrived in Fingal's Cave,
on the tiny island of Staffa. A later immigrant from Ireland,
St. Columba, founded an abbey on nearby Iona and urged the
community to grow barley. One and a half thousand years later, a
whisky called Iona was launched.

Both Staffa and Iona are off the island of Mull, where the harbor
village of Tobermory gives a home and a name to the local distillery.
(Lovers of trivia, albeit literary trivia, may know that this name was
also given to a talking cat by the Edwardian author Hector Hugh
Munro, better known by his pen-name Saki). The village was once
known as Ledaig (sometimes pronounced "ledchig," and meaning
"safe haven" in Gaelic). The distillery traces its origins to 1795, but has
a much interrupted history, peppered with many owners.

Those in charge of the distillery have at times used the name
Tobermory on a blended whisky and a vatted (blended) malt, but it
now appears on a clearly labeled single malt, produced after the
distillery reopened in 1989–90. This version has a peatiness, albeit
light, derived entirely from the water. The barley malt is not peated.
The name Ledaig was for some years used for older versions of the
whisky, employing peated malt. Ledaig—peated to between 30 and
40 ppm—now accounts for around half of the distillery's output.

The maritime character of the whiskies was diminished when the
warehouses were sold by previous owners during a financial crisis to
make room for apartments. However, in 2007, a small warehouse
facility was created at the distillery, so that some spirit could mature on
its native island.

HOUSE STYLE Faint peat, minty, sweet. Restorative.

TOBERMORY 10-year-old, 46.3 vol

COLOR Lemon gold.

NOSE Fresh and nutty, with citrus fruit and brittle toffee. A whiff of peat and hint of oak.

BODY Smooth.

PALATE Spicy fresh fruit, honey, delicate peat, and mixed nuts.

FINISH Medium in length, with salted caramel, ginger, and dark chocolate.

SCORE **76**

TOBERMORY 15-year-old, 46.3 vol

COLOR Chestnut.

NOSE Rich Scottish fruit pudding with orange, sherry, spicy milk chocolate, and a hint of peat.

BODY Full.

PALATE Sherry, rich fruitcake, toffee, and a sprinkling of pepper.

FINISH Long and luxurious, with chocolate-coated raisins.

SCORE **83**

TOBERMORY 20-year-old, PX Finish, 56.1 vol

Distillery-exclusive bottling.

COLOR Full amber.

NOSE Savory sherry, sweet, spicy, and leathery.

BODY Full.

PALATE Sweet sherry and lots of lively spice.

FINISH Golden raisins, drying sherry, and perpetual spice.

SCORE **83**

TOBERMORY 42-year-old, 48.5 vol

COLOR Deepest amber.

NOSE Complex; sherry, nutmeg, black currants, black pepper,
and York Peppermint Pattie.

BODY Soft and full.

PALATE Intensely fruity, dark berries, pepper, then licorice
and tannins develop.

FINISH Bitter oak balanced by persistent sherried frutiness.

SCORE 88

THE LEDAIG BOTTLINGS
LEDAIG 10-year-old, 46.3 vol

COLOR Lemon gold.

NOSE Soft peat, barley, and malt extract, with walnut,
a hint of iodine, plus dried fruit and nuts.

BODY Medium, oily.

PALATE Lively spice and peat smoke gather above charred oak.
Medicinal notes, plus vanilla and black pepper.

FINISH Medium in length, slightly smoky, with cloves and brine.

SCORE 76

LEDAIG 18-year-old, PX Finish, 57.1 vol

Distillery-exclusive bottling.

COLOR Full amber.

NOSE Old leather and fragrant sherry, and sweet spicy smoke,
with a hint of antiseptic.

BODY Rounded.

PALATE Lots of early fruit, then ginger and ashy peat emerge.

FINISH Medium to long, lively spices, sherry, and pipe tobacco smoke.

SCORE

LEDAIG 42-year-old, 47.7 vol

COLOR Dark amber.

NOSE Initially quite reticent, dry smoke, bung cloths, coal soot,
dark chocolate, and dried fruit.

BODY Soft.

PALATE Early dark sherry fruitiness is soon matched by tannins
and spicy peat.

FINISH Long, with wine-gum candies, ginger in syrup, and
mouth-drying oak.

SCORE

TOMATIN

PRODUCER The Tomatin Distillery Co. Ltd.
REGION Highlands   DISTRICT Speyside (Findhorn)
ADDRESS Tomatin, Inverness-shire, IV13 7YT
TEL 01808 511444   WEBSITE www.tomatin.com
EMAIL info@tomatin.co.uk   VC

STANDING BY THE UPPER REACHES of the Findhorn, Tomatin distillery was established in 1897, but saw its great years of expansion between the 1950s and 1970s. During this period, it became the biggest malt distillery in Scotland and was just a little smaller than Suntory's Hakushu distillery in Japan. Both of these distilleries have scaled down volume since those heady days: Tomatin by removing almost half of its stills, Hakushu by mothballing its biggest still-house. Tomatin might just remain the largest in Scotland; though it is pretty much neck-and-neck with Glenfiddich.

As a large distillery, Tomatin developed a broad-shouldered malt as a filler for countless blends during the boom years. It is neither the most complex, nor the most assertive of malts, but it is far tastier than is widely realized. For the novice wishing to move from lighter single malts to something a little more imposing, the climb to Tomatin will be very worthwhile.

HOUSE STYLE Malty, spicy, rich. Restorative or after dinner.

TOMATIN Decades, 46 vol

COLOR Light straw.
NOSE Initial musty peat notes give way to vanilla, peaches, and fresh leather.
BODY Medium to full.
PALATE Butterscotch, cinnamon, dark chocolate, and raisins.
FINISH Medium to long, spicy, drying oak.
SCORE **78**

TOMATIN Legacy, 43 vol

COLOR Light gold.

NOSE Fragrant, with honey, malt, melons, and a hint of molasses.

BODY Medium.

PALATE Fruity, with pineapple, freshly baked sponge cake, and white pepper.

FINISH Relatively dry, with ginger.

SCORE 75

TOMATIN 12-year-old, 40 vol

COLOR Bright, greeny gold.

NOSE Cookie sweetness. Vanilla. Soft mint candy.

BODY Smooth, velvety.

PALATE Mellow and round. Toffeeish. Pine nuts. Apples and pears.

FINISH Sweet, with a pleasant, refreshing mintiness.

SCORE 75

TOMATIN 14-year-old, Port Wood Finish, 46 vol

COLOR Gold, with rose facets.

NOSE Orchard fruit, toffee, and honey, developing deeper sweet cherry notes.

BODY Soft.

PALATE Sweet, with nutmeg, walnuts, and ripe damsons.

FINISH Medium in length, fruity, with a hint of oak.

SCORE 76

TOMATIN 15-year-old, 52 vol

3,150 bottles.

COLOR Light copper.

NOSE Canned fruit cocktail, salted caramels, milk chocolate, and vanilla.

BODY Rounded.

PALATE Rich fruit, bananas, and autumn berries, with toffee and a sprinkling of black pepper.

FINISH Long and nutty, creamy, with peppery oak.

SCORE 77

TOMATIN 18-year-old, 43 vol

Finished for a final 8 months in oloroso casks.

COLOR Antique brass.

NOSE Soft vanilla and cinnamon. Raisins.

BODY Full. Slightly oily.

PALATE Oak, raisins, honey, heather; a touch of cedar, a waft of smoke.

FINISH Medium. Spiced wood. Spicy.

SCORE 78

TOMATIN 30-year-old, 46 vol

COLOR Mid-gold.

NOSE Apricots, oranges, and an earthy note.

BODY Medium.

PALATE Orange wine-gum candies, soft oak, and ginger.

FINISH Lengthy, drying, developing aniseed.

SCORE 79

TOMATIN Cù Bòcan, 46 vol

Lightly peated.

COLOR Full gold.

NOSE Coconut, lemonade, and almonds, some earth, sweet smoke.

BODY Medium and soft.

PALATE Smoky malt, honey, cinnamon, and cloves.

FINISH Oak and dry peat smoke.

SCORE 78

TOMATIN 1989, Cù Bòcan, 53.2 vol

1,080 bottles.

COLOR Mid-gold.

NOSE Vanilla, furniture polish, apple, and wood smoke.

BODY Full and rounded.

PALATE Very focused orchard fruit, heather and light peat,
and a little earthiness.

FINISH Drying, with spicy smoke.

SCORE **80**

TOMATIN Cù Bòcan, Sherry Cask, 46 vol

6,000 bottles.

COLOR Bright gold.

NOSE Early mashy peat, then vanilla, sherry, and white pepper.

BODY Voluptuous.

PALATE Sweet spices and new leather, soft smoke, and autumn fruit.

FINISH Medium in length, malty, then drying nutty peat.

SCORE **80**

TOMATIN 1988, 46 vol

COLOR Straw.

NOSE Fragrant and gentle, strawberries, caramel, honey, and rich red wine.

BODY Supple.

PALATE Soft fruit, caramel, and smoky dark chocolate.

FINISH Lengthy, with ginger and discreet oak.

SCORE **82**

TOMINTOUL

PRODUCER Angus Dundee Distillers PLC
REGION Highlands DISTRICT Speyside (Livet)
ADDRESS Ballindalloch, Banffshire, AB37 9AQ
TEL 01261 812612 WEBSITE www.tomintouldistillery.co.uk

THE VILLAGE OF TOMINTOUL (pronounced "tom in t'owl") is the base camp for climbers and hikers in the area around the rivers Avon and Livet. Nearby, Cromdale and the Ladder Hills foreshadow the Cairngorm Mountains. It is about 8 miles (13 kilometers) from the village to the distillery, which is on the edge of a forest, close to the Avon River.

The distillery was built in the 1960s and is modern in appearance, with large warehouses and no pagoda roofline. The wildness of the surroundings contrasts with the delicacy of the district's malts. Tomintoul has traditionally seemed the lightest among them in flavor, although it has a little more body than its neighbor Tamnavulin.

HOUSE STYLE Delicate, grassy, perfumy. Aperitif.

TOMINTOUL 10-year-old, 40 vol

COLOR Full, sunny gold.

NOSE Grassy. Lemongrass. Orange-flower water.

BODY Light, smooth, and slippery.

PALATE Sweetish. Crushed barley. Potpourri.

FINISH Lively and lingering gently. Nutty. Lemongrass.

SCORE 77

TOMINTOUL 12-year-old, Oloroso Sherry Cask Finish, Limited Edition, 40 vol

Finished for 18 months in oloroso casks.

COLOR Pale to mid-amber.

NOSE Orange peel and rinds. Rhubarb, vegetal spice, and hints of sherry.

BODY Light, approaching medium. Smooth.

PALATE Malt, with traces of oak and vanilla and a touch of orange oil.

FINISH Spicy dryness. Lingering and warming.

SCORE **78**

TOMINTOUL 14-year-old, 46 vol

COLOR Pale gold.

NOSE Light, fresh, and fruity, with ripe peaches, pineapple cheesecake, delicate spice, and background malt.

BODY Medium.

PALATE Rounded, fruity, and fudgy.

FINISH Wine-gum candies, mild, gently spiced oak, malt, and a suggestion of smoke.

SCORE **79**

TOMINTOUL 16-year-old, 40 vol

COLOR Pale bright orange.

NOSE Orange icing on a cheesecake.

BODY Silky.

PALATE Finely grated, zesty citrus peel. Syllabub. Zabaglione. Nougat.

FINISH Refreshing but also warming, like sherry in an English trifle.

SCORE **78**

TOMINTOUL 21-year-old, 40 vol

COLOR Yellow gold.

NOSE Ripe honeydew melon, pears, warm spices, and barley sugar.

BODY Medium. Smooth.

PALATE Rich and spicy, with toffee and malt.

FINISH Medium to long, mildly mouth drying, with cocoa powder. Spicy to the end.

SCORE **80**

TOMINTOUL "With a Peaty Tang," No Age Statement, 40 vol

COLOR Dark straw with greenish tint.

NOSE Peat, with notes of barley mash. Malty.

BODY Light to medium. Smooth.

PALATE Full, very clean. Delicious maltiness.

FINISH Clean. Lingering moderately.
Complexity develops in the finish.

SCORE 80

TOMINTOUL 1981, 53.9 vol

COLOR Rich amber.

NOSE Malty, with grapefruit and white pepper.

BODY Rounded.

PALATE Nutty and spicy, with orange and more malt.

FINISH Sweet and peppery.

SCORE 82

TOMINTOUL 10-year-old, Old Ballantruan, 50 vol

COLOR Rich gold.

NOSE Sweet spices, vanilla, ginger, and smoky peat.

BODY Oily and full.

PALATE Malt and peat, oatcakes, smoked fish, and licorice.

FINISH Sweet malt notes merge with chili and drying peat.

SCORE 82

TORMORE

PRODUCER Chivas Brothers (Pernod Ricard)
REGION Highlands   DISTRICT Speyside
ADDRESS Advie by Grantown-on-Spey, Morayshire, PH26 3LR
TEL 01807 510244

T HE MOST ARCHITECTURALLY ELEGANT of all whisky distilleries, Tormore stands among the Cromdale Hills, overlooking the Spey. It was designed by Sir Albert Richardson, president of the Royal Academy, and erected as a showpiece in 1958–60, during a boom in the Scotch whisky industry. It looks somewhat like a spa.

The whisky was originally intended as a component of Long John, and later became an element of Ballantine's. Admirers find it aromatic, sweet, and easily drinkable, but the more cautious deem its firmness "metallic." The distillery does not have tours, which seems a wasteful denial of its original purpose as a visual celebration.

When Pernod Ricard acquired Allied Domecq in 2005, Chivas Brothers gained control of the distillery.

HOUSE STYLE Dry, fruity. After dinner.

TORMORE 14-year-old Batch No 1, 43 vol
COLOR Rich bronze.
NOSE Red berries. Lemon. Vanilla. Nutty.
BODY Sweet, sticky, and full.
PALATE Sweet, pleasant. Vanilla, toffee, and nuts. Candy sticks. Some orange and lemon notes. Trace of spice.
FINISH Long, sweet, and spicy.
SCORE 82

TORMORE 16-year-old Batch No 1, 48 vol
COLOR Golden.
NOSE An array of fruit, including orange. Clean and fresh. Well-balanced, with a hint of oak and spice but sweet fruit to the fore.
BODY Rich and full. Smooth.
PALATE Juicy and sweet, with bursts of ripe melon and pear.
FINISH Long with tannins and drying.
SCORE 85

TULLIBARDINE

PRODUCER Picard Vins & Spiriteux
REGION Highlands DISTRICT Midlands
ADDRESS Stirling Street, Blackford, Perthshire, PH4 1QG
TEL 01764 682252 WEBSITE www.tullibardine.com

TULLIBARDINE REOPENED FOR BUSINESS in the hands of a consortium in 2003, almost a decade after being mothballed. The success of that regime led to the distillery being acquired by French family company Picard in 2011, and two years later an entirely new range of single malts was launched.

Tullibardine Moor is in the Ochil hills. In this area, the village of Blackford is the source of Highland Spring bottled water. The hills and their springs have provided water for brewing since at least the 12th century. In 1488, a Tullibardine brewery brewed the ale for the coronation of King James IV at Scone. It is a former brewery site that accommodates the distillery.

There may have been whisky making there in the late 1700s, but it was not until 1949 that the present distillery was built. It was the work of Delmé-Evans, a noted designer of distilleries, whose functional styling can also be seen at Glenallachie and Jura. Evans was fascinated by breweries and distilleries. One of his enthusiasms was the "tower" brewery design, popular in the late 1800s. In this system, a water tank on the roof and a malt loft disgorge their contents, which flow by gravity, without pumps, through the processes that lead to a cellar full of beer. At Tullibardine, he sought to incorporate gravity flow into a distillery. Delmé-Evans died just before the distillery reopened.

HOUSE STYLE Winey, fragrant. With predinner pistachios. More sherried versions with a honeyed dessert (baklava?).

TULLIBARDINE Sovereign, 43 vol

COLOR Light gold.

NOSE Floral, with vanilla, malt, butter, hay, and light spices.

BODY Medium.

PALATE Milk chocolate and fresh fruit, malt, and cinnamon.

FINISH Cocoa powder, white pepper, and light ginger.

SCORE **77**

TULLIBARDINE 225 Sauternes Cask Finish, 43 vol

COLOR Gold.

NOSE Vanilla, citrus fruit, black pepper, and a background herbal note.

BODY Medium.

PALATE Ripe Jaffa orange, cereal, and spicy malt.

FINISH Medium to long, milk chocolate, and passion fruit.

SCORE **77**

TULLIBARDINE 228 Burgundy Cask Finish, 43 vol

COLOR Ruby red.

NOSE Milk-chocolate-covered Turkish delight, vanilla,
sweet chili, and a hint of char.

BODY Rounded and silky.

PALATE Nutty, with apples and sweet spices.

FINISH Relatively lengthy, with spicy damsons.

SCORE **79**

TULLIBARDINE 500 Sherry Cask Finish, 43 vol

COLOR Rich brown.

NOSE Caramel apples, new leather, autumn fruit, and vanilla.

BODY Smooth.

PALATE Toffee, vanilla, dates, orange peel, more leather, and cereal.

FINISH Fruity and spicy, medium in length.

SCORE **81**

TULLIBARDINE 20-year-old, 43 vol

COLOR Mid-gold.

NOSE Slightly oily, with cocoa, honey, and soft toffee.

BODY Creamy.

PALATE Milk chocolate, vanilla, strawberries and cream, light spices.

FINISH Lengthy, with vanilla and cocoa.

SCORE **85**

TULLIBARDINE 25-year-old, 43 vol

COLOR Golden red.

NOSE Apple pie, malt, and freshly planed wood.

BODY Viscous.

PALATE Orange marmalade, roasted almonds, and cocoa powder.

FINISH Spice and ripe bananas, then mild tannins develop.

SCORE **84**

UNSPECIFIED MALTS

A LIMITED NUMBER of bottlings do not carry the name of the distillery. It may be because an independent bottler has an arrangement with the distillery or, conversely, does not want a dispute with them. It may also be because the bottler wants to promote the flavor of the particular malt rather than the distillery per se. And some companies have used this approach to appeal to consumers put off by traditional labeling, as with Burnfoot, from Glengoyne.

AS WE GET IT 8-year-old, Cask Strength Highland
Ian Macleod, 58.9 vol

COLOR Dark amber.

NOSE Hot cocoa, fleeting balloon rubber, vanilla, prunes, and big, sweet sherry notes.

BODY Full.

PALATE Bold, spicy, and sugary sweet, with caramel and a fruity tang.

FINISH Drying, with a hint of Jaffa orange and dark spicy chocolate.

SCORE **87**

AS WE GET IT 8-year-old, Cask Strength Islay
Ian Macleod, 59.2 vol

COLOR Pale straw.

NOSE Sweet peat smoke, brittle toffee, and cereal.

BODY Oily.

PALATE Peppery peat, with vanilla and lively spices.

FINISH Lengthy; citrus fruit and lots of smoke.

SCORE **85**

CASK ISLAY A. D. Rattray, 40 vol

COLOR Pale gold.

NOSE Ozone, tide pools, shellfish, and then a hint of discreet smoke.

BODY Medium, soft.

PALATE Rich and sweet, with peat and chili.

FINISH Warm and lengthy, with persistent chili notes.

SCORE **86**

FINLAGGAN EILEAN MORE Vintage Malt Whisky Co, 46 vol

COLOR Light gold.

NOSE Sweet, with pears and mango, against a backdrop of peat smoke. Ozone develops in time.

BODY Full.

PALATE Sweet and fruit, with spicy peat and light iodine notes.

FINISH Peat, subtle oak, ginger, and tide pools.

SCORE 88

GLENKEIR TREASURES 13-year-old, Spcyside, 40 vol

COLOR Amber.

NOSE Orchard fruit, vanilla, and honey.

BODY Medium, supple.

PALATE Rich vanilla, ripe apples, pears, and freshly mown hay.

FINISH Softly spiced fruit and licorice sticks.

SCORE 87

LIDDESDALE 21-year-old (Batch 7) Adelphi, 46 vol

COLOR Mid-bronze.

NOSE Sherry, rolling tobacco, ripe oranges, and brine.

BODY Full and rounded.

PALATE Caramel, toffee, and relatively dry sherry.

FINISH Medium in length, with salted caramels.

SCORE 87

MACPHAIL'S 15-year-old, Gordon & MacPhail, 40 vol

COLOR Bright gold.

NOSE Cereal, fresh fruit, subtle wood smoke, and oak.

BODY Rounded.

PALATE Ripe peaches, soft sherry, fudge, and a hint of smoke.

FINISH Lengthy, with dried fruit and light smokiness.

SCORE 85

MASTER OF MALT 40-year-old, Speyside (Second edition), 43 vol

COLOR Copper.

NOSE Floral and fruity, with vanilla, honey, and fresh pineapple.

BODY Full and slightly oily.

PALATE Stewed fruit, old leather, pipe tobacco, and vanilla.

FINISH Long, nutty, and spicy, with dry sherry-soaked raisins.

SCORE 90

MASTER OF MALT 60-year-old, Speyside, 42.2 vol

COLOR Full gold.

NOSE Cocoa powder, malt, cherries, golden raisins, marzipan, and canned peaches. Finally, a hint of char.

BODY Full.

PALATE Drying oak, which never overwhelms. Fruit wine-gum candies and coconut milk lurk behind the wood.

FINISH Long and oaky, with spicy anise.

SCORE 88

PORT ASKAIG 19-year-old, Speciality Drinks Ltd., 45.8 vol

COLOR Yellow gold.

NOSE Maritime, with peat smoke, carbolic soap, malt, vanilla, and ripe peaches.

BODY Medium and slightly oily.

PALATE Medicinal and peaty, with brine, succulent red berries, and more vanilla and milk chocolate.

FINISH The chocolate note darkens, with sweet peat and rock salt.

SCORE 88

STRONACHIE 10-year-old, A. D. Rattray, 40 vol

COLOR Rich amber.

NOSE Mildly savory, with toffee and honey, followed by plums and prunes.

BODY Medium to full.

PALATE Spicy, with graham crackers and subtle yet zesty fruitiness.

FINISH Medium in length, with drying oak notes and persistent ginger.

SCORE 84

STRONACHIE 18-year-old, A. D. Rattray, 40 vol

COLOR Rich gold.

NOSE Floral, with toasted malt, stewed fruit, sweet sherry, honey, nuts, and wood smoke.

BODY Full.

PALATE Sweet, with more sherry and honey, ripe apples, fudge, and soft spices.

FINISH Medium in length, featuring a hint of peat, roasted malt, and pleasing tannins.

SCORE 87

BLENDED MALTS

Dominic Roskrow

B LENDED MALTS ARE NOT THE SAME THING as blended whiskies, and they have a place in this book because they are made up of only malted barley. They differ from single malt whiskies in that the malt comes from more than one distillery.

There is nothing new about this category, though the name was only recently enshrined in law. The style of whisky had been known as "vatted" but the Scotch Whisky Association somewhat controversially moved to outlaw the term in the United Kingdom, and replace it with one that is altogether more confusing. John Glaser of Compass Box, whose whiskies are included in this section, marked the occasion by mixing the last Scottish vatted malt on Westminster Bridge as Big Ben struck midnight.

The concept of mixing malts from different distilleries is not new. Malts have been mixed since the early 1800s and they were recognized in law as early as 1853. Even before Andrew Usher's earliest forays into the science of blending, he sought to achieve balance and quality with the use of malted whisky only, and his first big success—Usher's Old Vatted Glenlivet—was… well, there's a clue in the name.

In more recent times there has been a steady flow of vatted malt products. But it has never grown quite as much as it seemed likely to in the first part of the millennium, when it looked like it would blossom as a category, appealing to a new generation of drinker by ridding Scotch whisky of some of its historical baggage, and presenting it in a new and modern way. If malt whisky was the solo musician of the whisky world, and a good blended whisky like an orchestra, then vatted malts could be considered to be a rock group, breathing excitement and variety irreverently into the world of whisky.

When the revival in the category emerged there were two strong players. Jon, Mark, and Robbo's Easy Drinking Whisky Company replaced gravitas, heavy label titles, and age statements with modern and stylish labels. They tried to sell whiskies on their flavor, and the company's founders eschewed the normal whisky festival circuit and traditional trade magazine route, and took their whiskies to a more energetic demographic based around skiing, cycling, sailing, and climbing exhibitions instead.

John Glaser of Compass Box, on the other hand, brought whisky alchemy to the category, creating innovative boutique whiskies, which he packaged in stylish and eye-catching bottles and cartons.

And when William Grant & Sons maintained its reputation for staying close to the cutting edge of the industry when it launched Monkey Shoulder, it looked like the vatted malt category would break wide open. It is a mix of three malts dressed in fashionable packaging, and the name is ingenious because it allows its owners space to be creative when marketing it, but is actually soaked in traditionalism.

That it hasn't happened is at least in part due to the new name, and the confusion it causes in the mind of the consumer, who sets out to be a single malt whisky, and subconsciously brackets blended malts with what he (often mistakenly) thinks are inferior blended whisky products.

In recent years, we have seen a general shortage of single malt whisky, since whisky's popularity as an affordable luxury has expanded, and new markets have emerged for it. This, in turn, might once more open the door for blended malts. There are only two ways you can react to shortages of whisky: put it into a bottle at a younger age and risk devaluing the product, or wait. If you are going to put it into a bottle at a younger age, then why not combine it with another malt whisky to create a more exciting, and better tasting new blended malt?

The argument in favor of flavor over age has grown stronger in recent years for this reason. That plays toward blended malts. Let's hope we see more of them—the quality in this category can be quite outstanding.

BERRY BROS. & RUDD Blue Hanger 9th Release, Winter 2013, 45.6 vol

COLOR Rich gold.

NOSE Wispy smoke. Fresh fruit bowl. Vanilla. Custard.

BODY Sweet, rich, and full.

PALATE Unrelentingly flavorful. Smoke and peat. Huge wave of citrus fruit. Plum and raisin. Vanilla ice cream.

FINISH Long and fruity, with smoky tones.

SCORE **90**

COMPASS BOX The General, 53.4 vol

COLOR Bronze.

NOSE Floor polish. Dusty old oak office. Wispy. Church pew. Flowers.

BODY Medium, rounded, and sweet.

PALATE Sunday church. Sweet spices. Oak. Dried fruit. Squishy raisins. A surprising fruit-and-nut milk-chocolate back story.

FINISH Full. Sweet. Berry fruit.

SCORE **94**

COMPASS BOX Flaming Heart FH16MMVII, 48.9 vol

COLOR Pale gold.

NOSE Port Ellen ferry. Oil and smoke. Lemon. Intense.

BODY Rich, sweet, and oily, but very gentle.

PALATE Rooty, then smoky, with a big fruit compote fightback. A syrupy contest between smoke and plummy fruit.

FINISH A score draw. Perfectly balanced between strawberry and black-currant jam and a steam-engine festival.

SCORE **93**

COMPASS BOX Spice Tree 2014, 46 vol

COLOR Pale lemon.

NOSE Musty. Oily fish. Gentle seaweed and peat. Soy sauce.

BODY Rich, oily, and full.

PALATE Sweet and honeyed. Zesty citrus. Oaky tannins. Ginger. Paprika. Cumin. Tingling orange.

FINISH Long, with a battle between the fruit and spice.

SCORE **91**

COMPASS BOX Oak Cross 2014, 43 vol

COLOR Pale honey.

NOSE Tangerine zest. Nail polish. Aniseed.

BODY Rounded, quite savory, and full.

PALATE Rounded, more savory taste than of old. Earthier and more rustic. Sandalwood. Sweet and sour citrus. Grapefruit. Green fruit.

FINISH Medium, complex, and pleasant.

SCORE 90

COMPASS BOX The Peat Monster, 46 vol

COLOR Lemon yellow.

NOSE Rooty. Lemon zest. Wafting smoke.

BODY Creamy and peaty.

PALATE Sweet and balanced, with sugary fruit, preserved herring smoke, and sea notes.

FINISH Medium, balanced, and peaty.

SCORE 85

DOUGLAS LAING The Big Peat, 46 vol

COLOR Yellow.

NOSE Everything Islay. Seaweed. Oily rope. Big peat. Tar.

BODY Full, rich, and mouth coating.

PALATE Tons of peat. Sea notes. Some green fruit in the mix.
Sweet. Industrial.

FINISH Unrelenting, long, oily, and very peaty.

SCORE **90**

DOUGLAS LAING Big Peat Christmas, 54.9 vol

COLOR Straw yellow.

NOSE Smoke. Industrial. Tarry. Some citrus.

BODY Full, oily, and glutinous.

PALATE Earthy. Big peat and smoke. Steam engine.
Seashell. Tarry rope.

FINISH Massive. Full. Long. Very smoky.

SCORE **92**

DOUGLAS LAING Double Barrel, 4th Release
(Laphroaig/Mortlach), 46 vol

COLOR Light yellow.

NOSE Peat. Pepper. Grapefruit. Berries.

BODY Medium, sweet, and pleasant.

PALATE The Laphroaig dominates. Peat. Citrus. Sweet pear.
Underneath, the jagged peaty edges are taken off by a soft,
fruity landing. Quite gritty and grungy.

FINISH Medium and much fruitier and softer than palate.

SCORE **80**

DOUGLAS LAING Double Barrel
(Glenallachie/Bowmore), 46 vol

COLOR Light yellow.

NOSE Melon. Nectarine. Juicy berries. Wispy smoke.

BODY Light, soft, and agile.

PALATE Sweet and fruity. Bowmore peat is there but not dominant.
Surprisingly clean and refreshing. Apricot. Juicy golden raisins. Kumquat.

FINISH Fruity and peaty, all in equal measure.

SCORE **82**

DOUGLAS LAING Double Barrel (Talisker/Craigellachie), 46 vol

COLOR Pale gold.

NOSE Almond. Plum. Sour apple. Chili spice.

BODY Thin, punchlike.

PALATE Two malts split down the middle. Dry spice and lemon
on one side; berries, plum, and gooseberry fruit on the other.

FINISH Fruit and pepper fade quite quickly.

 SCORE 80

DOUGLAS LAING Scallywag, 46 vol

COLOR Light lemon.

NOSE Sappy. Green salad. Cucumber. Green fruit. Dusty. Buttered toast.

BODY Light, punchlike.

PALATE Lemon and lime. Some berry fruit. Orange. Lime-flavored punch.
Sharp pepper notes.

FINISH Medium. Fruity. Pleasant but not particularly assertive.

 SCORE 80

FAMOUS GROUSE Blended Malt, 40 vol

COLOR Orange.

NOSE Mix of honey, citrus fruit, and a chemistry set. Some orange.

BODY Smooth, soft, and rounded.

PALATE Clementine. Honey. Given depth by late peat and spice.

FINISH Medium and spicy.

 SCORE 72

MASTER OF MALT Reference Series I, 47.5 vol

COLOR Pale straw.

NOSE Light and floral. Manuka honey. Floral. Melon.

BODY Quite thin, but zesty and zippy.

PALATE Sweet and vibrant zesty peach, apricot, and pear.

Sweet malted barley. Traces of ginger.

FINISH Medium and sweet.

SCORE **89**

MASTER OF MALT Reference Series II, 47.5 vol

COLOR Slightly green-tinged yellow.

NOSE Spicy and zesty, with lemon and lime.

BODY Clean, buttery, rounded, and easy drinking.

PALATE Vanilla, canned pears, red berries. Sherry.

Dark chocolate. Candied cherries.

FINISH Medium, sweet, and flawless.

SCORE **89**

MASTER OF MALT Reference Series III, 47.5 vol

COLOR Golden yellow.

NOSE Sugared almonds. Some tangerine. Custard. Mint.

BODY Big, rich, and full.

PALATE Milk chocolate. Sweet breads. Earthy.

Big puréed peach and orange fruit.

FINISH Fruit. Salt. Spice and earthiness. Very strong all through.

SCORE **91**

POIT DHUBH BLIADHNAS 21-year-old, The Hive, 43 vol

COLOR Deep brown.

NOSE Coastal but controlled. Mild and temperate salt, spice, and peat.

BODY Medium and quite gentle.

PALATE Gentle peat and smoke. Fishing port. Grilled fish drizzled with lemon. Pleasant and rounded. Light honeycomb heart. Not very challenging.

FINISH Medium and gentle, with peat and savory and spice notes.

SCORE **80**

TASMANIAN HEARTWOOD 2013, 12-year-old,
Convict Redemption, 71.9 vol

COLOR Horse chestnut.

NOSE Big red berries. Black currant. Orange-flavored chocolate.
Cocoa. Wispy smoke.

BODY Full and creamy.

PALATE Puréed fruit. Red apples. Lots of berries. Big menthol
cough lozenge. A touch of sulfur earthiness. Complicated and intense.

FINISH Long with menthol and grungy earthiness.
Intense and unforgettable.

SCORE 90

TASMANIAN HEARTWOOD 2014, The Beagle, 68.3 vol

COLOR Rich red.

NOSE Winey. Cigarette ash. Complex. Fruit liqueur.
Mandarin. Berries. Licorice. Nutty.

BODY Full, oily, and intense.

PALATE In your face, like an Australian rugby player. Big port notes.
Peat. Berries including strawberry jam. Scottish camp coffee. Molasses.
Earthy. Bold. Plum. Complex, contradictory, and intense.

FINISH Feisty and with lots going on. Finish is long and the malt
is fighting with itself. One which you'll love or hate.

SCORE 88

TASMANIAN HEARTWOOD Vat Out Of Hell, 67.4 vol

COLOR Ruby brown.

NOSE Complex. Apple. Wispy smoke.

BODY Big, full, and oily. In your face.

PALATE Impressive mix of peat and sweetness. Earthy undertow.
Honey. Apple pit. Rugged and monstrous.

FINISH Huge oily, peaty, and fruity finish that lingers. Unforgettable.

SCORE 84

TASMANIAN HEARTWOOD Velvet Hammer, 68.8 vol

COLOR Reddish brown.

NOSE Apple. Tree bark. Menthol. Wispy smoke.

BODY Big, bold, and full.

PALATE Complicated and complex whisky going in lots of directions.
Earthy and rustic. Apple. Apple pit. Softens with water.
Vermouth and floral notes among the spice. Intriguing.

FINISH Long, full, and kicks out with attitude as it goes.

SCORE 82

THE SIX ISLES, 43 vol

COLOR Light gold.

NOSE Lime, lemon, grapefruit. Honeyed. Gentle wafts of peat and smoke.

BODY Quite full and assertive.

PALATE Much peatier and smokier than the nose suggests. Some fruit notes.

FINISH Medium full and peaty, with some peppery notes.

SCORE 80

WEMYSS MALTS 8-year-old, The Hive, 40 vol

COLOR Corn syrup.

NOSE Honey. Sweet. Refreshing. Fresh dough. Spring flowers.

BODY Rounded and smooth.

PALATE Honeyed. Puréed almond. Sweet. Canned apricots.
Kumquat. Rich and full.

FINISH Honeycomb, sweet, and quite long.

SCORE 86

WEMYSS MALTS 12-year-old, The Hive, 40 vol

COLOR Corn syrup.

NOSE Orange peel. Grapefruit traces. Musty. Savory tones.

BODY Medium and rounded.

PALATE Less sweet than eight-year-old. Spicier. Oakier.
More savory notes. Dates. Berries. Balanced.

FINISH Medium long, with orange hints and a late pepper and spice hit.

SCORE **84**

WEMYSS MALTS 8-year-old, Peat Chimney, 40 vol

COLOR Corn syrup.

NOSE Smoke. Light peat. Garden herbs. Citrus trace.

BODY Medium full and a touch oily.

PALATE Some peat. More pipe than chimney. Polite. Sweet fruit.
Well-married with soft sponge cake among the smoke.

FINISH Peat comes through the sweetness. Medium long.

SCORE **87**

WEMYSS MALTS 12-year-old, Peat Chimney, 40 vol

COLOR Corn syrup.

NOSE Light. Summer meadow. Lemon. Some wispy smoke.

BODY Light and inoffensive.

PALATE Sweet. Soft, overripe melon. Kiwi fruit. Some peat but not dominant. Pantry spices.

FINISH Medium, peaty, and sweet.

SCORE 82

WEMYSS MALTS 8-year-old, Spice King, 40 vol

COLOR Corn syrup.

NOSE Cumin, smoke, chili pepper, and fireplace. Sooty.

BODY Medium and earthy.

PALATE Earthy and feisty, with rooty and green-salad notes. Rustic. Savory. Light pepper.

FINISH Medium long, with rustic and earthy feel.

SCORE 82

WEMYSS MALTS 12-year-old, Spice King, 40 vol

COLOR Corn syrup.

NOSE Floral. Trace of lemon. Thyme. Dusty smoke.

BODY Light but quite complex.

PALATE Honey. Sweet. Melon. Soft peach. Light spice. Unusual. Complex.

FINISH Short, soft fruit, sweet.

SCORE 81

WILLIAM GRANT & SONS Monkey Shoulder, 40 vol

COLOR Honey gold.

NOSE Apples. Fresh and zesty. Grapefruit. Young.

BODY Light, soft, and rounded.

PALATE Green apples. Citrus fruit. Refreshing, with clean barley. Very rounded and balanced.

FINISH Medium and fruity, with some late fruit.

SCORE 88

CLOSED DISTILLERIES

Gavin D. Smith

L IKE ANY OTHER SPHERE OF COMMERCIAL ACTIVITY, the Scotch whisky industry is prone to periods of expansion and contraction, and while new distilleries are built and existing ones enlarged during "boom" times, the price of "bust" is often distillery closures.

The distilleries featured in the following pages were mostly victims of the period of Scotch whisky overproduction that characterized the late 1970s and early 1980s, and led the Distillers Company Ltd. (DCL) to make drastic cutbacks to its distilling portfolio during 1983 and 1985.

Despite the passage of time, bottlings of all the distilleries noted here are still available, principally from independent bottlers, but the individual expressions tend to change quite rapidly, since most are single cask or very limited edition bottlings. A few, such as Brora and Port Ellen, have achieved something close to cult status among collectors and consumers.

Most of the closed distilleries listed here produced malt spirit almost entirely for blending, and the issue of whether their whisky had desirable single malt profiles did not arise. Some were chosen for closure because they were comparatively old-fashioned, and required substantial investment to increase their efficiency, while others were selected because their "make" was not outstandingly individualistic.

A number of these closed distilleries are still readily identifiable today. Part of St. Magdalene in Linlithgow has been converted into housing units, retaining a malting pagoda roof, while Brora, Coleburn, Convalmore, Millburn, Port Ellen, and Rosebank all retain distinctive elements of their whisky-making antecedents.

On the other hand, developers have obliterated the likes of Glen Mhor and Glen Albyn in Inverness (shopping center), Stonehaven's Glenury Royal (housing development), and North Port in Brechin (supermarket). The most recent loss was Imperial, near Aberlour on Speyside, but at least it made way for Chivas Brothers' new Dalmunach distillery, which now occupies the site.

So the cycle continues, with new distilleries being created in good times, and the most vulnerable old ones being shut down when things turn bad. Hopefully, however, by the next edition of this book, there will have been no more casualties to report.

BANFF

PRODUCER DCL
REGION Highlands   DISTRICT Speyside (Deveron)
SITE OF FORMER DISTILLERY Inverboyndie, on B9139, 1 mile west of Banff

DATING FROM AT LEAST 1824, Banff closed in 1983, leaving a substantial amount of stock for independent bottlings. Its buildings have gradually been dismantled. The distillery stood near the adjoining towns of Banff and MacDuff, which face each other across the Deveron, where the river flows into the Moray Firth. Before being subsumed into Aberdeenshire, the county of Banffshire once formed the eastern flank of Speyside and embraced half the region's distilleries.

HOUSE STYLE Fragrant. Lemongrass. Sweet. Restorative or after dinner.

BANFF 1975, Celtic Heartlands, 48.1 vol

COLOR Pale gold with a greenish tinge.

NOSE Gentle. Pineapple. Exotic fruit. A touch of oak.

BODY Full. Creamy. Sweet.

PALATE Honey. Fruit syrup. Apricots. Late dryness.

FINISH Sugary sweetness remains but is joined by sweet spice. Quite long.

SCORE **83**

BANFF 1976, Connoisseurs Choice, 40 vol

COLOR Pale gold.

NOSE Fresh cut barley soaked in lemon juice. Old lady's perfume. Violets.

BODY Quite creamy. Soft and full.

PALATE Juicy barley. Soft fruit. Blemish-free. Lemon-and-lime bonbons.

FINISH Relatively short. Sweet lemon candy.

SCORE **86**

BANFF 37-year-old, Old & Rare, 53 vol

COLOR Pale gold.

NOSE Big. Crispy vegetables. Grapefruit.

BODY Medium and zesty.

PALATE Burned wood. Very sweet. A battle between citrus fruit and wood.

FINISH Medium. Drying. Spicy.

SCORE **70**

BRORA

REGION Highlands   DISTRICT Northern Highlands
ADDRESS Brora, Sutherland, KW9 6LR

BRORA WAS FOUNDED AS CLYNELISH DISTILLERY in 1819 by the Marquis of Stafford, later the 1st Duke of Sutherland, principally to provide an outlet for barley grown by the estate's tenants. It became part of the Distillers Company Ltd. (DCL) in 1925.

The "whisky boom" of the 1960s saw a new and larger distillery built alongside the original in 1967, and the Clynelish name was transferred to that. The old distillery was rechristened Brora, and operated until 1983, when it fell victim to the DCL's very large round of distillery closures. It is externally intact, and its two stills remain in situ. A number of its warehouses are still used for maturation purposes.

HOUSE STYLE Full-bodied, fruity, earthy, and coastal, with peat smoke.

BOTTLINGS OF BRORA MALTS
BRORA 30-year-old, 52.4 vol

COLOR Deep golden brown.

NOSE Halfway between a florist's and a fruit store.
Delightfully fruity, but with hints of spice
and peat. Smoky.

BODY Rich. Full. Very assertive.

PALATE Captivating. A perfectly balanced blend of pepper, peat,
big orangey fruit, and brine. Plenty of oak.

FINISH Perfectly balanced, peaty, fruity, and peppery.

SCORE **94**

BRORA 35-year-old Special Release 2014, 48.6 vol

COLOR Honeyed gold.

NOSE Burlap and hemp, ozone, discreet peat, and old tar. Fragrant,
with ripe apples and a hint of honey.

BODY Medium and waxy.

PALATE Waxy, sweet, and spicy, with heather and ginger.
Smoky and mildly medicinal.

FINISH Steadily drying to aniseed, black pepper, dark chocolate,
and fruity tannin.

SCORE **92**

BRORA 35-year-old Special Release 2013, 49.9 vol

COLOR Light amber.

NOSE Fresh and fruity; a hint of wax, plus brine, walnut fudge, and a wisp of smoke. Finally, wood resin.

BODY Oily.

PALATE Very fruity, with mixed spices, then dark chocolate, gentle peat smoke, and finally coal. Mildly medicinal.

FINISH Long, slowly drying, aniseed, and ashy peat.

SCORE **93**

BRORA 35-year-old Special Release 2012, 48.1 vol

COLOR Straw.

NOSE Lemon and contrasting vanilla, and honeycomb aromas. Musty malt and coal in the background.

BODY Medium to full.

PALATE The citrus and honey themes continue into the slightly earthy, peppery palate.

FINISH Drying, with French mustard and coal.

SCORE **92**

INDEPENDENT BOTTLINGS OF BRORA MALTS
BRORA 1982, Connoisseurs Choice, 43 vol

COLOR Pale yellow.

NOSE Lemon-flavored flu medicine and intense smoke.

BODY Rich. Intense. Oily.

PALATE Intense barley with some sweetness. Citrus. Peat.

FINISH Long. Sweet. Lemon and peat.

SCORE **83**

BRORA 27-year-old, Cask 1427,
Duncan Taylor, 53.8 vol

COLOR Lemon yellow.

NOSE Lemon zest. Clean. Traces of peat, but also rich and honeyed.

BODY Sweet. Oily. Full.

PALATE Chocolate-covered seafoam candy. Honeycomb. Soft and sugary. Intense barley.

FINISH Very pleasant. Rich honeyed barley. Very clean. A trace of late tannin. Very fruity.

SCORE **89**

CAPERDONICH

PRODUCER Chivas Brothers
REGION Highlands DISTRICT Speyside (Rothes)
ADDRESS Rothes, Morayshire, AB38 7BN

CAPERDONICH WAS MOTHBALLED IN 2002, and there are no current plans to reopen it. It is the lesser known partner to Glen Grant—the two distilleries stand across the street from one another in the whisky town of Rothes and share the same ownership. Caperdonich, founded in 1898, was rebuilt in 1965 and extended in 1967. Its name is said to indicate a "secret source." From the start, it has been a backup to Glen Grant. When young, the malts of both distilleries are light and fragrant in their bouquet, medium bodied, and nutty tasting.

Of the two, Caperdonich is perhaps a dash fruitier and slightly more smoky. It, too, is a component of the Chivas Regal blend. The Chivas group kept a tight control of its malts during the last years of its ownership by Seagram, of Canada. This policy was maintained following the takeover by Pernod Ricard, of France. There are no official bottlings of Caperdonich, and the independent bottlings tend to be from very old stock.

HOUSE STYLE Dried fruit, grainy, toasty. Breakfast? After dinner?

CAPERDONICH Aged 40 years, Old Malt Cask, 42.9 vol
COLOR Rich gold.
NOSE Rich and full. Orange and mandarin. Soft Jell-O. Honeycomb.
BODY Medium, sweet, and full.
PALATE Berries. Blood-orange marmalade. A battle for the fruit against wood and pepper.
FINISH Quite long and very spicy. Big oak notes.
SCORE **79**

CAPERDONICH 11-year-old, Provenance, 46 vol
COLOR Pale yellow.
NOSE Banoffee pie. Banana milkshake. Milk chocolate.
BODY Thin and unassertive.
PALATE Sweet. Minty. Ginger barley. Touch of citrus.
FINISH Short and sweet.
SCORE **65**

COLEBURN

REGION Highlands   DISTRICT Speyside (Lossie)
ADDRESS Longmorn by Elgin, Moray, IV38 8GN

THE USHER'S WHISKIES, pioneer blends, once relied heavily upon malt from this distillery. Coleburn was built in the booming 1890s. It closed in the grim 1980s, the year before its owners DCL were subsumed into United Distillers, which in turn became part of Diageo. The Coleburn distillery has not been licensed since 1992, and is unlikely to work again. There have been sporadic proposals to redevelop the site for other uses. Its whisky, always intended for blending, was never destined for solo stardom. A valedictory Rare Malts vintage was as enjoyable as any Coleburn to have been bottled in recent decades.

HOUSE STYLE Dry, fruity. Aperitif.

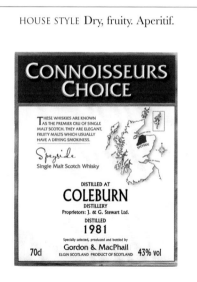

COLEBURN 1981, Connoisseurs Choice, 43 vol

COLOR Honey gold.

NOSE Shy. Oil paint. Rock-garden shrubs. Herb garden.

BODY Medium full. Sweet.

PALATE Peppery. Sweet barley sugar and diluted lemon and lime juice.
Then salt and pepper. Traces of oak.

FINISH Quite long and spicy.

SCORE 67

CONVALMORE

REGION Highlands   DISTRICT Speyside (Dufftown)
ADDRESS Dufftown, Banffshire, AB55 4BD

THE PAGODAS OF DUFFTOWN make an impressive congregation of landmarks, and Convalmore's is one of the most strikingly visible. Sadly, the distillery no longer operates.

For much of its life, Convalmore contributed malt whisky to the Buchanan/Black & White blends. The distillery was built in the 1870s; seriously damaged by fire, and rebuilt in 1910; modernized in 1964–65, but mothballed a couple of decades later by its owners at the time, DCL. Their successors, Diageo, still have the right to issue bottlings of Convalmore whisky from stock, but most appearances currently are independent bottlings. In 1992, the premises were acquired by William Grant & Sons, owners of nearby Glenfiddich and Balvenie, but their use is purely for warehousing.

HOUSE STYLE Malty, syrupy, fruity, biggish. After dinner.

CONVALMORE 1977, 36-year-old
(Diageo Special Releases 2013), 58 vol
Matured in European oak refill casks; 2,680 bottles.

COLOR Dark gold.

NOSE Fruit, brittle toffee, honey, and a little wood smoke.
Mildly herbaceous.

BODY Rounded.

PALATE Initially fruity, becoming earthier and more oaky,
with nutmeg and black pepper.

FINISH Grapefruit, then dark chocolate and malt
in the spicy, lengthy finish.

SCORE **90**

DALLAS DHU

PRODUCER DCL
REGION Highlands   DISTRICT Speyside (Findhorn)
ADDRESS Forres, Morayshire, IV36 2RR
TEL 01309 676548   VC

THE NAME MEANS "black water valley." This Dallas accommodates a hamlet somewhat smaller than its indirect descendant in Texas (named after US Vice-president George Mifflin Dallas, who seems to have been of Scottish origin). The Dallas Dhu distillery was established in 1899. Despite a fire in 1939, it does not appear to have changed greatly. Recently, its whisky appeared in the Benmore blends and vattings, and as Dallas Mhor single malt.

The distillery closed in 1983 and reopened to the public in 1988, under the aegis of Scotland's Historic Buildings and Monument Directorate. There are no plans to restart production, but the later batches continue to appear in independent bottlings.

HOUSE STYLE Silky, honeyish, sometimes chocolatey. After dinner.

DALLAS DHU 1981, 26-year-old, Duncan Taylor, 55.8 vol

COLOR Pale yellow.

NOSE Zesty lemon-and-lime sherbet. Lime soda. Perfumed bath salts.

BODY Medium full and pleasant.

PALATE Honey. Vanilla. Barley. Citrus fruit. Clean and refreshing.
Tastes sprightly for its years. Some late pepper.

FINISH A delightful mix of fruit, barley, and spice. Lengthy.

SCORE **86**

GLEN ALBYN

REGION Highlands   DISTRICT Speyside (Inverness)
SITE OF FORMER DISTILLERY Telford Street, Inverness,
Inverness-shire, IV3 5LD

A COMPUTER SUPERSTORE AND a home-improvement store now stand on the site in Inverness once occupied by Glen Albyn, a distillery for 140 years, founded by a Provost (Mayor) of the city generally regarded as the capital of the Highlands. Before the distillery, there was a brewery on the site. There is still a small pub, The Caley. The site is alongside one of Scotland's great feats of engineering, the Caledonian Canal, the dream of James Watt and Thomas Telford. The canal links the North Sea with the Atlantic by joining Loch Ness with a series of more lochs in the Great Glen (also known in parts as Glen Albyn or Glen Mor, More, or Mhor). There is an unconnected Glenalbyn pub pub in the center of Inverness. Albyn is a variation on Albion or Alba, old names applied to Scotland, especially the Highlands.

HOUSE STYLE Light. Fruity, nutty, dry. Aperitif.

GLEN ALBYN 1976, Rare Vintage (Gordon & MacPhail), 43 vol

COLOR Dark gold.

NOSE Soft fruit, sherry, malt, and ginger.

BODY Medium.

PALATE Fruity, with more sherry, resin notes, cocoa powder, and developing oak.

FINISH Relatively long and spicy, with cocoa.

 SCORE 78

GLENLOCHY

PRODUCER DCL/UDV
REGION Highlands   DISTRICT Western Highlands
SITE OF FORMER DISTILLERY North Road, Fort William,
Inverness-shire, PH33 6TQ

THE LOCHY IS A RIVER that flows through the town of Fort William, at the foot of the mountain Ben Nevis. In addition to the Ben Nevis malt distillery, which is still very much in operation, Fort William for many years had another, called Glenlochy. This was built at the end of the 19th century between 1898 and 1900, and it changed little over the decades in the first half of the 20th century. It passed to DCL in 1953, lost its railroad spur in the 1970s, and was closed in 1983. The equipment has long since gone, and the premises are now used as offices by unrelated businesses.

One sophisticated and geographically precise taster was reminded of Lebanese hashish by a Scotch Malt Whisky Society bottling of Glenlochy in the mid-1990s. The smokiness is less obvious in some bottlings, in which the wood seems tired, but more oxidation and ester notes emerge. In 1995, United Distillers released a Rare Malts edition, with a similar bottling the following year.

HOUSE STYLE Peaty, fruity, creamy. With dessert or a book at bedtime.

GLENLOCHY 27-year-old,
Rarest of the Rare, 54.8 vol

COLOR Ginger.

NOSE Chocolate-lime bonbons. Pineapple candy. Scottish camp coffee.

BODY Soft and sweet.

PALATE Barley sugar. Orange hard candy. Ginger cookies.
Hints of oak late on. Vanilla.

FINISH Sweet and spicy, but rounded and well-balanced.
Impressive.

SCORE **88**

GLEN MHOR

REGION Highlands   DISTRICT Speyside (Inverness)
SITE OF FORMER DISTILLERY Telford Street, Inverness, Inverness-shire, IV3 5LU

PURISTS PRONOUNCE IT the Gaelic way, "Glen Vawr," to rhyme with "law." The distillery, built in 1892 in Inverness and demolished in 1986, was one of several at which the poet, novelist, and pioneering whisky writer, Neil Gunn, worked as an exciseman. In his book, *Scotch Missed*, Brian Townsend writes that Gunn was inspired by Glen Mhor to let slip his observation that "until a man has had the luck to chance upon a perfectly matured malt, he does not really know what whisky is." Even in Gunn's day, Glen Mhor could be found as a single malt, and casks still find their way into independent bottlings.

HOUSE STYLE Aromatic, syrupy. Quite sweet. With dessert or after dinner.

GLEN MHOR 1989, Rare Vintage (Gordon & MacPhail), 43 vol

COLOR Pale gold.

NOSE Floral, with vanilla and soft oak, plus an edge of lemon.

BODY Medium, slightly oily.

PALATE Sweet and spicy, with cinnamon and orchard fruit.

FINISH Medium to long, with dry oak and a hint of mint.

SCORE **79**

GLENUGIE

REGION Highlands   DISTRICT Eastern Highlands
SITE OF FORMER DISTILLERY Peterhead, Aberdeenshire, AB42 0XY

THE CENTRAL STRETCH OF the East Coast has lost all its distilleries. This one was close to the remnants of a fishing village near Peterhead, where the river Ugie reaches the sea. The site incorporates the stump of a windmill. There had been distilling there since the 1830s, and the surviving buildings date from the 1870s.

The Whitbread brewing company, owners since the 1970s, gradually withdrew from the production of spirits during the 1980s, when the whisky industry was suffering one of its cyclical downturns. Industrial premises in Aberdeenshire were being snapped up by small engineering firms servicing the oil boom, and that was Glenugie's fate in 1982–83. Its whisky-making equipment was removed. There is still some stock to be found, and bottlings are still being made, though fewer as the years roll by.

HOUSE STYLE Flowery, resiny. Can be medicinal. Book-at-bedtime.

GLENUGIE 1980, 30-year-old, Deoch an Doras, 52.1 vol
COLOR Old gold.
NOSE Perfumed, with gentle sherry, cocoa powder, new leather,
black currants, caramelized peaches, and apricots.
BODY Oily.
PALATE Sweet, with fresh fruit, then old-fashioned cough drops
and licorice notes arrive.
FINISH Very long, spicy, and tannic.
SCORE **82**

GLENURY ROYAL

REGION Highlands   DISTRICT Eastern Highlands
SITE OF FORMER DISTILLERY Stonehaven, Kincardineshire, AB3 2PY

FOUNDED IN 1825, Glenury Royal stood on the east coast of Scotland, south of Aberdeen. The water for the whisky came from the Cowie River, and the distillery's name derived from the glen that runs through the Ury district. Its founder, Captain Robert Barclay, was an athlete known for an occasional achievement: he was the first man to walk 1,000 miles in as many hours without a break. He was also a local Member of Parliament. Barclay had a friend at court to whom he referred coyly as "Mrs. Windsor," and through whose influence he was given permission by King William IV to call his whisky "Royal." It was an excellent malt, judging from recent bottlings. The distillery was mothballed in 1985, and the site, later sold, became a housing development.

HOUSE STYLE Aromatic, spicy, fruity. Book-at-bedtime.

GLENURY 40-year-old (Diageo Special Releases 2011), 59.4 vol
Matured in American oak refill casks; 1,500 bottles.

COLOR Deep gold.

NOSE Worn leather, nutmeg, and malt, with developing vanilla and brittle toffee.

BODY Full, slightly oily.

PALATE Very fruity, with orange-flavored chocolate and cinnamon notes.

FINISH Lengthy, with black pepper, oak, and bitter orange.

SCORE 85

IMPERIAL

PRODUCER Allied Distillers Ltd.
REGION Highlands DISTRICT Speyside
ADDRESS Carron, Morayshire, AB34 7QP

MALT LOVERS THIRSTING FOR THIS underrated and rarely bottled Speysider have in recent years been permitted to satiate their desires through a number of independent bottlings.

The Imperial distillery is in Carron, just across the river from Dailuaine, with which it was historically linked. It was founded in 1897 and extended in 1965. It closed in 1985, but was reopened by Allied in 1989, then mothballed in 1998. The distillery was demolished during 2013 to make way from Chivas Brothers' new Dalmunach distillery. Imperial's unusually large stills make it hard to use flexibly.

HOUSE STYLE Big and (often sweetly) smoky.
After dinner or at bedtime.

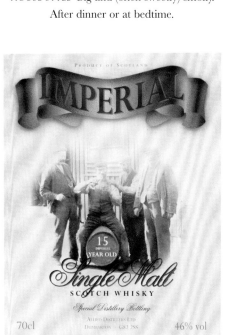

IMPERIAL 15-year-old,
Special Distillery Bottlings, 46 vol

COLOR Golden satin. Slight haze.

NOSE Lemon meringue pie. Key lime pie. Not only the fruit filling, but also the pastry. Slightly floury and dusty. Some cellar character.

BODY Thin but smooth. Falls away somewhat.

PALATE Lemon skins. Some sweet lemon, becoming quite intense, then drying. Rounds out with a little water.

FINISH Gently dry. Slight hint of smoky dryness.

SCORE **71**

IMPERIAL 13-year-old, Duncan Taylor N.C.2, 46 vol

COLOR Pale yellow.

NOSE Canned pineapple. Fruit hard candy. Clean. Vanilla. Fresh flowers.

BODY Soft and well-balanced.

PALATE Sugared barley. Fresh rich fruit. Some late spice.

FINISH Rich and spicy.

SCORE **80**

IMPERIAL 1990, 18-year-old, Cask No 354,
Duncan Taylor, 51.9 vol

COLOR Honey gold.

NOSE Spearmint. Lime. Refreshing and clean.

BODY Soft, pleasant, and rounded.

PALATE Sweet. Grapefruit and lime. Soft and pleasant. Syrupy fruit bowl.

FINISH Short and sweet, with the merest hint of wood.

SCORE **83**

IMPERIAL 1990, 18-year-old, Duncan Taylor, 55 vol

COLOR Rich orange.

NOSE Canned melon. Exotic fruit. Candied cherries. Vanilla. Sweet and clean.

BODY Full, sweet, and balanced.

PALATE Full and fruity. Exotic fruit, as with the nose, balanced by some underlying spice.

FINISH Medium, with sugar and spice, and very addictive. Delightful and balanced.

SCORE **90**

LITTLEMILL

PRODUCER Loch Lomond Distillery Co. Ltd.
REGION Lowlands   DISTRICT Western Lowlands
ADDRESS Bowling, Dunbartonshire, G60 5BG
TEL 01389 752781   EMAIL mail@lochlomonddistillery.com

UNTIL THE NINETEEN THIRTIES, Littlemill followed the Lowland practice of triple distillation. The surviving buildings date from at least 1817, but appear to be older. Littlemill was long believed to date from 1772, but more recent evidence suggests that it was already distilling in 1750. It is thus one of the several claimants, each with a slightly different justification, to being the oldest distillery in Scotland.

HOUSE STYLE Marshmallow-soft. A restorative, or perhaps with dessert.

LITTLEMILL 1990, 22-year-old, Cask No 21, 46 vol

COLOR Pale yellow.

NOSE Fresh and clean. Summer meadow. Daisies. Gentle fruit. Perfumed.

BODY Light and soft.

PALATE A touch of citrus. Summer orchard. Meadows. Delicate and complex.

FINISH Long, and very clean and light.

SCORE **79**

LOCHSIDE

REGION Highlands   DISTRICT Eastern Highlands

LOCHSIDE DISTILLERY was situated in the port of Montrose, and had the distinction of being converted from an 1890s "Brauhause" style tower brewery. Whisky was made there from 1957 to 1992, with pot stills for malt whisky distillation, and a continuous still for grain spirit production in place.

The former Deuchars brewery was owned for some years by Destilerias y Crianza of Spain, finally ending up in the Allied Distillers' portfolio. Allied deemed Lochside surplus to requirements, and despite a spirited campaign by conservation bodies to save the historic structure, permission was granted to demolish the distillery. During 2005, the site was cleared and redeveloped for residential use.

HOUSE STYLE Fruity, dry, gentle. Aperitif.

LOCHSIDE 1991, Gordon & MacPhail, 43 vol

COLOR Light gold.

NOSE Perfumed, nutty, malty, and sweet.

BODY Medium.

PALATE Spicy and sweet, with toasted malt and a herbal note.

FINISH Drying, with a faint hint of smoke.

SCORE **74**

MILLBURN

PRODUCER DCL
REGION Highlands   DISTRICT Speyside (Inverness)
SITE OF FORMER DISTILLERY Millburn Road, Inverness,
Inverness-shire, IV2 3QX

As THE TRAIN FROM LONDON finishes its 11-hour journey to Inverness, it glides by recognizable distillery buildings that are now a pub-steakhouse. At least there is still alcohol on the premises.

Millburn is believed to have dated from 1807, and its buildings from 1876 and 1922. It was owned for a time by Haig's. The distillery closed in 1985. Whiskies distilled a decade earlier have been released at 18 years and now 25, as Rare Malts.

HOUSE STYLE Smoky, aromatic. Nightcap.

MILLBURN 25-year-old, Distilled 1975, Bottled 2001, Rare Malts, 61.9 vol

COLOR Yellow.

NOSE Vegetal. Peppery. Aromatic.

BODY Dry, firm chewiness.

PALATE Flavor development. Medium dry. Sooty. Smoky oaky. Sappy. Orange pith and zest.

FINISH Surprisingly lively; spicy. Faintly medicinal.

SCORE 75

MILLBURN 18-year-old, Distilled 1975, Rare Malts, 58.5 vol

COLOR Greeny gold.

NOSE Oaky and aromatic.

BODY Lightly smooth.

PALATE Dryish, perfumy, and smoky.

FINISH Oaky and sappy.

SCORE **74**

MILLBURN 1978, Gordon & MacPhail, 46 vol

COLOR Pale gold with amber highlights.

NOSE Fragrant and fruity, with mildly smoked malt.

BODY Smooth.

PALATE Malt and peat, plus background ginger.

FINISH Drying quite swiftly to oak.

SCORE **75**

NORTH PORT

REGION Highlands   DISTRICT Eastern Highlands
SITE OF FORMER DISTILLERY Brechin, Angus, DD9 6BE

THE NAME INDICATES THE NORTH GATE of the small, once-walled city of Brechin. The distillery was built in 1820. The pioneering whisky writer Alfred Barnard, who toured Scotland's distilleries in the 1880s, recorded that this one obtained its barley from the farmers around Brechin, and its peat and water from the Grampian mountains. The late writer Derek Cooper reported that the condensers were cooled in a stream that ran through the distillery. North Port was modernized in the 1970s, and closed in 1983. It was subsequently demolished, and a supermarket now occupies the site. Some bottlings of this malt appear under the name Brechin.

HOUSE STYLE Dry, fruity, ginlike. Aperitif.

NORTH PORT 28-year-old, Brechin
(Diageo Special Releases 2006), 53 vol

2,040 bottles.

COLOR Gold.

NOSE Quite dry; almonds, bitter chocolate, and a whiff of smoke.

BODY Full.

PALATE Sherbet, then licorice, with some underlying wood smoke, morphing to creamy caramels.

FINISH Fudge and lingering hot spices.

SCORE **83**

PITTYVAICH

PRODUCER Diageo
REGION Highlands   DISTRICT Speyside (Dufftown)
SITE OF FORMER DISTILLERY
Dufftown, Banffshire, AB55 4BR

BULLDOZED IN 2002, after a short and unglamorous life, the industrial-looking distillery was built by Bell's in 1975. In the late 1980s, enthusiasts for single malts began to wonder whether the product would become available to them. Then independent bottler James MacArthur released a 12-year-old, revealing a perfumy, soft-pear house character. The same bottler then added a 14-year-old that more assertively pronounced its dry finish. A bottling of the same age from the Scotch Malt Whisky Society was similar, but seemed to have more spicy dryness on the nose. In 1991 there was finally an official bottling, at 12 years old, in the Flora and Fauna series. This had all the other characteristics, plus a hefty dose of sherry.

HOUSE STYLE Fruity, oily, spicy, spirity.
After dinner—a Scottish grappa, so to speak.

PITTYVAICH 21-year-old, Cadenhead, 54.3 vol
168 bottles released.

COLOR Rich gold.

NOSE Lemon. Linament. Medicine cabinet.

BODY Medium full and soft.

PALATE Fiery. Peach. Sugar beet and sugar barley. The merest hint of oak and spice. Not much depth.

FINISH Medium long and undramatic.

SCORE 64

PITTYVAICH 29-year-old, Rarest of the Rare, 50 vol

COLOR Yellow with a green hue.

NOSE Lime Starburst. Sweet barley.

BODY Sweet and creamy.

PALATE Sweet citrus. Rooty. Melon skin. Pleasant but two-dimensional.

FINISH Short, sweet, and citrusy.

SCORE 67

PORT ELLEN

PRODUCER Diageo
REGION Islay   DISTRICT South Shore
SITE OF FORMER DISTILLERY Port Ellen, Isle of Islay, PA42 7AH
WEBSITE www.malts.com

WHICH WILL BE THE FINAL VINTAGE of this cult whisky? As stocks at the distillery diminish, and the fashionability of Islay soars, speculation mounts. Port Ellen is the rarest of Islay malts, despite a surprising number of independent bottlings. The distillery, near the island's main ferry port, was founded in 1825, substantially rebuilt and expanded during the boom years of the 1960s, then closed during the downturn in the 1980s. In the last two or three years, the modern parts of the distillery have been demolished, but the original pair of malt kilns have been preserved, complete with pagodas.

Adjoining the distillery is a modern maltings. The malt is supplied, in varying levels of peatiness, to many of the other Islay distilleries, including those that make a proportion of their own.

In 1995, Diageo started marketing whiskies from silent distilleries as The Rare Malts, and three years later a 20-year-old (1978) expression of Port Ellen was released, followed in 2000 by a 22-year-old. Further bottlings appeared from 2001, with Rare Malts being replaced by annual Special Releases. Port Ellen has been a firm fixture in this range ever since, and the 2014 expression was the 14th annual release. At 35 years of age, it was also the oldest Port Ellen "house bottling" to date.

HOUSE STYLE Oily, peppery, salty, smoky, herbal. With smoked fish.

PORT ELLEN 1979, 22-year-old, Limited Edition Numbered Bottles, First Release 2001, 56.2 vol

COLOR Solid, greeny gold. Bright, refractive.

NOSE Fresh. Bison grass. Cereal grain. Oily.

BODY Firm, nutty, and malty.

PALATE Earthy. Peaty. Salty. Quite hard. Austere.

FINISH Pronounced salt. Dry smokiness. Intensely appetizing.

SCORE **92**

PORT ELLEN 1978, 24-year-old, Limited Edition Numbered Bottles, Second Release 2002, 59.35 vol

COLOR Lemony with golden hues.

NOSE Grassy and herbal. Dill, angelica, and camomile.
A pleasant earthiness comes through.

BODY Tender.

PALATE Surprisingly smooth and sweet. A refreshing coolness.
Smokiness slowly emerges and hovers on menthol and vanilla.

FINISH Pleasantly dry and slowly dying.

SCORE 90

PORT ELLEN 1979, 24-year-old, Limited Edition Numbered Bottles, Third Release 2003, 56.2 vol

COLOR Pale gold. Faint green tinge.

NOSE Herbal. Slightly sour. Seaweedy. Sea breezes.

BODY Soft, textured.

PALATE Edible seaweed. Salty flavors reminiscent of
some vermouths. Developing spicy notes.

FINISH Powerful, peppery, warming.

SCORE 91

PORT ELLEN 22-year-old, Distilled 1978, Rare Malts, 60.5 vol

COLOR Pale yellow.

BODY Big, textured.

NOSE Fruity, seaweed, bay leaves, and olive oil.

PALATE Big-bodied. Slightly sticky. Chewy. Edible seaweed. Parsley.

FINISH Hugely salty and equally peppery.

SCORE 85

PORT ELLEN 1978, Limited Edition Numbered Bottles, Fourth Release, 2004, 56.2 vol

COLOR Straw.

NOSE Bold, slightly spirity, smoky oak.

BODY Quite dry.

PALATE Powerful, complex, and salty-sweet. Brittle toffee and a
hint of licorice.

FINISH Long and smoky, slightly woody, dark chocolate,
and dry fruit.

SCORE 90

PORT ELLEN 32-year-old Special Release 2012, 52.5 vol

COLOR Old gold.

NOSE Maritime notes, sweet peat, leather, a whiff of chlorine,
damp soil, and cashew nuts. Becoming sweeter with time.

BODY Soft, slightly oily.

PALATE Slightly woody palate, with fruit, vanilla, and more leather emerging.

FINISH Bonfire smoke and cloth Band-Aids, finally drying very emphatically.

SCORE 91

PORT ELLEN 34-year-old Special Release 2013, 55 vol

COLOR Rich amber.

NOSE Waxy; initial savory notes and wood smoke, giving way to
tide pools and citrus fruit.

BODY Substantial.

PALATE Big smoke and lemon notes, followed by brine, honey,
old leather, and oak.

FINISH Big and lengthy, with earthy peat smoke, dark chocolate,
and licorice.

SCORE 91

PORT ELLEN 35-year-old Special Releases 2014, 56.5 vol

COLOR Mid-gold.

NOSE Coal tar, damp cloth Band-Aids, citrus fruit, golden raisins,
and warm leather.

BODY Voluptuous.

PALATE Pineapple and banana wrapped in peat smoke and ginger.
Brine and dark chocolate arrive in time.

FINISH Long, with oaky spices and smoky fruit.

SCORE 91

AN INDEPENDENT BOTTLING
PORT ELLEN 1982, Connoisseurs Choice, 40 vol

COLOR Pale gold.

NOSE Ozone and citric peat.

BODY Medium.

PALATE Fresh fruit, damped-down bonfires,
and developing maritime salt.

FINISH Peat ash and ginger.
Finally old-fashioned hospital dressings.

SCORE 82

ROSEBANK

PRODUCER Diageo
REGION Lowland DISTRICT Central Lowlands
SITE OF FORMER DISTILLERY Falkirk, Stirlingshire, FK1 5BW
WEBSITE www.malts.com

IN 2002, THE QUEEN OPENED The Falkirk Wheel, a rotating lift to hoist boats between the Union canal and the restored Forth-Clyde canal. There had been hopes that the development of the canalside at Falkirk would include a tourist distillery to replace the silent Rosebank, but this prospect has so far not materialized.

Roses once bloomed on the banks of the Forth-Clyde canal, and a great deal of very early industry grew there. The Rosebank distillery may have had its origins as early as the 1790s. From the moment the canals lost business to the roads, the distillery's location turned from asset to liability. The road awkwardly bisected the distillery and as the traffic grew, it was difficult for trucks to drive in and out of the distillery. Rosebank was closed in 1993.

Rosebank's whisky at its best (i.e., not too woody) is as flowery as its name. It was the finest example of a Lowland malt, and was produced by triple distillation, in the Lowland tradition. It is a grievous loss.

HOUSE STYLE Aromatic, with suggestions of clover and camomile.
Romantic. A whisky for lovers.

ROSEBANK Special Release 2014, 55.3 vol

COLOR Pale gold.

NOSE Hazelnut chocolate. Lemon and grapefruit. Summer meadow.
Daisies. Manuka honey. Buttered croissant.

BODY Soft, sweet, and full.

PALATE Very sweet citrus. Astringent. Dusty. Baked bread.
Spices late on.

FINISH Medium. Tangy lemon.

SCORE **87**

ST. MAGDALENE

REGION Lowland   DISTRICT Central Lowlands
SITE OF FORMER DISTILLERY Linlithgow, West Lothian, EH49 6AQ

THIS SITE ACCOMMODATED a leper colony in the 12th century, and later a convent, before a distillery was established, possibly in 1765. Production ceased in 1983 and some of the buildings have since been converted into apartments. The distillery has sometimes been known by the name of its hometown, Linlithgow, which lies west of Edinburgh, close to the Forth River.

HOUSE STYLE Perfumy, grassy, smooth. Restorative.

ST. MAGDALENE 1975, Rare Old (Gordon & MacPhail), 43 vol
COLOR Brass.

NOSE Evolves quickly. Raspberry sherbet. Wall garden. Primrose. Pachouli oil.

BODY Medium. Sweet.

PALATE Maple syrup. Honey. Citrus. Zesty. Some spice. Balanced.

FINISH Some fruit, but wrapped in oak and spice.

SCORE 83

NEW WORLD WHISKY

Dominic Roskrow

Greatest hits on New World whiskies

IT IS ALL BUT IMPOSSIBLE TO OVERSTATE how much whisky from outside the traditional territories has both grown and grown up since the last edition of The Malt Whisky Companion.

There was a world whisky section in the sixth edition, but it was a contained chapter that put all the world's emerging whisky nations together, and it is now completely out of date, not least because many of the whisky makers produced annual batches of spirit that have evolved rapidly.

Now, in the category that we may call "New World Whisky" there are countless whiskies, operating at several levels. The top world whiskies can and do match up to the very best whiskies from the traditional producers, such as Scotland and Ireland, and they have won awards at the world's top competitions. What's more, we're looking at the tip of an iceberg because scores of distilleries have opened since 2013 and won't bottle their first whiskies until at least 2016.

So the supply of New World whisky is there, but so is the demand. The Whisky Tasting Club, of which I am a director, has seen its miniature set of world whiskies go from novelty status to the most popular package on its site, beating even the likes of Islay whiskies and rare bourbons.

There are several reasons for this. First, the quality of New World whisky has massively improved in the last five years, and the world awards have not gone unnoticed. Some world whiskies are reaching ages that would be considered premium in Scotland, and many of them are aided by different climatic conditions, are using different size casks made of different oaks and even different woods, and are made with barley dried over materials other than peat.

Yoichi produces Japan's most respected single malts
Founder Masataka Taketsuru and his Scottish wife, Rita, lived in one of the distillery's neat, stone buildings.

The art of maturation
Oak barrels are used in the maturation of the spirit,
which is a traditional and highly skilled procedure.

They have a distinctive style, and that's the second reason for their growing success. The whisky-drinking public has accepted that these whiskies occupy a category of their own and shouldn't be compared to Scotch any more than bourbon is. They're not better or worse, just different, just as American football and English rugby union are different. And increasingly, people want different. World distilleries are increasingly exhibiting at the big whisky shows and are being welcomed with open arms.

So why would a Scottish whisky producer welcome a Finn or a Frenchman? Because they're helping to make the category highly exciting. They appeal to a younger drinker, and more women are attending whisky events because of them. Bring someone to whisky in their early 20s instead of their mid 30s, and they will discover Scottish single malts by their mid 20s. That's good for everyone in malt whisky. The competition isn't each other; it's vodka and gin drinkers.

And finally, economic circumstances have favored New World whiskies. With Scotch whisky in demand worldwide, many territories are struggling to get it. Drinkers have turned to the world whiskies stepping into their place, and they have been pleasantly surprised. There has been a sea change in attitude in a very short period of time, and many whisky lovers are taking pride in their national malts. Not only that, but local resources and production methods, such as drying malted barley over juniper twigs in Sweden, means that we are starting to see the development of regionalized world whiskies.

You will see in this section that there are a considerable number of whiskies, with very high scores, many of them higher than some very good Scottish single malts. But as we have said, such comparisons are irrelevant. And there's another factor: we have cherry-picked the biggest, most established, and best New World distilleries for this section, which means that they tend to produce the best New World whiskies.

There is a point to this. You may have to go to some effort to find some of these malts—how likely would you be to do that if we'd dismissed a whisky as poorly made, of indifferent quality, and not worth the purchase price? This is, then, a "greatest hits" of New World whisky. Most of these distillers make an array of whiskies that are not defined by a house style. For this reason we have not included a house style for the distilleries in this section.

One final comment. When we set out to update the sixth edition, there was some debate as to whether the book should evolve without Michael Jackson. This seventh edition shows exactly why it had to: Michael's last edition included none of the following whiskies. But he would have wanted them in and he would have pursued them as voraciously as we have. That's good enough for us.

Hot, dry Australian bush
The weather conditions of the Australian bush make it hostile to producing whisky, but along the temperate coast, distilling flourishes.

AMRUT

PRODUCER N. R. Jagdale Group
COUNTRY India   TEL 0044 191 233 6316
WEBSITE www.amrutwhisky.co.uk

INDIA IS THE LARGEST MARKET in the world for whisky, but nearly all of it is blended or made with molasses, and therefore, not whisky at all by European definition. Amrut in Bengaluru is a sizeable distillery, which makes spirits, including "whisky," for the domestic market. Amrut single malt came about as part of a "coals to Newcastle" project by Rick Jagdale while he was studying at Newcastle University. As part of his studies, he explored the possibility of marketing Indian whisky in Scotland. Since then, the malts have won countless awards and forced connoisseurs to take Indian and new world whiskies seriously. Amrut has carved a path for others to follow but a question mark remains over the distillery's next move, as at the time of writing, general manager for international operations Ashok Chokalingam was moving back to India.

AMRUT Two Continents (Second Edition), 46 vol

COLOR Orange.

NOSE Savory. Kitchen pantry. Doughy at first, then lime and orange zest. Subtle and intriguing.

BODY Light and gentle, refreshing, and cordial-like.

PALATE Citrus cordial. Exotic spices. Orange again. Ginger barley. All very clean and refreshing.

FINISH Medium and quite spicy.

SCORE **87**

AMRUT Intermediate Sherry Matured, 57.1 vol

COLOR Rich gold.

NOSE Strong sherry notes. Plum. Stewed dates. Soy. Chinese food wrapper. Cookie.

BODY Mouth coating and even with water. Big, bold, and rounded.

PALATE Big plum and apricot jam.

FINISH Rich, full, rounded, and fruity.

SCORE **92**

AMRUT Kadhambam Batch 1, 50 vol

COLOR Browny orange.

NOSE Autumnal. Forest floor—wild flowers and damp leaves.
Peat. Autumn berries. Some sporty sweet notes.

BODY Medium, savory, creamy, and spicy.

PALATE Quite dry. Very sherryish but with odd offshoots,
presumably due to the rum and brandy casks used for part of the
maturation. Some rum and raisin. Lovely spices and big orange fruit notes.

FINISH Long, warming, complex, and very good.

SCORE **86**

AMRUT 10-year-old, Greedy Angels, 50 vol

COLOR Deep bronze.

NOSE Clean, fresh, and about as fruity as it is possible to get.
Pineapple, orange, lemon, and lime. Enticing.

BODY Full. Fruity. Liqueurlike.

PALATE Big rumtopft fruits. Soft with no negative astringent notes,
particularly given the age—extremely old for Indian whisky.
Menthol whisky rancio is at its heart and the cask has given this depth.

FINISH Delightful sweet fruit and red licorice make the finish
long and outstanding.

SCORE **93**

AMRUT 8-year-old, Greedy Angels, Chairman's Reserve, 50 vol

COLOR Rich gold.

NOSE Tropical fruit. Gumdrop and fondant-candy mix. Sugared almonds.
Spiky spice. Crystallized pineapples.

BODY Full, firm, and fruity.

PALATE Big red licorice whisky, syrupy gumdrops, some mandarin,
cherry lozenge, and canned strawberries. Menthol rancio dominates.

FINISH Long and sweet with licorice, vanilla, and bourbon notes.

SCORE **94**

AMRUT Naarangi, 50 vol

COLOR Rich bronze.

NOSE Winey. Sherried. Berry compote. Mandarin orange.
Orange sponge cake. Some candied fruit.

BODY Big, rich, full, and earthy.

PALATE Beautiful. Soft, rounded, and quite peaty, with strawberry
and candied cherry. Puréed fruit. Dark chocolate.

FINISH Very soft but earthy, long, and waxy.

SCORE **92**

AMRUT 100, 57.1 vol

UK bottling; 100 bottles only.

COLOR Deep golden brown.

NOSE Smoky, dusty peat. Unassuming. Cupcake notes.

BODY Mouth coating with sweet and peat.

PALATE Lots of sugar, dancing spice, and puréed fruit,
and wave after wave of peat. By the end these are welded together.

FINISH Quite long, with dusty oily peat bouncing over a peach melba base.

SCORE **94**

BELGIAN OWL

PRODUCER Etienne Bouillion
COUNTRY Belgium   TEL 0032 4 247 3814
WEBSITE www.belgianwhisky.com

THESE ARE EXCITING TIMES for Etienne Bouillion and Belgian Owl. Until 2013 it was very much a steady-as-you-go process, but the distillery is expanding, all on one site, and demand for the whisky is growing.

Etienne learned his distilling skills from none other than Bruichladdich's legendary distiller Jim McEwan, and they have kept in touch ever since, with the Scotsman often traveling to Belgium to offer help and advice. Still, Etienne seems to be doing a pretty good job on his own. He started his distillery working from three separate sites and quickly tapped into a highly fruity, dessert-style whisky. But his dream was to operate from a rural farm site on which barley could be grown. The new Belgian Owl distillery lies close to Liege, a cultural melting pot with a reputation as a center for great food and spirits, and is equipped with stills from the demolished Caperdonich distillery in Scotland.

We're still waiting for the first whisky from them, but the Belgian Owl operation is a considerably expanded one and going on to the next. And despite the expansion, there are no plans to lose sight of the way the whisky is crafted in this stylish and scenic distillery.

BELGIAN OWL 4-year-old, 46 vol

COLOR Bright yellow-gold.

NOSE Vanilla, sweet apple, and pear.

BODY Rich and creamy.

PALATE Canned pear in syrup. squishy banana. Honey. Toffee. Buttered dough balls. Vanilla. A touch of sweet spice.

FINISH Rich, full, and sweet.

SCORE **83**

BELGIAN OWL Single Cask No. 4018707, 80 months, 50 vol

COLOR Lemon.

NOSE Tight and restrained. Sparkling alcohol. Dirty spices.

BODY Full and oily.

PALATE Lemon sherbet. Quite spicy and savory. Allspice.
Canned pears. Some tropical fruit. Clean and refreshing.

FINISH Full, fruity, and lingering.

SCORE **88**

BELGIAN OWL 2014, 5-year-old, 46 vol

COLOR Light lemon.

NOSE Sweet grape. Lemon. Floral. Spray cleaner. Sherbet.

BODY Sweet, full, and oily.

PALATE Milk chocolate-filled sweet lime candy. Some winey notes.
Poached pear. Clean, fresh, and sweet.

FINISH Medium long, with some spice appearing through the sweet fruit.

SCORE **90**

BLAUE MAUS

PRODUCER The Fleischmann family
COUNTRY Germany   TEL 0049 9545 7461
WEBSITE www.fleischmann-whisky.de

MANY OF THE DISTILLERIES of Germany, Switzerland, and Austria are not primarily whisky-making ones. They tend to make whisky in small quantities sporadically, but there are exceptions, and Blaue Maus is one of them. In fact, Robert Fleischmann is one of the earliest creators of German whisky, having started producing fruit liqueurs in 1978.

He first began producing whisky in 1983 with the help of the local customs and excise officer, of all people. The early efforts were not great but he stuck with it, and today the distillery produces a wide range of expressions. The names of the whiskies are partly due to a good-natured sense of humor and partly because of Robert's old links with the navy.

BLAUE MAUS Elbe 1, 40 vol

COLOR Clear honey.

NOSE Violin resin. Cooking oil. Nutty. Dried leaves.

BODY Medium.

PALATE Early on, sweet and rounded. Lime Starburst. Sappiness in the center. Finally, fermenting berries. Caramel. Hazelnut. Unusual. Marzipan.

FINISH Warming, soft, and sweet.

SCORE **86**

BLAUE MAUS Spinnaker, 40 vol

COLOR Gold.

NOSE Dirty and spicy with lemon notes. Cedar.

BODY Soft, light, and creamy.

PALATE Weird. Grape. Cedar. Forest floor. Red berries. Unusual spices. Some sappiness. Green fruit.

FINISH Short and unassertive.

SCORE **77**

BLAUE MAUS **Old Fahr, 40 vol**

COLOR Bright lemon.

NOSE Dusty office wood panels. Furniture polish. Citrus.

BODY Medium, earthy, and woody.

PALATE Delightful and sweet. Honey with pistachios

and nougat. Some pepper.

FINISH Quite short, with nougat and nut holding off the pepper.

SCORE **83**

BLAUE MAUS **Otto's Uisge Beatha, 40 vol**

COLOR Maple syrup.

NOSE Forest floor and polished wood. Nuttiness.

BODY Light and unassertive.

PALATE Sharp. Deep citrus. Dark molasses toffee. Hints of menthol.

Smoked cheese. Nougat and nuts. Very different.

FINISH Short with zesty fruit.

SCORE **86**

BUSHMILLS

PRODUCER Jose Cuervo Overseas
COUNTRY Ireland   TEL +44 (0) 28 207 33218
WEBSITE www.bushmills.com   VC

NORTHERN IRISH DISTILLERY has long been something of a misfit, and at the end of 2014 its checkered history took another unexpected turn when its owners Diageo exchanged it with Jose Cuervo for a tequila distillery. Before Diageo bought it, the distillery was part of the south-based Irish Distillers group, long before the Irish Troubles came to an end. Truth be told, Diageo had never really made the most of its Irish whiskey producer, although sales continued to grow rapidly during the spirits giant's tenure.

Bushmills is a pretty distillery situated close to the impressive Giant's Causeway. It makes both single malt and blended whiskey, offers a great tour, and has a stylish visitor center.

BUSHMILLS 10-year-old, 40 vol

COLOR Pale gold.

NOSE Fresh fruit. Peach. Juicy berries. Honey.

BODY Gossamer soft.

PALATE In two parts—initially, sweet grape, overripe red apples, and pleasant summer fruit; then bitter chocolate and pepper spice, giving definition to the overall taste.

FINISH Rounded and structured, with a nice balance of sweetness and spice. Impressive assertiveness.

SCORE **84**

CHICHIBU

PRODUCER Ichiro Akuto
COUNTRY Japan TEL 0081 494 624601
WEBSITE NA

JAPAN'S NEWEST DISTILLERY is a fulfilment, both of a dream and a long-held promise by owner Ichiro Akuto. Ichiro has a 400-year-old family association with distilling, and when the link was broken in the early 2000s, he promised he would one day open a distillery again. He chose to build it in Chichibu since it was where his family had been making sake since 1625.

Ichiro had made his name in Japanese whisky well before his new distillery produced its first whisky. He bought the remaining stock of highly acclaimed Japanese whisky Karuizawa, and was responsible for the bottling of some stunning whisky in the much sought-after "Card" series. Each bottling in this series had a different playing card on its label, making it easier for the consumers to remember what they liked.

Even at three years old, the new whisky has been excellent, and a range of different styles has now been released in a highly limited edition.

CHICHIBU The First, 61.8 vol

COLOR Light lemon yellow.

NOSE Shy, but with some apple, some lemon, and pineapple candy. Attractive.

BODY Well-rounded and balanced.

PALATE Clean and very palatable. Lemon meringue pie. Vanilla and honey.

FINISH Big and sweet, but too short. Definitely addictive.

SCORE 85

CHICHIBU Port Pipe, Bottled 2013, 54.5 vol

COLOR Pinky orange.

NOSE Dusty and sweet, with wafting smoke. Melon. Red fruit.

A touch of raspberry.

BODY Rich, full, and evolving.

PALATE Autumn berries, hints of smoke, berry compote, and tobacco.

FINISH Rural, citrussy, and earthy. Medium long.

SCORE **90**

CHICHIBU The Peated, 2013, 53.5 vol

COLOR Pale lemon juice.

NOSE Gooseberry, grape, and green salad. Some smoke.

BODY Big, full, and oily.

PALATE Sea spray, seaweed, and peat. Damp leaves. Autumn forest.

Dates. Damp fire hearth.

FINISH Medium, sappy, rustic, and with a touch of putty.

SCORE **80**

CHICHIBU Floor Malted, 2012, 50.5 vol

COLOR Lemony gold.

NOSE Sweet candy. Strawberry sherbet. Musk. Menthol.

BODY Medium, mouth coating, and rich.

PALATE Ginger barley. Menthol. Grapefruit and lemon.

An earthy underlay.

FINISH Medium long, with lemon and peat.

SCORE **86**

GLANN AR MOR

PRODUCER Jean Donnay   COUNTRY France
TEL 0033 52 7346500   WEBSITE www.glannarmor.com

Most of us associate France with wine, Champagne, and Cognac, but the northern part of the country has a strong tradition of cider, apple brandy, and beer. It is now establishing a reputation for whisky, too. There are now four distilleries in the Brittany region, and one each in Cognac and Alsace Lorraine. In Brittany the distilleries have little in common with each other, but the most rugged, Celtic and Scottish islandlike is Glann ar Mor, owned by Jean Donnay. The name of his distillery and his whiskies come from the Brêton language, which is closely linked to the Celt tongues spoken in Cornwall and Wales. Jean Donnay is very proud of his Celtic roots and his whiskies reflect this—they have a distinctly Scottish West Coastal tanginess. He uses peat to make Kornog, which could be from the Scottish island of Islay. This is no coincidence because in late 2012 Jean announced plans for a craft distillery on Islay itself, bringing new meaning to the term "Auld Alliance."

KORNOG Taouarc'h Kentan 2014, 57.1 vol

COLOR Lemon.

NOSE Broody smoke. Unripe apple.

BODY Full, mouth coating, and oily.

PALATE Big waves of industrial smoke, gooseberry, green fruit, peat, and chai spice. All very big and aggressive.

FINISH Long and peaty.

SCORE **89**

GLANN AR MOR Taol Esa 1st Edition Gwcch 2014, 46 vol

COLOR Straw yellow.

NOSE Hay and freshly cut meadow. Lemon. Spritely candy notes.

BODY Medium, clean, and fresh.

PALATE At first, quite sweet with citrus notes; then a more earthy center
with a rustic and peatlike base; and finally, some salt and pepper.
Evolves intriguingly.

FINISH Medium, with salt and pepper.

SCORE 85

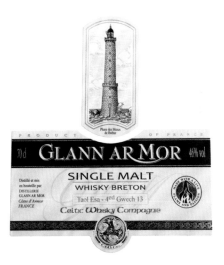

GLANN AR MOR Taol Esa 4th Edition Gwech 2014, 46 vol

COLOR Light lemon.

NOSE Green salad, barley, baking dough, and traces of vanilla and candy.

BODY Big, full, and rich.

PALATE Overripe apples, sea notes, and salt. Candy. Fruitcake.
Unusual and quite intriguing.

FINISH Medium and balanced, between savory and sweet.

SCORE 88

HAKUSHU

PRODUCER Suntory
COUNTRY Japan   TEL 0081 55 231 2722
WEBSITE www.suntory.com   VC

HAKUSHU IS JAPAN'S HIGHEST and most remote distillery, surrounded by natural forests with walking and cycling tracks in the Japanese Southern Alps. It takes about two and a half hours by fast train from Tokyo, and has a visitor center and a museum.

Not as well known as Suntory's other distillery, Yamazaki, Hakushu is nonetheless a fascinating whisky. The house style could be described as fresh, clean, and fruity, though there have been a a series of limited edition releases that have explored different flavors and cask types, including a heavily peaked version of the malt. The distillery is relatively young, having been built in 1973 to meet the growing demand for Suntory whiskies.

HAKUSHU Distiller's Reserve, 43 vol

COLOR Light gold.

NOSE Cucumber. Green salad. Kitchen pantry. Lime traces.

BODY Medium and sweet.

PALATE Clean, sweet, fresh, and spicy. Rustic notes.
Apples. Pepper. Vanilla.

FINISH Very short, clean, and fresh.

 SCORE **82**

HAKUSHU 12-year-old, 43.5 vol

COLOR Light bronze.

NOSE Clean, fresh, light, and fluffy. Freshly cut grass. Pine.

BODY Medium and pleasant.

PALATE Fresh and clean, with fresh barley, some spearmint,
and a cordial-like quality.

FINISH Medium and very easy drinking.

SCORE **85**

HELLYERS ROAD

PRODUCER Betta Milk Co-operative Ltd.
COUNTRY Australia   TEL 0061 3 6433 0439
WEBSITE www.hellyersroaddistillery.com.au

HELLYERS ROAD IS THE LARGEST DISTILLERY on Tasmania, but one that has kept a relatively low profile. It is located in the northwest of the island, away from the others, and is part of a large milk-making cooperative. It is said that it was opened to provide an alternative source of income, if cheaper milk from the mainland ever threatened that from Tasmania. The whisky is very different from other Tasmanian malts, which tend to be big and powerful. Hellyers Road whiskies tend to have more in common with a floral and light Scottish Lowland style of whisky. The distillery does a peated and lightly peated version and matures some of its malts in casks that have been previously used for Pinot Noir.

HELLYERS ROAD 10-year-old, 46.2 vol

COLOR Pale gold.

NOSE Damson. Plum. Chardonnay. Sweet grape. Citrus.

BODY Quite thin, sweet, and refreshing.

PALATE Easy drinking and sweet whisky. Gooseberry, apricot, and summer fruit. Perfumed. Medicine cabinet. Simple and addictive.

FINISH Short and sweet.

SCORE *82*

HELLYERS ROAD 12-year-old, 46.2 vol

COLOR Pale gold.

NOSE Pine. Fresh polish. Fir tree. Gooseberry. Green melon.
Refreshing and earthy.

BODY Light, clean, and fresh.

PALATE Clean. Grapey. Sour apple. Easy drinking.
Light, with mild but late spice.

FINISH Short and a tad feisty.

SCORE 80

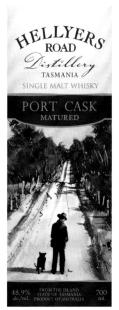

HELLYERS ROAD Port Cask Matured, 48.9 vol

COLOR Red-tinged orange.

NOSE Very fruity, almost cordial-like, with strawberry,
red currants, and summer fruit.

BODY Light, clean, and pleasant.

PALATE Light, sweet, and very fruity. Like black-currant soda.
Vanilla. Jell-O and English trifle. Very pleasant.

FINISH Quite short, but sweet and attractive.

SCORE 82

JOHN DISTILLERIES

PRODUCER Paul John Distilleries
COUNTRY India   TEL 0091 80 2860 0630
WEBSITE www.jdl.in

PAUL JOHN IS A HUGE DISTILLED SPIRITS PRODUCER with more than 2,000 employees and several properties and distilleries in India. Although single malt whisky is a relatively new venture, the company made a big impact when the first whiskies were released in late 2012. The standard bottlings—an unpeated, lightly peated, and a strongly peated version—have received a string of awards and been widely praised by whisky writers. However, it is the single cask limited releases that have put this distillery at the very forefront of the world whisky revolution. The distillery swept the board in the 2014 Wizards of Whisky World Whisky Awards.

PAUL JOHN Brilliance, 46 vol

COLOR Deep reddish brown.

NOSE Sweet and fruity. Zesty.

BODY Rich, full, and sweet.

PALATE Young but not immature, with a pleasant sweet and zesty shape to it. Lime and citrus Starburst, sweet candy, and some powdered sugar.

FINISH Medium, tropical fruit, and mild spice.

SCORE **88**

PAUL JOHN Edited, 46 vol

COLOR Deep reddish brown.

NOSE Cinnamon. Dried fruit. Lemon. Medium peat.

BODY Medium, peaty, and sweet.

PALATE Intense fruit flavors, particularly green apples. Medium sooty smoke. Herbal notes. Fireplace smoke. A touch of cumin and chili spice. There's also cinnamon on the palate.

FINISH Big, full, smoky, and spicy.

SCORE **86**

PAUL JOHN Peated Select Cask, 55.5 vol

COLOR Deep gold.

NOSE Green fruit. Crab apple. Fluttery, wispy smoke.

BODY Medium and mouth coating.

PALATE Acerbic and cutting smoke. Baked apples with
mincemeat. Dried fruit. Raisins. Sweet incense smoke.

FINISH Medium. Sharp smoke and incense.

SCORE **84**

PAUL JOHN Single Cask No. 777, 59.2 vol

COLOR Deep gold.

NOSE Seashells. Damp boathouse. Salty. Seaside. Fireplace embers.

BODY Full, savory, and oily.

PALATE Pungent smoke and chili up front, then licorice.
Beyond that, puréed canned apricots and peach. Lots of smoke
and peat. Sweet walnut and dates. Chutney. Perfumed.

FINISH Long, sweet, and smoky.

SCORE **86**

PAUL JOHN Single Cask No. 1444, 59.7 vol

COLOR Amber.

NOSE Floral. Black currant. Raisin. Vague wispy smoke. Perfumed.
Dusty. Violet candy.

BODY Firm, full, and oily.

PALATE Lemon candy dipped in sherbet. Sherbet. Orange Jell-O,
puréed almond, and then white pepper.

FINISH Quite short. Dusty and citrus.

SCORE **86**

LANGATUN

PRODUCER Hans Baumberger
COUNTRY Switzerland TEL 0041 79 336 0017
WEBSITE www.langatun.ch

URRENT OWNER HANS BAUMBERGER is at the helm of a family business that is nearly 160 years old. Having studied as a brewer in Munich, Jakob Baumberger established a distillery on his father's farm, bought a brewery a few years later, and made a success of both enterprises. He also acquired the rights to a spring in the hills above the distillery, and to this day that spring provides the water for the making of the whisky.

Local barley is also used but stout yeast is imported from England. There are other extras here, too. The spirit is triple distilled and various wine casks are used for maturation. The combination works because all the whiskies included here are astounding.

LANGATUN Old Eagle, 40 vol

COLOR Orangey gold.

NOSE Lemon polish and polished oak. Rich fruit.

BODY Rich, full, and punchy.

PALATE Lime. Polished wood. Sweet vanilla and honey.
Peach. Intense smoke.

FINISH Stylish balance of sweet and spice.

SCORE **90**

LANGATUN Old Bear, 40 vol

COLOR Rich gold.

NOSE Very fruity with wafting smoke. Summer garden.

BODY Light and refreshing.

PALATE Light smoke and green fruit. Bladnoch-like. Mango. Peach.
Pear. Light wispy smoke. Beautifully made.

FINISH Sweet and fruity with some peat.

SCORE **92**

LANGATUN Young Bear, 64 vol

COLOR Clear.

NOSE Peat. Cereal. Grainy. Fresh. Sweet.

BODY Rich, full, and dominant.

PALATE Smoky. Surprisingly rich and fruity. Cereal. Mint.
Pepper. Complex.

FINISH Big, smoky, and fiery.

SCORE **80**

LARK

PRODUCER Bill Lark
COUNTRY Australia   TEL 0061 3 6231 9088
WEBSITE www.larkdistillery.com.au

H E MUST BE SICK TO DEATH of hearing it, but Bill Lark is the godfather of whisky making in Tasmania. He is well known for having overturned the country's ancient prohibition laws with the help of an amused customs and excise department who found the quest more fun than the usual red tape and bureaucracy.

Bill has shared his expertise with almost all of the 20 or so distilleries on the island, reflecting the influence he has on the whisky industry here. His distillery, however, remains the first and the best. His whiskies have acquired distinctive and high quality characteristics, and he has defied naysayers by producing excellent and recognizable whiskies in a fraction of the time it would take to do so in Scotland. The distillery is on farmland outside Hobart, but there is a waterside Cellar Door in the middle of the city's picturesque port.

LARK Cask Strength, Cask LD31, 58 vol

COLOR Chestnut.

NOSE Fine pepper dust. Savory. Furniture varnish. Unusual.

BODY Sweet, soft, and rich.

PALATE Soft, thick honey. Overripe plum and pepper.
Touches of salt and pepper.

FINISH Gentle and rounded. Different, but balanced and impressive.

SCORE **83**

LARK Distiller's Selection Cask, 46 vol

COLOR Deep gold.

NOSE Sweet lemon and honey cough drop.
Fruity hard candy. Complex.

BODY Oily. Very soft. Mouth coating.

PALATE Gooseberries. Plums. Lots of other fruit.
Complex but gentle. A trace of pepper.

FINISH Quite long. Graceful, honeyed, and soft.

SCORE **85**

LIMEBURNERS

PRODUCER The Great Southern Distilling Company
COUNTRY Australia   TEL 0061 8 9842 5363
WEBSITE www.distillery.com.au

L IMEBURNERS IS A WHISKY whose time is now. In the last decade or so its malts have evolved into full, fruity, and specially made malts that rival the best in Australia. The secret to its success lies in maintaining the values of craft distilling and an emphasis on quality over quantity. The distillery uses local barley, claiming that barley from Southwestern Australia is among the best in the world. It is malted in Perth and then combined with hard water from a local limestone aquifer and soft water collected from the local rainfall. All whisky is made in small batches in 100-liter and 200-liter casks that have previously held Australian sherry, port, and tokay. Some casks have an 80-year-old history dating back to prewar Kentucky. Small batch runs can be anything from 100 to 320 bottles, but the distillery tries to have a 43 percent, a cask strength, and a peaked whisky available at all times.

LIMEBURNERS Single Malt M76, 43 vol

COLOR Deep gold.

NOSE Big, winey noted. Berries. Some candy and vanilla.

BODY Full, aggressive, and oily.

PALATE Oily with fruit and floral notes. A trace of young green barley and menthol. Licorice. Spicy cardamom.

FINISH Quite long, with menthol, spice, and some fruit.

SCORE **84**

LIMEBURNERS Single Malt M79, 61 vol

COLOR Russet.

NOSE Fig and dates. Honey. Overripe peach and apricot. Molasses.

BODY Full, creamy, and powerful.

PALATE Hard-hitting and forceful, but complex. More fig and dates to the fore, baked peach, and crystallized brown sugar. Creamy, rich, some menthol, and cough drop.

FINISH Big, long, and bold.

SCORE **87**

MACKMYRA

PRODUCER Mackmyra
COUNTRY Sweden   TEL 0046 855 602 580
WEBSITE www.mackmyra.se

MACKMYRA IS ONE OF THE ORIGINAL PIONEERS of nontraditional world whiskies and one of the first to break into export markets. Originally set up by a bunch of friends as an experiment after a conversation on a ski vacation, the distillery's early runaway success has seen it expand rapidly over the years. The distillery uses a traditional distillation process and local peat, which was under the Baltic sea, so it lends a salty taste to the malt—a taste suited to the Swedish palate. Some of the barley is also dried over juniper twigs as Swedish food often is, so there are some distinctive regional characteristics in the whisky, too. There's something deliciously kooky about Mackmyra. It has warehouses in various parts of the country so that people purchasing quarter casks don't have to travel too far to visit them. And it matures some of its whisky in an underground mine and in old armories on islands off the coast of Stockholm.

MACKMYRA Iskristall Swedish Single Malt, 46.1 vol

COLOR Pale orange.

NOSE Damp wood bark. Musty. Peat. Grapefruit.

BODY Medium sweet and sour.

PALATE Banana, bourbon cask, candy, vanilla, but also smoke and ash.

FINISH Medium sweet, spicy, and smoky.

SCORE **88**

MACKMYRA Svensk Rök, 46.1 vol

COLOR Lemon yellow.

NOSE Big smoke. Tarry and with charcoal. Maritime notes. Mustiness.

BODY Quite full, mouth coating, and oily.

PALATE Grungy industrial smoke. Lots of savory notes. Gooseberry. Chili spice. Delicatessen. Anchovy.

FINISH Long and peaty.

SCORE **88**

MACKMYRA Midvinter Swedish Single Malt, 46.1 vol

COLOR Straw lemon.

NOSE Pineapple fritters. Sweet citrus Jell-O and cream.

BODY Light. Cordial-like.

PALATE Citrus Starburst. Lime and orange sherbet.

Quite delicate. Sweet peppers.

FINISH Medium. Clean. Refreshing. Citrus.

SCORE **85**

MACKMYRA Midnattssol Swedish Single Malt, 46.1 vol

COLOR Rich lemon.

NOSE Massive waft of banana and vanilla. Sweet. Dusty spice.

BODY Full, sweet, and spicy.

PALATE Lots of banana and vanilla. Tropical fruit.

Then biting sweet chili spice.

FINISH Long, sweet, and spicy. Dessert whisky. Very well made.

SCORE **90**

MACKMYRA Moment Gold, 51.2 vol

COLOR Rich honey.

NOSE Sweet apple and pears. Wispy smoke.

BODY Rich, full, and mouth coating.

PALATE Pleasant peat but also summer fruit. Sweet apples.

Juniper. Black currant, while cinnamon plays a role, too. Subtle.

FINISH Quite long, refined, and complex.

SCORE **88**

MACKMYRA Moment Maveld, 52.2 vol

COLOR Straw lemon.

NOSE Lots of bourbon notes, with candy, vanilla, and honey.

BODY Big, flavorful, and intense.

PALATE A dessert and cigar whisky. Melon, banana, and vanilla

on one level; and chili spice and earthy, smoky malt on another.

FINISH Long and more of the same. A firecracker of a whisky.

SCORE **89**

THE NZ WHISKY COMPANY

PRODUCER The NZ Whisky Company
COUNTRY New Zealand   TEL 0064 3 434 8842
WEBSITE www.thenzwhisky.com

WHETHER THE NZ WHISKY COMPANY should be included in this chapter is debatable because while the company has a distillery and whisky for sale in the market, the distillery hasn't produced any of the whisky for sale. The NZ Whisky Company is actually owned by Tasmanian Greg Ramsay and he has bought up the old stock of the now closed Willowbank Distillery at Oamaru. A new distillery is operating but it has yet to bottle its first release. We decided to include it though because the whiskies have been repackaged and improved, and the company is making a splash by exporting premium old malt across the world to great success.

THE NZ WHISKY COMPANY 18-year-old, 40 vol

COLOR Light lemon.

NOSE Grapes. Grapefruit. Prickly spices. Quite light.

BODY Medium full, citrus.

PALATE Big mix of citrus fruit, particularly lemon. Salt and pepper. Grape. Hickory. Melon. Peat. Later, an oak buildup. Quite oily.

FINISH Long and peppery.

SCORE **81**

THE NZ WHISKY COMPANY 21-year-old, 40 vol

COLOR Bronze.

NOSE Buttery. Orange Jell-O. Pantry spices. Mushy peas.

BODY Medium and cordial-like.

PALATE Peppered fish drizzled with lemon. Earthy and gutsy. Some green fruit. Oaky. Tannins. Lacking in assertiveness.

FINISH Medium, rooty, and pleasant, but a tad too quiet.

SCORE **80**

THE NZ WHISKY COMPANY 1989, Single Cask, 53 vol

COLOR Rich lemon.

NOSE Lemon and grapefruit. Light, with some wispy smoke.

BODY Big, full, and oily.

PALATE Big manuka-honey hit, then a big wave of peat. The sweet and peaty mix continues throughout. Honey and lemon. Clean and stylish.

FINISH Medium long, sweet, and clean.

SCORE **91**

THE NZ WHISKY COMPANY 1993, Single Cask, 55.4 vol

COLOR Deep yellow.

NOSE Spearmint. Green banana. Pine needles. Green salad. Melon.

BODY Big and aggressive.

PALATE Big hickory and menthol. Sweet fruit. Toffee. Gentle and soft, until some earthiness arrives later.

FINISH Oaky, spicy, earthy, and medium long.

SCORE **89**

PENDERYN

PRODUCER Penderyn Whisky Company
COUNTRY Wales   TEL 0044 1685 810651
WEBSITE www.welsh-whisky.co.uk

WHEN PENDERYN BROUGHT WHISKY PRODUCTION back to Wales for the first time in more than a century, it made the decision to make something that very clearly wasn't Scotch. The distillery itself looks different from a Scottish distillery, the distinctive bottle sets it apart, and so does the taste. There are several reasons for this. The distillery has a unique still that was specially invented for it, a hybrid of a pot still and column still. Hopless beer is brought in from Brains Brewery in Cardiff and treated to give it the necessary sourness found in distiller's beer. After distillation the spirit is matured for four years in three cask types—about half of it in ex-Madeira casks, a quarter in ex-bourbon casks, and a quarter in casks that have been used for nonpeated Scottish single malt. All stock is bottled month to month, so variations do exist between different bottlings.

PENDERYN Single Malt, 46 vol

COLOR Rich gold.

NOSE Lemon and lime sherbet candies. Light toffee.

BODY Quite light. Gentle.

PALATE Wispy. Light and floral. Vanilla. Perhaps a trace of apricot. Later, lime liqueur.

FINISH Surprisingly long, with gentle Starburst lime and sweet spice.

SCORE *82*

PENDERYN Portwood, 60.6 vol

COLOR Reddish brown.

NOSE Wine-gum candy. Stewed fruit. Berries.

BODY Mouth coating, rich, full, and dominant.

PALATE Big red fruit and citrus. Complex mix of cinnamon, clove, nutmeg, and other spices. Raspberry and black currant. Sweet spices. Fruit rumtopf.

FINISH Rich and liqueur-like.

SCORE *92*

PENDERYN Peated, 46 vol

COLOR Greeny brown.

NOSE Distinctive, but not heavy on the peat.

Youthful cereal and hay. Vegetal.

BODY Medium full.

PALATE Gentle peat. Almost flowery. Root vegetable. Spice.

FINISH Smoky and rooty. Not much complexity.

SCORE **75**

PENDERYN Sherrywood, 46 vol

COLOR Rich golden brown.

NOSE Prickly. Red currant and berries. Rich sherry.

BODY Quite full.

PALATE Red fruit. Pear-flavored hard candy. With water, green apples.

Hard pear. Fruit zest. Refreshing.

FINISH Clean and fruity. Crisp, with a delightful sweetness.

SCORE **80**

ST. GEORGE'S

PRODUCER The English Whisky Company   COUNTRY England
TEL 0044 1953 717939   WEBSITE www.englishwhisky.co.uk

WHEN FATHER AND SON TEAM James and Andrew Nelstrop decided to make the first English whisky in more than 100 years, they didn't hang around. They received planning permission for their greenfield site in February and were producing spirit in November of the same year. That was a decade ago, and since then the whisky has gone from strength to strength so that now it is producing world-class whisky. Although the distillation method is traditional, the distillery uses a wide range of casks to produce a diverse selection of whiskies, including heavily peaked ones.

The whiskies are named by chapter, which can be quite confusing. The first releases were Chapter 6 and 9 because "Works in Progress" had been released previously. Chapter 13 is released as a different whisky every St. George's Day, and in 2014 Chapter 7 from a rum cask was rereleased just after Chapter 15. Got it?

ST. GEORGE'S God Save the Queen 60th Anniversary, 46 vol

COLOR Honey gold.

NOSE Toffee. Unripe bananas. Deli spices. Spring onion.

BODY Medium. Cordial-like. Quite refreshing.

PALATE Cooking apple. Peat smoke. Savory. Burned meat.
Grungy and feisty.

FINISH Medium, pepper smoke. Quite long.

SCORE **83**

ST. GEORGE'S Lest We Forget 1914–18, 46 vol

COLOR Pale lemon.

NOSE Pineapple. Guava. Baked apple. Traces of lemon and
lime sherbet. Grape.

BODY Medium, clean, sweet, and pure.

PALATE Clean and sweet. Soft banana. Melon. Fruity panna cotta.
Late sweet spice.

FINISH Sweet, medium, and spicy.

SCORE **88**

ST. GEORGE'S Chapter 14, 46 vol

COLOR Straw.

NOSE Pineapple. Tropical fruit. Clean and sweet. Honey. Vanilla.

BODY Rich, sweet, and full.

PALATE Banana. Pineapple. Battenberg cake. Vanilla. Vanilla ice cream.
Milk-chocolate cookies. Some menthol. Gentle spice.

FINISH Sweet and dessertlike.

SCORE **92**

ST. GEORGE'S Chapter 15, 46 vol

COLOR Pale lemon.

NOSE Saline. Bonfire smoke. Quite gentle with grapefruit
and drizzled lemon.

BODY Oily, full, and sweet.

PALATE Citrus fruit. Surprisingly rounded and clean. Lots and lots
of peat but gentler flavors come through. Melon and apple.

FINISH Sweet citrus and peat. Rounded and quite long.

SCORE **91**

ST. GEORGE'S Chapter 16, 46 vol

COLOR Golden orange.

NOSE Sherry. Red currant. Quite shy.

BODY Medium, crispy, and spicy.

PALATE Earthy and fruity. Red berries. Rounded.
Strawberry. Christmas cake.

FINISH Perfectly balanced. Medium long, with both smoke
and fruit in the mix.

SCORE **89**

SULLIVAN'S COVE

PRODUCER The Tasmania Distilling Company
COUNTRY Australia TEL 0061 3 6248 5399
WEBSITE www.sullivanscovewhisky.com

SULLIVAN'S COVE HAS HAD AN INCREDIBLE two years, culminating with the title for its French Oak malt as the world's best single malt whisky in the World Whiskies Awards, beating the finest Scottish and Irish malts along the way.

The distillery has improved massively from its earliest bottlings, and having moved into bigger premises, it has started to export to markets across the world. The whisky is produced in batches so there is considerable variety between the whiskies in each, so make sure you're tasting a recent bottle. The spirit is made in the traditional manner and matured in both American and French oak casks.

SULLIVAN'S COVE Double Cask 68, 40 vol

COLOR Lemon.

NOSE Vanilla. Soft toffee. Oranges.

BODY Creamy, rich, and full.

PALATE Clean, with soft spicy notes. Tangerine. Kumquat.
Powdered sugar. Traces of peppermint.

FINISH Medium, sweet, and pleasant.

SCORE **89**

SULLIVAN'S COVE Double Cask 71, 40 vol

COLOR Gold.

NOSE Honey. Sweet. Early evening at a rock festival site.
Raspberry sherbet. Lemon bonbon.

BODY Gentle, soft, and rounded.

PALATE An easy drinking whisky with a feisty and spicy side to it.
Quite sweet, but there's a meaty sherry component, and
the sherbety qualities pep it up.

FINISH Medium and sweet.

SCORE **86**

SULLIVAN'S COVE Double Cask 72, 40 vol

COLOR Lemon.

NOSE Dark leaves, late Autumn orchard. Marzipan. Currants.

BODY Rich, full, and intense.

PALATE A wave of dark fruit. Molasses. Black coffee.
Traces of honey and pepper spice. Complex and evolving.

FINISH Long and sweet.

SCORE **87**

SULLIVAN'S COVE American Oak HH2432, 47.5 vol

COLOR Light copper.

NOSE Overripe fruit on an orchard lawn. Feisty, with traces
of meaty sulfur.

BODY Earthy, medium full, and syrupy.

PALATE Stewed berries. Blood orange. Grungy and rustic,
with some earthy spices.

FINISH Sweet and medium long.

SCORE **83**

SULLIVAN'S COVE French Oak HH401, 47.5 vol

COLOR Mahogany.

NOSE Autumnal. Red and dark berries. Forest floor. Musty wine cellar.

BODY Rich, intense, mouth coating, and delightful.

PALATE Fantastic balance of berries and orange fruit. Fruit rumtopft.
Some nuttiness. Lemon and intense orange. Rich and sweet.

FINISH Outstanding. Long and almost liqueurlike.

SCORE **92**

YAMAZAKI

PRODUCER Suntory
COUNTRY Japan   TEL 0081 75 962 1423
WEBSITE www.suntory.com

YAMAZAKI, JAPAN'S FIRST DISTILLERY, was set up in 1923. It was here that the philosophy of making high-standard single malt whisky, in a Scottish style, was combined with the desire to push whisky boundaries with new and innovative flavors.

There are six stills here, all of different shapes and sizes, and with the use of different yeasts and a mix of cask types, it is believed that more than 100 different whiskies can be made here. In recent years we have been able to see some of that diversity with releases of the whiskies that make up the standard 10-year-old.

YAMAZAKI Bourbon Barrel, 48.2 vol

COLOR Bright yellow.

NOSE Typical bourbon wood, with candy, sandalwood, leather saddle, vanilla, and lots of tropical fruit.

BODY Rich, sweet, and assertive.

PALATE Fabulous mouth delivery. Soft and sublime. Vanilla ice cream in caramel sauce and with crushed hazelnuts. Overripe melon.

FINISH Medium, sweet, and utterly addictive.

SCORE **90**

YAMAZAKI 10-year-old, 40 vol

COLOR Orangey brown.

NOSE Vanilla, overripe fruit. Very enticing.

BODY Soft and sweet.

PALATE Squishy banana. Fluffy apple. Sweet vanilla. Ginger barley. Toffee.

FINISH Sweet fruit, toffee, and vanilla. Medium long.

SCORE **84**

YAMAZAKI 18-year-old, 43 vol

COLOR Rich bronze.

NOSE Mango, kiwi, vanilla, and oak. Venerable.

BODY Big, bold, and rich.

PALATE Oak, exotic spices, and some earthiness join the tropical fruit from the nose to make for an excellent and complex whisky. Very enjoyable. Wonderful.

FINISH Complex, long, and with hints of Japanese umami.

SCORE **93**

YAMAZAKI 25-year-old, 43 vol

COLOR Full amber.

NOSE Sweet sherry, plum jam, fruit compote, and bitter chocolate.

BODY Full and rounded.

PALATE Dry sherry, molasses, tannic oak, smoke, and dried fruit.

FINISH Long and drying.

SCORE **88**

ZUIDAM

PRODUCER The Zuidam family
COUNTRY Netherlands   TEL 0031 13 507 8470
WEBSITE www.zuidam.eu

ZUIDAM IS A FAMILY COMPANY that has been making fruit liqueurs and Jenevers for more than 50 years. It makes about 600 different drinks and doesn't cut corners, using the finest fresh ingredients to make high-class spirits. It has been making an array of whiskies for more than 15 years and includes in its portfolio a 100 percent malted rye. Zuidam distills in the same way as Scotland does, and uses an array of casks to produce big-flavored malts.

MILLSTONE Rye 100, 50 vol

COLOR Rich golden brown.

NOSE Swirling spice. Hickory. Menthol.

BODY Big, sweet, and balanced.

PALATE Sugar and spice interplay. Soft toffee. Honey. Apricot and peach. Ginger cookies. Delightful and playful. Prickly spices.

FINISH Delightfully sweet and spicy. Very addictive.

SCORE **93**

MILLSTONE Lightly Peated, 40 vol

COLOR Rich orange.

NOSE Shy. Some pear. Wood shavings. Dry. Cinnamon. Where's the peat?

BODY Rich, big, and creamy.

PALATE Ah, there we are. Wafting but only medium peaty and
not acerbic or industrial. Softer and almost spicy. Ginger cake.
Menthol, and later, a lemon and lime mix.

FINISH Medium and peaty, and certainly the firmest justification
for the name of the whisky.

SCORE **83**

MILLSTONE Pedro Ximénez Cask, 46 vol

COLOR Orangey red.

NOSE Intense and liqueurlike. Raisins. Dried fruit.
molasses toffee. Scottish camp coffee.

BODY Also intense. Full and slightly oily.

PALATE Liquerlike. Plummy fruit. Damson jam. Gooseberry.
But also, fragrant, with a dusting of cocoa and some pepper.

FINISH Medium, with apricot jam notes.

SCORE **86**

MILLSTONE 12-year-old, Sherry Cask, 46 vol

COLOR Deep orange.

NOSE Big sherry notes. Stewed prunes. Overripe red
and black berries. Canned mandarins.

BODY Big, full, and fruity.

PALATE Speyside sherried whisky. Lots of sherry notes. Some oak
and pepper. Christmas cake. Orange- and black-cherry liqueur.

FINISH Long and warming. Very impressive.

SCORE **93**

US WHISKEYS

HISTORICALLY, WHISKEY has been a fringe player in the United States, and although the distilleries are very large, traditionally there have been very few of them. In fact, not long ago, American whiskey outside of the bourbon producers of Kentucky, consisted only of some important distilleries in Tennessee, a couple of bit players in Portland, Oregon, and another two in the San Francisco area. Why whiskey-making has had such a limited impact is a mystery. Perhaps it's partly because the indigenous whiskey is so far removed from the much sought-after Scotch and Irish whiskies, that the American middle class has tended to give it a wide berth over the generations, condemning local liquor to the bottom shelf as an inferior blue-collar drink.

BALCONES DISTILLERY
BALCONES Texas Single Malt Special Release, August 2014, 53 vol

COLOR Horse chestnut.

NOSE Bourbony notes. Candy stick. Fruit gumdrops. Cherry. Very rich and liqueurlike.

BODY Big, smooth, and mouth coating.

PALATE Big, plummy, syrupy fruit. Intense flavors. Oaky anise and spice. Very sweet and honeyed. Sandalwood. Vanilla.

FINISH Long, fruity, and with cinnamon spice.

SCORE **93**

BALCONES Texas Single Malt French Oak Finish Single Cask, 60.6 vol

COLOR Deep reddy brown.

NOSE Less sweet than the Special Release. Chicory. Dark chocolate with cherries. Overripe fruit.

BODY Big, rich, and spicy.

PALATE Less sweet and with a lot more spice. Chili and coriander spices. Smoky. Scottish camp coffee. Candy sticks. Lots of liqueurlike fruit. Powerful.

FINISH Very rich, spicy, and warming.

SCORE **90**

CORSAIR DISTILLERY
CORSAIR Ryemeggadon, 46 vol

COLOR Chestnut brown.

NOSE Toffee. Molasses. Soft fudge. Surprisingly soft and reluctant spicy rye notes.

BODY Mouth coating, rich, and full.

PALATE Honey. Cocoa. Citrus fruit. Soft toffee. Spicy rye is there, but hardly a Ryemeggadon. Very nice though.

FINISH Soft, some spices, pleasant.

SCORE **87**

CORSAIR Triple Batch, Small Batch, 40%

COLOR Chestnut brown.

NOSE Smoke and pear-flavored hard candy. Sweet wood smoke. Candy apple. Enticing.

BODY Medium sweet and soft.

PALATE Fascinating mix of sweet wood hearth smoke, and a more traditional bitter and phenolic industrial peat. Lots of fruit, especially apple and pear.

FINISH Sweet and oily smoke cut with lingering sweet fruit.

SCORE **88**

CORSAIR Quinoa, 46 vol

COLOR Chestnut brown.

NOSE Polished wood, sweet chestnut. Chinese takeaway. Soy.
Far-East spices. Damp leaves. Some fragrance.

BODY Medium full and oily.

PALATE Very spicy, with crab apple, apple pits, and baked bread. Soft peach.
Some herbal notes.

FINISH Sharp, spicy, warming, and long.

SCORE **82**

OTHERS

THE TRICKLE OF QUALITY world whisky has become a flood in recent years, and it is almost impossible to keep up with it. There are 50–100 distilleries in Germany, Switzerland, and Austria alone, many with generations of experience of spirit making, now being adapted to whisky production. Across the world, spirits makers are tinkering with definitions, and raising big questions for the future. For instance, is a 100 percent malted rye whisky a single malt? The answer is surely yes, but that takes us into new territory. That's for the future though. For now here are some of the best New World whiskies from smaller producers.

AUSTRALIAN MALTS

BAKERY HILL Peated Malt, Cask Strength, 59.8 vol

COLOR Deep orange.

NOSE Greenhouse. Intense green vegetable. Unripe tomatoes.
Wafts of peat smoke.

BODY Sweet and soft.

PALATE Intense version of the standard malt. Green fruit, big bursts
of flavor. Restrained but noticeable earthy peat.

FINISH Fresh. Quite long. Peaty.

SCORE **86**

BAKERY HILL Double Wood, 46 vol

COLOR Rich yellow.

NOSE Fragrant. Canned fruit in syrup. Sweet melon.

BODY Medium full.

PALATE Clean exotic fruit. Refreshing. Canned pear. Honeyed.

FINISH Medium, very soft, sweet, and pleasant.

SCORE 83

HEARTWOOD The Beagle, August 2014, 68.3 vol

COLOR Rich red.

NOSE Winey. Liqueur fruit. Cigarette ash. Berries. Mandarin. Kumquat.

BODY Huge. Aggressive and in your face, like an Aussie fast bowler in cricket.

PALATE Big port, peat, and berry notes. Would make a good cigar malt.
Earthy, ashy, bold alcoholic prune juice. Plummy. Fig.

FINISH Pulls in different directions. Confusing. Feisty and peaty.
Long and full.

SCORE 88

HEARTWOOD **Convict Redemption December 2013, 71.9 vol**

COLOR Deep reddy brown.

NOSE Big. Red berries. Black currant. Orange-flavored chocolate. Cocoa. Cherry. Wispy smoke.

BODY Full, rich, and aggressive.

PALATE Puréed fruit. Big red apple. Lots of berries. Touch of earthy sulfur. Melon. Big menthol cough drop. Huge and hard to pin down.

FINISH Long. Menthol. Peat. An all-or-nothing whisky.

SCORE **91**

ENGLISH MALTS

ADNAMS **Copper House Triple Grain No 2, 43 vol**

COLOR Yellow.

NOSE Dusty, light spices, and perfumey and winey notes.

BODY Creamy and medium full but with soft toffee.

PALATE Quite two-dimensional. Not a lot of body but with soft toffee. Orange-flavored chocolate, oaky tannins, and some pepper spice.

FINISH Quite short but very pleasant.

SCORE **82**

ADNAMS **Copper House Single Malt No 1, 43 vol**

COLOR Yellow.

NOSE Malty. Ginger. Wood shavings. Vanilla. Honey.

BODY Quite light and cordial-like.

PALATE Lots of vanilla with oaky notes and pepper.

FINISH Medium, with vanilla and oak. Pleasant.

SCORE **83**

IRISH MALTS

TEELING 21-year-old, 57.5 vol

COLOR Bright gold.

NOSE Complex and disorienting. Soft fruit. Fresh summer meadow. Honey. Green fruit.

BODY Medium, assertive, and intriguing.

PALATE Flip-flops. A bit madcap. Grape. Honey. Cocoa. Dates. Peach. Goooseberry. Some apple and pear late on.

FINISH Refreshing and pleasant. Quite dry.

SCORE **91**

TEELING 26-year-old, Gold Reserve Old White Burgundy, 46 vol

COLOR Liquid honey.

NOSE Citrus. Salty. Apricot. Some spice. Dough.

BODY Intense, sharp, and full.

PALATE Big apple notes. Lots of oaky tannins and spice. With water, softens and is a mix of vanilla, marzipan, soft apples, and sweet pears.

FINISH Medium, with a hint of fruit, oak, and spice.

SCORE **85**

TEELING 30-year-old, Platinum Reserve, 46 vol

COLOR Pale lemon.

NOSE Musty, slight, some yellow fruit but not very giving and a bit tired.

BODY Big and rich.

PALATE A total turnaround. Crystallized sweet fruit including lime and black currant. Red licorice, whisky rancio, liqueurlike, complex. Late pepper.

FINISH Long, big, and bold.

SCORE **90**

TEELING Small Batch, 46 vol

COLOR Golden yellow.

NOSE Deceptively sweet. Vanilla. Canned fruit.

BODY Rich, creamy, and medium full.

PALATE Sweet. Typically Irish sweet fruit. Toffee notes. Some tropical fruit. Delicious rum raisin and milk chocolate. Some cutting spices. Not too cloying.

FINISH Medium sweet, very fruity.

SCORE **89**

TAIWANESE MALTS

KAVALAN Solist Fino Cask Strength, 58.3 vol

COLOR Deep russet brown.

NOSE Sweet. Full sherry. Currants. Berries. Coffee.

BODY Rich, sweet, and mouth coating.

PALATE Sweet. Gooey plums. Juicy raisins. A light pepper dusting
late on. Some green banana notes.

FINISH Short, soft, and sweet.

SCORE **89**

KAVALAN Solist Vinho Barrique Cask Strength, 59.2vol

COLOR Deep reddy brown.

NOSE Soda. Sweet summer fruit. Pineapple. Strawberry.

BODY Creamy, rich, and full.

PALATE Big bold flavors. Kumquat liqueur. Tropical fruit.
Black currants. Strawberries and cream. Candy.

FINISH A big finish with the sweet fruit combined with Far-East spices.

SCORE **92**

KAVALAN Solist Bourbon Cask 57.1 vol

COLOR Bright lemon.

NOSE Dancing vanilla, prancing tropical fruit, and rampant spices.

BODY Very rich, full, and sweet.

PALATE More of the same. Zippy and zesty. Vanilla. Coconut.
Tropical fruit. Pineapple. Overripe banana, all sprinkled
with powdered sugar and cinnamon.

FINISH Wonderfully over the top. Big canned fruit cocktail.

SCORE 94

KAVALAN Solist Vinho Barrique, 60 vol

COLOR Rich amber.

NOSE Big and full, with mango, melon, and papaya. Sherbetlike dustiness.
Some floral notes.

BODY Rich, full, and mouth coating.

PALATE Bright, even with water. Water turns this is into a huge
oral rainbow, with tropical fruit, big sweet, and soft spices, all tempered
by toffee and cocoa.

FINISH Long, rich, and lingering with big fruit.

SCORE 91

KAVALAN Solist Fino, 57.6 vol

COLOR Marmalade orange.

NOSE Firm and fruity. Fresh juicy grapes. Some citrus notes.
Spicy. Faintly dusty.

BODY Full, sharp, and assertive.

PALATE Full and sweet, this evolves during the taste journey. Early
on plummy sweet fruit. But then drying sherry and some pepper notes.

FINISH Medium long, with grapey fruit.

SCORE 87

KAVALAN Bourbon Oak, 46 vol

COLOR Bright lemon.

NOSE Tropical fruit. Squishy overripe melon. Vanilla ice cream.
Banana split.

BODY Full, sweet, and rich.

PALATE Gentle waves of tropical fruit. Vailla. Honey. Apple pie
and cream developing into licorice and menthol.

FINISH Rich, fruity, and with those menthol notes lingering.
Very impressive.

SCORE 92

KAVALAN Podium, 46 vol

COLOR Rich bronze.

NOSE Soft and gentle. Vanilla. Toffee.

BODY Gentle and sweet.

PALATE Banoffee pie. A dessert whisky. Maple syrup. Fruit Starburst.
Nuanced and subtle. Candy.

FINISH Relatively short, sweet, and pleasant.

SCORE **88**

KAVALAN Sherry Oak, 46 vol

COLOR Reddy brown.

NOSE Typically sherried. Big plum and red berries. Some orange notes.

BODY Big, sweet, and mouth coating.

PALATE Big and very sherried. Juicy plums. Prunes. Stewed fruit compote.
Late autumn damp forest notes. Lots of tannins and a touch of spice.

FINISH Big, rich, and plummy.

SCORE **87**

WELSH MALTS

PENDERYN Single Malt, 46 vol

COLOR Rich gold

NOSE Lemon-lime powdered candy. Light toffee.

BODY Quite light. Gentle.

PALATE Wispy. Light and floral. Vanilla. Perhaps a trace of apricot.
Later, lime liqueur.

FINISH Surprisingly long, with gentle Starburst lime and sweet spice.

SCORE **82**

PENDERYN Peated, 46 vol

COLOR Greeny brown.

NOSE Distinctive, but not heavy on the peat.
Young cereal and hay. Vegetal.

BODY Medium full.

PALATE Gentle peat. Almost flowery. Root vegetable. Spice.

FINISH Smoky and rooty. Not much complexity.

SCORE **75**

FURTHER READING & RESOURCES

BOOKS

The Whisky Opus,
Dominic Roskrow and
Gavin D. Smith, Dorling
Kindersley, 2012

Whisky: What To Drink Next,
Dominic Roskrow, Sterling
Epicure, 2015

*1001 Whiskies You Must
Taste Before You Die,*
Universe, Dominic
Roskrow 2012

The World's Best Whiskies,
Dominic Roskrow,
Stewart, Tabori and
Chang, 2010

A-Z of Whisky, Gavin D.
Smith, NWP, (3rd edition),
2009

Discovering Scottish Distilleries,
Gavin D. Smith, GW
Publishing, 2010

*Stillhouse Stories, Tunroom
Tales,* Gavin D. Smith,
NWP, 2013

*The Whisky Distilleries of the
United Kingdom,* Alfred
Barnard. (1887 classic,
reprinted 2008)

Malt Whisky, Charles
MacLean. Mitchell Beazley,
1997, revised edition 2006

*Eyewitness Companion to
Whisky,* Editor-in-Chief
Charles MacLean. Dorling
Kindersley, 2008

Handbook of Whisky, Dave
Broom. Hamlyn, 2001

*Jim Murray's Complete Book
of Whisky,* Jim Murray.
Carlton, 1997

The Whisky Bible,
Jim Murray. Dram Good
Books, published annually

The Malt Whisky Yearbook,
Editor: Ingvar Ronde.
MagDig Media,
published annually

*The Scotch Whisky Industry
Review* (annual),
Alan S. Gray.
Sutherlands, Edinburgh.
(Industry statistics,
financial analysis and
commentary)

*The Scottish Whisky
Distilleries,* Misako Udo.
Black and White
Publishing, 2006

The Whisk(e)y Treasury,
Walter Schobert. Neil
Wilson Publishing, 2002.
(A–Z lexicon of owners,
distilleries, industry terms)

The World Guide to Whisky,
Michael Jackson. Dorling
Kindersley, 1987, reprinted
2005. (Scotch, Japanese,
US, and Irish whiskies.)

Scotland and its Whiskies,
Michael Jackson. Duncan
Baird, 2001. (Photography:
Harry Cory Wright)

*Whisky: the Definitive World
Guide,* Michael Jackson.
Dorling Kindersley, 2005

Appreciating Whisky, Phillip
Hills. HarperCollins, 2000,
reprinted 2002. (Physiology
and chemistry of taste)

Collins Gems: Whiskies,
Dominic Roskrow.
Harper Collins, 2009

*Need To Know? Whiskies:
from Confused to Connoisseur,*
Dominic Roskrow.
Harper Collins, 2008

*The Connoisseur's Guide to
Whisky,* Helen Arthur.
Apple Press, 2002

MAGAZINES & WEBSITES

Whisky Magazine
(Published in the United
Kingdom)
www.whiskymag.com

Whisky Advocate
(Published in the
United States)
www.maltadvocate.com

SPECIALIZED MALT RETAILERS IN THE UK

Milroy's, Greek Street,
London www.milroys.co.uk

The Vintage House, Old
Compton Street, London
www.sohowhisky.com

The Whisky Exchange at
Vinopolis, London www.
thewhiskyexchange.com

Royal Mile Whiskies,
London and Edinburgh
www.royalmilewhiskies.com

The Whisky Shop, 15
outlets across England
and Scotland
www.whiskyshop.com

The Wine Shop in
Leek, Staffordshire
www.wineandwhisky.com

The Whisky Shop in
Lincoln www.
lincolnwhiskyshop.co.uk

Loch Fyne Whiskies,
Inveraray www.lfw.co.uk

Whisky Shop, Dufftown
www.thewsd.co.uk

AUTHORS' ACKNOWLEDGMENTS

For their generous time and effort in helping with this and past editions of the book, the authors would like to thank the following.

Pauline Agnew, Rob Allanson, Rolf Andersen, Nick Andrews, Raymond Armstrong, Bridget Arthur, Elaine Bailey, Sarah Bailey, David Baker, Duncan Baldwin, Ian Bankier, Liselle Barnsley, Rachel Barrie, Pat Barrow, Owen D. L. Barstow, Michael Barton, Sonia Bastian, Micheal Beamish, Paul Beevis, Thierry Benitah, Bill Bergius, Jérôme Bordenave, David Boyd, Neil Boyd, Stephen Bremner, Dave Broom, Derek Brown, Lew Bryson, Emily Butcher, Ian Buxton, Alec Carnie, Ian Chapman, Karen Christie, Rick Christie, Neil Clapperton, Paula Cormack, Isabel Coughlin, Simon Coughlin, David Cox, Ronnie Cox, Jason Craig, Katherine Crisp, Andrew Crook, Jim Cryle, Peter Currie, Bob Dalgarno, Stephen Davies, Jancis Davis, Jürgen Deibel, Jean Donnay, Lucy Drake, Jonathan Driver, Gavin J. P. Durnin, Anthony Edwards, Hans-Jürgen Ehmke, Joel Elder, Kate Enis, Gable and Ralph Erenzo, Amy Felmeister, Robert Fleming, John Glaser, John Glass, Alan Gordon, Jim Gordon, Steve Gorton, Lesley Gracie, Heather Graham, George Grant, Alan S. Gray, Peter Greve, Natalie Guerin, Anna Hall, Nick Harris, Donald Hart, Ian Henderson, Dennis Hendry, Stuart Hendry, Robert Hicks, Sandy Hislop, David Hume, Brigid James, Richard Jones, Caitriona Kavanagh, Frances Kelly, Sheila Kennedy, Edward Kinsey, Ed Kohl, Kiran Kuma, Mari Laidlaw, Fred Laing, Stewart Laing, Bill Lark, Christine Logan, Lars Lindberger, Richard Lombard-Chibnall, Jim Long, Bill Lumsden, Neil Macdonald, Lorne Mackillop, Dennis Malcolm, Lauren Mayer, Fritz Maytag, Anthony McCallum-Caron, Stephen McCarthy, Jim McEwan, Frank McHardy, Douglas McIvor, Ian Macmillan, Stephen Marshall, Carla Masson, Annabel Meikle, Claire Meikle, Marcin Miller, Keita Minari, Euan Mitchell, Matthew Mitchell, Shuna Mitchell, Mike Miyamoto, Glen Moore, Lindsay Morgan, Nicholas Morgan, Malcolm Mullin, Stuart Nickerson, Margaret Nicol, B. A. Nimmo, Martine Nouet, Rebecca Painter, The Patel Family, Richard Paterson, Lucy Pritchard, Annie Pugh, John Ramsay, Stuart Ramsay, Kevin Ramsden, Robert Ransom, Kirsty Reid, Mark Reynier, Rebecca Richardson, Damian Riley-Smith, Pat Roberts, Dave Robertson, Pamela Robertson, Amy Robson, Geraldine Roche, Chris Rodden, Colin Ross, Fabio Rossi, Imogen Russell-Taylor, Colin Scott, Jacqui Seargeant, Catherine Service, Euan Shand, Rubyna Sheikh, Raj Singh, Sukhinder Singh, David Smith, Rory Steel, David Stewart, David Stirk, Elizabeth Stubbs, Kier Sword, Andrew Symington, Jack Teeling, Elodie Teissedre, Jens Tholstrup, Graeme Thomson, Pippa Thomson, Margaret Mary Timpson, Hide Tokuda, Robin Torrie, Gerry Tosh, Rich Trachtenberg, Robin Tucek, Cathy Turner, The Urquhart Family, Alistair Walker, Billy Walker, Karen Walker, Rick Wasmund, Ian Weir, Amy Westlake, Cristina Wilkie, Michelle Williams, Alan Winchester, Arthur Winning, Lance Winters, Gordon Wright, Kate Wright, Vanessa Wright, Ken Young, Ron Zussman.

Dorling Kindersley would like to thank the following distilleries and drinks companies for supplying their images, labels or bottles for use as illustrations in this book: Allied, Angus Dundee, Isle of Arran, Beam Global, Ben Nevis, Benriach, Bladnoch, Bruichladdich, Burn Stewart, Campari group, Chivas Brothers, John Dewar & Sons, Diageo, Duncan Taylor, Edradour, Edrington Group, Glenfarclas, Glenmorangie, Gordon & MacPhail, Ian Macleod, Inver House, J & G Grant, Kilchoman, La Martiniquaise, Loch Lomond, Mark Tayburn, Mitchell's Glengyle Ltd., Morrison Bowmore, Picard Vins & Spiriteux, Remy Cointreau, Signatory Vintage, Speciality Drinks, Speyside Distillers Co., Springbank, Suntory holdings, Tomatin, Whyte & Mackay, William Grant & Sons.

Photography: pp1–3 Michael Ellis; pp6–69 Ian O'Leary (except p35 Diageo, p44 Edrington Group); p70 Paul Harris.

INDEX